# Swordsmen

# SWORDSMEN

## The Martial Ethos in
## the Three Kingdoms

ROGER B. MANNING

OXFORD

UNIVERSITY PRESS

# OXFORD
UNIVERSITY PRESS

Great Clarendon Street, Oxford OX2 6DP

Oxford University Press is a department of the University of Oxford.
It furthers the University's objective of excellence in research, scholarship,
and education by publishing worldwide in

Oxford New York

Auckland Bangkok Buenos Aires Cape Town Chennai
Dar es Salaam Delhi Hong Kong Istanbul Karachi Kolkata
Kuala Lumpur Madrid Melbourne Mexico City Mumbai Nairobi
São Paulo Shanghai Taipei Tokyo Toronto

Oxford is a registered trade mark of Oxford University Press
in the UK and in certain other countries

Published in the United States
by Oxford University Press Inc., New York

© Roger B. Manning 2003

The moral rights of the author have been asserted
Database right Oxford University Press (maker)

First published 2003

British Library Cataloguing in Publication Data
Data available

Library of Congress Cataloging in Publication Data
Data available

ISBN 0-19-926121-0

1 3 5 7 9 10 8 6 4 2

Typeset 10/12pt Sabon by Graphicraft Limited, Hong Kong
Printed in Great Britain
on acid-free paper by
Biddles Ltd.,
Guildford and King's Lynn

To Anne

# Acknowledgements

ONE INCURS MANY debts of gratitude in undertaking a new research project and writing a book crossing several disciplines. Financial assistance for travel and research was provided by a senior fellowship from the National Endowment for the Humanities, Fletcher Jones and Mellon fellowships awarded by the Huntington Library, and a sabbatical leave and grants from the College of Graduate Studies of Cleveland State University. Research was carried out in the British Library, the Institute of Historical Research, the Public Record Office, Chancery Lane, the Cleveland Public Library, the Huntington Library, the Newberry Library, and the College of Law and University Libraries of Cleveland State University, and I wish to thank the archivists and librarians of those worthy institutions for many kindnesses beyond the bounds of duty.

Colleagues and friends have been especially helpful and encouraging. Edward Berry, Samuel Clark, and Jane Ohlmeyer read the entire manuscript. Robert Bucholz, Barbara Donagan, Edward Furgol, and Pamela McVay read individual chapters. They, as well as the anonymous readers of the Oxford University Press, offered much encouragement and many helpful suggestions. I also wish gratefully to acknowledge the kind reception and helpful criticism of the members of the Seminar in Courts, Households and Lineages of the Newberry Library, where I read an earlier version of Chapter 1. Others have assisted in many varied but no less important ways, especially Harry Andrist, Paul Hardacre, David Evett, Scott Hendrix, Michael MacDonald, Joyce Mastboom, Donald Ramos, Robert Ritchie, and Robert Shoemaker. My very good friends Barrett Beer, Jacob Price, Earl Reitan, Clayton Roberts, and James Sack endured many hours of discussion of this topic with patience and good humour, as did my students both graduate and undergraduate. I also wish to thank Scott Hendrix, Ryan Moore, and Linda Petranek, graduate students past and present, for research assistance in compiling and encoding the database of peers of the Three Kingdoms.

The history editors of the Oxford University Press, Ruth Parr, Anne Gelling, and Kay Rogers, saw this book through the various stages of review and production in a most professional and helpful manner. Once again, Hilary Walford has taken on the daunting task of copy-editing, which she does so well.

As always, my greatest debt of gratitude is owed to my wife, Anne Brown Manning, who never ceased to encourage me and provide the leisure to write this book.

R.B.M.

*Cleveland, Ohio*
*March 2003*

# Contents

# List of Illustrations

# List of Tables

# Abbreviations

| | |
|---|---|
| *Acts P.C.* | *Acts of the Privy Council of England*, ed. J. R. Dasent, 46 vols. (London, 1890–1964) |
| BC | Bannatyne Club |
| *BIHR* | *Bulletin of the Institute of Historical Research* |
| BL | British Library |
| *Cal. S.P., Dom.* | *Calendar of State Papers, Domestic Series, Charles II*, ed. M. A. E. Green, 24 vols. (London, 1860–1947) |
| CS | Camden Society |
| *DNB* | *Dictionary of National Biography*, 22 vols. (Oxford, 1990 edn.) |
| *EHR* | *English Historical Review* |
| ESTCT *or* ESTCN | English Short Title Catalogue, 1701–1800 (online) |
| GEC | G. E. Cockayne, *The Complete Peerage of England, Scotland, and Ireland, Great Britain and the United Kingdom, Extant, Extinct, or Dormant*, 13 vols. (rev. edn.; London, 1910–40) |
| HEH | Henry E. Huntington Library |
| *HJ* | *Historical Journal* |
| *HLQ* | *Huntington Library Quarterly* |
| HMC | Historical Manuscripts Commission |
| *HR* | *Historical Research* |
| *IS* | *Irish Sword* |
| *JBS* | *Journal of British Studies* |
| *J. Mod. Hist.* | *Journal of Modern History* |
| NRS | Navy Records Society |
| *OED* | *Oxford English Dictionary* |
| *P&P* | *Past and Present* |
| PRO | Public Record Office, London |
| *SHR* | *Scottish Historical Review* |
| SHS | Scottish Historical Society |
| STC | *A Short-Title Catalogue of English Books Printed in England, Scotland & Ireland and of Books Printed Abroad, 1475–1640*, comp. A. W. Pollard and W. G. Redgrave, 3 vols. (2nd edn.; London, 1976–91) |

| | |
|---|---|
| *Trans. R. Hist. Soc.* | *Transactions of the Royal Historical Society* |
| Wing | *Short-Title Catalogue of Books Printed in England, Scotland, Ireland, Wales and of English Books Printed in other Countries, 1641–1700*, comp. D. G. Wing, 3 vols. (2nd edn.; New York, 1972–88) |

# Note on the Text

THE SPELLING, PUNCTUATION, and capitalization of all quotations used in the text and taken from contemporaneous manuscripts and printed books have been modernized. However, the actual spelling of titles of books printed before 1800 has been retained in footnote citations and in the bibliography, although the punctuation and capitalization have been modernized. Where the author has used different editions of the same work, the actual edition consulted is cited in the footnotes, but only the earliest edition or the most accessible modern edition, or editions cited more than once, are listed in the Bibliography.

The year is assumed to begin on 1 January rather 25 March. The day and the month are given according to old style where such precision is possible.

# Introduction

Every man thinks meanly of himself for not having been a soldier, or not having been to sea . . . The profession of soldiers and sailors has the dignity of danger. Mankind reverence those who have got over fear, which is so general a weakness.

(James Boswell, *The Life of Samuel Johnson*, ed. C. P. Chadsey (New York, 1945), 449–50)

Whatever be the causes and incitements to courage, its actual exertions will always meet with admiration, because men look up to its achievements with a degree of fear and respect; and they pay a deference to its possessor, because they either feel themselves secure under his protection or dread the effects of his prowess.

(Charles Moore, *A Full Inquiry into the Subject of Suicide, to which are added . . . Two Treatises on Duelling and Gaming*, 2 vols. (London, 1790) [ESTCT 111258], ii. 262)

The soldier, we are told, has his point of honour and a fashion of thinking, which he wears with his sword.

(Adam Ferguson, *An Essay on the History of Civil Society* (Edinburgh, 1767; repr. New York, 1971), 229)

War was not regarded as pathological or abnormal before 1914, but was viewed as an 'acceptable' and usual way of settling international disputes. In late-medieval and early modern Europe, war was a way of life and an integral part of aristocratic culture. As such it required little justification and was endemic throughout mainland Europe in the sixteenth and seventeenth centuries.[1] During the period of time examined in this volume, from 1585 (the date of the official English intervention in the Spanish–Dutch or Eighty Years War) until 1702 (the death of William III), a war was going on somewhere in Europe for all but a little more than three years. In western Europe, Spain, France,

---

[1] Sir Michael Howard, *The Causes of War and Other Essays* (Cambridge, Mass., 1983), 9, 11–13.

and the Netherlands were at war approximately two out of every three years; in eastern Europe, Sweden, Russia, and Poland engaged in armed struggles four out of every five years. The Three Kingdoms of England, Ireland, and Scotland were relatively peaceful, since they were at war for only forty-nine of those 117 years. The long-term trend in early modern Europe was to fight less frequently from the sixteenth through the eighteenth centuries—probably because the number of civil wars and rebellions generally decreased and because war became more and more expensive. For the Three Kingdoms the long-term trend was to become more involved in continental European and colonial wars during the early modern period. The North American colonies were also at war during nearly half of the years between 1607 and 1702.[2] Other than a few peripheral campaigns to clear the French out of Scotland (1560–73) and to suppress the Northern Rebellion (1569–70), Elizabethan England was spared the destruction and turmoil of warfare for a generation. Queen Elizabeth I avoided projecting a bellicose image, and, knowing the cost of war, preferred diplomatic methods of resolving disputes.[3] The English people enjoyed several decades of peace, and the English aristocracy became largely demilitarized for want of opportunities to pursue their favourite pastime.[4]

[2] Historians and social scientists who have attempted to calculate how much war there was in early modern Europe have been unable to agree upon a set of criteria for defining war. Some, such as André Corvisier, include only wars between great powers and exclude rebellions and civil wars such as the Eighty Years War (1568–1648) before 1621 and the British and Irish civil wars or Wars of the Three Kingdoms (1638–51). At the other extreme, a Quaker social scientist, Lewis F. Richardson, includes all acts of aggression such as banditries, group murders and feuds, mutinies and insurrections, as well as 'wars small and large' (André Corvisier, 'Guerre et mentalités au XVII$^e$ siècle', XVII$^e$ siècle, 148 (1985), 2220–1; Jack S. Levy, 'Historical Trends in Great Power War, 1495–1975', International Studies Quarterly, 26.2 (1982), 289; Francis A. Beer, How Much War in History: Definitions, Estimates, Extrapolations and Trends (Sage International Studies Series, 3; Beverley Hills, Calif., 1974), 8, 12–14; Lewis F. Richardson, Statistics of Deadly Quarrels (Pittsburgh and Chicago, 1960), 5–6, 175; E. W. Carp, 'Early American Military History: A Review of Recent Work', Virginia Magazine of History and Biography, 94.3 (1986), 260–1. It would appear that whether or not a conflict qualifies as a war can depend upon one's ethical code, ideology, and national or ethnic perspective. I have included civil wars as well as sustained and armed rebellions in my calculations of how much war there was in mainland Europe and the British Isles during the late-sixteenth and seventeenth centuries.
[3] Mark Charles Fissel, English Warfare, 1511–1642 (London, 2001), 114–36; Ben Lowe, Imagining Peace: A History of Early English Pacifistic Ideas, 1340–1560 (University Park, Pa., 1997), 300–5; R. B. Wernham, Before the Armada: The Emergence of the English Nation, 1485–1588 (repr. New York, 1972), 235–43.
[4] Lawrence Stone, The Crisis of the Aristocracy, 1558–1641 (Oxford, 1965), 256.

The peace did not persist. Presented with the threat of an increasingly hostile Spain in the Low Countries, Elizabeth decided to intervene and send assistance to the Dutch in their struggle to gain freedom from the Spanish Habsburgs, and a military expedition under the command of Robert Dudley, earl of Leicester, was dispatched to the Netherlands in the late autumn of 1585. This was the first of a series of military and naval expeditions that were sent to the Low Countries, the Rhenish Palatinate, Northern France, the Iberian Peninsula, Ireland, and the West Indies over the next forty-three years. Many English, Scots, and Irish not only accompanied these expeditions but also fought in the armies of both Catholic and Protestant powers and rebel groups of mainland Europe as gentlemen volunteers, officers, and impressed soldiers. Since England itself remained unscathed by war until the Battle of Newburn in 1640 (during the Second Bishops' War), the experience of warfare in the modern mode remained largely hidden from the English people except for the disruption caused by higher levels of taxation, the impressment and discharge of considerable numbers of soldiers and mariners, the billeting of the same upon civilian households, and the proclamation of martial law to deal with the resulting disorders.

Then came the Wars of the Three Kingdoms, otherwise known as the civil wars of England, Ireland, and Scotland, which rudely demonstrated how interwoven the politics and military cultures of Europe and the British Isles had become. Rival armies were raised in each of the Three Kingdoms, that were kept standing and fought one another for a decade before the Parliamentarian and Cromwellian forces prevailed. The Gaelic societies of the more remote and hilly regions of the British Isles had retained warrior classes and had long been characterized by species of private warfare that included clan conflict, blood feuds, cattle raiding, and the like. These private conflicts could be bloody enough, but had been largely fought with the medieval weapons of sword, bow, and axe, and their casualties paled in comparison with the fearful tolls that the more modern mode of warfare of mainland Europe extracted through slaughter, famine, and disease. Returning English, Scottish, and Irish veterans of the continental European conflicts introduced this new style of warfare into the British Isles, which employed larger and more permanent armies, more advanced firearms, siege warfare, and the more systematic exploitation of economic resources.

At the end of the British and Irish civil wars, each of the Three Kingdoms retained small standing armies, which gradually became more integrated under English control, while the English navy of the Interregnum and Restoration periods was deployed further and further from home waters and engaged in a number of naval wars— most notably with the Dutch Republic in the third quarter of the seventeenth century. William III's descent on England and his conquest of Scotland and Ireland in 1689–92, together with the Glorious Revolution, placed a soldier-king on the thrones of the Three Kingdoms and dragged the peoples of the British Isles into a series of European and colonial wars that persisted for more than a century. At the beginning of the period under discussion, when England intervened in the Eighty Years War, the Three Kingdoms were second- and third-rate powers in a backwater of Europe; at the time of William III's death in 1702 the Three Kingdoms were coalescing into a unified entity that by reason of its military and naval forces and an efficient system for exploiting its economic resources could lay claim to great-power status in Europe and beyond. The arrival at the threshold of great-power status of the Three Kingdoms cannot be explained only by the development of a fiscal system, which gathered into the government's hands the sinews of war and allowed it to wage war on an unprecedented scale;[5] the politically active peoples of the British Isles had first to undergo a cultural change that exposed them to the martial ethos of the mainland European aristocracies. As a consequence of this cultural transformation, the English aristocracy was remilitarized, and the Scottish and Irish aristocracies, which had never been demilitarized, came to realize that greater opportunities lay waiting beyond the myopic world of clan rivalries, blood feuds, and cattle raiding. By the beginning of the eighteenth century those swordsmen of Protestant persuasion had come to embrace the new opportunities that service in the British army offered for honour, glory, and professional careers.

Among the gentlemen volunteers, officers, and soldiers from the British Isles who had fought in the various armies and navies of mainland Europe prior to the civil wars and continued to serve in those forces thereafter a distinctive set of experiences, attitudes, customs, and traditions accumulated. During the late-sixteenth and seventeenth centuries a martial culture developed among those who were employed

---

[5] For examples of this approach, see John Brewer, *The Sinews of Power: War, Money and the English State, 1688–1788* (New York, 1989), and James Scott Wheeler, *The Making of a World Power: War and the Military Revolution in Seventeenth-Century England* (Stroud, 1999).

as soldiers overseas that was largely alien to courtier, urban, and provincial cultures and stood outside the mainstream of recent English,
Irish, and Scottish experience. Since those who sought adventure and
pursued the military life before 1640 (other than in the Irish wars)
were usually obliged to do so in the mainland European wars, they
were brought into contact with a distinctly European martial culture,
which flourished in the camps and courts of martialists such as the
princes of Orange, who commanded the Dutch army, and Gustavus
Adolphus, king of Sweden, as well Ambrose Spinola, commander of
the Spanish Army of Flanders. In pursuit of virtue and honour as well
as booty, they grew accustomed to hazarding their lives and testing
their valour. Violence was their stock in trade. When they returned
home—often congregating in the taverns of London in the winter
months between the campaigning seasons—they became aware that
their values and way of life were distinctive and different from those
of courtiers and those who stayed at home. Courtier culture they
regarded as effeminate, and 'carpet knights' and gownsmen were
beneath contempt. Swordsmen frequently resorted to violence to
punish infractions of their professional code and they punished trans-
gressors in a characteristically military way.[6]

Warfare, like sports, possesses its own sets of rules, which encodes
values that reveal various martial cultures arising in different times
and places. By the end of the Middle Ages two concepts of warfare
had emerged in Europe: one was an agonistic kind of war fought
according to the rules of chivalry by noblemen and gentlemen who
regarded their enemies as worthy opponents. Feudal warriors derived
their status from the possession of hand-wielded edged weapons
that required prowess gained by long practice in the exercise of
arms. Such swordsmen and gallants considered themselves to be the
equals of all others armed in the same way. Armies composed of such
warriors tended to be impermanent, possessed of little organization
and less discipline. Warriors who came out of the feudal tradition
tended to regard war as a ritual that served to emphasize their status
and validate their honour rather than as an instrument to gain

---

[6] See Edward A. Shils, 'Introduction', in Georges Sorel, *Reflections on Violence*,
trans T. E. Hulme and J. Roth (1950; repr. New York, 1961), 14–15: 'Heroism and
a sense of the sublime are the highest virtues—they are military virtues whether
practiced inside the society in the case of civil war or outside the society in the case of
national wars; they raise the dignity of the individual and endow him with the pride
which dignity requires.'

military and political objectives. A newer kind of instrumental war, or 'war to the death', in which the enemy was an evil force or an obstacle to be destroyed, was ushered in by commoners who spurned the values of the feudal aristocracy and whom amateur swordsmen regarded as mercenaries. Their mercenary status reflected not so much that they were paid to fight, because the nobility were often paid in late-medieval and early modern wars, but rather their lower social status in the eyes of the military nobility. The advent of soldiers who wielded missile weapons such as longbows, crossbows, muskets, cannons, and the like had a levelling effect in military affairs and favoured the advancement of those persons who possessed technical expertise in missile weapons systems, military engineering and fortification, and logistics—some of the innovations that came to be associated with the so-called military revolution.[7] This provoked a reaction among swordsmen and gallants who clung to the older values and the use of traditional edged weapons such as swords and pikes. This reaction is associated with what historians and literary scholars call the 'chivalric revival', and can be dated to the re-entry of England into the continental European wars *circa* 1585.[8] The persistence of the older martial values hampered the technological innovations associated with the military revolution, asserted that social hierarchies remained more important than military hierarchies, and thus delayed the professionalization of the officers corps of the armies of the Three Kingdoms.[9] Under royal leadership, because

[7] Anthony Grafton, 'Introduction: Notes from the Underground on Cultural Transmission', in Anthony Grafton and Ann Blair (eds.), *The Transmission of Culture in Early Modern Europe* (Philadelphia, 1990), 4; André Corvisier, *Armies and Societies in Europe, 1494–1789*, trans A. T. Siddall (Bloomington, Ind., 1979), 98–9; Martin van Creveld, *Technology and War from 2000 BC to the Present* (New York, 1989), 140–1; Geoffrey Parker, *The Military Revolution: Military Innovation and the Rise of the West, 1500–1800* (2nd edn.; Cambridge, 1996), 1–4; James A. Aho, *Religious Mythology and the Art of War: Comparative Religious Symbolisms of Military Violence* (Westport, Conn., 1981), 9.

[8] Arthur B. Ferguson, *The Indian Summer of English Chivalry: Studies in the Decline and Transformation of Chivalric Idealism* (Durham, NC, 1960); id., *The Chivalric Tradition in Renaissance England* (Cranbury, NJ, 1986); Richard C. McCoy, *The Rites of Knighthood: The Literature and Politics of Elizabethan Chivalry* (Berkeley, Calif., 1989); J. S. A. Adamson, 'The Baronial Context of the English Civil War', *Trans. R. Hist. Soc.*, 5th ser., 40 (1990); id., 'Chivalry and Political Culture in Caroline England', in Kevin Sharpe and Peter Lake (eds.), *Culture and Politics in Early Stuart England* (Stanford, Calif., 1993), 161–97.

[9] Christopher Storrs and H. M. Scott, 'The Military Revolution and the European Nobility, c.1600–1800', *War in History*, 3 (1996), 1–2.

the king's honour demanded it, high-ranking peers who were military amateurs tended to monopolize positions of command in these
seventeenth-century military forces, while experienced veterans of
continental European wars of lesser rank were relegated to subordinate positions (except under the Commonwealth and Protectorate and
during the reign of William III).

The conflict between social hierarchies and military hierarchies was
at the heart of the collision between the archaic values of a revived
code of chivalry and the need to compel warfare to serve political
and strategic ends by making efficient use of modern military technology. Treva Tucker has argued that French noblemen who fought
in the religious and civil wars of that country in the latter part of
the sixteenth century preferred to serve in the *gens d'armes*, or heavy
cavalry, because they perceived that this particular service maintained
their privileged status and provided opportunities to demonstrate
honour and valour and to enhance their reputations.[10] That light or
medium cavalry was more useful for military purposes did not signify.
The nobleman preferred hand-to-hand combat where he could display his individual prowess, and he did not readily adapt to fighting
as part of a group to secure agreed-upon military objectives.[11] Not
only French noblemen, but also aristocrats from the Three Kingdoms,
continued to have difficulty distinguishing between *duellum* and
*bellum*—that is, between private combat and public war declared by
authority of a sovereign or a state. On more than one occasion as late
as the English civil wars, English peers offered to fight individual
combats to determine the outcome of battle.[12] Under Leicester's command in the Netherlands, English swordsmen continued to show a
preference for capturing enemies of equal social rank in order to
ransom their captives. At first sight, the courtly ritual of jousting appears
to be remote from the tactical needs of modern cavalry warfare with
its emphasis upon group action and discipline, but it may have been
closer to the reality of how noblemen fought, since they continued
to show a fondness for individual displays of prowess.[13] Because of
the shortage of warhorses in England and the cost of shipping whole

[10] Treva J. Tucker, 'Eminence over Efficacy: Social Status and Cavalry Service in Sixteenth-Century France', *Sixteenth Century Journal*, 32.4 (2001), 1090–1.
[11] Sydney Anglo, 'Introduction', in Sydney Anglo (ed.), *Chivalry and the Renaissance* (Woodbridge, 1990), pp. xiv–xv.
[12] Adamson, 'The Baronial Context of the English Civil War', 104–5.
[13] Tucker, 'Eminence over Efficacy', 1090–1.

cavalry troops overseas, only a minority of swordsmen from the Three Kingdoms who served in mainland European armies fought in mounted forces, and they had to accept the reality that most opportunities for battle were to be found in the foot. Even then, officers and volunteers in the foot retained a preference for fighting with edged weapons—swords and pikes—until as late as the Nine Years War (1688–97).

Linda Colley has pointed out that the stereotype of the British as an insular people is not a true reflection of men and women who travelled widely. In the eighteenth century the travels of the British took the form of aggressive commercial and military enterprise.[14] In the seventeenth century the peoples of the British Isles travelled and lived abroad for a variety of reasons, including seeking military adventure and career opportunities in the service of foreign princes and states and the necessity of seeking religious and political refuge. At the beginning of the seventeenth century, wealthy aristocrats from the British Isles also began undertaking prolonged grand tours, which typically included equestrian studies and swordsmanship in France, observing modern fortifications in the style of the *trace italienne* in Italy, and perhaps serving as gentleman volunteers for a campaigning season or two in the Low Countries.[15] Those who sought a longer military apprenticeship and perhaps opportunities as professional soldiers gravitated towards three armies in particular. The most esteemed were the courts—in reality peripatetic military camps—of Maurice of Nassau, prince of Orange, and his younger brother and successor, Frederick Henry, in the Dutch Republic; of Gustavus Adolphus, king of Sweden, who campaigned extensively in the Baltic and Germany; and, for English and Irish Catholics, the Spanish Army of Flanders—especially under the capable leadership of the Italian general, Ambrose Spinola, marquis of Balbeses. Under Maurice of Nassau, the organization and training of the Dutch army, the conduct of war, and the army's logistical services were transformed by a series of innovative reforms that introduced standards of professional competence based upon a system of merit under which officers and men were judged by results rather than social status—although

---

[14] Linda Colley, *Britons: Forging the Nation, 1707–1837* (New Haven, 1992), 8–9, 370–1.

[15] Sir Robert Dallington, *A Survey of the Great Duke's State of Tuscany . . . in 1590* (London, 1605) [STC 6201], 8–11; id., *This View of France* (1604; repr. Oxford, 1936), sigs. S3–4; J. W. Stoye, *English Travellers Abroad, 1604–1667: Their Influence in English Society and Politics* (London, 1952; repr. 1968), 262–3.

the officer corps of the States' Army in most other respects retained an aristocratic military culture. Having served their military apprenticeships overseas, many of these swordsmen from the British Isles later became the commanders and officers of the various armies that fought in the Wars of the Three Kingdoms, and they were also the instruments by which the innovations of the military revolution were transmitted to the British Isles. Also, in the Dutch and Swedish armies in particular, officers and volunteers from England and Scotland often served together for many years—sometimes in the same regiments—and thus learned to regard one another as allies in the same Protestant cause. English and Scottish regiments of the Anglo-Dutch and Scots Brigades of the States' Army formed the core of William III's invasion force that landed at Torbay in November 1688. Later, during the Nine Years War and the War of Spanish Succession, this fellow feeling among Scots and English officers, which included a shared military culture and a growing sense of professionalism, helped to lay the foundations for a common British identity.

Following the end of the late-Elizabethan wars with Spain in 1604, many members of the aristocracies of the Three Kingdoms rejected the peace with the Habsburgs that James VI and I tried to preserve by his refusal to be drawn into the continental religious wars. Numerous peers and gentlemen volunteered as individuals or raised regiments for mainland European armies, while military writers and Puritan clerics condemned peace as an aberration that bred effeminacy, sloth, and neglect of the exercise of arms. Gentlemen returning from the grand tour or from service in continental European armies also imported Italian and French fashions of duelling, which helped to perpetuate old habits of feuding and interpersonal violence among the aristocracies and gave them a baroque formality. Young gentlemen felt that it was a necessary rite of passage to seek out danger and verify their honour on both the battlefield and the field of honour. Again, the martial culture that was shaped by these common experiences did not make a clear distinction between public and private combat, and the tendency of many aristocrats to view war in personal terms persisted. Parliament refused to make duelling *per se* illegal, and, while the Stuart monarchs feebly attempted to discourage the practice, none possessed the political will to eradicate the practice altogether. As long as armies were led into battle by aristocratic officers, monarchs still had need of swordsmen who could stare death and danger in the face and present an example of courage to their men.

James VI and I's policy of avoiding being drawn into the continental European wars was based upon a personal abhorrence of war, a distaste for rebels such as the Dutch Protestants or the Bohemian Estates that had elected his son-in-law, Frederick, the Elector Palatine, as their new king, and a recognition that his kingdoms lacked the financial resources to fight long wars. James ignored the mood of bellicosity that was widespread in the political nation. Many of his subjects believed that James's failure to assist the mainland European Protestants or even to help his own son-in-law, Frederick, regain his thrones in Bohemia and the Rhineland Palatinate in the opening phase of the Thirty Years War brought shame upon his dynasty and harmed the cause of international Protestantism. Believing that the king undervalued the valour of the nobility, many peers and gentlemen became openly critical of the Jacobean peace and continued to volunteer and serve in the armies of other Protestant princes against Habsburg might.

The neglect of military exercises and preparedness by James VI and I and Charles I not only deprived their subjects of the traditional and reassuring image of a warrior-king, but also contributed to the disastrous outcome of the various military and naval expeditions of the 1620s. Royal neglect of the militia also left the realm of England ill-prepared to repel or resist the invasion and occupation of the north of England by the Scots Covenanting Army during the Second Bishops' War of 1640. In both instances, Charles I had entrusted command of the royal forces to amateur gallants and courtiers rather than to experienced professional soldiers, because it was thought that the king's honour required that his military commanders should be of high social rank, and the weakness and ineptitude of the king and the military forces that he had raised were revealed to all.

During the civil wars the Three Kingdoms were flooded with professional soldiers returning from abroad to fight for their chosen causes. In the long run, victory tended to favour the experienced professionals and those who could raise and command permanent and disciplined armies. Many noblemen and gentlemen who became amateur soldiers or remained active in civilian politics acquired a distrust for professional soldiers as mercenaries. Civilians learned to hate standing armies, and the Interregnum governments discovered how difficult it was to control standing armies and ambitious generals. The events of the civil wars, of course, merely confirmed old prejudices. The preference for a select militia, based upon the lords lieutenant and office-holding gentry of each county raising a military force from among substantial yeomen and husbandmen, and the prejudice against mercenary soldiers and standing armies had been confirmed by reading the works of Cornelius Tacitus and Niccolò Machiavelli, who praised the ideal of a citizen army, which was associated with the Roman Republic, and warned against the dangers of a professional standing army, which was inextricably linked in their minds with political absolutism and tyranny.[16]

The Restoration of the monarchy in 1660 gave Charles II command of a small standing army in each of the Three Kingdoms. They were not large enough to play a significant role in the mainland European wars, but they were more than adequate for crushing religious dissent and rebellion. The English army had been limited by Parliament to guards and garrisons, and, since the former were posted to London, they constituted a visible and noisy presence in the metropolis, where their officers, who had abundant leisure, spent their free time brawling in the taverns and streets and duelling in the fields and parks. The pre-1640 dichotomy between swordsmen and courtiers had largely disappeared as the experience of war and exile spread military culture widely among the aristocracies of the British Isles, and made it requisite for amateur gallants to demonstrate valour either as volunteers during the Anglo-Dutch wars, or in continental European armies, or on the field of honour. Many of the veterans of the civil wars found employment overseas, and the British Isles of the Restoration period continued to be a major source of military manpower. Although the choice of which army a swordsman served in when abroad did not invariably reflect individual religious beliefs, Catholic soldiers from the Three Kingdoms did tend to serve in the military and naval forces of Spain, France, and Imperial Austria. Protestant swordsmen continued to gravitate towards the armies of Sweden and the Netherlands. Old Cromwellians, in particular, appear to have found a refuge in the military and naval forces of the Dutch Republic. The rulers of Denmark–Norway and Russia placed a premium on military expertise, and appear to have been willing to tolerate Catholics in their fighting forces.[17]

---

[16] The classic discussion of the persistent English prejudice against standing armies and professional soldiers is found in Lois G. Schwoerer, *'No Standing Armies!' The Antiarmy Ideology in Seventeenth-Century England* (Baltimore, 1974).

[17] See the database compiled by Steve Murdoch and Alexia Grosjean, which contains the names of more than 6,000 men and women, including a high proportion of military and naval officers, who migrated to or lived in Russia and Scandinavia in the seventeenth century ('Scotland, Scandinavia and Northern Europe, 1580–1707', database @ www.abdn.ac.uk/history/datasets/ssne). See also Dimitry Fedosov, *The Caledonian Connection: Scotland–Russia Ties, Middle Ages to Early Twentieth Century* (Aberdeen, 1996), 45.

The accession of a soldier-king to the English throne in 1689 and William III's subsequent conquest of Scotland and Ireland led to the participation of the Three Kingdoms—after 1707 the Kingdoms of Great Britain and Ireland—in the allied war effort against Louis XIV. This provided an abundance of opportunity in the armies of the Three Kingdoms and Great Britain for Protestant swordsmen seeking military adventure, glory, and careers. The entry into the cockpit of mainland European wars reflected a new direction in the politics of the Three Kingdoms, and this reorientation of British politics and foreign and military policy was surely made possible by the remilitarization of the English aristocracy and the integration of the English, Scottish, and Irish aristocracies into the European military world. At the same time, the failure to accommodate Catholic swordsmen in the British armies of the eighteenth century provided many able soldiers from the British Isles for the armies of Catholic monarchs and those more tolerant princes who gave a higher priority to professional competence than religious conformity.

# PART I

# Aristocratic Society and Martial Culture, 1585–1702

# CHAPTER ONE

# Swordsmen, Gownsmen, and Courtiers

To obtain estate of gentleness through service done in your sovereign's wars, to the defence of the church, your king or country, is of all human actions most excellent and worthy.

(Sir John Ferne, *The Blazon of Gentrie* (London, 1586)
[STC 10824], 37)

The military profession has in all ages been esteemed the most honourable from the danger that attends it. The motives that lead mankind to it must proceed from a noble and generous inclination since they sacrifice their ease and their lives in the defence of their country.

(Humphry Bland, *A Treatise of Military Discipline*
(London, 1727) [ESTCT 160420], 114)

The English antiquarian and legal scholar John Selden reminded his readers that noble status originally derived from the martial exploits of a warrior class. Kings came to recognize this nobility, and, although in more recent times they also conferred noble status on men of the long robe, Selden insisted that military men had a special quality that the king could not confer. The king could create peers, but he lacked the power to make a gentleman. Moreover, by licensing peers, knights, and esquires to display coats of arms with military insignia, the monarch put the recipient on notice that 'being a gentleman, he is supposed also to either be a soldier or ready upon occasion to be one . . .'[1]

---

[1] John Selden, *Titles of Honour* (2nd edn.; London, 1631) [STC 22178], II. vii. 855, 864, 866. See also Matthew Carter, *Honor Redivivus, or An Analysis of Honor and Armory* (London, 1660) [Wing C659], 12.

  Later in the seventeenth century, Algernon Sidney warned: 'Nothing makes the king's power to be so adored as evidence that in a moment he can raise a favourite from the lowest condition to far above what ancient nobles had arrived unto, or what

Selden's pointed reminder about the military origins of the noble estate in England as well as the rest of Europe was part of a clarion call issued by antiquarians, poets, dramatists, military writers, memoirists, fencing masters, and clergymen declaring that noble status and honour had to be revalidated in every generation. Sir John Ferne thought that gentle status, based upon 'bare nobleness of blood', was the meanest 'kind of gentry' because it derives only from heredity and not from the mind, where virtue (that is, valour) and reason reside. The civil laws everywhere have always assigned priority of place to men of arms over men of the law because the former status was obtained by knighthood on the battlefield.[2] Vincent Saviolo, an Italian fencing master in the service of Robert Devereux, second earl of Essex, stated that through the ages men had advanced themselves by arms and letters, but martial deeds have always been more highly esteemed —especially by poets. True nobility acquired by martial deeds and valour was always to be preferred to that which rested only on birth.[3] Matthew Carter explained that the knight would always have precedence over the lawyer or divine because the peace that permitted the latter two to enjoy their studies was a product of the sword of the knight.[4] Edward Molyneux's memoir of Sir Philip Sidney asserted that Sidney possessed 'the invincible mind of an ancient Roman' whose martial exploits were 'the only true mark of nobility'.[5] After standing armies came into existence in the British Isles in the middle of the seventeenth century, it became axiomatic that possession of a military commission constituted evidence of gentle status.[6]

These contemporaneous assertions of the primacy of martial values, spanning the late Elizabethan period into the eighteenth century, do not accord well with recent historiographical opinion, which posits

their ancestors in many cases had purchased by their services or blood . . . Our court way to it is easy and pleasant; the way of rising by war is with difficulty and danger' (*Court Maxims*, ed. H. W. Blom, E. H. Mulier, and R. Janse (Cambridge, 1996), 68).

[2] Sir John Ferne, *The Blazon of Gentrie* (London, 1586) [STC 10824], 15, 36–7.

[3] *Vincentio Saviola his Practice: In Two Bookes, the First Intreating Use of the Rapier and Dagger, the Second, of Honor and Honorable Quarrels* (London, 1595) [STC 21788], sigs. A³ʳ, B1ʳ⁻ᵛ; See also Carter, *Honor Redivivius*, 9–10; [Nicholas,] Sieur Faret, *The Honest Man: or, The Art to Please in Court* (London, 1632) [STC 21788], 23–5; Louis de Gaya, sieur de Tréville, *Gaya's Traité des Armes, 1678*, ed. Charles Ffoulkes (Oxford, 1911).

[4] Carter, *Honor Redivivius*, 13–14.

[5] Raphael Holinshed, *Chronicles*, 3 vols. in 2 parts (London, 1587) [STC 13569], iii. 1551–2.

[6] Carter, *Honor Redivivius*, 16–17.

a demilitarization of the English aristocracy in the Tudor period. In the medieval period the English aristocracy were as thoroughly martial as any in Europe, and led military expeditions into France, Flanders, the Rhineland, Italy, and the Iberian kingdoms, as well as Ireland and Scotland.[7] At the time of the Battle of Bosworth (1485), every English nobleman could be regarded as a military peer, but by 1576 only one-quarter of the English peerage had any experience of war. According to Lawrence Stone, English peers had lost their martial spirit and did not adapt well to modern conditions of war; only younger sons and impoverished peers continued to seek military adventure or careers. Few opportunities for military adventure presented themselves to the English aristocracy before the 1580s, and so they remained at home and managed their estates or were attracted to court life.[8] Up to the latter period, Professor Stone's assessment of the demilitarization of the Elizabethan English peerage is not far off the mark, but when he says that in the early seventeenth century 'only about one peer in five' had experienced battle, his conclusions must be challenged.[9]

My calculations of the proportion of English peers who had experience of battle, sought military adventure, or pursued military careers in the period 1585–1702 (that is, from the official English intervention in the Dutch war of independence, more commonly known as the Eighty Years War, to the death of William III) suggest a very different trend from that described by Professor Stone. By my calculations, 40 per cent of the English peerage in 1585 may be classified as military peers, with the proportion dropping to 36 per cent in 1595 and 1600. But thereafter the proportion of military peers begins to rise steeply: 45 per cent in 1605, 54 per cent by 1620, 63 per cent in 1630, and 69 per cent on the eve of the civil wars in 1640.[10] One would

---

[7] Perry Anderson, *Lineages of the Absolutist State* (repr. London, 1979), 116–17; J. P. Cooper, 'Retainers in Tudor England', in G. E. Aylmer and J. S. Morrill (eds.), *Land, Men and Beliefs: Studies in Early Modern History* (London, 1983), 79.

[8] Lawrence Stone, *The Crisis of the Aristocracy, 1558–1641* (Oxford, 1965), 265–6; Lawrence and Jeanne C. Fawtier Stone, *An Open Elite? England, 1540–1880* (Oxford, 1984), 257; Anderson, *Lineages of the Absolutist State*, 125–6.

C. S. L. Davies questions Professor Stone's thesis about the decline of the martial spirit among the Tudor nobility, particularly as exemplified by early and mid-Tudor peers ('The English People and War in the Early Sixteenth Century', in A. C. Duke and C. A. Tanse (eds.), *Britain and the Netherlands*, vol. vi: *War and Society* (The Hague, 1977), 10–12).

[9] Stone, *Crisis of the Aristocracy*, 266.     [10] See Table 1.1.

TABLE 1.1. *Total number of peers of the Three Kingdoms and the proportion classifed as military peers, 1585–1700*

| Year | Total English peerage | English military peers | | Total Irish peerage | Irish military peers | | Total Scots peerage | Scots military peers | |
|------|------|------|------|------|------|------|------|------|------|
| | | No. | % | | No. | % | | No. | % |
| 1585 | 62 | 25 | 40 | 29 | 19 | 67 | 49 | 25 | 51 |
| 1590 | 63 | 23 | 37 | 31 | 21 | 68 | 56 | 27 | 48 |
| 1595 | 58 | 21 | 36 | 29 | 23 | 79 | 56 | 25 | 45 |
| 1600 | 58 | 22 | 36 | 27 | 21 | 78 | 61 | 27 | 44 |
| 1605 | 77 | 35 | 45 | 32 | 23 | 72 | 68 | 29 | 43 |
| 1610 | 88 | 42 | 48 | 35 | 25 | 71 | 80 | 31 | 39 |
| 1615 | 87 | 43 | 49 | 34 | 23 | 68 | 77 | 35 | 45 |
| 1620 | 94 | 51 | 54 | 42 | 27 | 64 | 86 | 41 | 48 |
| 1625 | 103 | 59 | 57 | 63 | 43 | 68 | 85 | 47 | 55 |
| 1630 | 128 | 80 | 63 | 95 | 50 | 53 | 94 | 53 | 56 |
| 1635 | 127 | 82 | 65 | 97 | 56 | 58 | 108 | 66 | 61 |
| 1640 | 123 | 85 | 69 | 91 | 65 | 71 | 106 | 77 | 73 |
| 1645 | 149 | 106 | 71 | 98 | 68 | 69 | 114 | 88 | 77 |
| 1650 | 156 | 107 | 69 | 96 | 67 | 70 | 122 | 91 | 75 |
| 1655 | 187 | 98 | 52 | 98 | 64 | 65 | 126 | 89 | 71 |
| 1660 | 140 | 94 | 67 | 99 | 61 | 62 | 122 | 85 | 70 |
| 1665 | 149 | 99 | 66 | 110 | 63 | 57 | 130 | 78 | 60 |
| 1670 | 151 | 94 | 62 | 110 | 63 | 57 | 124 | 73 | 59 |
| 1675 | 153 | 93 | 61 | 111 | 63 | 57 | 127 | 67 | 53 |
| 1680 | 152 | 95 | 63 | 109 | 62 | 57 | 127 | 64 | 50 |
| 1685 | 153 | 96 | 63 | 105 | 60 | 57 | 123 | 59 | 48 |
| 1690 | 158 | 91 | 58 | 112 | 66 | 59 | 132 | 65 | 49 |
| 1695 | 163 | 86 | 53 | 112 | 63 | 56 | 122 | 62 | 51 |
| 1700 | 162 | 79 | 49 | 109 | 59 | 54 | 137 | 73 | 53 |

*Note*: The most important criterion for designation as a military peer is service as a gentleman volunteer or a commissioned officer in any army or navy of the Three Kingdoms or any other state. See n. 11.

expect the proportion of peers taking up arms or having experience of battle to increase substantially with the beginning of hostilities in the Wars of the Three Kingdoms, but that is not the case. The proportion of swordsmen among English peers rises only to 71 per cent in 1645 and then declines to 52 per cent in 1655—probably reflecting deaths in battle and by natural causes and fewer peerage creations in the 1650s, when Charles II was in exile.[11]

The explanation for this remarkable remilitarization of the English peerage in the decades preceding the Wars of the Three Kingdoms is, I would suggest, a rechivalrization of English aristocratic and gentry culture, as younger sons, heirs of peers, and peers themselves heeded the call of John Selden and others to validate their honour upon the field of battle. Since they could not do so in England, they served as gentlemen volunteers and military officers, together with their counterparts from the Irish and Scottish aristocracies, in the armies of the Dutch Republic, Spanish Flanders, the Holy Roman Empire, Denmark, Sweden, and France, as well as in the Nine Years War (Tyrone's Rebellion) in Ireland, or as naval officers and privateers upon the high seas. This brought them into contact with a European martial culture that reinforced what they learned from Selden, Ferne, and other writers, as well as exemplars of martial virtues such as Sir Philip Sidney and the second and third earls of Essex.

The Restoration of Charles II in 1660 provided the opportunity to reward faithful followers in arms, but, in fact, the total number of English peers decreased from 187 in 1655 to 140 in 1660, although the proportion of military peers rose from 52 per cent to 67 per cent. Thereafter, the absolute number of military peers remained fairly steady and the proportion slowly declined to about half of the English peerage in 1700. Although Professor Stone reminds us that the number of

[11] The database from which the statistics in Table 1.1 are drawn comprises 1902 individuals who held titles from 1585 to 1702 inclusive in the peerages of England, Ireland, and Scotland as listed in GEC.

The criteria for designation as a military peer include service as a gentleman volunteer or a commissioned officer in any army or navy of the Three Kingdoms or any other state. Also included are those who fought in any battle or participated in any armed privateering expedition, engaged in and led their retainers and tenants in any violent, private feud (duelling and poaching excluded) or participated in any armed rebellion or suppression of any rebellion. I have excluded Cromwellian peers, but have included Jacobite peers created by James VII and II after 1688. Also excluded from the database are the twenty heirs of peers who were killed in battle or otherwise pre-deceased their fathers. Those who served as lords lieutenant or militia officers are also excluded and classified as non-military peers unless they meet the above criteria.

The non-military peers comprise those who do not meet the criteria for military peers. From this category I have excluded the few peers who were ordained clergy and those who are known to have been underage (below 18 years of age) before 1702, or were mentally defective or physically handicapped.

The main sources for this database are those found in GEC, but I have also added in information from numerous contemporaneous sources.

military and colonial offices expanded after 1690,[12] my calculations suggest that English peers did not benefit from any largesse under William III, who did not trust English and Scots officers unless they had served in the Dutch Army under his command. (Of course, he did not trust the Irish at all—whether Protestant or Catholic.) In the eighteenth century, younger sons of the peerage frequently chose the army as a career, but not until 1830 did more than half of the officers of the British home army come from members of the landed aristocracy and gentry.[13]

What needs to be stressed is that the increase in the proportion of English military peers is not based on the rewarding of out-standing military commanders with new peerages (although that did occasionally happen), but rather reflects a long-term remilitariza-tion of the existing peerage in the period preceding the Civil Wars. Dr P. R. Newman calculates that, among the many regimental colonels in the Royalist army during the first Civil War, only sixteen received English peerages, while four received Irish titles and two were made Scottish peers.[14] Recruitment to the peerage on this scale will hardly suffice to explain a doubling of the proportion of military peers in England in the early seventeenth century.

How is one to explain the neglect of such an important phenomenon as the remilitarization of the English peerage by both contemporane-ous and modern historical writers? Lamenting the low reputation of soldiers in the middle of the Elizabethan period, Geoffrey Gates con-tended that, if England were a continental country 'environed with mighty nations', the soldier would be more highly esteemed than the lawyer or merchant.[15] Lord Burghley, on the other hand, thought that a soldier in peacetime was particularly useless. He strongly dis-approved of educating one's sons in military matters, and believed that professional soldiers could hardly be honest men or good Christians.[16] Sir Francis Bacon maintained that being of the royal council conferred

---

[12] Stone and Stone, *An Open Elite?*, 281.

[13] Ibid. 290 n.
In 1769, more than half the colonels of regiments were peers, sons of peers, or were married to daughters of peers (John Cannon, *Aristocratic Century: The Peerage of Eighteenth-Century England* (Cambridge, 1984), 120).

[14] P. R. Newman, *The Old Service: The Royalist Regimental Colonels and the Civil Wars, 1642–46* (Manchester, 1993), 99–107.

[15] Geoffrey Gates, *The Defence of Militarie Profession* (London, 1579) [STC 11683], 18.

[16] William Cecil, Lord Burghley, *Certaine Preceptes or Directions for the Well Ordering of and Carriage of a Man's Life . . . Left by a Father to his Sonne at his Death* (Edinburgh, 1618) [STC 4898], 10–11.

a higher degree of honour than that possessed by military commanders, although he was willing to concede that those who won honour on the battlefield should be more highly esteemed than mere favourites, courtiers, and office-holders.[17] The peerage and the armigerous gentry had assumed administrative and judicial duties, and had steeped themselves in classical learning. They were no longer merely 'the sword-arm of the body politic'. Moreover, knights and peers had ceased to be the principal means of defending the realm, as modern warfare demanded more technical expertise, and this weakened chivalric culture.[18] Queen Elizabeth never quite trusted martial men, and she made it a practice to play the men of the long robe off against the swordsmen without allowing one faction to become dominant. Peers with military experience were not well represented on the Privy Council, and the younger generation of peers felt excluded.[19] Although professional soldiers did exist in Elizabethan England, they were usually referred to disparagingly as 'mercenaries' and 'soldiers of fortune'. Because they did not meet the criteria of modern professions—that is, they did not undergo formal training or initiation or meet legally regulated qualifications—modern historians have been slow to study this group systematically.[20]

There were also more fundamental reasons why the military profession was slighted in Elizabethan and Stuart England. As a result of imbibing Roman history—especially as filtered by Tacitus and Machiavelli—many educated Englishmen had come to have an ungovernable prejudice against professional soldiers and standing armies as an order set apart from the ordinary citizen. In a republic, a citizen takes up arms to defend the laws and is only a part-time soldier; in a monarchy, martialists seek glory, honour, and fortune, and it is dangerous to give too much power to such persons. Montesquieu

[17] Sir Francis Bacon, Viscount St Albans, 'Of Honour and Reputation', in *The Essayes or Counsels, Civill and Moral*, ed. Michael Kieran (Cambridge, Mass., 1985), 165.
[18] Arthur B. Ferguson, *The Indian Summer of English Chivalry: Studies in the Decline and Transformation of Chivalric Idealism* (Durham, NC, 1960), 104–5.
[19] Simon Adams, 'Favourites and Factions at the Elizabethan Court', in Ronald G. Asch and Adolf Birke (eds.), *Princes, Patronage and tthe Nobility: The Court at the Beginning of the Modern Age, c.1450–1650* (London, 1991), 281–2; Linda Levy Peck, 'Peers, Patronage and the Politics of History', in John Guy (ed.), *The Reign of Elizabeth I: Court and Culture in the Last Decade* (Cambridge, 1995), 91–2.
Algernon Sidney thought that nothing was so 'destructive' to absolute monarchy as 'an ancient, powerful, virtuous and warlike nobility' (*Court Maxims*, 68).
[20] Barbara Donagan, 'Halcyon Days and the Literature of War: England's Military Education before 1642', *P&P* 147 (May 1995), 68–9.

was not the only political theorist who thought of England as a republic disguised as a monarchy in this regard. Consequently, civil employments were accorded more honour in public discourse.[21] With the exception of the expedition to LeHavre in 1562 and the Scottish expeditions of 1560–1 and 1573, which afforded small opportunity for military adventure, England had been at peace for twenty-five years when, in 1585, Elizabeth decided to intervene in the Low Counties to assist the Dutch against their former masters. England now had need of swordsmen, and the queen's honour required that the military expedition dispatched to the Netherlands be commanded by a nobleman of at least the rank of earl.[22] From among a diminishing pool of English peers with actual military experience, Elizabeth chose her favourite, Robert Dudley, earl of Leicester, to command in the Netherlands. When Leicester began to recruit volunteers for this expedition, the English nobility were experiencing a crisis characterized by a decadent way of living among the sons of the nobility, who ought to have offered their swords without hesitation. Thomas Moffet, a follower of Sir Philip Sidney and, later, of the second earl of Essex, remarked:

One was horrified to observe that many youths sprung from the ranks of nobles were—what shall I say?—sons of Mars? Nay, rather nephews of Venus! So unmanned were they by ease, delicacies, drunkenness, and sensual pleasures that they preferred to pursue their debaucheries at home, staying up all night to lead dances instead of to cross the sea for the sake of the commonwealth and in assistance of neighbours . . . To live in clover at home, to hunt wild animals, to watch a hawk, to enjoy abundantly every sensual pleasure far surpassed going down to the sea in ships for the sake of aiding a neighbouring country, and gratuitously running into fire upon reaching shore.[23]

---

[21] Charles Louis de Secondat, baron de la Brède et de Montesquieu, *The Spirit of the Laws* (1748), trans. and ed. A. M. Cohler, B. C. Miller, and H. S. Stone (Cambridge, 1989), 69–70, 328; Charles Moore, *A Full Inquiry into the Subject of Suicide, to which are Added . . . Two Treatises on Duelling and Gaming*, 2 vols. (London, 1790) [ESTCT 111258], ii. 69–70. Patrick Abercrombie (*The Martial Achievements of the Scots Nation*, 2 vols. (Edinburgh, 1711) [ESTCT 86819], i. 216–17) believed that Elizabeth I neglected the English nobility and allowed the House of Commons to get the upper hand; consequently Parliament was better able to maintain armies than the Crown in the civil wars.

[22] M. C. Fissel, *English Warfare, 1511–1642* (London, 2001), 85–6, 114–22, 131–6; Stone, *Crisis of the Aristocracy*, 265; Anne McLaren, 'The Quest for a King: Gender, Marriage and Succession in Elizabethan England', *JBS* 41.3 (2002), 282–8.

[23] Thomas Moffet, *Nobilis, or a View of the Life and Death of a Sidney*, trans. V. B. Heltzel and H. H. Hudson (San Marino, Calif., 1940), 87.

1. Engraved frontispiece from Thomas Venn, *Military and Maritine Discipline* (London, 1672) [Wing V192]. Detail depicting a pikeman triumphant over cupid (or lust) and a musketeer triumphant over bacchinalian excess. Huntington Library. The pikeman and the musketeer represent military virtue or valour banishing vice.

Elizabeth always displayed an ambivalence towards men of the sword; after the beginning of the war with Spain she needed men of martial spirit, but feared having them serve in foreign armies. The attempts by Leicester, his nephew Sir Philip Sidney, Sir John Norris, the second earl of Essex, Lord Mountjoy, and other Elizabethan military leaders to recruit gentlemen volunteers was taken by many gallants and courtiers

as an invitation to win honour together with their mistress's favour by exposing themselves in the wars, especially when the queen and the affairs of the kingdom stood in some necessity of the soldier. For we have many instances of the sallies of the nobility and gentry, yea, and of the court and her prime favourites that had any touch or tincture of Mars in their inclinations and to steal away without licence and the queen's privity, which had like to have cost some of them dear, so predominant were their thoughts and hopes of honour grown in them . . .[24]

Just as the monarch's honour required that his armies be commanded by peers of the rank of earl or higher, military writers asserted

[24] Sir Robert Naunton, *Fragmenta Regalia, or Observations on Queen Elizabeth, her Times and Favorites*, ed. J. S. Cervoski (1641; repr. Washington, 1985), 55–6.

that troops of horse must always be commanded by persons of noble birth, while other military offices should always be awarded to peers or gentlemen in preference to 'common people'. Henry Peacham thought that the highest ranking military commanders, so chosen, should also be of the prince's council of war and be the only ones to carry the royal standard into battle.[25] Although the development of the county trained bands during the Elizabethan period may have cut into the aristocracy's monopoly on raising and maintaining soldiers, the trained bands were for home defence only, and peers and magnates continued to be necessary for finding and furnishing soldiers for overseas military expeditions until the development of standing armies in the latter part of the seventeenth century.[26] Even then, they retained an important recruiting function and regiments continued to be named for their colonels-proprietors into the early eighteenth century.

Like the English peerage of the seventeenth century, the aristocracies of Scotland and Ireland also responded to the opportunities for military adventure or careers in the continental wars. The Scots aristocracy had remained feudal in nature in the Lowlands, and was based upon clanship—a Scottish adaptation of feudalism—in the Highlands, while the Irish peerage became colonial in nature as the Stuart monarchs created titles for English and Scots planters and adventurers. William III later gave out Irish titles to French Huguenot and Dutch generals who helped him to subdue Ireland.[27] In 1585, twenty-five of the forty-nine Scots peers were military. James VI and I was clearly trying to reduce the power of martial men among the Scots peerage, and the proportion of swordsmen dropped to 39 per cent in 1610, but thereafter the proportion began to rise: 48 per cent in 1620; 56 per cent in 1630; and 73 per cent in 1640. Again, as in the case of the English peerage, the largest increase occurred before the outbreak of the Wars of the Three Kingdoms, and reflects a reassertion of martial values among Scots aristocratic families rather than a deliberate policy of rewarding men of the sword. The proportion of military peers remains

---

[25] Henry Hexham, *The Second Part of the Principles of the Art Militarie Practiced in the Warrs of the United Provinces* (London, 1638) [STC 13264.2], 38–9; Henry Peacham, *The Compleat Gentleman* (London, 1622; repr. Amsterdam, 1968), 13–14.

[26] M. L. Bush, *The English Aristocracy: A Comparative Synthesis* (Manchester, 1984), 50–1.

[27] Keith M. Brown, *Kingdom or Province? Scotland and the Regal Union, 1603–1715* (New York, 1992), 47; Allan I. Macinnes, *Clanship, Commerce and the House of Stuart, 1603–1788* (East Linton, East Lothian, 1996), 1–3.

above 70 per cent until the Restoration in 1660, but thereafter declines to a low of 53 per cent in 1700 (including in the database the Jacobite peers).[28] Although a few new peerages were bestowed on professional soldiers of distinction, such as Alexander Leslie, earl of Leven, and James King, Lord Eythin, who had held high command in the Swedish Army, most of the new Scottish peers (an increase of 74 per cent between 1600 and 1640) were recruited from among the families of existing peers and holders of landed estates, who shared the same values as the older peers. In addition, 10 per cent of the Scottish peerages created during the seventeenth century went to Englishmen.[29]

In Scotland, a parliamentary peerage had come into existence only in the middle of the fifteenth century. Otherwise noble status derived from holding land by freehold, and anyone with a sufficient quantity was considered to be noble. Thus, lairds were also considered to be noble, although they lacked titles. The Scottish nobility, prior to the creation of the peerage, consisted of earls, barons, freeholders, or 'other nobles'. Most of the latter two would have had the status of lairds, but were not comparable to gentry in the English sense. Being a Scottish peer did not confer any special territorial jurisdiction that lairds and clan chieftains did not already possess. It is paradoxical that this distinction in status between lord and laird was so insignificant, considering how obsessed the Scots were with social rank. One mark of the continuing feudal nature of Scottish society was the extraordinary ability of lords, lairds, and clan chieftains to recruit their tenants as soldiers—something that English observers often remarked upon.[30]

From the Scottish civil wars of the 1560s until the beginning of the Bishops' Wars in 1638, the Lowlands were not organized for war and may have become partially demilitarized. However, the Scottish

[28] See Table 1.1.

[29] Brown, *Kingdom or Province?*, 35–6.

[30] Alexander Grant, 'The Development of the Scottish Peerage', *SHR* 57 (1978), 1–2; Brown, *Kingdom or Province?*, 34–5; Jenny Wormald, 'Lords and Lairds in Fifteenth-Century Scotland: Nobles and Gentry?', in Michael Jones (ed.), *Gentry and Lesser Nobility in Late Medieval Europe* (New York, 1986), 181; Allan I. Macinnes, *Charles I and the Making of the Covenanting Movement, 1625–1641* (Edinburgh, 1991), 2–3; Maureen M. Meickle, 'The Invisible Divide: The Greater Lairds and the Nobility of Jacobean Scotland', *SHR* 17 (1992), 70–1; Geoffrey Holmes, *The Making of a Great Power: Late Stuart and Early Georgian Britain, 1660–1722* (London, 1993), 22–3; Daniel Szechi and David Hayton, 'John Bull's Other Kingdoms: The English Government of Scotland and Ireland', in Clyve James (ed.), *Britain in the First Age of Party, 1680–1750: Essays Presented to Geoffrey Holmes* (London, 1987), 243–4.

nobility retained a martial reputation by engaging in private warfare in the form of blood feuds and cattle raiding—pursuits that were especially prevalent on the Borders until 1603 and in the Highlands throughout the seventeenth century.[31]

Otherwise, few opportunities for military service at home presented themselves to the Scottish aristocracy before the formation of the Scots Covenanting Army in 1638–9, and Scots lords and lairds were driven by a lack of opportunity for honourable employment at home and overpopulation to seek careers in the armies of Denmark, Sweden, the Dutch Republic, France, Spain, the Holy Roman Empire, and elsewhere. The presence of large numbers of Scots officers and soldiers in north European armies reflected more than poverty at home; this military migration also reflected an enthusiasm and a respect for the martial ethos that was encouraged by the education of Scottish youth in the exercise of arms and that grew out of a long military tradition. When the Bishops' Wars broke out, the Scottish Estates called for the return of Scots officers and soldiers in Swedish service. At Newcastle-upon-Tyne, Sir Alexander Leslie ran into no fewer than twenty-five veterans of the Swedish Wars.[32] Thereafter, peers usually filled the positions of command at the regimental level and higher in succeeding Scottish armies.[33] Not all Scots returned home from Sweden in the 1640s. Some eighty Scots were ennobled by the Swedish Crown during the seventeenth century. While not all were soldiers, those who were tended to come from distinctly military families.[34]

In late-Elizabethan Ireland, the number of peers ranged between twenty-seven and thirty-one, but between two-thirds and four-fifths of the Irish peers were swordsmen.[35] James VI and I wished to

[31] Julian Goodare, 'The Nobility and the Absolutist State in Scotland, 1584–1638', *History*, 78 (1993), 180–1; Keith M. Brown, 'Scottish Identity in the Seventeenth Century', in Brendan Bradshaw and Peter Roberts (eds.), *British Consciousness and Identity: The Making of Britain, 1537–1707* (Cambridge, 1998), 245–6; id., 'From Scottish Lords to British Officers: State Building, Elite Integration and the Army in the Seventeenth Century', in Norman MacDougall (ed.), *Scotland and War* (Savage, Md., 1991), 141; id., *Noble Society in Scotland: Wealth, Family and Culture, from Reformation to Revolution* (Edinburgh, 2000), 90.

[32] T. A. Fischer, *The Scots in Sweden* (Edinburgh, 1907), 114.

[33] Brown, *Kingdom or Province?*, 43–4.

[34] Fischer, *The Scots in Sweden*, 120, 259–64. Sweden had a service nobility, and by the 1650s most army officers of the rank of captain or above were noble (A. F. Upton, 'The Swedish Nobility, 1600–1772', in H. M. Scott (ed.), *The European Nobilities in the Seventeenth and Eighteenth Centuries*, 2 vols. (London, 1995), ii. 21–2.

[35] See Table 1.1.

curb the power of the native Catholic aristocracy—especially those who had been less than loyal in the Tyrone Rebellion—and so he began creating new peers from amongst the English and Scottish settlers resident in Ireland in order to tie the new aristocracy closer to his regime.[36] Not surprisingly, many of these new peers, such as Arthur, Lord Chichester, were planters and military men, and the proportion of military peers remained at about two-thirds until 1630, when it dropped to 53 per cent.[37] But a few were also Catholic recusants. Richard Burgh, fourth earl of Clanricarde, led a double life as a courtier in England and a landed magnate and governor of Connaught in Ireland. As the stepfather of the third earl of Essex he had strong connections with that circle of swordsmen and during his lifetime was able to ward off attempts to colonize Connaught. Randall MacDonnell, earl of Antrim, having helped to defeat the the earl of Tyrone in the Irish Nine Years War, was another Catholic peer who enjoyed promotion and favour under the patronage of the royal favourite Charles Villiers, first duke of Buckingham. James began the practice of selling Irish peerages in 1616 to raise money. Under Buckingham's influence, the Crown sold peerages to Catholics and former rebels; and, consequently, the Irish peerage doubled during the 1620s.[38] During the Civil Wars Charles I created new Irish peerages or conferred new titles on existing peers as a reward for military service or financial assistance, and between 1640 and 1650 the proportion of military men among the Irish peerage again rose to between 69 and 70 per cent.[39]

The belief that the English aristocracy had become demilitarized in the seventeenth century turns out to be a myth supported by very little historical evidence. Instead, a large part of the peerage and gentry, who had come to form one social class by the Elizabethan period,[40] were rediscovering their martial heritage and asserting these values in a measurable way in the first decades of the seventeenth century. This trend can be demonstrated quantitatively in the English

---

[36] Charles R. Mayes, 'The Early Stuarts and the Irish Peerage', *EHR* 73 (1958), 227–8.
I do not find Mayes's statistics on the Irish peerage to be reliable. I suspect that he counted each title held by Irish peers rather than each peer, however many titles he possessed, which has been my practice.
[37] See Table 1.1.
[38] Victor Treadwell, *Buckingham and Ireland, 1616–1628* (Dublin, 1998), 107, 109; Mayes, 'The Early Stuarts and the Irish Peerage', 238, 241.
[39] Ibid. 246–7; See also Table 1.1 above.
[40] Stone and Stone, *An Open Elite?*, 257.

peerage and is comparable to similar trends among the peerages of Scotland and Ireland. The peerages of each of the Three Kingdoms had been remilitarized to a significant degree before 1640.

These men of the sword attempted to assert that they were in possession of a distinctive culture and value system, and this insistence upon distinctiveness became embedded in the English language. In the early modern period military aristocrats throughout Europe persisted in their age-old attachment to edged weapons in preference to missile weapons and the use of gunpowder. This western aristocratic preference for swords employed in face-to-face combat belongs to what Martin van Creveld calls 'irrational technology', and the continuing association of the sword with war survives in linguistic usage.[41] Thus, the term 'swordsman', which dates from about 1601, and which means a 'military man', is also used to distinguish a man devoted to military exploits from a 'pen-gentleman'.[42] A Lincolnshire man, who was an admirer of the late earl of Essex, recently executed, said in 1601 that the Cecils, referring to the deceased Lord Burghley and his second son, Sir Robert, later earl of Salisbury, were no 'better than pen-gentlemen', and the whole Privy Council was packed with 'goose-quill gentlemen'.[43] 'Gownsman', which *The Oxford English Dictionary* says dates from about 1579, was a less pejorative term. Professor Stone admits that a distinction could be made between a *noblesse de robe* and a *noblesse d'épée* among the English aristocracy, but he does not think that English peers and gentlemen employed such labels.[44] However, Sir Francis Vere, who commanded the English contingent of the Dutch Army at the Battle of Ostend (1601), uses the terms 'swordsman' and 'gownsman',[45] and Thomas Adams, a chaplain to the Honourable Artillery Company of London, did not hesitate to use the more sarcastic label 'carpet knight', and idenified such individuals with 'effeminacy'.[46] Although he was not above extracting

---

[41] Martin van Creveld, *Technology and War from 2000 BC to the Present* (New York, 1989), 72–3.

[42] *OED.*   [43] HMC, *Salisbury*, xi. 586.

[44] Stone, *Crisis of the Aristocracy*, 60. This is because Professor Stone chose to read only the writings of gownsmen and their stewards rather than the writings of swordsmen.

[45] *The Commentaries of Sir Francis Vere* (1657), in *Stuart Tracts, 1603–1693* (Westminster, 1903; repr. Wilmington, Del., 1973), 183.

[46] Thomas Adams, *The Souldier's Honour . . . Preached to the Worthy Compagnie of Gentlemen that exercise in the Artillerie Garden* (London, 1617) [STC 22184], sigs. B2$^{r-v}$.

favours from the king's Scottish favourite the earl of Somerset, John Holles, earl of Clare, told Francis, Lord Norris, that 'the new courtiers believe more than they have cause, and like skillful shopkeepers magnify their wares beyond their worth'.[47] Barnabe Rich also expressed his contempt for 'battle-less knights' who 'have greater desire to be practiced in carpet trade'.[48] Sir Robert Naunton was aware that distinctions of culture and career patterns could be made between swordsmen and gownsmen or courtiers, but he preferred to call them by the more learned and polite terms of *militia* and *togati*.[49]

Naunton does not use the terms in a mutually exclusive sense. Lord Burghley was ranked 'amongst the *togati*, for he had not to do with the sword more than as the great paymaster and contriver of the war [in the Netherlands]'. Thomas Radcliffe, earl of Sussex, Leicester's rival, 'was indeed one of the queen's martialists, and did her very good service in Ireland . . . till she recalled him to the court'. 'But he played not his game with the cunning and dexterity that Leicester did, which was the more facile courtier, though Sussex was thought the honester man and far the better soldier.' Although Leicester gathered about him a group of gallants eager for military adventure and honour, Naunton classified Leicester as one of the *togati* because 'he had more of Mercury than Mars'.[50]

Writers of the seventeenth century understood that a distinction could be made between swordsmen and gownsmen. Henry Peacham, tutor to the children of Thomas Howard, second earl of Arundel, and a noted writer on heraldry, assumed that a state was 'preserved [by] *armis & consilio*', which he rendered as 'military and civil discipline'. With the first he associated 'valour and greatness of spirit', and with the second 'justice [and] knowledge of the laws'.[51] Such writers, however, had greater difficulty distinguishing swordsmen from courtiers, although they agreed that each category represented distinct values.

---

Sylvanus Morgan (*The Sphaere of Gentry* (London, 1661) [Wing M2743], sig. B1ʳ), says that 'carpet knights' were so called because they were summoned and knighted at court in time of peace.

[47] *Letters of John Holles, 1587–1637*, ed. P. R. Seddon, 3 vols. (Thoroton Soc., 31, 35, 36; Nottingham, 1975–86), i. 71.

[48] Barnabe Rich, *Alarme to England Foreshewing What Perilles are Procured where the People Live Without Regarde of Martiall Lawe* (London, 1578) [STC 20978], sig. Giiijʳ.

[49] Naunton, *Fragmenta Regalia*, 48, 52; Richard C. McCoy, *The Rites of Knighthood: The Literature and Politics of Elizabethan Chivalry* (Berkeley, Calif., 1989), 9–10.

[50] Ibid. 48, 52, 55.     [51] Peacham, *The Compleat Gentleman*, repr. 3–4.

Lorenzo Magalotti suggests that such divisions existed at the court of Charles II, although he states that Henry Jermyn, earl of St Albans, who had been a soldier, but was later thought of as a courtier, had managed in the course of a long career to offend both factions.[52] Mandeville saw a fundamental dichotomy between courts and camps. The first taught feminine accomplishments and virtues; the second promoted masculine virtues such as honour, frankness, 'and humanity peculiar to military men of experience, and such a mixture of modesty and undauntedness, as may bespeak them both courteous and valiant'.[53] George Lauder felt more comfortable among military men than at court:

> The camp's my court, wherein a corslet clad,
> I find more ease of mind, and walk more glad
> Than he who lac'd in gold and velvet goes
> Proud of the silken gloss of fading clothes.[54]

Jacques de Callières followed Castiglione in assuming that the education of a soldier and a courtier should be the same. When a young gentleman reached the age of 16 or 17, he should devote himself to such practical endeavours as the exercise of arms, horsemanship, geometry, geography, fortifications, Roman and French history, and Latin and modern languages. The more 'sublime sciences' studied by men of the long gown were 'too tedious and difficult', and might damage the minds of young soldiers and courtiers.[55] Although the boundaries between martial and courtly culture may have been blurred, military peers did not miss the opportunity to put down those who were not descended from a martial background. Thomas Howard, second earl of Arundel, could not resist reminding Robert, first Lord Spencer, that his ancestors once kept sheep. The latter retorted that, when his ancestors herded sheep, Arundel's ancestors 'were plotting treason'.[56]

[52] *Lorenzo Magalotti at the Court of Charles II: His 'Relazione d'Inghilterra' of 1688*, ed. and trans. W. E. Knowles Middleton (Waterloo, Ont., 1980), 59.

[53] [Bernard Mandeville,] *The Fable of the Bees: or, Private Vices, Publick Benefits* (London, 1714) [ESTCT 77573], 94–5.

[54] [George Lauder,] *The Scottish Souldier, by Lawder* (Edinburgh, 1629) [STC 15312], sig. B1ʳ; *DNB*, *sub* George Lauder (*fl.* 1677).

[55] Jacques de Callières, *The Courtier's Calling* (London, 1675) [Wing C301], 149–50.

[56] Arthur Wilson, *The Life and Reign of James I, the First King of Great Britain* (1653), repr. in [White Kennett,] *The Complete History of England*, 3 vols. (London, 1706) [ESTCT 145258], ii. 737a.

As swordsmen of the British Isles reasserted the values of their martial culture, the model that they most frequently looked to and imitated was that of the French *noblesse d'épée*. It had been traditional for the French nobility to spend some time in military service —especially younger sons—but the coming of peace to France in 1559 meant unemployment, which contributed to a crisis of status and identity among the French nobility. The age of the Religious Wars witnessed the spread of those values associated with the professional soldier—technical proficiency and skill—while the culture of French military aristocrats, derived from neostoicism, tended to place more emphasis on moral qualities in the education of a soldier. Thus, the French military nobility were driven to redefine their values, perceptions of status, and means of educating young gentlemen in the acquisition of military skills. The French example led many English and Scottish aristocrats to display neostoic values and professional ethics in the pursuit of war and a commitment to religious causes whether Catholic or Protestant. Skill in the exercise of arms revived and continued to be part of the education of young Scottish and English gentlemen in the late sixteenth and seventeenth centuries.[57]

Some chose to place greater emphasis upon lineage and feats of arms, whether or not they pursued the profession of arms. But Montaigne reminded his readers that nobility was still defined by function, and in late-sixteenth-century France that meant following the profession of arms and displaying virtue, which, in a military context, meant valour. The assumption that war was the proper occupation of a nobleman led to the further assumption that the *noblesse d'épée* were inherently superior to men of the robe.[58] At

---

[57] Ellery Schalk, *From Valour to Pedigree: Ideas of Nobility in France in the Sixteenth and Seventeenth Centuries* (Princeton, 1986), 10–11, 202–7; Davis Bitton, *The French Nobility in Crisis, 1560–1640* (Stanford, Calif., 1969), 2–3; Jay M. Smith, *The Culture of Merit: Nobility, Royal Service and the Making of Absolute Monarchy in France, 1600–1789* (Ann Arbor, 1996), 45; Brown, *Noble Society in Scotland*, 1–2; Cooper, 'Retainers in Tudor England', 79.

[58] M. L. Bush, *Rich Noble, Poor Noble* (Manchester, 1988), 51; Jonathan Dewald, *Aristocratic Experience and the Origins of Modern Culture: France, 1590–1715* (Berkeley, Calif., 1993), 7–8; Roger Mettam, 'Definitions of Nobility in Seventeenth-Century France', in Penelope J. Corfield (ed.), *Language, History and Class* (Oxford, 1991), 80, 85; André Corvisier, 'La Noblesse militaire: Aspects militaires de la noblesse française du XVᵉ et XVIIIᵉ siècles', *Histoire sociale/Social History*, 11 (1978), 341; John A. Lynn, *Giant of the Grand Siècle: The French Army, 1610–1715* (Cambridge, 1997), 87.

the same time, French martialists were compelled to accept the fact
that the changing art of war required higher educational standards,
and they turned to classical writers who had important things to
say about the organization, discipline, and tactics of deploying large
masses of foot soldiers.[59]

In actuality, the differences between robe and sword were often
based upon individual choice and circumstance, but the increasingly
specialized educations for the different careers forced individuals
into different cultural and mental worlds. Pascal thought that the
*noblesse de robe*, as well as magistrates and physicians, must dress up
in elaborate costumes because their authority rested, at least in part,
upon illusion; soldiers did not need to disguise themselves or wear
uniforms because their authority rested upon force.[60] The use of
violence, whether in war or in duelling, gave the military nobleman
a special knowledge that the gownsman lacked, and it was for this
reason that La Rochefoucauld thought that bravery was appropriate
only for the *noblesse d'épée*, although gownsmen and magistrates
might show resolution in the face of danger.[61] Not surprisingly,
this antagonism between robe and sword in France led to feuding,
duelling, litigation, and scurrilous language. Increased competition
in the political arena led noblemen to become more ambitious and to
think more about individuality and less about dynastic continuity,
which could not help but undermine patriarchal authority.[62]

There was really no other model in Europe to which the aristocracies of the Three Kingdoms could turn for inspiration than the
French *noblesse d'épée*. The nobility of Castile still paid lip-service
to serving the king in a military capacity, but lineage and descent
from those who had participated in the *Reconquista* of the fifteenth
century counted for more than actual military service, and, by default,

[59] Ibid. 8; J. J. Supple, 'François de la Noue and the Education of the French
"Noblesse d'Épée" ', *French Studies*, 36.3 (1982), 270–1.
In his *Discours politiques et militaires* (1587), in which he discusses the education
of the sword nobility, La Noue proposed the erection of four royal academies for
this purpose that would concentrate on moral philosophy, the art of governing, and,
especially, the art of war. His students would study mathematics, geography, and
fortification. The classics from the ancient world would also be included, but read
in translation (François de la Noue, *Discours politiques et militaire*, ed. F. E. Sutciffe
(1587; repr. Genera, 1967).
[60] Blaise Pascal, *Pensées*, trans. A. J. Krailsheimer (Harmondsworth, 1966; repr. 1986),
39–41.
[61] Dewald, *Aristocratic Experience*, 66–7.
[62] Ibid. 8; Bush, *Rich Noble, Poor Noble*, 51.

the Spanish Army had become 'proletarianized'.[63] The nobility of Holland appear to have lost their military significance with the rise of mercenary armies.[64] The German nobility were more well known to the Scots than to the English or the Irish, and, in any case, French was the language most frequently spoken in the polyglot military camps of Europe.[65] But Sir Robert Dallington could hold up the French nobility as exemplars of valour and courtesy, and thought that there was no better way for a young gentleman to acquire polish than by beginning his grand tour in France. Sir Edward Harwood praised the custom of the French nobleman of serving in the wars and learning 'good and perfect use of his arms'. Dallington thought that it was also important for swordsmen to be scholars as well, so that the prince's government would not be left in the hands of men of the long robe: 'I count him a very lame gentleman that cannot serve his country in peace and war.'[66] Sir Walter Raleigh, who had experience of war in both France and Ireland, said that an armed nobility was useful for overawing peasants, but then remembered that France was never free of civil strife.[67]

Exemplars of military virtues were even more important to the shaping of a revived martial culture than the writers on heraldry, chivalry, and the exercise of arms. As early as the 1560s, gentlemen who regarded themselves as 'born to arms and not idleness', began to think themselves obliged to validate their honour by serving as

[63] I. A. A. Thompson, 'Neo-Nobility: Concepts of *Hidalguía* in Early Modern Castile', in his *War and Society in Hapsburg Spain* (Aldershot, 1992), 382–4; id., '*Hidalgo* and *Pechero*: The Language of "Estates" and "Classes" in Early Modern Castile', ibid. 64–5.

[64] H. F. K. van Nierop, *The Nobility of Holland: From Knights to Regents, 1500–1650*, trans. Martin Ultee (Cambridge, 1993), 175–6; J. L. Price, 'The Dutch Nobility in the Seventeenth and Eighteenth Centuries', in H. M. Scott (ed.), *The European Nobilities in the Seventeenth and Eighteenth Centuries*, 2 vols. (London, 1995), i. 83, 95.

However, the lists of officers of the Dutch cavalry in F. J. S. ten Raa and F. de Bas, *Het Staatsche Leger*, 8 vols. (Breda, 1911–80), ii–iv, indicate that men with noble names continued to predominate, although they may have come from families located in parts of the United Provinces other than Holland.

[65] *The Appollogie of the Illustrious Prince Ernestus, Earle of Mansfield* (Heidelberg, 1622) [STC 24915], preface.

[66] Sir Robert Dallington, *This View of France* (1604; repr. Oxford, 1936), sigs. S3ᵛ–4ʳ, R4ᵛ-S1ʳ; *The Advice of that Worthy Commander, Sir Edward Harwood, Colonel. Written by King Charles's Command* (1642), in *The Harleian Miscellany*, ed. William Oldys and Thomas Park, 10 vols. (London, 1808–13), iv. 273.

[67] Sir Walter Ralegh, *The Works*, ed. Thomas Birch, 8 vols. (London, 1751; repr. Oxford, 1829), viii. 163, 183–4.

volunteers in foreign wars.[68] The exercise of arms belonged 'principally and properly' to noblemen and gentlemen of substantial revenues; to achieve fame by martial feats was the main characteristic of 'true nobility'.[69] In a book dedicated to Henry, earl of Pembroke, the Irish soldier Robert Barret assumed that the son of a peer would, because of his noble birth, have a disposition to 'war and arms'.[70] By their devotion to the exercise of arms, the nobility could provide an example to the humbler sort that would encourage them to practise their skills with weapons appropriate to their station.[71] John Hooker, the antiquarian, regarded Sir Philip Sidney as the leading exemplar of martial virtue in his generation.[72] Sidney was also widely admired as a model gentleman in the context of courtly culture, and thus was one of the very few men who could move comfortably between court and camp. He was an excellent horseman, a courageous and able soldier, an extraordinarily good poet, a man of scholarly tastes, a steadfast Protestant, and a skilful player in the game of politics. Despite the myths constructed by Fulke Greville and others, Sidney remained a genuine hero to those who knew him.[73] Leicester's stepson, Robert, second earl of Essex, had also gone to the Netherlands as an 18-year-old general of the horse; he was created a knight banneret on the battlefield at Zutphen, where Sidney received his fatal wound in 1586. Sidney bequeathed Essex his favourite sword, and Essex claimed Sidney's widow as well. Ambitious from the start, Essex also retained Sidney's personal physician, Thomas Moffet, who was on terms of intimacy with a number of sword families and was one of perhaps nine or ten authors employed by Essex. By shaping a suitable *persona* for Sidney, which would allow him to serve as a hero for swordsmen, Essex hoped to gather Sidney's admirers into his own circle.[74] Matthew

[68] William Camden, *The History of the Most Renowned and Victorious Princess Elizabeth* (3rd edn.; London, 1675) [Wing C362], 82.
[69] [Thomas Proctor,] *Of the Knowledge and Conducte of Warres* (London, 1578) [STC 20403], preface; Raphael Holinshed, *Chronicles of England, Scotland and Ireland*, 6 vols. (London, 1807–8), iv. 879–82.
[70] Robert Barret, *The Theoricke and Practicke of Moderne Warres* (London, 1598) [STC 1500], sig. ¶ 2ʳ⁻ᵛ.
[71] Proctor, *Of the Knowledge and Conducte of Warres*, preface.
[72] Holinshed, *Chronicles* (1807–8 edn.), iv.879–82.
[73] W. A. Ringer, 'Sir Philip Sidney: The Myth and the Man', in Jan van Dorsten, Dominic Baker-Smith, and Arthur F. Kinney (eds.), *Sir Philip Sidney: 1586 and the Creation of A Legend*, (Leiden, 1986), 9–10; Moffet, *Nobilis*, pp. xiv–xv, fo. 5ʳ⁻ᵛ.
[74] McCoy, *Rites of Knighthood*, 79–80; Moffet, *Nobilis*, pp. xv–xvi, xix–xxiv, fos. 94–5.

Sutcliffe, who had served as judge-advocate-general in Leicester's expedition to the Netherlands, said that he and all English soldiers looked to Essex to fulfil their aspirations and to be accorded the glory that stay-at-home courtiers continued to deny them.[75] In 1599, Essex carried with him to Ireland a great crowd of 'gallants', who included seven peers besides himself, three sons of peers, and several hundred knights and gentlemen.[76] The Essex legend survived his execution for treason in 1601, and Gervase Markham praised his son Robert, the third earl, as the heir to his father's position of exemplar of all military virtues in the succeeding generation: 'Indeed, being the son of that father, the very naming of his name was enough to raise an army to gaze upon him.'[77]

Customarily, it was the gaze of the sovereign that recognized and validated the military virtue of noblemen and knights, but, since Elizabeth I and James VI and I neglected to foster martial values, such validation in the British and Irish context had to come from the followers of a military leader. The need to observe and depict heroic actions, to present evidence of the presence and efficacy of military virtue yielding deeds worthy of military glory, called forth a new breed of writers who could depict warfare as theatre. Despite the increase in the scale and destructiveness of modern warfare, an awareness of its histrionic aspects developed not only amongst aristocrats but also townsmen.[78] The increasing number of publications about war in the late sixteenth and early seventeenth centuries, including military treatises, manuals on the exercise of arms, translations of classical writers and historians on military topics, newsbooks and newspapers, sermons preached to military societies, depictions of war in the graphic arts, not to mention chivalric romances—all testify to the spreading militarization of both aristocratic and popular cultures.[79]

Particularly noteworthy among the new varieties of martial literature was the memoir—both autobiographical and biographical.

<hr/>

[75] Matthew Sutcliffe, *The Practice, Proceedings, and Lawes of Armes* (London, 1593) [STC 23468], sig. B2ʳ; H. J. Webb, *Elizabethan Military Science: The Books and the Practice* (Madison, Wis., 1965), 62–3.

[76] *The Letters of John Chamberlain*, ed. N. E. McClure, 2 vols. (Philadelphia, 1939), i. 62–3.

[77] Gervase Markham, *Honour in his Perfection* (London, 1624) [STC 17361], 32; Wilson, *The Life and Reign of James, the First King of Great Britain*, ii. 736a–737a.

[78] Dewald, *Aristocratic Experience*, 58–9; Smith, *The Culture of Merit*, 4–6.

[79] James A. Freeman, *Milton and the Martial Muse: Paradise Lost and the European Traditions of War* (Princeton, 1980), 34.

In France it was assumed that no one could write authentic military history unless he had been in battle, but in England, because not every soldier lived to tell his story, military chaplains, wives, and secretaries were sometimes pressed into service. Among the earliest of modern military memoirs were the *Commentaires* of Blaise de Monluc, a French Catholic nobleman who placed great stress on personal merit and ambition. The translator of the first English edition, Charles Cotton, claimed that Monluc's *Commentaries* 'has been allowed by all to be the best soldier's book, that is, the best book for the instruction of a soldier that ever was writ'.[80] Among the classic military memoirs written by or about swordsmen from the British Isles in the seventeenth century were those by Robert Monro, Sir James Turner, James Touchet, third earl of Castlehaven, and Lucy Hutchinson, wife of Col. John Hutchinson.[81] An eager reading public expected accounts of battles and sieges to indicate that brave deeds were performed in the face of danger against a worthy enemy and to depict the profession of arms as a noble endeavour. All these literary devices had become conventionalized by the end of the sixteenth century. There was, of course, no substitute for the actual experience of war, because deliberate exposure to danger separated military noblemen from other people, and war wounds constituted an anticipated rite of passage for young gentlemen volunteers.[82]

Implicit in the assumption that one could not demonstrate virtue and win glory except when engaged against a worthy enemy was the further assumption that there existed a European brotherhood of arms sharing the same values. This is the reason why military noblemen often engaged in displays of magnanimity towards their enemies

[80] The first English translation is [Blaise de Lasseran-Massencome, seigneur de Monluc, marshal of France,] *The Commentaries of Messire Blaize de Montluc, Mareschal of France*, trans. Charles Cotton (London, 1674) [Wing M2506]. The standard modern French edition is Blaise de Monluc, *Commentaires, 1521–1576*, ed. Paul Couteault (Paris, 1964); an abridged modern English edition has been translated and edited by Ian Roy (*Commentaires: English Selections* (Hamden, Conn., 1972)).

[81] Robert Monro, *Monro, his Expedition with the Worthy Scots Regiment called Mac-keys*, ed. W. S. Brockington (London, 1637; repr. Westport, Conn., 1999); Sir James Turner, *Memoirs of his Own Life and Times (1632–1670)* (BC 28; Edinburgh, 1829); *The Earl of Castlehaven's Review: Or his Memoirs . . . of the Irish Wars* (London, 1684) [Wing C1237]; Lucy Hutchinson, *Memoirs of the Life of Colonel Hutchinson*, ed. C. H. Firth (London, 1906).

[82] Orest Ranum, *Artisans of Glory: Writers and Historical Thought in Seventeenth-Century France* (Chapel Hill, NC, 1980), 60, 88–9, 95, 253–4; Dewald, *Aristocratic Experience*, 65–6.

during the interludes of battle. In one of the most remarkable of early seventeenth-century memoirs, Lord Herbert of Cherbury recounts how, when he was serving as a volunteer under the command of Maurice, prince of Orange, at the siege of Juliers[83] in 1610, he had occasion to go, under flag of truce, into the camp of Ambrosio Spinola, marquis of Balbases, commander of the Spanish Army of Flanders. Spinola entertained Herbert at dinner with great courtesy. During the conversation Spinola asked Herbert how Sir Francis Vere, late commander of the English forces in the Dutch army, had died. Herbert replied that he had died of peace and boredom. Spinola said, 'it is enough to kill a general', and added, sympathetically, that he regretted that Vere 'died not in time of war but of peace'.[84]

That swordsmen had values, assumptions, and traditions that set them apart from gownsmen should now be evident, but, at the same time, it needs to be emphasized that martial society and courtly society were not mutually exclusive. Numerous writers agree that the distinction arose out of individual choice, age, and circumstance as well as family tradition. Aristotle had assumed that men who were soldiers in their youth would acquire the experience and maturity to become councillors in their riper years.[85] In the latter part of the seventeenth century, the Scots martialist Sir James Turner assumed that, since few gentlemen could sit at the council table, most would have to seek military careers.[86]

Arthur Wilson, gentleman-in-waiting and secretary to the third earl of Essex, was perhaps one of the first to point out that there existed in England a group of peers who had inherited a martial tradition from Sidney and the second earl of Essex. Wilson described them as being opposed to the court party. Among the martialists whom he identifies were his own master, the third earl of Essex, Henry Wriothesley, third earl of Southampton, and Henry de Vere, eighteenth earl of Oxford, all of whom commanded regiments in the Palatinate Expedition and in the Dutch army; Robert Rich, second

---

[83] Jülich or Gulik.

[84] *The Life of Edward, First Lord Herbert of Cherbury, Written by Himself*, ed. J. M. Shuttleworth (London, 1976), 72.

[85] *The Politics of Aristotle*, trans. Ernest Barker (Oxford, 1946), bk. vii, ch. 9 (pp. 301–2).

[86] Sir James Turner, *Pallas Armata: Military Essayes of the Ancient Grecian, Roman, and Modern Art of War, Written in the Years 1670 and 1671* (London, 1683) [Wing T3292], unpaginated epistle to the reader.

earl of Warwick, acquired his martial laurels by way of privateering and, later, command of the Parliamentary Navy. Wilson thought that Warwick was a swordsman by taste, whereas his younger brother, Henry, Lord Kensington and later earl of Holland, although he had soldiered, was more comfortable in the atmosphere of the early Stuart Court. Another member of Wilson's 'country party' was Robert, first Lord Spencer, who, although he did not hesitate to attack courtiers, was no swordsman. In Wilson's view, what tied this disparate group together was that they 'supported old English honour, and would not let it fall to the ground'.[87]

R. M. Smuts also recognizes the difficulty in defining courtly culture when he says that the court had 'a distinct nucleus but a vaguely defined periphery'.[88] If court culture displayed only a limited degree of unity, the same could be said of martial culture. While all swordsmen in the British Isles shared certain values characteristic of European military culture, their experiences differed, and one must take into account the existence of a number of martial subcultures within the aristocracies of the British Isles that had been shaped by service in Ireland, in the Dutch and Swedish armies, as well as in those of France, the Empire, and Spanish Flanders, as well as by the peculiar circumstances of their own native lands. Although this is not the place to explore the question, it is perhaps not too fanciful to suggest that these varying experiences did much to shape allegiance in the wars of the Three Kingdoms and during the Glorious Revolution and the Williamite Wars, which also partook of the nature of civil and religious wars.

Professional soldiers in Elizabethan and early Stuart England were becoming isolated from court culture because they had to seek employment elsewhere, and, like Sir Francis Vere, spent most of their time in camps.[89] They became bitter about stay-at-home courtiers who seemed to reap all the rewards, and these dichotomies and tensions between court and camp are evident in contemporary writings. John Clapham equated being 'a good courtier' with being 'a cunning dissembler'. He had Leicester in mind when he said this, and he felt

---

[87] Wilson, *The Life and Reign of James, the First King of Great Britain*, ii. 736a–737a.
[88] R. M. Smuts, *Court Culture and the Origins of a Royalist Tradition in Early Stuart England* (Philadelphia, 1987), 3–4.
[89] Arthur B. Ferguson, *The Chivalric Tradition in Renaissance England* (Cranbury, NJ, 1986), 103–4; Naunton, *Fragmenta Regalia*, 84.

that Leicester did not make a good soldier because he preferred the 'ease and delights of the court' to 'service in the field', and it was only ambition that drove him to the Low Countries Wars. While in the Netherlands he spent most of his time 'in shows of triumph and feasting'.[90] By contrast, when he was at court, Sir Philip Sidney had the reputation of surrounding himself with soldiers and never living like a 'carpet knight'. Martialists also admired Sidney for the forthright manner in which he offered unwelcome advice to the queen; this afforded a striking contrast to the toadyism of the courtiers. George Whetstone thought Sidney 'a perfect mirror for the followers of both Mars and Mercury'.[91] The second earl of Essex was also presented as an alternative role model to the dissolute lives of courtiers: Clapham depicts him as one who hated both flattery and dissembling, 'esteemed soldiers', and always shared his gifts of patronage with those who served with him.[92] Raleigh was typical of many younger sons who began their careers as soldiers. Although he achieved success as a courtier, he retained the reputation of being 'valiant' in military affairs and became captain of the queen's guard. However, he lacked the affability of Essex and was as much 'hated' as Essex was 'beloved'.[93]

The same dichotomies and tensions are evident in Sir Robert Naunton's description of Elizabeth's court. The former lord deputy of Ireland, Sir John Perrot, was an archetypal swordsman who could not bridle his tongue and was unable to adapt to courtier society.[94] Peregrine Bertie, Lord Willoughby, 'was one of the queen's finest swordsmen':

I have heard it spoken that had he not slighted the court he might have enjoyed a plentiful part of her grace, and it was his saying (and it did him no good) that he was none of that *reptilia*, intimating that he could not creep and crouch. Neither was the court his element, for, indeed, as he was a great soldier, so he was of a suitable magnanimity and could not brook the obsequiousness and assiduity of the court.[95]

---

[90] *Elizabeth of England: Certain Observations concerning the Life and Reign of Queen Elizabeth by John Clapham*, ed. Evelyn Plummer Read and Conyers Read (Philadelphia, 1951), 90–1.
[91] Sir Fulke Greville, Lord Brooke, *Life of Sir Philip Sidney* (1652), ed. Nowell Smith (Oxford, 1907; repr. 1971), 60–3; George Whetstone, *Sir Philip Sidney, his Honorable Life, his Valiant Death* (London, 1578) [STC 25349], title page and sig. B2ᵛ.
[92] *Elizabeth of England*, 94–6.      [93] Ibid. 92–6.
[94] Naunton, *Fragmenta Regalia*, 65–7.      [95] Ibid. 61–2.

Sir Francis Vere was a soldier of formidable reputation, which derived from his deeds rather than his descent. He rarely came to court; Elizabeth both respected and envied him, but she found his independent manner subversive.[96] Henry Carey, first Lord Hunsdon, was Elizabeth's cousin and lord chamberlain. Although Naunton classified him as one of the *togati*, he had extensive military experience and had held high command more than once, and 'loved sword and buckler men'.[97] Two of Margaret, duchess of Newcastle's brothers were professional soldiers: 'for though they might have lived upon their own estates very honourably, yet [they] rather chose to serve in the wars under the States of Holland than to live idly at home in time of peace.' One brother, Sir Thomas Lucas, commanded a troop of horse in the States' Army, and his younger brother, Sir Charles, served under his command as a volunteer. The eldest brother, John, Lord Lucas, remained at home as head of the family and purchased a peerage. Although his inclinations were scholarly, he was also skilled in the use of the sword. The three brothers, when they gathered together, used

to exercise themselves with fencing, wrestling, shooting, and such like exercises, for . . . they did seldom hawk or hunt, and very seldom or never dance or play music, saying it was too effeminate for masculine spirits. Neither had they skill or did use to play . . . at cards or dice or the like games, nor [were they] given to any vice . . . unless to love a mistress was a crime . . .[98]

All of the seven younger brothers of Lucy Hutchinson's grandfather, John Apsley of Pulborough, Sussex, fought in the wars in Ireland and the Low Countries. They were all dead by the time she was born and left no issue. Her father, Sir Allen Apsley, gave up the life of a courtier after he had developed an excessive fondness for gambling, and followed the second earl of Essex on the Cadiz Expedition of 1596.[99]

The Civil Wars exacerbated the cleavage between swordsmen and gownsmen. When Aubrey de Vere, twentieth earl of Oxford,

---

[96] Ibid. 84.    [97] Ibid. 69–71.

[98] Margaret Cavendish, duchess of Newcastle, *The Life of William Cavendish, Duke of Newcastle* (1667), ed. C. H. Firth (London, 1906), 158–9; Edward Hyde, earl of Clarendon, *The History of the Rebellion and Civil Wars in England*, ed. W. D. Macray, 6 vols. (Oxford, 1888; repr. 1958), iv. 108.

[99] Hutchinson, *Memoirs of the Life of Colonel Hutchinson*, ed. Firth, 7–10.

was informed that the troopers in his Regiment of Horse Guards were subject to the common law just like everyone else, he angrily demanded where the gownsmen were during the Civil Wars when Charles I needed the help of his loyal subjects.[100] Charles II's supporters in exile were polarized into factions of swordsmen, courtiers, and gownsmen. Some of these tensions eased following the Restoration, perhaps because so many aristocrats, like their king and the duke of York, had experience of battle and were respected soldiers. Numerous courtiers actually fought with the fleet as volunteers during the second and third Anglo-Dutch Wars, and more than a few lost their lives.[101] Christopher Codrington was an unusual figure in the seventeenth century in that he moved easily between academic life and camp life in a way that could not have happened 100 years earlier. He had been elected a fellow of All Souls College, Oxford, on the basis of merit, and he subsequently began a career in the army without cutting his ties with the university. He joined King William's army in 1694 and campaigned in Flanders as an officer in the First Foot Guards. Following the end of the campaigning season, Codrington returned to Oxford and All Souls, and acted as public orator when William III visited the university. Later, William made him governor of the Leeward Islands.[102]

The values of martial culture appealed to a wider audience than peers and gentry. In 1592, Richard Johnson, who called himself an apprentice, gathered together the names and biographical details of nine men, who began their careers as London apprentices and achieved knighthood, but were not content to remain 'carpet knights', and subsequently achieved fame by martial exploits. For each he wrote a heroic poem. Among the more familiar of these names were those of Sir William Walworth, fishmonger and lord mayor at the time that he killed Wat Tyler at Mile End during the Great Revolt of 1381, and Sir John Hawkwood, merchant taylor,

[100] *The Autobiography of Sir John Bramston* (CS, old ser., 32; London, 1845), 126-7.
[101] John Sheffield, 3rd earl of Mulgrave and 1st duke of Buckingham and Normanby, 'Memoirs', in *Works*, 2 vols. (London, 1740) [ESTCT 86931], ii. 4; Roger Palmer, earl of Castlemaine, *A Short and True Account of the Material Passages in the Late War between the English and the Dutch* (London, 1671) [Wing C1247], sig. A3ʳ.
In France, the sword nobility also learned to get along better after experiencing the civil wars of the Frondes (1648-53) and discovering that they had common interests (Mettam, 'Definitions of Nobility in Seventeenth-Century France', 94-5).
[102] Vincent T. Harlow, *Christopher Codrington, 1668-1710* (London, 1928), ch. 5.

who was pressed to serve in France and later became a mercenary captain in Italy.[103]

The mercenary motives of the Scots who served in foreign armies have undoubtedly been exaggerated. In the absence of a royal court in Scotland after 1603, military service provided an outlet for the energies of many gentlemen. Numerous officers and soldiers who served in the regiments of Sir Andrew Grey and Colonel Seton at the beginning of the Thirty Years War in Bohemia were gentlemen volunteers who professed a personal loyalty to James VI and I's daughter, Elizabeth of Bohemia.[104] As in other countries, Scots soldiers volunteered for a variety of reasons. Charles Middleton, later second earl of Middleton, took up a military career not out of inclination, but because of financial necessity and partly to cut a figure at court where, during the Restoration, martial achievements came to be more highly regarded than formerly.[105] The first Viscount Stair fled Scotland after killing his father's murderer and forfeiting his estates; he became a soldier overseas and returned to command cavalry troops under Oliver Cromwell and, later, the earl of Glencairn.[106] Andrew Fletcher of Saltoun, who had himself been a soldier of fortune in Hungary where he fought the Turks, later condemned the martial heritage of Scotland and the tradition of younger sons serving as mercenary soldiers. Fletcher thought such a way of life was idle, debauched, and 'for the most part criminal'.[107]

---

[103] Richard Johnson, *The Nine Worthies of London: Explaining the Honourable Exercise of Armes, the Vertues of the Valiant and the Memorable Attempts of Magnanimous Minds; Pleasaunt for Gentlemen, not unseemely for Magistrates, and most profitable for Prentises* (1592), in *The Harleian Miscellany*, ed. William Oldys and Thomas Park, 10 vols. (London, 1808–13), viii. 437, 440–3, 456–7; William Hunt, 'Civic Chivalry and the English Civil War', in Anthony Grafton and Ann Blair (eds.), *The Transmission of Culture in Early Modern Europe* (Philadelphia, 1990), 206.

[104] Steve Murdoch, 'The House of Stuart and the Scottish Professional Soldier', in Bertrand Taithe and Tim Thornton (eds.), *War: Identities in Conflict, 1300–2000* (Stroud, 1998), 44–5.

[105] George Hilton Jones, *Charles Middleton: The Life and Times of a Restoration Politician* (Chicago, 1967), 18–19.

[106] Sir James Dalrymple, *Memoirs of Great Britain and Ireland*, 2 vols. (London, 1771–3) [ESTCT 145644], I. i. 216; *DNB, sub* Sir James Dalrymple, 1st Viscount Stair (1619–95).

[107] Andrew Fletcher of Saltoun, *Two Discourses concerning the Affairs of Scotland* (Edinburgh, 1698), repr. in *Political Works*, ed. John Robertson (Cambridge, 1997), 46; John Robertson, *The Scottish Enlightenment and the Militia Issue* (Edinburgh, 1985), 31; *DNB, sub* Andrew Fletcher (1665–1716).

Sir Robert Naunton states that a distinct pattern of marital alliances set the *militia*, or nobility of the sword, apart in the latter part of the Elizabethan period. The example that he seizes upon to make this point is the marriage of Frances, daughter and sole heir of Sir Francis Walsingham, to Sir Philip Sidney, and, after his death, to the second earl of Essex, and, after his execution, to Richard Bourke or de Burgh, fourth earl of Clanricarde and earl of St Albans in the English peerage, a prominent Irish Catholic and the stepfather of the third earl of Essex. In the case of Clanricarde, martial and marital bonds could overcome differences of religion. Despite the fact that he and his son and heir Ulick, the fifth earl, were Catholic recusants, the third earl of Essex grew very close to them. During the civil wars Essex, although much esteemed by Protestants, did his best to protect the properties of his half-brother Ulick, although formally they were adversaries. Frances Walsingham seemed to Naunton 'a lady destined to the bed of honour', and all her husbands were 'persons of the sword and otherwise of great honour and virtue'.[108] Sir George Holles was a fairly typical younger son of an aristocratic family with numerous relationships to other sword families. He was a younger brother of John, first earl of Clare, and by maternal descent he was related to the earls of Mulgrave. He was also a kinsman of the Veres, whose heads, the earls of Oxford, were military peers in at least four succeeding generations of the sixteenth and seventeenth centuries. Sir George began his military career trailing a pike in the company of 'his famous kinsman, Sir Francis Vere'. His first posting as a lieutenant was to the company of Sir Edward Cecil (later Viscount Wimbledon), whom he did not appear to like, and next he was lieutenant to Sir Thomas Knollys, a younger son of Sir Francis Knollys. By 1615, he had become sergeant-major-general of the English Brigade of the States' Army.[109]

Lord Herbert of Cherbury was very conscious of belonging to a sword family. Having spent his patrimony at court, his grandfather became a soldier in the Habsburg-Valois Wars in France and helped suppress rebellions during the mid-Tudor period with such good success that he refounded the family fortunes. Two uncles and

---

[108] Naunton, *Fragmenta Regalia*, 59; Patrick Little, ' "Blood and Friendship": The Earl of Essex's Protection of the Earl of Clanricarde's Interests, 1644–6', *EHR* 112 (1997), 927–41.

[109] Gervase Holles, *Memorials of the Holles Family, 1493–1656*, ed. A. C. Wood (CS, 3rd ser., 60; London, 1937), 73–5.

his brother William soldiered in the Dutch wars, and his autobiography opens with a boastful recounting of their exploits in both battles and duels. Another brother, Sir Henry, became a courtier and master of the revels under Charles I. Because he was not a soldier, he felt obliged 'to give several proofs of his courage in duels'. A third brother, Thomas, began his career in the camp of Sir Edward Cecil and campaigned in Germany; he later served as a volunteer in several naval expeditions.[110]

The Holles family was at the centre of a network of sword families. Sir John Holles, later Lord Houghton and first earl of Clare, maintained a lifelong aversion to the court. Just before he sailed with the second earl of Essex and Sir Francis Vere on the Azores Expedition of 1597, Lord Burghley reprimanded him for his familiarity with Lady Hatton, Lord Burghley's grandchild. Holles wrote an angry reply just before his departure, and only Lord Burghley's death in 1598 prevented him from making a Star Chamber case of it. In the reign of James I, Holles had to pay for his titles with plunder just like any other new peer. The barony of Houghton cost £10,000 and the earldom of Clare cost another £5,000. In 1620, he wrote to the lords commissioners for the office of earl marshal complaining that he had been affronted and his honour and that of the whole peerage touched by the manner in which Sir Edward Coke had ordinary subpoenas served upon him in a Star Chamber case instead of requesting his presence by private and personal letter. Clare regarded Coke as a man devoid of courtesy, and asked the Court of Chivalry to take cognizance of the case and to confer with the College of Heralds in order to preserve the dignity of the nobility of England. He lost favour in the eyes of Charles I because he avoided the court and because of the action of his younger son Denzil in preventing the speaker of the House of Commons from rising from his chair to prorogue Parliament. Clare's son and heir, Lord Houghton, married the daughter and coheir of Sir Horace Vere, Lord Vere of Tilbury, and his daughters made similar alliances. As head of the Holles clan, Clare discouraged his kinsman, Gervase Holles, from becoming a soldier because he was the only son of a dead father; Gervase became a barrister and an antiquarian instead, but he did not give up fighting duels. During the Civil Wars, Gervase finally fulfilled his ambition to become a soldier, and saw considerable

[110] *Life of Edward, First Lord Herbert of Cherbury*, 3–4, 8–9, 85.

action.[111] The earl of Clare also helped Ferdinando, second Lord Fairfax, place his son, the future Parliamentary general and later third Lord Fairfax, as a volunteer in Lord Vere's company at Dordrecht, where Lord Houghton, Clare's heir, promised to watch over him. When he arrived in 1629 at the age of 17, Thomas Fairfax was the third generation of his immediate family to serve in the Dutch Army. He later married Anne, the other daughter of Lord Vere.[112]

The Norths were a family who made the transition from gownsmen to swordsmen in the late Elizabethan wars and continued to maintain that status through five generations in the seventeenth century. Edward, first Baron North, was a barrister and chancellor of the Court of Augmentations. Roger, second Lord North, at the age of 55, volunteered for service in the Netherlands and, with his two sons, John and Henry, accompanied Leicester's expedition. Dudley, the third lord, also served in the Netherlands, while Dudley, the fourth lord, volunteered for the Palatinate Expedition in 1620. Charles, the fifth lord, became governor of Portsmouth. William, sixth Lord North and second Lord Grey of Rolleston, was the first of his family who could be described as a professional military officer. He began his career as a gentleman volunteer in Flanders in 1691, served with great distinction under Marlborough, and ultimately became a lieutenant general in 1710.[113] A similar rededication to martial values occurred in the family of Henry, Lord Norris of Rycote, ambassador to France between 1566 and 1570. Six of his sons, including the lord general, Sir John Norris, all became professional soldiers.[114]

[111] Holles, *Memorials*, 92–3, 106–7, 109; *DNB*, *sub* Gervase Holles (1606–75); C. R. Mayes, 'The Sale of Peerages in Early Stuart England', *J. Mod. Hist.* 29.1 (1957), 23–4; HMC, *Fourth Report*, part I (De La Warr MSS), 304a; *Letters of John Holles*, ed. Seddon, ii. 237–8.

[112] *The Fairfax Correspondence*, ed. G. W. Johnson, 2 vols. (London, 1848), i. 160; BL, Add. MS 18,979 [Fairfax Correspondence], fo. 15[r–v]; J. W. Stoye, *English Travellers Abroad, 1604–1667: Their Influence in English Society and Politics* (London, 1952; repr. 1968), 262–3.

[113] Harold H. Davis, 'The Military Career of Thomas North', *Huntington Library Quarterly*, 12 (1948–9), 317–18; *DNB*, *sub* Dudley North, 3rd Baron North (1581–1666), Dudley North, 4th Baron North (1602–70), Edward North, 1st Baron North (1496?–1564), Roger North, 2nd Baron North (1530–1600), *et* William North, 6th Baron North (1678–1734); GEC ix. 657–60.

[114] Naunton, *Fragmenta Regalia*, 63–4; Emmanuel van Meteren, *A True Discourse Historicall of the Succeeding Governors in the Netherlands and the Civill Warres there Begun in the yeere 1565*, trans Thomas Churchyard (London, 1602) [STC 17846], 54; *DNB*, *sub* Sir Edward Norris (d. 1603), Sir Henry Norris, 1st Baron Norris of Rycote (1525?–1601), Sir John Norris (1547?–1597), *et* Sir Thomas Norris (1556–99).

The Wakes were a family of Northamptonshire baronets who, for a period of 300 years, almost invariably sent their younger sons into either the army or the church.[115]

The record of military service of certain Scottish noble families is particularly impressive. All five surviving sons and an illegitimate son of Arthur, tenth Lord Forbes, fought in the Thirty Years War and four were killed. Alexander, eleventh Lord Forbes, rose to the rank of lieutenant general in the Swedish army and also served as a military recruiter and a diplomat. In the 1630s, seven Lindsay cousins of the houses of Crawford, Spynie, and Balscho were soldiers—six of them in the Swedish army and the seventh, Ludovic, sixteenth earl of Crawford, became a Catholic and commanded a regiment in Spanish service. The other Lindsay cousins included the fourteenth and fifteenth earls of Crawford and Alexander, second Baron Spynie. Only Ludovic and Lord Spynie survived the war and all died unmarried and without children.[116] John Blackader, lieutenant colonel of the Cameronian Regiment, came from a Berwickshire family, whose members, following the end of the Anglo-Scottish border wars, served in Spain under Ludovic Lindsay, sixteenth earl of Crawford, with Gustavus Adolphus in Sweden, with the Royalists and Charles I, and participated in the earl of Glencairn's uprising in 1653. His father was the heir to a baronetcy, but never claimed it and became instead an itinerant preacher who fled to the Netherlands after the defeat of the Covenanters at Bothwell Bridge, where his family became involved in Orangist conspiracies.[117]

It is possible to detect in the individual endeavours of gentlemen volunteers who went off to distant places to authenticate their honour a re-emergence of the medieval tradition of knight-errantry. Maurice Keen views this chivalric revival as being closely linked to the fact that many aristocrats could never fully acknowledge their subservience to sovereign monarchs. This aristocratic individuality manifested itself in a readiness of swordsmen to become rebels—whether *frondeurs*,

[115] Stone and Stone, *An Open Elite?*, 235–6.

[116] Alistair and Henrietta Tayler, *The House of Forbes* (Spalding Club, 3rd ser., 8; Aberdeen, 1937), 168–9; Alexander Lindsay, Lord Lindsay, *Lives of the Lindsays*, 3 vols. (London, 1849), ii. 53–7; Steve Murdoch and Alexia Grosjean, 'Scotland, Scandinavia and Northern Europe, 1580–1707' (database @ www.abdn.ac.uk/history/datasets/ssne), nos. 177, 1616, 2086.

[117] Andrew Crichton, *The Life and Diary of Lieut. Col. J. Blackader of the Cameronian Regiment* (Edinburgh, 1824), 13, 14, 17, 26–7.

Parliamentarians, Williamites, or Jacobites. The pursuit of personal goals such as building a military career in a foreign army and enhancing one's reputation and fortune could not help but subvert allegiance or lead to frequent changes of loyalty. That was a negative aspect of the influence of martial culture on the aristocracy and gentry, but it also inspired martialists to lead military and colonizing expeditions into Asia and the New World.[118]

As the careers of the second and third earls of Essex demonstrate, there was an inherent conflict in aristocratic culture and society between the pursuit of honour and the performance of duty that severely tested the allegiances of proud aristocrats and disposed them to rebellion.[119] Another direction in which this could lead was a rivalry between aristocratic amateurs and professional soldiers for import-ant offices such as military governorships and garrison commands. When Edmund, third Lord Sheffield, resigned as governor of the Dutch cautionary town of Brill, there were numerous applicants, including peers, for this office, which was in the queen's gift. The queen chose to appoint Sir Francis Vere in 1598 because he was an experienced commander who was the colonel of a regiment in the States' Army and had numerous victories to his credit. Essex, who headed the faction of gallants, or military amateurs and peers, ambitious for command, opposed the choice. Elizabeth's distribution of patronage also undermined the assumption that peers should always be given preference in the distribution of military commands.[120] After another dispute with the queen over the patronage of the lord deputyship of Ireland, the second earl of Essex turned his back on the queen, who cuffed him in the ear, whereupon Essex placed his hand on the hilt of his sword. Being advised to apologize, Essex made matters worse by refusing to admit that princes cannot err.[121] The conflict over

---

[118] Maurice Keen, *Chivalry* (New Haven, 1984), 250; André Corvisier, *Armies and Societies in Europe, 1494–1789*, trans. A. T. Siddall (Bloomington, Ind., 1979), 99; Roger Chartier, *A History of Private Life*, iii: *Passions of the Renaissance*, trans. Arthur Goldhammer (Cambridge, Mass., 1989), 22–4.

[119] Richard C. McCoy, ' "A Dangerous Image": The Earl of Essex and Elizabethan Chivalry', *Journal of Medieval and Renaissance Studies*, 13.2 (1983), 316–17.

[120] W. T. MacCaffrey, 'Place and Patronage in Elizabethan Politics', in S. T. Bindoff, J. Hurstfield, and C. H. Williams (eds.), *Elizabethan Government and Society: Essays Presented to Sir John Neale* (London, 1961), 107–8; William Camden, *Annales: Or the History of the Most Renowned and Victorious Princesse Elizabeth* (3rd edn.; London, 1635) [STC 45011], 465.

[121] Ibid. 493–4.

patronage was linked to the need of Essex to reward his followers, and engaged him in a struggle with the Cecils, Lord Burghley and Sir Robert, over the distribution of patronage. It also involved a dispute between the Cecilians and the Essexians over whether to make peace with Spain. Essex had united under his leadership a considerable number of martialists who believed that peace with Spain was utterly inconsistent with their values of honour and virtue. Camden regarded Essex's followers as 'swordsmen, bold confident fellows, men of broken fortunes, discontented persons, and such as saucily used their tongues in railing against all men'.[122] Essex, like so many swordsmen as they were depicted by Naunton and Clapham, was too candid and rash to compete effectively in court circles; his loss of influence drove him to appeal to the support of followers in the City of London and among the commonalty, and so down the path to treason.[123]

Not everyone was persuaded that the second earl of Essex's actions constituted treason. During the Christmas season after the earl's execution, a pall fell over the court. Essex's friends still gathered together and avoided the court: Sir John Harington, one of Essex's knights, entertained the earls of Rutland, Bedford, and Pembroke together with Sir Robert Sidney and others at his house in Rutlandshire. Following the accession of James I, the verdict of treason against Essex was questioned and, in retrospect, he became a Protestant hero. His son and heir, Robert, the third earl, together with the second earl's co-conspirator, Henry Wriothesley, third earl of Southampton, became a more successful focal point for discontent than the second earl had ever been. The circle of the third earl included not only those aristocrats who resented the thwarting of their military ambitions with the coming of peace and who hated the upstart carpet knights at court, but also attracted underemployed and unemployed military officers, City of London Puritan ministers, antiquarians and Oxford classical scholars, plus a number of poets and playwrights who were characterized by anti-absolutist sentiments and were committed to

---

[122] Camden, *History of the Most Renowned and Victorious Princess Elizabeth* (1675 edn.), 303.
[123] Margot Heinemann, 'Rebel Lords, Popular Playwrights and Political Culture: Notes on the Jacobean Patronage of the Earl of Southampton', *The Yearbook of English Studies: Politics, Patronage and Literature in England: Special Number*, 21 (1991), 67, 70–1; Blair Worden, 'Ben Jonson among the Historians', in Kevin Sharpe and Peter Lake (eds.), *Culture and Politics in Early Stuart England* (Stanford, Calif., 1993), 78.

anti-Spanish, Protestant nationalist, expansionist policies. Although denied patronage at James I's court, the Essexians found posts in the courts of Queen Anne and Henry, prince of Wales, where they were able to have plays produced that expressed their sentiments.[124] Thus was a fully developed Elizabethan martial culture passed on to a new generation of swordsmen who would volunteer in their numbers to fight in the mainland European wars of the seventeenth century, and who would be ready to take up arms when they returned home at the beginning of the Wars of the Three Kingdoms.[125]

It is difficult to obtain precise figures on the proportion of swordsmen to be found among the aristocracies of continental countries in the seventeenth century, but it does appear that the peerages of the Three Kingdoms were more thoroughly militarized than many of those of western Europe, and at least as martial as that of France.[126] While the English peerage had become demilitarized in the early and mid-Elizabethan periods, the stunning increase in the proportion of military peers by the beginning of the Civil Wars reflected a resurgence of a martial ethos among the English aristocracy that owed little or

[124] A. L. Rowse, *An Elizabethan Garland* (London, 1954), 73; Robert Codrington, *The Life and Death of the Illustrious Robert Earle of Essex* (London, 1646) [Wing C4877], 2–5; Vernon F. Snow, *Essex the Rebel: The Life of Robert Devereux, the Third Earl of Essex, 1591–1646* (Lincoln, Neb., 1970), 39–40; Heinemann, 'Rebel Lords, Popular Playwrights and Political Culture', 64–5, 70–1.
[125] Charles Carlton, *Going to the Wars: The Experience of the British Civil Wars, 1638–1651* (London, 1992), 19.
[126] Samuel Clark, *State and Status: The Rise of the State and Aristocratic Power in Western Europe* (Montreal, 1995), 160, 203.
The distinction between sword and robe nobility remained fluid in seventeenth-century France, and it was not unusual for the sons of robe families such as the Colberts to serve in the army. The proportion of noblemen who saw actual military service varied greatly in France by region and chronological period. In the Beauce region, in the latter part of the seventeenth century, it was 16%; in the Bourbonnais it was as high as 93%. In the bailiwick of Amiens in 1675, only ninety-two heads of noble households out of 390 surveyed (24%) could claim that they had served in the army or had an eldest son serving in the army. For all of France in the seventeenth century, André Corvisier estimates that between one-third and one-half of the French nobility served in the army. By 1775, Corvisier estimates that no more than a quarter of French noblemen served in or had served in the Royal Army (*Armies and Societies in Europe*, 102–3; Lynn, *Giant of the* Grand Siècle, 261 and n.; Jean Bérenger, 'Noblesse et absolutisme de François Ier à Louis XIV', in Béla Köpeczi and Éva H. Balázc (eds.), *Noblesse française, noblesse hongroise, XVIᵉ–XIXᵉ Siècles* (Budapest and Paris, 1981), 20). J. H. M. Salmon ('Storm over the Noblesse', *J. Mod. Hist.* 53 (1981), 254) assumes that among the French aristocracy the robe nobles were always more numerous than those of the sword.

nothing to royal distribution of titles and honours. The Irish and Scots peerages had never become demilitarized to the same degree as the English peerage, but they also reflect the same trend towards a remilitarization of values and culture prior to the Wars of the Three Kingdoms.

The noble classes of the Three Kingdoms may not be perfectly comparable groups, but it is possible to state quantitatively what proportion of the parliamentary peerages acted upon the values of martial culture at some point in their lives. While some were professional soldiers throughout their whole careers, others served as volunteers for only one or a few campaigning seasons, and subsequently became courtiers, or, more rarely, gownsmen in their more mature years, or simply retired to their estates. Some peers, such as the third earl of Essex, or John, earl of Clare, belonged to a hard core of martial men who showed a lifelong distaste for courtier culture and society. Others, like the earl of Holland, made an easy transition between camp and court, and we can say that both martial and court cultures had hard cores and soft peripheries that could and did overlap. The ranks of the gentry and lairds are more difficult to delineate and thus quantify, but it seems clear that many of them followed the example of their titled kinsmen, patrons, and colleagues, and were drawn into the ranks of the swordsmen.

There came to exist within the military society of Europe a growing dichotomy between the values and assumptions of professional soldiers, who expected advancement based upon experience and merit, and amateur gallants, who took it for granted that the choice of a commander should be based upon birth and social status. This fundamental clash between hereditary social rank and military hierarchies was resolved only when aristocrats integrated themselves into professional military cultures by education, experience, and acceptance of the merit system. That process was more drawn out in the British Isles than in Prussia or France, and could be completed only after the abolition of the purchase system of military commissions in the third quarter of the nineteenth century.

CHAPTER TWO

# Honour and Martial Culture

The winning of honour is but the revealing of a man's virtue and worth.

> (Sir Francis Bacon, 'Of Honour and Reputation', in
> *The Essayes or Counsels, Civill and Moral*,
> ed. Michael Kieran (Cambridge, Mass., 1985), 163)

High honour is not only gotten and born by pain and danger, but it must be nursed by the like, else it vanisheth as soon as it appears to the world.

> (*Aphorisms of Sir Philip Sidney*, 2 vols. (London, 1807), i. 34)

He that chooseth the profession of a soldier ought to know withal that honour must be his greatest wages and his enemy his surest paymaster.

> (George Monck, duke of Albemarle, *Observations upon
> Military and Political Affairs* (London, 1671) [Wing A864], 2)

The meaning of honour depends upon 'example, gender, class, occupation, religion and geographical location'.[1] In the martial culture of the early modern British Isles, which did not differ significantly from that of continental Europe, all gentlemen of whatever rank, from princes to lords to plain gentlemen, were presumed to belong to the community of honour. The first qualification for membership was ancient lineage and honourable descent, but honour could be retained only by deeds—the most usual and acceptable being to test one's honour on the field of battle.[2] 'Honour is that ardent heat, which inflameth the mind of men to glorious enterprises, making him audacious against enemies and to vices timorous.' Imperfect honour derives from 'man's

---

[1] Conference on 'Honour and Reputation in Early-Modern England', *Trans. R. Hist. Soc.*, 6th ser., 6 (1996), summary, 248.

[2] Mervyn James, *English Politics and the Concept of Honour, 1485–1642* (*P&P* Supplement, 3; Oxford, 1978), 22.

incorruptible state of nature and is retained as long as one does nothing disloyal, cowardly or unjust. Perfect honour is acquired only by valour on the battlefield, and is authenticated by the opinion of men.'[3] Henry Peacham, emphasizing the martial aspects of nobility, insisted that 'all virtue consisteth of action, and . . . honour is the reward of virtue and glorious action only . . .'[4] Shakespeare's history plays reveal much about what the playwright and his audience thought about honour. Ancient lineage and sound moral education conferred a predisposition to honour and yielded exalted rank and exceptional virtue (that is, valour). These qualities were necessarily manifested through displays of force, violence, and physical courage. A precondition of such exertions was martial prowess, and the best evidence of the quest for honour and glory was the testimony of wounds.[5] As Shakespeare has Richard, third duke of York, demand of Edward Beaufort, duke of Somerset, in *Henry VI, Part 2* (III. i): 'Show me one scar character'd on thy skin: / Men's flesh preserved so whole do seldom win.'

In Scotland as in other parts of Europe, writers on the subject of nobility argued about whether to give primacy to blood and birth or virtue as the source of nobility. The humanists, following Aristotle, tended to emphasize virtue. In the early seventeenth century, the poet Patrick Hannay believed that a noble who did not add virtue to the family's accumulation of virtue lost honour, while it was possible for a commoner to acquire virtue by deeds.[6] The more typical view of honour among the Scottish nobility tended to be less individualistic and more collective than was the case in England; honour derived from lineage, and, being less demilitarized than the English nobility of the Elizabethan period, the Scots nobility remained confident that they were possessed of martial prowess and capable of brave deeds. David Hume of Godscroft celebrated the House of Douglas, which for three centuries had brought forth warriors who were 'all singular in their valour'. Sir James Douglas, second earl of Douglas,

---

[3] [Count Annibale Romei,] *The Courtier's Academie*, trans. John Kepers (London, 1598) [STC 21311], 78–84.
[4] Henry Peacham, *The Compleat Gentleman* (London, 1622; repr. Amsterdam, 1968), 2–3. See also Thomas Hobbes, *Leviathan* (1651; repr. Oxford, 1967), 73–5.
[5] Curtis Brown Watson, *Shakespeare and the Renaissance Concept of Honor* (Princeton, 1960), 176–7, 218–19, 241.
[6] *The Poetical Works of Patrick Hannay, A.M., MDCXXII* (New York, 1875; repr. 1968), 35–6 157, 225–8, 235. Hannay, a Galloway poet, accompanied Sir Andrew Gray's expedition to Bohemia in 1620 in the company of Sir John Hepburn and Sir John Ramsay.

had engaged in single combat with Harry Hotspur, son of the earl of Northumberland. He won the Battle of Otterburn in 1388, although he lost his life. Godscroft asserted that the generations of Douglases had done more to defend Scotland against English incursions than all the military assistance from France. This is essentially what Sir James Balfour of Denmilne, Lyon king-of-arms to Charles I, meant when he insisted that nobility derived from ancient lineage of not less than four generations.[7]

The rules of honour constituted a public code that had nothing to do with private morality. The man of honour remained unsullied unless there was a public attribution of misconduct.[8] Sir John Ferne was not alone in thinking that a gentleman 'of blood' who was possessed of virtue 'is to be preferred before all others in the receiving of a dignity, office or rule in a commonweal . . .'[9] At the beginning of the eighteenth century Bernard Mandeville went so far as to say that gentlemen who were possessed of a sense of honour and understood their military duties would always make good officers, even if they were 'dissolute reprobates'. Such a person would always know what to do in the face of danger.[10] Eighty years later, Charles Moore found that men who possessed valour without any other virtues to 'sweeten' them were 'very pernicious to civil society'. This was because the moral balance achieved in politics by alloying justice and honesty with valour was upset by the greater emphasis upon honour that accompanied the fashion for duelling that came into England at the end of the sixteenth century and continued into Moore's own time and beyond.[11]

Because honour existed in the public sphere and concerned men of valour, it had to be protected from sentimentality and what Sir John Reresby called 'women's kindness'. Reresby was annoyed by his wife

[7] Keith M. Brown, *Noble Society in Scotland: Wealth, Family and Culture, from Reformation to Revolution* (Edinburgh, 2000), 4–5; David Hume of Godscroft, *The History of the House of Douglas and Angus* (Edinburgh, 1648) [Wing H3659], 92–101; Gawin Douglas, bishop of Dunkeld, *The Palis of Honoure* (London, 1553?) [STC 7073], unpaginated; Patrick Abercrombie, *The Martial Achievements of the Scots Nation*, 2 vols. (Edinburgh, 1711) [ESTCT 86819], vol. i, preface.

[8] James, *English Politics and the Concept of Honour*, 28.

[9] Sir John Ferne, *The Blazon of Gentrie* (London, 1586) [STC 10824], 23.

[10] [Bernard Mandeville,] *The Fable of the Bees: or, Private Vices, Publick Benefits* (London, 1714) [ESTCT 77573], 94–5.

[11] Charles Moore, *A Full Inquiry into the Subject of Suicide, to which are Added . . . Two Treatises on Duelling and Gaming*, 2 vols. (London, 1790) [ESTCT 111258], ii. 261 n.

because she was 'sometimes so mistaken as to wish a husband's safety before his honour and preferment'.[12] Bulstrode Whitelocke dealt with this bother by not informing his wife when he marched off to war in 1642.[13]

In the Restoration period, Sir James Turner, by his own admission a Scottish soldier of fortune, addressed his *Pallas Armata* to 'young lords and gentlemen . . . whose birth entitles you to martial exercises'. He told them:

The ancientest of you all derive your pedigree from those who bore arms; it is by arms you had your honour; and it is by arms you are now bound to maintain it . . . I shall entreat you to follow the footsteps of your martial ancestors, and account it more honour for you by war-like exploits to show you are worthy successors than to pretend it only by a vain muster of their old charters, patents and commissions.[14]

Many military peers were of the opinion that their social position could be maintained only by frequent opportunities to validate their honour on the battlefield; to be able to ignore danger and display courage was what distinguished the nobility from ordinary men. Archibald Campbell, first marquis of Argyll, thought that a prince should go to war even if it meant suffering defeat in order to provide opportunities for his nobles to earn honour; to remain at peace was a less desirable alternative because it meant granting patronage and pensions to courtiers.[15]

In English martial culture, chivalric values generally continued to favour individual ambition over public interests throughout the seventeenth century. Sir Philip Sidney thought that 'high honour' could be achieved only 'by pain and danger', and was sustained only by continuing exposure to the like, 'else it vanisheth as soon as it appears to the world'. This never sat well with Christian humanists,

[12] *Memoirs of Sir John Reresby*, ed. Andrew Browning (Glasgow, 1936; repr. 1991), 382–3.

[13] *The Diary of Bulstrode Whitelocke, 1605–1675*, ed. Ruth Spalding (British Academy, Records of Social and Economic History, NS 13; London, 1990), 140.

[14] Sir James Turner, *Pallas Armata; Military Essayes of the Ancient Grecian, Roman, and Modern Art of War, Written in the Years 1670 and 1671* (London, 1683) [Wing T3292], unpaginated preface. See also Thomas and Dudley Digges, *Foure Paradoxes and Politique Discourses concerning Militarie Discipline* (London, 1604) [STC 6872], 98.

[15] Archibald Campbell, 1st marquis of Argyll, *Instructions to a Son* (London, 1661) [Wing A3657], 129, 150. This book was written during Argyll's confinement just prior to his execution for treason in 1661.

and Sidney's Huguenot friend and mentor, Hubert Languet, was appalled by the 'wholesale slaughter' that was consequent upon seeking honour in violent deeds.[16]

Much of the hostility between the adherents of martial culture and courtly culture had disappeared in Restoration England as the latter became more influenced by the former. Books aimed at courtiers emphasized that it was highly desirable, if not requisite, to perform some valiant service. There were two ways of advancing one's fortune —to go to court or to serve as a soldier. The former was less sure because princes were whimsical and often bestowed 'their favours and caresses on persons that please them, rather than on such as advantageously serve them'.[17] If a man had the disposition, war was a surer way to both renown and fortune. It was not necessary to 'make arms their proper profession'; 'it was enough that they had once shown themselves . . . to be esteemed valiant'.[18] Although not every gentleman would have the occasion to experience battle, yet it was necessary for the preservation of the realm for every gentleman 'to know how to defend his king and country'.[19] Thus, as soon as he had arrived at court, John Wilmot, second earl of Rochester, looked about for an opportunity 'to hazard his life in the defence and service of his country', which he found in 1665 as a gentleman volunteer in the navy during the Second Anglo-Dutch War. Rochester went out of his way to risk his life, and fellow volunteers such as Thomas, Lord Clifford, had nothing but praise for his deeds.[20]

It was widely assumed in aristocratic circles that 'every man hunts after honour and wealth; these are the two grand wheels upon which the whole world is moved . . .'[21] The proper 'endeavour' of

---

[16] *Aphorisms of Sir Philip Sidney*, 2 vols. (London, 1807), i. 34; *The Correspondence of Sir Philip Sidney and Hubert Languet*, ed. S. A. Pears (London, 1845), 154; Edward Berry, *The Making of Sir Philip Sidney* (Toronto, 1998), 145; Arthur B. Ferguson, *The Chivalric Tradition in Renaissance England* (Cranbury, NJ, 1986), 111–12.

[17] Jacques de Callières, *The Courtier's Calling* (London, 1675) [Wing C301], 18–19; James Cleland, *The Institution of a Young Nobleman* (1611), ed. Max Molyneux, 2 vols. (repr. New York, 1948), i. 230; *The Triumphs of Nassau*, trans. W. Shute (London, 1613) [STC 17677], 76.

[18] De Callières, *The Courtier's Calling*, 20–1.

[19] Jean Gailhard, *The Compleat Gentleman*, 1 vol. in 2 pts. (London, 1678) [Wing G118], ii. 139.

[20] Gilbert Burnet, *Some Passages of the Life and Death of . . . John, Earl of Rochester* (1680), repr. in Vivian de Sola Pinto (ed.), *English Biography in the Seventeenth Century*, ed. (London, 1951), 100–1.

[21] De Callières, *The Courtier's Calling*, 8–9.

a gentleman is to seek honour; only the vulgar 'labour to become rich'.[22] This maxim rested, of course, upon the assumption that the gentleman in pursuit of honour was a person of substantial means. Only a very few military peers and gentlemen possessed the financial resources to sustain such a lofty and idealistic freedom from the taint of profit seeking. While all aristocratic soldiers hoped for glory and acknowledgement by their sovereign of this distinction as a reward, they also, by custom, believed that valour entitled them to ransom and booty as well.[23] At the beginning of the seventeenth century, most armies remained mercenary in nature and were expected to be more or less self-supporting; soldiers' wages, if paid, were invariably in arrears. Only in the Dutch army was the pay reasonably regular. Reflecting the values of a bourgeois society that did not tolerate the spoliation of property, officers and soldiers in Dutch service were expected to be content with their pay.[24] Clearly, there was ambivalence about the rewards of honour. Sir William Monson told his son that only a small proportion of soldiers survived long enough to enjoy preferment. George Monck, who served as an officer in the States' Army, thought that the pay was so insignificant that the soldier could expect little reward besides honour.[25] Selden, who observed that in ancient Rome soldiers were exempt from taxes as were the French *noblesse d'épée*, remarked that 'the soldiers say they fight for honour, when the truth is they have their honour in their pocket'.[26]

The quest for honour and the regard for reputation was thought to be a powerful incentive on the battlefield. A gentleman was known by his heroic virtues, which constituted a reputation known to and

[22] Sir William Segar, *Honor, Military and Civil* (London, 1602) [STC 22164], preface; Samuel P. Huntington, *The Soldier and the State: The Theory and Politics of Civil–Military Relations* (Cambridge, Mass., 1964), 20.

[23] Fritz Redlich, *De Praeda Militari: Looting and Booty, 1500–1815* (Vierteljahrschrift für Sozial- und Wirtschaftsgeschichte, 39; Wiesbaden, 1956), 2–5; *The Triumphs of Nassau*, 76.

[24] Maury D. Feld, 'Middle-Class Society and the Rise of Military Professionalism: The Dutch Army, 1589–1609', in Feld (ed.), *The Structure of Violence: Armed Forces as Social Systems* (Beverley Hills, Calif., 1977), 173–4.

[25] *The Naval Tracts of Sir William Monson*, ed. M. Oppenheim, 5 vols. (NRS, 22, 23, 43, 45, 49; London, 1902–1915), i. 103; George Monck, 1st duke of Albemarle, *Observations upon Military and Political Affairs* (London, 1671) [Wing A864], 2.

[26] John Selden, *Titles of Honor* (2nd edn.; London, 1631) [STC 22178], ii. vii. 864; *The Table-Talk of John Selden*, ed. S. W. Singer (1855 edn.; repr. Freeport, NY, 1972), 163.

discussed by everyone.[27] Gentlemen made better officers 'than men of
obscure birth' because they were stirred by 'a greater expectation of
advancement' and fear of shame.[28] Matthew Carter thought that the
display of honour required contrast: for that reason, some men were
born so base and ignoble that their dishonour emphasized the honour
of the gentleman or nobleman.[29]

From the belief that only noblemen and gentlemen possessed virtue
and honour flowed the assumption that their example and reputation
could be the only source of courage in their soldiers. Sidney could
not have put it more bluntly when he said: 'A brave Captain is as
a root, out of which (as into branches) the courage of his soldiers doth
spring.'[30] This assumption may have derived, in part, from exposure
to classical histories. Roman historians recounted the custom of
commanders, on the eve of battle, of exhorting their soldiers, with all
the rhetorical skills that they could muster, to be brave and perform
their duty.[31] The practice of reminding soldiers before going into
battle that they could bring home honour or shame led to the belief,
among some commanders at least, that honour was not peculiar to
officers only, but was an attribute of all good soldiers. Just prior
to sailing for Flanders in 1691, an English colonel told his men that
'honour is such an inseparable qualification of a soldier that when
the honour is gone the soldier dies though the man may drag on a
miserably despised life'.[32] If the ordinary soldier possessed a kind
of derivative honour, then it followed, thought Matthew Sutcliffe,
that commanders needed to reward soldiers for valour, including
those in the ranks. On the other hand, the failure to pay soldiers in a
timely fashion caused them to 'lose their courage', which fell back on
the assumption that base-born persons and ordinary soldiers would

[27] Matthew Carter, *Honor Redivivius, or An Analysis of Honor and Armory*
(London, 1660) [Wing C659], 1–2.
[28] Sir Edward Cecil, Lord Wimbledon, 'The Duty of a Private Soldier', BL, Harley
MS 3638, fo. 159ᵛ.
[29] Carter, *Honor Redivivius*, 1–2.
[30] *Aphorisms of Sir Philip Sidney*, i. 71.
[31] *A Myrrour for English Souldiers: Or, an Anatomy of an Accomplished Man at
Armes* (London, 1595) [STC 10418], sigs. C2ᵛ–C3ʳ, E1ᵛ; [Thomas Proctor,] *Of the
Knowledge and Conduct of Warres* (London, 1578) [STC 20403], fos. 37ᵛ–39ᵛ;
George Whetstone, *The Honourable Reputation of a Souldier* (London, 1585)
[STC 25339], sig. B1ʳ.
[32] *A True Copy of a Speech Made by an English Colonel to his Regiment,
Immediately before their Late Transportation for Flanders at Harwich* (n.p., 1691)
[Wing T2633], 1.

fight only for profit or plunder.[33] It remained difficult to unite officer and private soldier under a single code of conduct, and the distinction persisted between the code of honour of an officer and a gentleman and a private soldier's honour.[34]

Alfred Vagts argued that aristocrats in the British Isles as well as other parts of Europe attempted to maintain a monopoly on the culture of honour.[35] It must be answered that they did so with less than perfect success. Military service enhanced social status faster than any other activity, and was chosen by rising families as a career for sons that would acquire or maintain gentle status.[36] Although chivalric values and behaviour were usually associated with high-born status, the popular literature of chivalry asserted that true honour derived from 'virtuous deeds' rather than noble ancestry. Thus, London apprentices were persuaded that men of humble birth could achieve martial honour through service in the trained bands.[37] George Whetstone maintained that, since antiquity, service as a soldier had always conferred a certain degree of honour—even upon the most humble of men—and Alexander the Great and Julius Caesar were wont to encourage soldiers of whatever rank by calling them 'friends and companions'. Like many professional soldiers of the sixteenth and seventeenth centuries, Whetstone cherished the notion that there was a rough equality among soldiers: 'save that (by your election) I command, there is no difference between you and me, and therefore the meanest that best deserveth may one day step into my place.'[38] Whetstone provides many examples of Roman soldiers and other martial men of antiquity who became kings and emperors, and yet were of humble birth (which is undoubtedly one reason why noblemen of the early modern period so often distrusted and despised soldiers of fortune).

---

[33] Matthew Sutcliffe, *The Practice, Proceedings and Lawes of Armes* (London, 1593) [STC 23468], 298–9; *A Myrrour for English Souldiers*, sig. B1ᵛ.

[34] André Corvisier, *Armies and Societies in Europe, 1494–1789*, trans. A. T. Siddall (Bloomington, Ind., 1979), 183–4; James Turner Johnson, *Just War Tradition and the Restraint of War: A Moral and Historical Inquiry* (Princeton, 1981), 185.

[35] Alfred Vagts, *A History of Militarism* (rev. edn.; New York, 1959), 51.

[36] Ferne, *The Blazon of Gentrie*, 366–7; Gregory Hanlon, *The Twilight of a Military Tradition: Italian Aristocrats and European Conflicts, 1560–1800* (New York, 1998), 263–4; Keith M. Brown, *Kingdom or Province? Scotland and the Regal Union, 1603–1715* (New York, 1992), 43–4.

[37] William Hunt, 'Civic Chivalry and the English Civil War', in Anthony Grafton and Ann Blair (eds.), *The Transmission of Culture in Early Modern Europe*, (Philadelphia, 1990), 208.

[38] Whetstone, *The Honourable Reputation of a Souldier*, sig. B1 r–v.

Other writers also asserted that the truly valourous need not be ashamed of humble parentage. More than one writer recounts the story of the Scottish volunteer in Sir Andrew Gray's Regiment named William Edmonds, who was proud of being the son of a baker and freeman of Edinburgh. While camped along the Danube, Edmonds swam the river with a sword between his teeth, penetrated the lines of the Imperialist forces, captured their commander, the count de Bucquoi, and presented him to the prince of Orange as a prisoner. Edmonds was a favourite of Prince Maurice, who made him a colonel some time later. On a visit to Scotland, Edmonds built a manse in Stirling, where he displayed three baker's peels on his coat of arms.[39] Bulstrode Whitelocke insisted that being a lawyer did not disable a man from being a soldier and displaying the appropriate martial virtues. The son of a judge, Whitelocke had planned to become a soldier when he was a young man, and had actually been offered the command of a troop of horse in the French Army in Picardy, but was forced to abandon his intention to pursue a military career by family problems and studied law instead.[40] Sir Thomas Kellie, an Edinburgh lawyer, also insisted that men of his profession could make good soldiers; he urged his fellow advocates 'to do service to your country as well by the sword as the gown'.[41]

One of the most important sources of the remilitarization of the English aristocracy was the so-called chivalric revival. To what extent this cultural phenomenon was a revival and how much it owed to survivals from an earlier age is less clear. Chivalry originated in feudal society as a code of conduct for a warrior aristocracy, but it was not dependent on feudal tenures or fealty to a feudal monarch. It reached its fullest development even as classical feudalism was disintegrating and the aristocracy were displaying renewed bellicosity amidst the chaos of the Wars of the Roses. The demilitarization of the

---

[39] James Grant, *The Memoirs and Adventures of Sir John Hepburn* (Edinburgh, 1851), 14–15; Peacham, *The Compleat Gentleman*, 5. The *DNB*, *sub* Sir William Edmonds (d. 1606), says that Edmonds commanded one of the Scots Regiments in the States' Army at the Battle of Leffingen in 1601, and was killed at Rheinberg in 1606. The official history of the Dutch army (F. J. S. ten Raa and F. de Bas, *Het Staasche Leger*, 8 vols. (Breda, 1911–80), ii. 162) lists William Edmonds as a colonel as early as 1599. Although the biographical details of William Edmonds do not perfectly agree, the point of these stories remains the same.

[40] *The Diary of Bulstrode Whitelocke*, 80–1, 187–8.

[41] Sir Thomas Kellie, *Pallas Armata, or Militarie Instructions for the Learned* (Edinburgh, 1627; repr. Amsterdam, 1971), sig. ¶2$^r$.

English aristocracy in the mid-Tudor and early Elizabethan periods (in so far as they were demilitarized) was the result of assertive royal government, which ended the opportunities for the aristocracy to test their martial skills in civil wars and rebellions at home, but, at the same time, disengaged from continental wars by the loss of Calais. Those who did make their way overseas in search of military adventure found that the nature of war was changing; under the influence of firearms and modern fortifications in the Italian style the pitched battle as a chivalric exercise was giving way to siege warfare.[42]

Most scholars situate the chivalric revival in the Elizabethan period because the Elizabethans were still close to their medieval past but, at the same time were exposed to many other influences. One strain of chivalry derived from the Burgundian Court in the Netherlands and emphasized obedience to the sovereign and the development of martial skills and virtues to exercise in the service of the sovereign.[43] But, as Elizabethan aristocrats, in search of adventure under the new conditions of war, began to read Roman writers in order to learn how Roman military commanders managed and manoeuvred large masses of infantry, they also exposed themselves to the values of Tacitus and others who were less sympathetic to monarchy than the writers of chivalric romances.[44]

Although, in origin, chivalry may have owed something to Christian values, it became in the late-sixteenth-century revival a secular code of conduct and a culture that emphasized the martial function of the aristocracy. Perhaps the most important contribution of the revival of chivalric values was the concept of honour, which furnished the approbation for this code of conduct. It emphasized that a gentleman

[42] Ferguson, *The Chivalric Tradition*, 16–17; Richard C. McCoy, *The Rites of Knighthood: The Literature and Politics of Elizabethan Chivalry* (Berkeley, Calif., 1989), 17–18; Malcolm Vale, *War and Chivalry: Warfare and Aristocratic Culture in England, France and Burgundy at the End of the Middle Ages* (London and Athens, Ga., 1981), 71–4.

[43] Thomas Churchyard reminisced about memories of his youth: 'In the renowned reign of that noble prince Henry the Eighth, whose famous memory shall last while the world standeth, all chivalry was cherished, soldiers made of and manhood so much esteemed that he was thought happy and most valiant that sought credit by the execise of arms and discipline of war. Which did so animate the noble minds of men that . . . he was counted nobody that had not been known to be at some valiant enterprise' (*A Generall Rehearsall of Warres, Called Churchyarde's Choise* (London, 1579) [STC 5235], sig. A1ʳ).

[44] Ferguson, *The Chivalric Tradition*, 12–13; Maurice Keen, *Chivalry* (New Haven, 1984), 236–7.

must be courtly to women, display valour, and possess skills in swords-manship, equitation, and hunting. Above all, he must be a man of his word and hold his honour very dear—dearer than his life—which is why his sword was always at hand so that he might challenge any man who impugned his reputation.[45]

Mervyn James thought that the attempt to revive a culture of honour failed to survive the Bishops' Wars of 1638–40 because the peers entrusted with command of King Charles's army were incompetent, failed to win victories, and forfeited the confidence bestowed in them.[46] However, only professional soldiers thought in that mode; amateur gallants, if they fought a worthy enemy, could achieve personal honour by individual displays of valour and prowess without actually grasping victory.[47] The pursuit of personal honour and glory rather than discipline and military success was what distinguished the amateur gallant, such as the third earl of Essex, from the professional soldier. There were also, of course, soldiers in the civil wars who, like Oliver Cromwell, thought of the enemy as the personification of evil and a thing to be destroyed.[48] Dr James argues that after 1640 honour tended to become a subculture and a personal code of military men, but he may have buried aristocratic honour before it was quite dead.[49]

The practice of peers and gentlemen serving as volunteers in organized military units, which persisted to the end of the seventeenth century, argues that chivalric values and the belief that a gentleman needed to authenticate his honour on the field of battle in an agonistic war lasted longer than historians have generally supposed.

[45] Ibid. 239, 249–50, 252–3; J. R. Hale, *War and Society in Renaissance Europe, 1450–1620* (New York, 1985), 37–8.
[46] James, *English Politics and the Concept of Honour*, 88. More recently, Dr James has argued that this aristocratic culture based upon honour and chivalry collapsed with the Essex Revolt of 1601 ('At the Crossroads of the Political Culture: The Essex Revolt of 1601', in his *Society, Politics and Culture: Studies in Early Modern England* (Cambridge, 1986), 416–17). J. S. A. Adamson ('The Baronial Context of the English Civil War', *Trans. R. Hist. Soc.*, 5th ser., 40 (1990), 104–5) maintains that a chivalric culture survived among English peers and gentry, which made possible a temporary revival of baronial power during the first phase of the English civil wars.
[47] Using the typology of war devised by Hans Speier (*Social Order and the Risks of War* (New York, 1952), ch. 18), Gerke Teitler (*The Genesis of the Professional Officer Corps* (Beverley Hills, Calif., 1977), 3–4) distinguishes between an 'agonistic armed conflict', in which 'the enemy is held in esteem and the aim of the conflict is to gain honour and renown', and an 'instrumental armed conflict', where the enemy is viewed as an 'obstacle' to be removed.
[48] Ibid.    [49] James, *English Politics and the Concept of Honour*, 88.

The secular code of honour that grew out of the chivalric revival was self-validating. In the value system of martial culture, honour needed no justification other than vindication; it ranked above religion, morality, and allegiance.[50] This rationalization of the heedless and violent behaviour of swordsmen had particular application to the fashion for duelling and persisted long after the chivalric code of honour had become an empty shell. The more cerebral of martialists insisted that honour had its own laws, which might be contrary to and above divine and positive law. This attitude grew out of the belief that positive law was meant for inferior sorts of persons and had been debased by the pettifogging arguments and interpretations of lawyers. In the sixteenth century swordsmen believed that the law of honour was based upon natural law and reason and prescribed a morality better suited to achieve martial virtue.[51] When Robert Crichton, eighth Lord Sanquhar, was put on trial in 1612 for having the fencing master who had accidentally put out his eye murdered, he defended himself by saying: 'I considered not my wrongs upon terms of Christianity . . . but being trained up in the courts of princes and in arms, I stood upon terms of honour.'[52]

Castiglione thought that honour once stained with the shame of cowardice could never be restored: 'The fame of a gentleman that carrieth a weapon, if it be once tarnished with cowardice, or any other reproach, doth evermore continue shameful in the world . . .'[53] In British martial cultures there were ways of retrieving lost honour, but the path was thorny. The Irish Jacobite volunteer John Stevens recites a couple of examples from James II's Irish Army during the Williamite War. Peter Barnewall, a disgraced lieutenant colonel, retrieved his honour from the imputation of cowardice 'at the expense of his life' by

---

[50] *Vincentio Saviola his Practice: In Two Bookes, the First Intreating Use of the Rapier and Dagger, the Second, of Honor and Honorable Quarrels* (London, 1595) [STC 21788], sig. B2$^v$; Charles Louis de Secondat, Baron de La Brède et Montesquieu, *The Spirit of the Laws* (1748), trans. and ed. A. M. Cohler, B. C. Miller, and H. S. Stone (Cambridge, 1989), 33–4; Robert Harding, *Anatomy of a Power Elite: The Provincial Governors of Early Modern France* (New Haven, 1978), 68.

[51] Ruth Kelso, *The Doctrine of the English Gentleman in the Sixteenth Century* (Univ. of Illinois Studies in Language and Literature, 14.1–2; Urbana, Ill., 1929), 99–100.

[52] T. B. Howell (ed.), *A Complete Collection of State Trials*, 33 vols. (London, 1809–26), ii. col. 747; Keith M. Brown, *Bloodfeud in Scotland, 1573–1625: Violence, Justice and Politics in an Early Modern Society* (Edinburgh, 1986), 26.

[53] Count Baldasare Castiglione, *The Book of the Courtier*, trans. Sir Thomas Hoby (1561; repr. New York, 1967), 48.

accompanying private soldiers in a counter-attack against a breached wall during the Siege of Limerick in 1690. At the Battle of Aughrim in 1691, Lieutenant Colonel James O'Neill of Cormack O'Neill's Regiment was 'obliged to carry a musket in the same regiment for quitting his post and running shamefully away at Athlone . . . the whole regiment by his example basely abandoning the works and flying in such disorder that they lost considerable number of their arms'.[54]

In the Royal Navy the operation of the code of honour in dealing with the imputation of cowardice is well documented. An outright accusation led the accused either to demand a court martial to clear his name or to challenge his accuser to a duel.[55] However, the oblique accusations of rumours were more difficult to dispel. In 1665, a naval court martial tried and convicted Edward Nixon, captain of the *Elizabeth* frigate, for breaking off an engagement with two Dutch men-of-war of above thirty guns each. The lord admiral the duke of York attended the trial and expressed the view that the king and the nation had been 'wounded' by Nixon's conduct and asked for the severest penalty. The court pronounced the death sentence, although a minority of the members of the court thought that the penalty was too extreme.[56] Sir William Berkeley, having been accused of 'a want of courage' after an engagement of the previous season, was so determined to live down the accusation that during the Battle of the North Foreland in June 1666 it affected his judgement, and he took unnecessary risks and lost his life. Although his fellow officers believed that Berkeley had recovered his reputation by his valiant death, he also lost his ship to the Dutch, and some of his crew were also killed because of his unnecessary risks.[57] In the Third Anglo-Dutch War, Edward Montagu, first earl of Sandwich, was unjustly blamed for failure to destroy the Dutch East India fleet after it had sheltered in the harbour of Bergen, Norway. He convinced himself that 'nothing short of his death in action' could restore his reputation and satisfy his enemies, the duke of York, the duke of Albemarle, and Sir Thomas

[54] *The Journal of John Stevens Containing a Brief Account of the War in Ireland, 1689–1691*, ed. R. H. Murray (Oxford, 1912), 180.

[55] J. D. Davies, *Gentlemen and Tarpaulins: The Officers and Men of the Restoration Navy* (Oxford, 1991), 62–3.

[56] *The Journal of Edward Montagu, First Earl of Sandwich, 1659–1665*, ed. R. C. Anderson (NRS 64; London, 1929), 214–15.

[57] *The Rupert and Monck Letter Book, 1666*, ed. J. R. Powell and E. K. Timings (NRS 112; London, 1969), 213, 288.

Coventry. Sandwich was killed in the Battle of Solebay in August 1672 as his flagship the *Royal James* engaged the *Groot Hollandia*.[58]

Much of this was, of course, a legacy of the legends surrounding the death of Sir Philip Sidney, because one of the core values of English martial culture was that there was no hero quite so admirable as a dead hero. Although Sidney found that the war in the Netherlands consisted largely of protracted sieges, he searched out occasions for face-to-face combat such as the night raid on Axel and the skirmish at Zutphen, which cost him his life.[59] Although by the standards of the day, and certainly in contrast to his uncle Leicester, Sidney was a competent (if not exceptional) military commander, what particularly marked out his 'noblesse and chivalry' was his manner of dying. According to Fulke Greville, he had offered part of his armour to a fellow officer who had none and thereby exposed himself to the wound in his thigh that, after much suffering, caused his death. He refused to lie down and die, but remained seated upon his horse. Though extremely thirsty and in great pain, he offered his last drink to a wounded soldier lying along his path. W. A. Ringler believes that Greville fabricated a number of details about Sidney's death.[60] A strikingly similar incident is associated with Roger, second Lord North, who was also wounded at Zutphen. North refused to leave the scene of battle for treatment of his wounds, but had himself lifted back on his horse and went on fighting.[61]

Sidney played another important role in the revitalization of English martial culture. He was strongly attracted to the Burgundian courtly tradition of service under princes who displayed that virtue that inspired men to draw their swords and fight on behalf of a worthy cause. The Burgundian court culture flourished at the court of William I, prince of Orange, and animated the Dutch struggle for independence from

[58] Ibid. 213; *The Diary of John Evelyn*, ed. E. S. de Beer, 6 vols. (Oxford, 1955), iii. 616–19; Richard Ollard, *Cromwell's Earl: A Life of Edward Montagu, 1st Earl of Sandwich* (London, 1994), 134–5, 139, 255.

[59] Hubert Languet had warned Sidney that young gallants who lusted after honour and glory were apt to rush incautiously into battle and by their deaths 'deprive themselves of the power of serving their country; for a man who falls at an early age cannot have done much for his country' (quoted in Berry, *The Making of Sir Philip Sidney*, 45).

[60] W. A. Ringler, 'Sir Philip Sidney: The Myth and the Man', in Jan van Dorsten, Dominic Baker-Smith, and Arthur F. Kinney (eds.), *Sir Philip Sidney: 1586 and the Creation of a Legend* (Leiden, 1986), 8.

[61] Harold H. Davis, 'The Military Career of Thomas North', *Huntington Library Quarterly*, 12 (1948–9), 317–18.

Spain. The absence of this virtue at Elizabeth's court and her failure to support Protestant causes, such as that of John Casimir, Count Palatine, caused Sidney to transfer his loyalties to the Orangist cause. It was, according to Gordon Kipling, this shared legacy of Burgundian chivalry that drew Sidney and other English and Scots swordsmen to seek honour and glory in the Dutch war of independence, and provided Sidney with the opportunity to become 'the British Scipio'.[62] Fulke Greville died in 1628, without publishing his *Life of Sir Philip Sidney*. The Commonwealth government printed it in 1652, because Greville's book endorsed the concept of service to the state, and because it could be used to depict the Stuart court as effeminate.[63]

The pursuit of war as an instrument of the modern state with specified military objectives required that officers accept discipline and pursue those military objectives as a group effort. Few Elizabethan swordsmen resolved the conflict between the individual pursuit of honour on the battlefield and the ideal of service to king and country and vindication of a worthy cause. Chivalric culture fostered individual displays of prowess and valour, but modern warfare was becoming more impersonal in so far as it was determined by considerations of policy, strategy, and logistics. Such considerations were alien to the mentality of the late medieval knight, and Elizabethan swordsmen such as Sidney, the second earl of Essex, and (despite the fact that he was a professional soldier) Sir Francis Vere absorbed few lessons from the great outpouring of military writing in the late sixteenth century. Moreover, this mentality persisted well into the seventeenth century among amateur gallants such as the third earl of Essex and the first marquis of Argyll.[64]

---

[62] Blair Worden, *The Sound of Virtue: Philip Sidney's* Arcadia *and Elizabethan Politics* (New Haven, 1996), pp. xxii–xxiii, 23, 30–1; Wallace T. MacCaffrey, *Queen Elizabeth and the Making of Policy, 1572–1588* (Princeton, 1981), 228–9, 234, 236, 309, 399–400; Thomas Moffet, *Nobilis, or a view of the Life and Death of Sidney*, trans. V. B. Heltzel and H. H. Hudson (San Marino, Calif., 1940), 78–9; Gordon Kipling, *The Triumph of Honour: Burgundian Origins of the Elizabethan Renaissance* (The Hague, 1977), 169–70.

[63] Adriana McCrea, 'Whose Life Is It, Anyway? Subject and Subjection in Fulke Greville's Life of Sidney', in T. F. Mayer and D. R. Woolf (eds.), *The Rhetorics of Life-Writing in Early Modern Europe: Forms of Biography from Cassandre Fidele to Louis XIV* (Ann Arbor, 1995), 316.

[64] Ferguson, *The Chivalric Tradition*, 39–40; Geoffrey Parker, *The Military Revolution: Military Innovation and the Rise of the West, 1500–1800* (2nd edn.; Cambridge, 1996), 16; Sydney Anglo, 'Introduction', in Sydney Anglo (ed.), *Chivalry and the Renaissance* (Woodbridge, 1990), pp. xiv–xv.

Sieges were replacing pitched battles in the modern mode of warfare generated by the military revolution, and the infantryman was assuming more importance in strategy and tactics than the mounted knight. It was difficult for the individual knight to subordinate the enhancement of his reputation to the requirements of military discipline. A desire on the part of the aristocracy to win honour by displays of courage on the battlefield stood in the way of their accepting the responsibilities of command and avoiding unnecessary personal risks. Languet told Sidney (in vain, it would seem): 'It is the misfortune, or rather folly of our age, that most men of high birth think it honourable to do the work of a soldier rather than a leader, and would rather earn a name for boldness than judgment.'[65] Even in the latter part of the seventeenth century La Rochefoucauld thought that most swordsmen were more concerned with their reputations than with winning or losing a battle: 'Most men take sufficient risks in war to maintain their honour, but few are willing to take the further risk necessary to achieve victory.'[66] The first marquis of Argyll's mentality provides a very good example of why overmighty noblemen were not amenable to discipline; he thought commanders in the field should be prepared to seize opportunities and not wait for orders from their governments. In any case, Argyll believed that the outcome of battle depended solely on Divine Providence.[67] After the Battle of Zutphen, Leicester's official report emphasized his assessment that the day had ended with more honour accrued by English noblemen than Spanish, but it is unclear what the military objectives of the battle were, or whether they were achieved. Leicester did express regrets about not capturing more noblemen to hold for ransom.[68]

The pursuit of honour on the battlefield was a personal and individual endeavour, and gave rise to the assumption by many Elizabethan swordsmen that honour was indivisible and could not be shared. Just before the attack on Gravelines, Sidney's fellow officers and gentlemen volunteers vied with one another for a chance to accompany him, but Sidney was unwilling to share the honour with them, and he chose only one subaltern officer 'from the inferior sort of captains . . . by dice upon a drum's head'. He 'kept this steady counsel in his own bosom' because so many laboured 'on every side

---

[65] *Correspondence of Sidney and Languet*, ed. Pears, 137.
[66] François, duc de La Rochefoucauld, *Maximes* (1778; repr. Paris, 1959), no. 219.
[67] Campbell, 1st marquis of Argyll, *Instructions to a Son*, 155–6.
[68] Georgina Bertie, *Five Generations of a Noble House* (London, 1845), 110–13.

to obtain the honour of this service'. Sidney told the other English officers 'that his own coming thither was to the same end, wherein they were now his rivals; and therefore assured them that he would not yield anything to any men which by right of his place was both due to himself, and consequently [a] disgrace for him to execute by others . . .'[69] Robert Ashley thought that to desire more honour than was appropriate and 'proportionate' for one's social station was ambitious and inconsistent with the true nature of honour: 'as if he should desire the place of a general . . . and should take upon him[self] to rule and command his equals and superiors.'[70]

Sidney's determination to garner all honour was not unique. Sir Francis Vere always considered the effect upon his military reputation when making a strategic decision. This obsessive concern with his own honour led him to be careless in the expenditure of the lives of his soldiers. Sir John Ogle, Vere's second-in-command, recalled a conversation that he had with Vere about the surrender of towns and the honour of the commander of defending a garrison: 'Rather than you should ever see the name of Francis Vere subscribed in the delivery of a town committed to his custody . . . had I a thousand lives, I would first bury them all in the rampire!'[71] When Vere was defending Ostend in 1601, he conducted a parley with the Spanish governor of the Netherlands, Archduke Albert of Austria, in order to buy time for the arrival of a relief expedition. Sir John Ogle and Captain Charles Fairfax were sent to the Spanish as pledges. When Fairfax discovered that Vere, whom he called 'the Fox', was putting their lives at risk for such a stratagem, he was highly offended.[72] The conventional military wisdom about laying siege to fortresses was that any assault on the ramparts should be preceded by digging lines of circumvallation and artillery bombardments, but Vere preferred frontal assaults with scaling ladders and little or no artillery preparation. The question of whether the assault was successful and how many lives it cost was subordinated to the preservation or enhancement of Vere's honour.[73]

[69] Sir Fulke Greville, Lord Brooke, *Life of Sir Philip Sidney* (1652), ed. Nowell Smith (Oxford, 1907; repr. 1971), 121–3.

[70] Robert Ashley, *Of Honour*, ed. V. B. Heltzel (San Marino, Calif., 1947), 42.

[71] *The Commentaries of Sir Francis Vere* (1657), in *Stuart Tracts, 1603–1693* (Westminster, 1903; repr. Wilmington, Del., 1973), 91–2, 187. William Dillingham, the Latin poet and seventeenth-century editor of Vere's memoirs, gave them the title *Commentaries* because he likened them to Julius Caesar's *Commentaries* (ibid. 84).

[72] Ibid. 193–7.     [73] Ibid. 92–105.

MEDIO ET TEMPORE

Sr Francis Vere

2. Engraved portrait of Sir Francis Vere (1560–1609) by William
Faithorne the elder. National Maritime Museum. Vere commanded the
English and Scottish forces in the States' Army.

Believing that honour was indivisible, Vere, in his highly partial account of the Battle of Nieuwpoort, which was fought in June 1600 as part of the campaign to relieve the Dutch garrison at Ostend, refused to share the honour achieved by the victory over the Spanish with the Dutch or his own English officers. The States had gathered together an army of 12,000 foot and 3,000 horse under the command of Maurice of Nassau. Vere commanded 1,600 English soldiers, 2,500 Frisians, and ten cornets or troops of cavalry. Vere's men were fully engaged in the fighting and he rode amongst them so that he was 'in their eyes both doing the office of a captain and a soldier'. The Dutch forces were successful, but half of Vere's English soldiers and eight captains were slain. Vere himself was wounded four times and had his horse shot from beneath him. Vere insisted that the English bore the brunt of the fighting and offended the Dutch by slighting them. The only English officers mentioned in Vere's dispatches were Sir Horace Vere and Sir Robert Drury, who had saved Vere's life by pulling him out from under his dead horse. Vere mentioned none of the slain officers. His lieutenant colonel, Sir John Ogle, who wrote a separate account attached to Vere's *Commentaries* when they were published in 1657, was particularly offended because he was one of those who had helped save Vere's life.[74]

Most soldiers and military writers of the late-Elizabethan period rejected the idea that honour was indivisible. William Blandy, who served in the Netherlands under Sir John Norris, commander of the States' forces in Friesland, stated that a good general should assign credit for a victory first to God, and then share the honour with his officers and, finally, with his soldiers.[75] Sir Roger Williams, a seasoned soldier, reminded his readers that Julius Caesar, although 'highly ambitious', always made a point of apportioning honour among his lieutenants.[76] The case for a general distributing honour gained upon the battlefield was eloquently argued by the anonymous author of the account of Sir John Norris's expedition sent to assist the Huguenot assault on Guinganp in Brittany in 1591. The account was

[74] Ibid. 144–60, esp. 157, 161–4; Charles Dalton, *Life and Times of General Sir Edward Cecil, Viscount Wimbledon*, 2 vols. (London, 1885), i. 51–2, 56.
[75] William Blandy, *The Castle, or Picture of Policy* (London, 1581) [STC 3128], sig. A2ʳ.
[76] Sir Roger Williams, *A Brief Discouse of Warre* (London, 1590) [STC 225732], sig. A3ʳ.

intended to ensure that Norris's officers and gentlemen volunteers received their due acclaim:

A martial man principally devoteth himself to hazard his limbs and life in the service of his prince and country for honour and crowns. As it were shame to eclipse him the one, so it is injury to scant him the other. For the surest whetstone of valour and virtue is renown and glory. In defrauding the soldier of his pay, you cut his purse and rebate his edge. In depraving his honour, you cut his throat and strike him stone dead.[77]

The second earl of Essex had difficulty grasping the idea that modern war had become a group effort requiring some attention to strategy, tactics, and logistics. His military career consisted of a series of antique chivalric displays and tableaux vivant. In 1589, during the attack on Lisbon, Essex challenged any nobleman of his rank from the garrison to engage in single combat. Camden thought the expedition a great victory because Essex and his men returned to England 'with 150 pieces of great ordnance and a very rich booty'.

Most men thought the English to have sufficiently revenged themselves, and gotten honour enough, having in so short a time forced one town by scalado, valiantly assaulted another, put to flight the forces of a most potent king, landed in several places, marched through the enemies' country seven days in battle array with colours displayed, attempted a great city with a small power of men, lodged three whole nights in the suburbs thereof, beaten back the enemy that sallied forth unto the very gates, taken two cities lying upon the sea, and deprived the enemy of his provision of war.[78]

Never mind that the English lost 6,000 of the 12,000 who sailed with the fleet, failed to destroy the Spanish naval forces that were being rebuilt in the ports of northern Spain, and failed to intercept the annual Spanish treasure fleet, which were the main military objectives as specified in the expedition's orders.

Again, in 1591, when he led an expedition to Normandy to assist at the Huguenot siege of Rouen, Essex, who like so many amateur gallants had no patience for that sort of warfare, challenged the governor of Rouen to single combat—without receiving the satisfaction of an

[77] *The True Reporte of the Service in Britanie Performed lately . . . by Sir John Norreys and other Captaines and Gentlemen Souldiers before Guingand* (London, 1591) [STC 18655], sigs. A2ʳ, A3ᵛ–A4ʳ.
    Sir James Turner (*Pallas Armata*, 351) makes much the same point and cites the French soldier Blaise de Monluc.
[78] William Camden, *The History of the Most Renowned and Victorious Princess Elizabeth* (4th edn.; London, 1688; repr. New York, 1970), 432.

answer. Such irresponsibility did invite the attention of the queen, who rebuked Essex on both occasions for placing the forces that he commanded in jeopardy. The example of gallants such as Sidney and Essex was not without effect; Sidney, Sir Roger Williams, and Sir William Russell once led a band of 500 knights and gentlemen volunteers to the picket lines of the duke of Parma's camp to challenge him to battle. For these gallants, *bellum*, or public war, was hardly distinguishable from *duellum*, or private war, and the tiltyard merged into the battlefield.[79]

The influence of the chivalric revival on aristocratic society and culture was profound, and it would be surprising if the image of monarchy had remained unaffected. The primary function of the medieval king had been to serve as a military leader in time of war and that image persisted into the Renaissance. Machiavelli wrote that the study of and preparation for war should be the principal concern of a prince when he was not actually at war. Princes could preserve their honour only by martial deeds; those who became more preoccupied with luxury than with war usually forfeited their crowns.[80] Henry VIII may not have read Machiavelli, but the legacy of the Burgundian code of chivalry, much in evidence at the Tudor court, would have taught Henry that honour was achieved through war, and that is why he led the military expedition of 1544 to France in person. Richmond Palace was one of Henry's favourite residences, and the portraits and Flemish tapestries hanging in the Great Hall at Richmond proclaimed that kings were expected to behave like 'bold and valiant knights'.[81]

Faced with this long tradition of warrior-kings, female rulers such as Mary I, Elizabeth I, and Mary, queen of Scots, were at a distinct disadvantage. From the 1580s onwards plays such as *Henry V*, poems such as *The Faerie Queen*, and chivalric romances like *Amadis de Gaul* portraying medieval warrior-kings and glorifying war established a model of kingship that Elizabeth and the early Stuart monarchs could not compete with. The increasingly bellicose sentiments of the English aristocracy raised the threat of civil war as in France, and

[79] Richard C. McCoy, ' "A Dangerous Image": The Earl of Essex and Elizabethan Chivalry', *Journal of Medieval and Renaissance Studies*, 13.2 (1983), 315–16; id., *The Rites of Knighthood*, 83–4; Anthony Esler, *The Aspiring Mind of the Elizabethan Younger Generation* (Durham, NC, 1966), 93–4, 110–11; Martin van Creveld, *Technology and War from 2000 BC to the Present* (New York, 1989), 72–3.

[80] Niccolò Machiavelli, *The Prince*, trans. Thomas G. Bergin (Arlington Heights, Ill., 1947), 41–2.

[81] Steven Gunn, 'The French Wars of Henry VIII', in Jeremy Black (ed.), *The Origins of War in Early Modern Europe* (Edinburgh, 1987), 35, 59; Kipling, *Triumph of Honour*, 3, 59–61.

Elizabeth's fear of ambitious noblemen hungry for glory led her to be very sparing in granting honours to swordsmen.[82]

Both Charles I and Charles II were aware that a king's presence on the battlefield helped rally supporters in times of civil war. George Monck thought that sovereigns who went to the field in person were more likely to succeed in war than those who relied on their lieutenants.[83] Putting aside what we know of the reign of James II, his earlier career affords evidence that he was regarded by many fellow soldiers as an honourable and brave commander who was generous to his followers. He had earned his honour on the battlefield, which he understood to be the only source of true honour. As duke of York, he had believed not only in leading his troops or the fleet into battle in person, but to be seen leading them. Thus, he took many risks in exposing himself to danger.[84] Indeed, his appearance on the battlefield in 1688 might have helped rally his army in a time of need. As it was, his opponent, William of Orange, was a monarch who was one of the most able and experienced commanders in Europe and never shrank from danger on the field of battle.

When kings ventured upon the battlefield, there inevitably arose the question of how to apportion the honour of victory. Jean Bodin noted that in a monarchy rulers would inevitably want to claim for themselves the honour and glory of victories won by soldiers and generals, but in a republic the honour, although perhaps won by soldiers, would be claimed by generals, and thus was more widely shared amongst martial men than in a monarchy. Bodin also claimed that in a military culture, where martial men read Roman writers, they would tend to favour a republic because they would see that in such a commonwealth honour is more widely distributed.[85] Locke thought that absolute monarchies rested upon 'the title of the sword' and must construct myths that ignored the honour acquired by those officers and soldiers who assisted the first conquering monarch.[86]

---

[82] R. M. Smuts, *Court Culture and the Origins of a Royalist Tradition in Early Stuart England* (Philadelphia, 1987), 20–1; Sir Robert Naunton, *Fragmenta Regalia, or Observations on Queen Elizabeth, her Times and Favourites*, ed. J. S. Cervoski (1641; repr. Washington, 1985), 26, 42–3.

[83] Monck, *Observations upon Military and Political Affairs*, 11.

[84] Turner, *Pallas Armata*, unpaginated epistle to reader; *The Memoirs of James II: His Campaigns as Duke of York, 1652–1660*, trans. A. L. Sells (London, 1962), 236–7.

[85] Jean Bodin, *The Six Bookes of a Commonwealth*, ed. K. D. McRae (1606; repr. Cambridge, Mass., 1962), 586.

[86] John Locke, *Two Treatises of Government*, ed. Peter Laslett (1690; repr. New York, 1965), 434.

The Elizabethan chivalric revival, which roughly coincides with the English intervention in the Dutch war of independence, reiterated the traditional belief that war was the usual occupation of princes and nobility, and it became necessary to idealize those martial activities in poetry, songs, drama, and graphic images. The leading spokesmen of the literary aspect of the chivalric revival were Sir Philip Sidney and Edmund Spencer, who sanctioned service in the Huguenot and Dutch forces, raids on Spanish treasure fleets, and the military conquest and plantation of Ireland as a militant new Protestant knight-errantry. By romanticizing this crusade, Sidney and Spenser helped persuade gentlemen volunteers that the military glory that they craved could be equated with honour.[87]

In Sidney's youth poetry had been regarded as a courtly pastime suitable only for the amusement of ladies, and therefore usually aimed at a female audience. Sidney had sought military adventure at least ten years before he went to the Netherlands with his uncle Leicester. His restlessness and impetuosity had sought outlets in duelling, privateering, and volunteering to fight against the Turks, but he was repeatedly frustrated in each attempt to demonstrate his virtue in battle. So he sought to redefine poetry in the classical heroic mode as a means of celebrating military triumphs. Although war was horrible in itself, yet poetry that described the displays of valour in battle would provide young gallants with models to emulate. 'Poetry is the companion of camps' and 'will never displease a soldier', Sidney insisted. By promoting heroic poetry and the ideals of a martial class, Sidney hoped to remedy England's effeminacy and military weakness in the face of Spanish power. He also revealed his ambition to become a soldier like his father and grandfather.[88]

Besides undertaking an apprenticeship in arms, military writers agreed that the best way to breed valour in a young gentleman was to have him read classical historians such as Homer, Xenophon, and Virgil. Not only would this motivate the young gallant to emulate heroes who had attained 'soldierlike immortal virtue', but, by making him aware of what to expect in hand-to-hand combat, it would give

---

[87] Hanlon, *Twilight of a Military Tradition*, 329; Ferguson, *The Chivalric Tradition*, 66, 70–2, 74.

[88] Berry, *The Making of Sir Philip Sidney*, 143–4; Victor Skretkowicz, 'Chivalry in Sidney's *Arcadia*', in Anglo (ed.), *Chivalry in the Renaissance*, 162–3; Robert Codrington, *The Life and Death of the Illustrious Robert Earle of Essex* (London, 1646) [Wing C4877], 2; Sir Philip Sidney, *An Apology for Poetry, or The Defence of Poesy* (1595), ed. Geoffrey Shepherd (Manchester, 1965), 114.

him the stomach to perform valourous deeds in the face of death.[89] When Sir Henry Sidney was lord president of the Council in the Principality and Marches of Wales, he commissioned an English translation of Caradog of Llancarvan's *The Historie of Cambria* to show his son Philip the path to true nobility by the example of ancient Welsh princes and their 'politic and martial acts'.[90]

The more wealthy gallants, such as Sir Philip Sidney and the second earl of Essex, employed scholars to search the classics for guidance and examples on how ancient martialists formulated policy, devised tactics, and behaved in battle. Sidney retained the poet Gabriel Harvey in this capacity, and with his circle of friends he made it a practice to meet with Harvey and other scholars to discuss appropriate action and behaviour during the enforced idleness prior to the English intervention in the Netherlands and elsewhere. Another group of swordsmen, who gathered for such interactive discussions with Harvey to discuss what he had gleaned from Livy, met at Hill House, Theydon Mount, Essex, the home of Sir Thomas Smith and his son, Sir Thomas the younger.[91] John Sadler, the English translator of the Roman military writer Vegetius, appears to have functioned as a reader to Sir Edmund Brudenell and probably also to Francis Russell, fourth earl of Bedford, to whom the translation of Vegetius was dedicated. Classical writers such as Vegetius were useful to Elizabethan swordsmen because they not only furnished examples of feats of valour, but also supplied detailed knowledge about training and disciplining multitudes of foot soldiers.[92]

The classical humanist tradition emphasized the importance of valour, and this did much to shape the martial cultures of the British

[89] Robert Ward, *Animadversions of Warre* (London, 1639) [STC 25025], 181; *A Myrrour for English Souldiers*, title page.

[90] Caradog of Llancarvan, *The Historie of Cambria*, trans. Humphrey Llwyd, ed. David Powell ([London,] 1584) [STC 4606], fo. iii.

[91] Lisa Jardine and Anthony Grafton, 'Studied for Action: How Gabriel Harvey Read his Livy', *P&P* 129 (Nov. 1990), 35–41.

Another preparation for war when England was at peace was hunting and poaching (Roger B. Manning, *Hunters and Poachers: A Cultural and Social History of Unlawful Hunting in England, 1485–1640* (Oxford, 1993), ch. 2). The subsequent generation of Smiths, represented by Sir William and his son William, acted as the leaders of a notorious gang of poachers based at Hill House (Ibid., 74, 173).

[92] *The Four Bookes of Flavius Vegetius Renatus . . . of Martiall Policye, Feates of Chivalrie, and Whatsoever Pertayneth to Warre*, trans. John Sadler (London, 1572; repr. Amsterdam, 1968), dedication; H. J. Webb, *Elizabethan Military Science: The Books and the Practice* (Madison, Wis., 1965), 11–12; Markku Peltonen, *Classical Humanism and Republicanism in English Political Thought, 1570–1640* (Cambridge, 1995), 19.

Isles. Although he was a gownsman all his life, Sir Francis Bacon had been part of the circle of the second earl of Essex in the 1590s. More significant than these associations, which he transcended, Bacon had read deeply in the writings of Roman authors as well as those of Machiavelli, Lipsius, and Giovanni Botero. Bacon insisted that the valour and martial disposition of a people and their application to the exercise of arms were the keys to greatness in a state. Although both ancients and moderns thought that money furnished the sinews of war, and many modern military writers stressed the importance of the most up-to-date weapons, fortifications, and other engines of war, Bacon never abandoned his emphasis on martial virtue and courage, which, in turn, generated the kind of reputation of an army that caused their enemies to fear their onslaught. Thus, the true sinews of war were to be found in the martial valour of an armed citizenry, not in the treasure of a state. No amount of treasure could save a nation that had sunk into effeminacy. This belief that the greatness of a state depended on the valour of its citizens rather than upon money was reiterated by James Harrington. Marchamont Nedham's reading of Roman history, as filtered by Machiavelli, carried this line of reasoning a step further: republics fostered virtue and military glory; kings were associated with corruption, langour, and effeminacy.[93]

By the early seventeenth century an acquaintance with classical historians and military writers could be supplemented by the memoirs of modern English and French soldiers. *The Actions of the Low Countries*, by Sir Roger Williams, was rewritten in the classical or humanist mode by the historian Sir John Hayward because Williams's reticence and modesty made him appear to be an observer of the events described instead of the participant that he actually was.[94] A coarser and more explicit appeal to impressionable young men

[93] Sir Francis Bacon, 'Of the True Greatness of the Kingdom of Great Britain', in *Works*, ed. James Spedding, R. L. Ellis, and D. D. Heath, 14 vols. (London, 1857–74; repr. Stuttgart, 1963), vii. 48–9, 55–6; Peltonen, *Classical Humanism and Republicanism*, 202–13, 312; Marchamont Nedham, *The Case of the Commonwealth of England, Stated*, ed. P. A. Knachel (Charlottesville, Va., 1969), 112–15.

[94] Sir Roger Williams, *The Actions of the Low Countries*, ed. Sir John Hayward (London, 1618) [STC 25731], preface to reader; William Camden, *Annales: or the History of the Most Renowned and Victorious Princesse Klizabeek* (3rd edn.; 1635) [STC 4501], 507.

My colleague John J. Manning tells me that Hayward rewrote *The Actions* in the style of Tacitus and polished the rhetoric in humanist fashion, but it was unlikely that he altered the substance of Williams's account.

to seek military adventure was provided by Captain John Smith's *True Travels* and *The Generall Historie of Virginia*. These writings awakened in would-be gallants a martial ardour and pride in the exploits of Englishmen who were fighting a very different sort of war from what was to be found in the Netherlands. Smith tried to per-suade his readers that fighting savages and barbarians, as he termed the Turks, Irish, and American Indians, also presented opportunities to perform heroic deeds. An outrageous boaster, Smith added that ladies of all nations found him and other soldiers irresistible.[95] In the Restoration period, military memoirs and travel adventures were supplemented by picaresque novels, such as Charles Croke's *Fortune's Uncertainty*, which was apparently semi-autobiographical. This novel appealed to Restoration gallants, who were interested in horse riding and military adventure. Having become bored with university life, the author joined his older brother's cavalry troop as a gentleman volunteer during the Cromwellian period. Because of a reduction in the size of the army, Croke was obliged to look for military adventure in Portugal.[96]

A few swordsmen were driven by a higher motivation than the pursuit of military adventure. Sir Philip Sidney and his circle played a significant role in bringing English martialists into contact with European neostoicism.[97] An important link between Sidney and the continental neostoics was Samson Lennard, who fought alongside Sidney at Zutphen and later translated *The Mystery of Iniquity* (1611) by Philippe Duplessis-Mornay, which blamed the papacy for the plague of religious wars. Mornay was another of Sidney's Huguenot

[95] *The True Travels, Adventures and Observations of Captaine John Smith in Europe, Asia, Africa and America, from 1593 to 1629* (London, 1630), in *Travels and Works of Captain John Smith*, ed. Edward Arber and A. G. Bradley, 2 vols. (Edinburgh, 1910; repr. New York, 1967), ii. 89; Captain John Smith, *The Generall Historie of Virginia* (1624), in ibid. i. 276–7; James A. Freeman, *Milton and the Martial Muse: Paradise Lost and the European Traditions of War* (Princeton, 1980), 38–9.

[96] [Charles Croke,] *Fortune's Uncertainty or Youth's Unconstancy* (London, 1667; Luttrell Soc. Reprints, 19; Oxford, 1959), introduction, pp. v–vii.

[97] Neostoicism, particularly associated with Justus Lipsius, drew upon classical learning to teach the military virtues of discipline, prudence, and engagement with the political issues of the day (Adriana McCrea, *Constant Minds: Political Virtue and the Lipsian Paradigm in England, 1584–1650* (Toronto, 1997), p. xxiii).

Other useful works on neostoicism include: Gerhard Oestereich, *Neostoicism and the Early Modern State* (Cambridge, 1982), Mark Morford, *Stoics and Neostoics: Rubens and the Circle of Lipsius* (Princeton, 1991), and Anthony Grafton, 'Portrait of Justus Lipsius', *American Scholar*, 56 (1986–7), 382–90.

friends, and his call to arms provided a justification for mounting an international Protestant crusade against Habsburg power. Another very influential book was *The Politicke and Militarie Discourses of the Lord De La Nowe*. François de La Noue was an experienced Huguenot military commander, who had a reputation for learning and chivalry at least equal to that of Sidney, but possessed twice the judgement of that knight errant. The determination to go to the aid of beleaguered Protestants helped shape an emerging political awareness in early Stuart England—especially in matters of foreign policy. Although the early Stuart monarchs were indifferent to such sentiments, the patronage of neostoic ideas by the second and third earls of Essex and Henry, prince of Wales, helped to provide a justification for a number of military expeditions sent to Brittany, Normandy, Bohemia, the Rhenish Palatinate, the Isle of Rhé, and elsewhere between the 1590s and the 1620s.[98]

Swordsmen and gallants would sometimes gather at country houses to discuss classical writers on war, to hunt, or just to socialize. In London, there were certain taverns that they frequented, and, later in the seventeenth century, coffee houses. Undoubtedly, the largest public gatherings of martialists in London occurred at public funerals. The Honourable Artillery Company helped to promote this practice, and one of their members quoted Tacitus to the effect that funerals for military heroes helped to propagate an admiration for martial culture and instructed young men in 'the soldier's bloody game'.[99] When Sir Roger Williams died in 1596, his funeral at St Paul's Cathedral was attended by the second earl of Essex dressed in black 'and as many military men as were in the City'.[100] Although Sir George Holles died unmarried and without landed estate, the martialists seized upon the occasion of his funeral to make a statement about military and foreign policy under the early Stuart monarchs. His kinsman Gervase Holles recollected that

[98] J. H. M. Salmon, 'Stoicism and the Roman Example: Seneca and Tacitus in Jacobean England', *Journal of the History of Ideas*, 50 (1989), 206–7; id., *The French Religious Wars in English Political Thought* (Oxford, 1959), 26, 184; François de La Noue, *The Politicke and Military Discourses of the Lord De La Nowe*, trans. Edward Aggas (London, 1587) [STC 15215]. The English translation was dedicated to George Clifford, 3rd earl of Cumberland.
[99] Richard Niccols, *London's Artillery: Briefly Containing the Noble Practice of that Worthy Society* (London, 1616) [STC 18522], 13.
[100] William Camden, *Annales: Or a History of the Most Renowned and Victorious Princesse Elizabeth* (3rd edn.; London, 1635) [STC 4501], 45.

his funeral was the greatest and most solemn that I have ever seen; to which the advantage both of time and place added much. For it happened soon after the term in Parliament time and a little before the expedition to Rhé[101] when the City was full of nobility, gentry and commanders. All the City trained bands were present. The hearse was borne by four and twenty colonels and field officers, eight at a time, the rest encompassing it. His brother, the earl of Clare, and the Lord Vere were the chief mourners, a great train of nobility and gentry followed it, and an infinite concourse of people were the spectators.[102]

In the days before military academies, riding schools functioned as places where the concepts of honour and martial values were inculcated. In 1574–5, Sir Philip Sidney and Edward Wotton, later first Lord Wotton, accompanied an embassy to the Imperial Court in Vienna, where they studied horsemanship under John Pietro Pugliano, from whom they learned 'that soldiers were the noblest estate of mankind, and horsemen the noblest of soldiers'. Although Sidney credited the beginning of his conversion from a mere courtier to a man of action to the lessons he learned from Pugliano, that transition did not happen all at once, but was fed by his subsequent reading of Roman historians.[103] The duke of Newcastle, who was a notable horseman, always linked menage with the exercise of arms and practised them both every day.[104] To be able to master the art of horsemanship and to sit well on a horse was a highly valued achievement because it gave an aristocrat 'A martial look, posture and countenance . . .' Horsemanship was a princely passion and was more likely to catch the eye of a prince than 'skill of government'.[105]

Martialists, being men of action, seldom reflected upon or concerned themselves about the nature of honour in a bellistic society. When John Stevens, a gentleman volunteer in James II's Irish Army, was marching into Dublin in May 1689, he was troubled by the fact that he was 'covered with dust, having lived there sometime before in esteem and spendour, and fearing to meet with many who had formerly known me in a prosperous condition'. He consoled

---

[101]   Actually, the Isle of Rhé expedition occurred in 1627.

[102]   Gervase Holles, *Memorials of the Holles Family, 1493–1656*, ed. A. C. Wood (CS, 3rd ser., 60; London, 1937), 77.

[103]   Sidney, *An Apology for Poetry*, 95.

[104]   Margaret Cavendish, duchess of Newcastle, *The Life of William Cavendish, Duke of Newcastle* (1667), ed. C. H. Firth (London 1906), 112–13.

[105]   Gailhard, *The Compleat Gentleman*, ii. 50–1; Sidney, *An Apology for Poetry*, 95.

himself with the thought that they would recognize him to be 'a
signal sufferer for my religion, my king, for justice and loyalty'. Then
his thoughts turned to the nature of honour and its emphasis on
outward appearances and upon the perception of virtue rather than
its actual possession. 'Most men aspire not to be truly virtuous, but
to be esteemed so; even those who are endowed with any peculiar
virtues do place the greatest satisfaction in having them known,
and study how to make them shine the brighter in the eyes of the
world.'[106]

Among those English gallants who came into contact with the European military world in the late sixteenth and early seventeenth
centuries, the swordsman's sense of honour was a highly individual
and personal concept, and hindered his acceptance of the principles
and practices of modern warfare; it also delayed his assimilation into
a professional officer corps with its values of promotion by merit,
technical expertise, and corporate endeavour. In its most extreme
form this mentality assumed that honour could not be shared, and,
consequently, the morale of worthy subalterns and soldiers suffered
under the obsession of noble commanders with their own reputations. Although the subject begs for more study, it also appears that
the Scots and Irish, because of their more collectivist view of honour
being rooted in the kindred, took a more relaxed approach to sharing
honour with their subordinates. This may help to account for the
professional success of Irish and Scottish soldiers serving in other
armies.

The martialist's concept of honour had nothing to do with Christian
morality, and he cared not about military victory or defeat or the
achievement of stated military objectives. He preferred the agonistic
war of classical Greek and Roman writers to the realities of modern
warfare with its concepts of instrumental or absolute conflict. For
the swordsman, there was little glory to be gained from fighting an
unworthy opponent and therefore it did not make sense to regard
the enemy as the personification of evil or utterly to destroy him. He
could not conceive of perpetual or even long-term peace because peace
generated effeminacy and ultimately brought the downfall of nations.
War was, therefore, the most natural of institutions and afforded the
occasion to make virtue manifest and thus gather honour.

[106] *The Journal of John Stevens*, 51–2.

The influence of Roman writers, usually read in translation, introduced British swordsmen to the practice of Roman commanders sharing honour in order to motivate and exhort their subordinates and soldiers to victory. British martialists also learned that military honour and glory tended to be more widely dispersed in republics than monarchies, and they had the opportunity to observe that, prior to the civil wars, their monarchs no longer shared the same martial culture with them.[107] The question of whether martial honour could be apportioned among many or attributed to only one individual was one that continued to divide the professional soldier from the amateur gallant well into the seventeenth century.

---

[107] Markku Peltonen says that humanism did not decline in Tudor England but continued to furnish a republican vocabulary during the Elizabethan and early Stuart periods. This can be demonstrated by the continued translation and reprinting of Italian humanist and other mainland European political treatises into English (*Classical Humanism and Republicanism*, 19).

CHAPTER THREE

# The Regulation of Aristocratic Status

El rey no puede hazer hidalgo.

> (Spanish aphorism quoted by John Selden, *Titles of Honour*
> (2nd edn.; London, 1631) [STC 22178], II. vii. 866)

Knighthood, in former times, was a peculiar and honourable
reward of military men, and that which is conferred in the field
in time of action is assuredly the most honourable.

> (Sir James Turner, *Pallas Armata*
> (1683; repr. New York, 1968), 351)

Throughout the aristocratic societies of early modern north-western
Europe, disagreement arose over the question of whether monarchs
were the source of honours and titles of nobility or whether they
merely recognized the prior existence of honour and nobility. After
the chivalric revival began in the Elizabethan period, swordsmen—
especially in England—began to resent the pretensions of gownsmen
and courtiers and to insist that honour could be gained or validated
only on the battlefield. The Tudor and Stuart monarchs sought to
monopolize and regulate the granting of titles and armorial bearings
and to adjudicate disputes about points of honour. This they did
through the College of Heralds, which granted and authenticated
coats of arms and conducted visitations by heralds in an attempt to
suppress spurious claims to armigerous status; they also revived the
Court of Chivalry, which claimed an exclusive jurisdiction over affairs
of honour in an unsuccessful attempt to prohibit the widespread
practice of duelling. Peers and gentlemen resented the sale of peerages
and baronetcies by James I and the duke of Buckingham, but the
conflict about the regulation of aristocratic status was more basic
than any dispute concerning royal venality. The basic issue was the

persistent belief among swordsmen that only the community of honour could recognize gentle or noble status.

Thus, the assertion by the Tudor and Stuart monarchs that they could confer noble status by creating peers, dubbing knights, and granting coats of arms conflicted with an older and still widespread view that the Crown could merely recognize noble status.[1] The belief that the nobility was based upon the military vocation, although weakened by the consolidation of royal power and the attempts to pacify the countryside, had not disappeared and was in fundamental conflict with the newer belief that noble status rested upon birth and lineage.[2] Moreover, the reception in the British Isles of a continental European martial tradition derived from Renaissance Italy, France, and the Burgundian Netherlands emphasized the concept of virtue displayed on the battlefield in a worthy cause.

Henry VIII had insisted that he was the sole fount of honour. This he did by an assertion of the royal prerogative rather than by an Act of Parliament. A royal commission of 1530 granted the heralds the authority to inspect and issue coats of arms, and they continued to conduct visitations until 1686.[3] While few disputed the king's right to create peerages (as well as baronets and knights), some English writers on honour believed that nobility extended beyond the peerage. Sir William Segar, who became Garter King-of-Arms in 1603, considered any gentleman who could claim three generations of gentry descent on both his paternal and maternal sides to be noble.[4] Sir Thomas Smith distinguished between the *nobilitas major*, or peerage, and the *nobilitas minor*, or gentry.[5] Sir John Ferne went so far as to insist that, without inward virtue and merit in the recipient, the king could not confer nobility, grant arms, or call a person a gentleman. Such noble or gentle status was 'forged', because, without the manifestation of virtue, the king's grant could constitute only 'a gentleman of paper and wax'.[6]

---

[1] Samuel Clark, *State and Status: The Rise of State and Aristocratic Power in Western Europe* (Montreal, 1995), 174–5, 182–3.

[2] Mervyn James, *English Politics and the Concept of Honour, 1485–1642* (P&P Supplement, 3; Oxford, 1978), 22–3.

[3] Felicity Heal and Clive Holmes, *The Gentry in England and Wales, 1500–1700* (Stanford, Calif., 1994), 28; A. R. Wagner, *Heralds and Heraldry in the Middle Ages* (2nd edn.; Oxford, 1956), 2–4.

[4] Sir William Segar, *Honor, Military and Civil* (London, 1602) [STC 22164], iii. 121.

[5] Sir Thomas Smith, *The Commonwealth of England* (1635 edn.), quoted in Peter Laslett, *The World We Have Lost* (3rd edn.; New York, 1984), 31.

[6] Sir John Ferne, *The Blazon of Gentrie* (London, 1586) [STC 10824], 60–1.

In the seventeenth century the Stuart monarchs could confer a peerage on any subject or, indeed, any foreigner, in any or all of the Three Kingdoms. But even they seem to have accepted the widely circulated maxim that a king could not make a gentleman. Military men possessed a special quality that the king could not confer and that could be earned only on the battlefield. James I supposedly told his old nurse when she asked him to make her son a gentleman: 'A gentleman I could never make him, though I could make him a lord.'[7] Daniel Defoe cited Charles II to similar effect: 'Well did Charles II say he could make a knight, but could not make a gentleman.'[8] Selden thought that this maxim derived from the Spanish, 'El rey no puede hazer hidalgo'. La Rochefoucauld enunciated a similar aphorism: 'L'air bourgeois se perd quelquefois à l'armée, mais il ne se perd jamais à la cour' [Bourgeois manners can sometimes be shed in the army, but never at court].[9]

Margaret, duchess of Newcastle, was as staunch a royalist as any, but she also insisted that the king could not make a gentleman: 'My father [Sir Thomas Lucas] was a gentleman, which title was grounded and given by merit, not princes; and it was the act of time, not favour.' She added that her father could have afforded to purchase a peerage, and was encouraged to do so, but 'did not esteem titles, unless they were gained by heroic actions'.[10] Gervase Markham thought that the Vere earls of Oxford were as ancient as the Roman caesars, and therefore could hadly owe their titles to the kings of England. If any magnate owed his title to another, he insinuated, it was the house of Lancaster (meaning Henry VII), since John, thirteenth earl of Oxford, was 'the best sword and buckler man' who ever fought for that monarch while he was still earl of Richmond. David

---

[7] John Selden, *Titles of Honour* (2nd edn.; London, 1631) [STC 22178], II. vii. 866; Matthew Carter, *Honor Redivivus, or An Analysis of Honor and Armory* (London, 1660) [Wing C659], 12; Louis B. Wright, *The First Gentlemen of Virginia: Intellectual qualities of the Early Colonial Ruling Class* (San Marino, Calif., 1940), 6. There is a slight rhetorical exaggeration here. A substantial landowning family, whose heads lived like gentlemen, and came to be so reputed by their neighbours, could be accepted as such by the royal heralds on their visitations. However, this process could take several generations. The demonstration of valour on the battlefield was the faster way of achieving the personal status of gentleman.

[8] Daniel Defoe, *The Compleat English Gentleman*, ed. K. D. Bülbring (London, 1890; repr. 1972), 25.

[9] François, duc de La Rochefoucauld, *Maximes* (1778; repr. Paris, 1959), no. 393.

[10] Margaret Cavendish, duchess of Newcastle, *The Life of William Cavendish, Duke of Newcastle* (1667), ed. C. H. Firth (London, 1906), 155–6.

Hume of Godscroft, an antiquarian who enjoyed the patronage of the earls of Angus in the early seventeenth century, insisted that the Douglases were noble long before Sir James Douglas became a companion of King Robert I. The Scots nobility were better at avoiding biological failure in the male line and they usually based their claims to honourable ancestry upon descent from ancestors who had been companions of the ancient kings of Scotland.[11]

The Scots mercenary Robert Monro observed that some of his fellows thought that military service was the fastest way to achieve noble status, and the plunder of war the best way to support such pretensions. Monro disapproved because he thought that those who obtained wealth 'by unlawful means' merely 'counterfeited . . . nobility'.[12] By the latter part of the seventeenth century there were difficulties in guarding the boundaries of honourable status. Sir James Turner rejected the idea—current among professional military men —'that all soldiers are gentlemen . . .' He thought that titles of honour, including recognition of gentle status, should be given only to commissioned officers. However, accepting reality, Turner recognized that the king cannot be restricted to granting titles and dignities of honour only to swordsmen.[13] In the Royal Navy of the Restoration period, questions of honour both united and divided gentlemen officers and 'tarpaulins', or those who had been promoted from the lower deck. Tarpaulins argued that the king's commission conferred honour and made them gentlemen. Gentlemen officers insisted that honour came only from breeding and that the courage that made an officer stand steady in time of battle was innate.[14]

Status was viewed as a form of power, and that was why early modern monarchs tried to control the recognition of honour and the granting of arms. The Tudor and Stuart monarchs succeeded

[11] Gervase Markham, *Honor in his Perfection* (London, 1624) [STC 17361], 10–11; Keith M. Brown, *Noble Society in Scotland: Wealth, Family and Culture, from Reformation to Revolution* (Edinburgh, 2000), 5; Gawin Douglas, bishop of Dunkeld, *The Palis of Honoure* (London, 1553?) [STC 7073], unpaginated.

[12] Robert Monro, *Monro, his Expedition with the Worthy Scots Regiment (called Mac-keyes Regiment) levied in August 1626 by Sir Donald Mac-key Lord Rhees*, 2 vols. (London, 1637) [STC 18022], ii. 20.

[13] Sir James Turner, *Pallas Armata: Military Essayes of the Ancient Grecian, Roman, and Modern Art of War. Written in the Years 1670 and 1671* (London 1683; repr. New York, 1968), 350.

[14] J. S. Davies, *Gentlemen and Tarpaulins: The Officers and Men of the Restoration Navy* (Oxford, 1991), 62–3; Edward Ward, *The Wooden World* (1707) (5th edn.; 1755; repr. London, 1929), 26, 30.

in controlling entry into the peerage more effectively than they did in regulating gentle status and knighthood, but the whole process was a continual source of friction and resentment. The values of the chivalric tradition could be exploited by monarchs to glorify the expression of dynastic power, and the ambitions of monarchs subordinated the individual gentleman's quest for honour and reputation to the political needs of the monarchy. In the Elizabethan period and after, knighthood could no longer be justified solely by military service; knights were also expected to carry a heavy burden of judicial and administrative duties as justices of the peace. Expressions of individualism that had been tolerated in battle in earlier times could no longer be allowed among civil magistrates or military officers, and this justified a tighter control by the monarch on the distribution of knighthoods and other honours.[15]

Chivalry in England had long been oriented towards serving the monarch. Elizabeth had attempted to exploit this in a number of ways. She sought to depict herself as a lady knight, a concept not unfamiliar to those who were acquainted with Edmund Spencer's Britomart in *The Faerie Queene*, and she also played this role when she donned a silver cuirass and reviewed the trained bands and aristocratic retinues mustered at Tilbury in 1588 to repel any Spanish invaders. She also revived the Order of the Garter with the intention of uniting aristocrats in a brotherhood of Protestant knights who pledged their allegiance to the Crown and undertook to defeat the papal dragon. However, she herself made few knights—and they were mostly of the carpet variety and never enough to satisfy anything like the demand—and she never succeeded in reining in her military commanders in the field or her deputies in Ireland in their distribution of battlefield knighthoods.[16]

Just as Elizabeth's parsimony in distributing battlefield honours bred resentment, the royal institutions for granting and regulating noble and honourable status also generated conflict because they appeared to involve extensions of the royal prerogative. In the Middle Ages, the Court of the Constable and Marshal had originated as a military court that controlled the royal army in the field when the king's

---

[15] Clark, *State and Status*, 362–3; Arthur B. Ferguson, *The Chivalric Tradition in Renaissance England* (Cranbury, NJ, 1986), 13–14, 107–9.

[16] Ibid. 75–6; Garrett Mattingly, *The Defeat of the Spanish Armada* (Harmondsworth, 1965), 364–6.

banner was unfurled and regulated military matters outside the realm and thus beyond the jurisdiction of the common law. These functions included the conduct of sieges and tournaments and the trial of disputes concerning matters of honour.[17] In the seventeenth century, the overseas functions of the Earl Marshal's Court, also known as the Court of Chivalry, came to be exercised by councils of war or courts martial established by the authority of the military commander in the field. The domestic functions of the Court of Chivalry were now confined to adjudicating disputes about armorial bearings and questions concerning honourable status. As a commissioner for the office of earl marshal, Henry Howard, first earl of Northampton, attempted to stem the inflation of honours by reforming abuses by heralds who sold arms to those who had no claim to be gentlemen. He also undertook a campaign against duelling, which was enforced in both the Court of the Earl Marshal and the Court of Star Chamber. Northampton died in 1614, but, when his nephew and heir, Thomas Howard, second earl of Arundel and Surrey, became earl marshal in 1621 and proposed reviving a statute of 1 Henry IV, which would allow the Earl Marshal's Court to condemn those who fought duels outside England and beyond the reach of the common law, common lawyers and members of Parliament condemned the Earl Marshal's Court as another species of obnoxious prerogative court.[18]

Although James I apparently believed that he could not make a gentleman, this did not prevent the Court of Chivalry from degrading gentlemen. In 1624, Arundel, sitting in the Earl Marshal's Court, declared that Sir Thomas Harris, a Shropshire baronet, was 'no gentleman'; at the same time Arundel discovered that his authority did not extend to undubbing the baronet because that honour had been granted by 'patent under the under the great seal of England'.[19] Tension also developed between king and Parliament over the question of who could degrade a knight. In April 1621, Parliament

---

[17] Wagner, *Heralds and Heraldry in the Middle Ages*, 20–1.
   The office of high constable fell into disuse after 1521, and thereafter the earl marshal became the presiding officer of the court (P. H. Hardacre, 'The Earl Marshal, the Heralds, and the House of Commons, 1604–1641', *International Review of Social History*, 2 (1957), 108).
[18] G. D. Squib, *The High Court of Chivalry* (Oxford, 1959), pp. xxxv–xxxvi; Linda Levy Peck, *Northampton: Patronage and Policy at the Court of James I* (London, 1982), 160–1.
[19] *The Letters of John Chamberlain*, ed. N. E. McClure, 2 vols. (Philadelphia, 1939), ii. 590.

impeached and convicted Sir Francis Michell, the monopolist, on a charge of corruption. However, the sentence against Michell of degradation from knighthood was handed down by the lord chief justice in the Court of King's Bench. The royal heralds carried out the ritual of degradation, which included having Michell ride a horse backwards through the City of London and having his sword broken over his head.[20] In 1627, the government of Charles I devised a plan to tax knights and baronets, and declared the intention of degrading those who refused to pay. Although Charles backed off from this scheme, medals were struck to be distributed and worn around the neck by those who had paid the tax—rather like a modern dog licence.[21]

The reputation of the Court of Chivalry was at a low ebb in the early seventeenth century, yet many still believed it to be necessary to prevent arms being granted to and borne by upstarts. Henry Peacham stated that without the 'outward ensigns and badges of virtue' it was difficult to 'discern and know an intruding upstart, shot up with last night's mushroom, from an ancient and deserved gentleman, whose grandsires have had their shares in every foughten field . . . since Edward the First'. During the personal rule of Charles I, when Parliament did not meet, the criticism of the Earl Marshal's Court abated, but in 1641, in the *Grand Remonstrance*, the Long Parliament denounced the jurisdiction of the court as arbitrary and illegal, but Parliament did not go so far as to abolish it as it did the Court of Star Chamber.[22]

Courts in early modern England required substantial written evidence to put a claim beyond dispute. The Court of Chivalry was no different, and would not accept the mere possession of a coat of arms as proof of honourable status, but preferred evidence that the individual in question was reputed to be a gentleman and lived like a gentleman. Sir John Doderidge, justice of the Court of Common Pleas, assumed that coat armour and claims to gentility were often spurious,

[20] *A Pepysian Garland: Black-Letter Broadside Ballads of the Years 1595–1639, Chiefly from the Collection of Samuel Pepys*, ed. H. E. Rollins (Cambridge, 1922), 144–9.

[21] Thomas Birch, *The Court and Times of Charles I*, ed. R. F. Williams, 2 vols. (London, 1848), i. 193.

[22] Hardacre, 'The Earl Marshal, the Heralds, and the House of Commons', 108–10; Henry Peacham, *The Compleat Gentleman* (London, 1622; repr. Oxford, 1906), 160–1.

and looked for further evidence of honourable blood, good parents, or some exploit in war or peace that would entitle the individual to the status claimed.[23] In Scotland, Sir James Balfour, Lord Lyon king-of-arms, thought that virtue and a long pedigree were an insufficient proof of nobility unless confirmed by a royal patent or charter. This, of course, placed a heavy emphasis upon the royal prerogative in recognizing nobility. However, in the Highlands oral memorials and even mythological genealogies were accepted as proof of noble status when recited by Gaelic bards on festive occasions.[24]

As the royal heralds became less involved in arbitrating the rules of engagement upon the battlefield during the fifteenth century, they took upon themselves the duties of prescribing, directing and recording the rituals observed at the funerals of peers and knights. They appeared at such funerals, whether invited or not, because this function had become an important source of the heralds' income. The rituals observed, such as carrying the helm and crest, sword and targe or buckler in the cortège probably contributed to the survival of martial culture among the gentry and peerage, since such funerals were important social gatherings for military men and served to impress young gentlemen who aspired to honour and adventure. Noble funerals in Scotland also became more extravagant, and might be attended by as many as 2,000 persons, who joined in a demonstration of hierarchy and kinship and a celebration of the deceased's martial reputation.[25]

Under Elizabeth the rule was that no English subject could claim titles of honour and dignity except those conferred by English monarchs. Camden records that 'some there were which thought that the rewards bestowed in respect of virtue by what prince soever are to be admitted, for virtue languisheth unless well-deservers be encouraged by rewards'. Camden also recited instances of English monarchs, as recent as Henry VIII, who accepted and recognized foreign titles. The Scottish kings had thought that such titles redounded to the honour

---

[23] Squib, *The High Court of Chivalry*, 171–5.
[24] Allan I. Macinnes, *Clanship, Commerce and the House of Stuart, 1603–1788* (East Linton, East Lothian, 1996), 5; Brown, *Noble Society in Scotland*, 5.
[25] Malcolm Vale, *War and Chivalry: Warfare and Aristocratic Culture in England, France and Burgundy at the End of the Middle Ages* (London and Athens, Ga., 1981), 92–3; Charles Hughes, 'Introduction', in Sir Henry Knyvett, *The Defence of the Realme* (Oxford, 1906), pp. xxii–xxiii; William Camden, *Annales: Or the History of the Most Renowned and Victorious Princesse Elizabeth* (3rd edn.; London, 1635) [STC 4501], 451; Brown, *Noble Society in Scotland*, 262–3.

of the kingdom. The contrary argument, advanced by those who could not abide the thought of the queen's Catholic subjects serving in the armies of Catholic monarchs, was that the titles in question were given to withdraw the queen's subjects from their allegiance to her.[26] The most famous test case involved Thomas Arundell, who served in the Imperial Army against the Turks and was made a count of the Holy Roman Empire in 1595 for his bravery in assaulting several fortified cities and fortresses occupied by the Turks in Hungary. When Arundell returned home, Elizabeth imprisoned him for accepting the title on the pretext that the English nobility had been offended by his presumption since he was only the son of a knight. The Emperor Rudolph II wrote to Elizabeth asking her to restore Arundell to favour, and Arundell himself pleaded that she had given him leave to serve against the Turks in Hungary for two years. He also added that the English nobility could not expect the nobility of the Holy Roman Empire to recognize their titles if there was not reciprocity. James I was less grudging and bestowed upon him the title Baron Arundell of Wardour in 1605.[27]

Another swordsman whom Elizabeth imprisoned for accepting a foreign honour was Sir Anthony Sherley, the most famous of the three sons of Sir Thomas Sherley. Sir Anthony had accompanied Peregrine Bertie, thirteenth Lord Willoughby, to France as a volunteer in 1589, where his gallantry attracted the attention of François de La Noue, the distinguished Huguenot commander. In 1591, he returned from France, where he was to command a regiment until 1595. While at home on leave Elizabeth committed him to prison for accepting a knighthood in the order of St Michel from Henri IV, and he was questioned about whether accepting the honour did not oblige him to swear allegiance to the king of France and the Catholic faith. Pressure was put upon him to renounce the knighthood, but Sherley refused to yield. Eventually, a compromise was reached whereby he returned the insignia of the Order of St Michel, but was allowed to continue styling himself as a knight. Subsequently, Sherley secretly married Frances Vernon, whose sister Elizabeth Henry Wriothesley,

---

[26] W. H. Dunham, 'William Camden's Commonplace Book', *Yale University Library Gazette*, 43 (1969), 151; Camden, *Annales* (3rd edn.), 467–8.

[27] Ibid. 'Thomas Arundel, Count Arundel (afterwards Lord Arundel of Wardour), his Apologie, upon Confinement for Accepting the Honor *Comes Imperii*, without the Queen's Leave', in Francis Peck, *Desiderata Curiosa*, 2 vols. (London, 1732–5) [ESTCT 97524], II. vii. 50–6.

third earl of Southampton, had also married without the queen's permission. As a consequence, the queen banished both Sherley and Southampton from court.[28]

There were only a limited number of civil and military offices available to noblemen and knights in the Three Kingdoms, and it was considered a disgrace not to be able to serve one's prince. Consequently, many young gentlemen and peers who were attracted to martial culture were driven to seek honour, glory, and adventure abroad in the service of foreign princes. When they were awarded titles and honours by those same princes they expected their own princes to recognize that status or to confer equivalent honours upon them.[29]

Following the second earl of Essex's return from his expeditions to Cadiz and the Azores, he grew dissatisfied with his inability to compete with the Cecils for office and patronage, and he set his eye on the office of earl marshal, which had been in commission since the death of George Talbot, sixth earl of Shrewsbury, in 1590. Sir Francis Bacon had warned Essex, who was his patron, that it was dangerous to seek so powerful a military office, and advised him to ask for a civil office instead. Essex not only persisted in going after the office of earl marshal, but withdrew from court until the queen yielded to his demands. Then he had the audacity to complain that the letters patent granting him the office of earl marshal did not sufficiently praise his reputation—thus failing to make the distinction between that honour earned by Essex on the battlefield and the honour that the queen's commission purported to bestow upon him—a distinction between 'native' and 'dative' honour.[30] Not content to rest there, Essex began to employ antiquarians to research the ancient usage of the office and to suggest ways of enhancing its powers. The antiquarians told Essex that he might ask that the office of constable, which had lapsed with the execution of Edward Stafford, duke of

[28] D. W. Davies, *Elizabethans Errant: The Strange Fortunes of Sir Thomas Sherley and his Three Sons* (Ithaca, NY, 1967), 35–9; R. B. Wernham, *After the Armada: Elizabethan England and the Struggle for Western Europe, 1588–1595* (Oxford, 1984), 165; *DNB*, *sub* Sir Anthony Shirley *or* Sherley (1565–1635?) *and* Henry Wriothesley, 3rd earl of Southampton (1573–1624).

Sherley later also accepted the title count of the Holy Roman Empire from Rudolph II for diplomatic services rendered.

[29] Caroline Hibbard, 'The Theatre of Dynasty', in R. M. Smuts (ed.), *The Stuart Court and Europe: Essays in Politics and Political Culture* (Cambridge, 1996), 162–3.

[30] Richard C. McCoy, 'Old English Honour in an Evil Time: Aristocratic Principle in the 1620s', in Smuts (ed.), *The Stuart Court and Europe*, 88–9.

THE REGULATION OF ARISTOCRATIC STATUS 91

Buckingham, for treason in 1521, be revived and combined with the office of earl marshal. Such talk had a ring of sedition about it, and, needless to say, Elizabeth turned a deaf ear to the proposal.[31]

The second earl's supporters had continued to meet privately after his execution in 1601, and never ceased to honour his name. In the 1620s, this adulation became more open. The revival of the political and military legacy of the second earl of Essex made honour an integral part of the political discourse of the 1620s. This provided a set of principles to guide political conduct and suggests that the factional struggles of this period did not rest entirely upon personal interest and systems of patronage and clientage. The issue that brought the group together was the sale of peerages, baronetcies, and other dignities, offices, and honours throughout the Three Kingdoms to the highest bidder for the profit of the king and the duke of Buckingham, which, of course, was at odds with the Essexian principle of granting titles only to recognize the prior existence of virtue and honour. The sale of honours began in the reign of James VI and I, and the prices escalated under Buckingham. During the Parliament of 1621, the third earl of Essex and the third earl of Southampton led a group of thirty-three English peers in drawing up 'The Humble Petition of the Nobility of England', which they presented to James I.[32]

The king was much offended by 'The Humble Petition'. It was more than an attack on the royal favourite, the duke of Buckingham, for the king perceived it as a challenge to his prerogative, and pretended to see behind it the spectre of aristocratic revolt. Although the petition was indeed humble in tone, and did not question the king's right to create peers and bestow other honours, James must have found the very thorough discussion of what constituted honour to be very disturbing. While James did refrain from creating so many peers thereafter, he also expostulated with the thirty-three petitioning peers one by one, treating 'some of them roughly'. The third earl of Essex had not actually signed the petition, but James was aware that he was one of the prime movers behind it. Arthur Wilson says

---

[31] Ibid. 90–5.
[32] Arthur Wilson, *The Life and Reign of James, the First King of Great Britain* (1653), repr. in [White Kennett,] *The Complete History of England*, 3 vols. (London, 1706) [ESTCT 145258], ii. 747a & b; Vernon F. Snow, *Essex the Rebel: The Life of Robert Devereux, the Third Earl of Essex, 1591–1646* (Lincoln, Neb., 1970), 104–6; Victor Treadwell, *Buckingham and Ireland, 1616–1628* (Dublin, 1998), 104–5; McCoy, 'Old English Honour in an Evil Time', 140–1.

that James told Essex: 'I fear thee not Essex, if thou wert as well beloved as thy father, and had forty thousand men at thy heels.'[33]

It might be argued that the second earl of Essex had helped contribute to the inflation of honours with his free hand (as the queen thought) in dubbing knights at Cadiz, in Ireland, and elsewhere. In fact, Essex made at most 175 knights during his whole career. This number seems large in comparison to the meagre 160 knights that the queen personally dubbed during the time of the war with Spain and the intervention in the Netherlands between 1585 and 1603. No other military or naval commander, or lord deputy of Ireland, being a subject, created anywhere near as many knights. Essex was advancing an entirely different set of criteria for bestowing honours, and, despite the queen's orders to desist from making more knights on the battlefield, he persisted in challenging the royal prerogative by doing so. Essex's knights did, at least, earn their knighthoods on the battlefield, and presumably had demonstrated virtue in the eyes of their fellow swordsmen. Whether these military and naval expeditions were successful is, by the standards of the time, irrelevent. James VI and I, by contrast, indiscriminately knighted 929 individuals in 1603 alone.[34] Whereas Elizabeth created an average of not quite nine knights per year during the war years (and only six during the year of the Armada), James made something like forty-five knights per year during peacetime (if we omit the extraordinary year of 1603 from our calculations). Charles I dubbed an average of not quite thirty-five knights for the five years of 1625, 1630, 1635, 1640, and 1645. The number of knights that he created in each of these years appears to have no correlation to the years of peace and the years of war, but, after the assassination of Buckingham in 1628, he certainly made fewer. Although Irish knighthoods were usually conferred to raise money for the Crown, the distribution of honours in Ireland was also linked to the various institutions, customs, and culture that made up what the English called 'civility', or the adoption of English ways. Of the 258 knighthoods handed out between 1603 and 1629, not quite a third were bestowed on Old Irish and Old English gentry, while over two-thirds went to the New English and Scots adventurers

---

[33] Ibid. Wilson, *The Life and Death of James, the First King of Great Britain*, ii. 747a & b.

James dealt with the earl of Southampton by imprisoning him after the dissolution of Parliament.

[34] See Table 3.1.

and planters.[35] Charles II created 223 knights in the year of his Restoration, but thereafter made new knights at the not ungenerous rate of thirty-two per year. William III, a soldier-monarch if there ever was one, made even fewer knights per year than Elizabeth I, which amply demonstrates the contempt that he had for officers of the English army.[36]

Despite Elizabeth's calculated neglect of the honour of knighthood, the belief persisted that knighthood was more honourable when conferred on the battlefield.[37] At the beginning of Elizabeth's reign, the number of knights stood at about 600, but declined to approximately 300 in 1580. During the war years from 1585 to 1602, 529 new knights were made.[38] Thomas Wilson estimated that there were 500 knights in England in 1600, but he made a point of excluding from that total the knights made by the second earl of Essex on the battlefield, who 'are scornfully called Cales [Cadiz], Rouen or Irish knights'. Wilson thought many of them were adventurers who could hardly be considered gentlemen, and he sneered that they were 'made knights for the credit of their country and to induce them to live in a more honourable manner, both for their own credit and the service of their prince and country, than perhaps they would otherwise do'. For Wilson, the qualifications for knighthood were based upon wealth; he thought that knights should possess estates worth between £1,000 and £2,000 p.a.[39] It is difficult to tell how many impecunious swordsmen Wilson deleted; between 1585 and 1602 the number of knights created by military and naval commanders was 165, and the number dubbed by the various lords deputy and lords justices of Ireland for the same period was 179. The greatest number of knights created by a lord deputy of Ireland was made, not by Essex, but by Sir Henry Cary, first Viscount Falkland, who made eighty-three between 1622 and 1629. However, the second earl of Essex made eighty-one as lord lieutenant of Ireland in 1599 during one four-month campaigning season.[40]

---

[35] Heal and Holmes, *Gentry in England and Wales*, 193; Treadwell, *Buckingham and Ireland*, 105–6.

[36] See Table 3.2.     [37] Turner, *Pallas Armata*, 351.

[38] Lawrence Stone, *The Crisis of the Aristocracy, 1558–1641* (Oxford, 1965), 71–2; See Table 3.1.

[39] 'The State of England Anno Dom. 1600, by Thomas Wilson', ed. F. J. Fisher, *Camden Miscellany XVI* (CS, 3rd ser., 52; London, 1936), 23.

[40] William A. Shaw, *The Knights of England*, 2 vols. (London, 1906), i, p. li.

TABLE 3.1  *Creation of English knights bachelors, 1584–1603*

| Year | Knights bachelors Created by | Number | Total |
|---|---|---|---|
| 1584 | Lord president of Wales | 1 | 17 |
|  | Lord deputy of Ireland | 7 |  |
|  | Queen Elizabeth | 9 |  |
| 1585 | Lord deputy of Ireland | 13 | 22 |
|  | Queen Elizabeth | 9 |  |
| 1586 | Lord deputy of Ireland | 2 | 53 |
|  | Lord Leicester, governor of Netherlands | 37 |  |
|  | Queen Elizabeth | 14 |  |
| 1587 | Lord deputy of Ireland | 2 | 22 |
|  | Leicester | 6 |  |
|  | Lord admiral | 1 |  |
|  | Queen Elizabeth | 13 |  |
| 1588 | Leicester | 3 | 26 |
|  | Lord Willoughby, governor of Netherlands | 11 |  |
|  | Lord admiral | 6 |  |
|  | Queen Elizabeth | 6 |  |
| 1589 | Lord deputy of Ireland | 6 | 13 |
|  | Queen Elizabeth | 7 |  |
| 1590 | None created |  | 0 |
| 1591 | Lord deputy of Ireland | 4 | 65 |
|  | Lord admiral | 7 |  |
|  | King of France | 5 |  |
|  | Essex before Rouen | 2 [26[a]] |  |
|  | Queen Elizabeth | 23 |  |
| 1592 | Lord deputy of Ireland | 1 | 22 |
|  | Queen Elizabeth | 21 |  |
| 1593 | Lord deputy of Ireland | 13 | 17 |
|  | Queen Elizabeth | 4 |  |
| 1594 | Lord deputy of Ireland | 5 | 23 |
|  | King of Scots | 17 |  |
|  | Queen Elizabeth | 1 |  |
| 1595 | Lord deputy of Ireland | 4 | 9 |
|  | Queen Elizabeth | 5 |  |
| 1596 | Lord admiral and Essex at Cadiz | 33 | 77 |
|  | Essex at Cadiz | 31 |  |
|  | Queen Elizabeth | 13 |  |
| 1597 | Lord deputy of Ireland | 10 | 19 |
|  | Essex on Azores Expedition | 4 |  |
|  | Queen Elizabeth | 5 |  |

TABLE 3.1 *(cont'd)*

| Year | Knights bachelors Created by | Number | Total |
|------|------------------------------|--------|-------|
| 1598 | Lords justices of Ireland | 7 | 13 |
|      | Queen Elizabeth | 6 | |
| 1599 | Lords justices of Ireland, | 2 | 94 |
|      | Essex, lord lieutenant of Ireland | 81 | |
|      | Queen Elizabeth | 11 | |
| 1600 | Lord deputy of Ireland | 8 | 18 |
|      | Queen Elizabeth | 10 | |
| 1601 | Lord deputy of Ireland | 2 | 24 |
|      | Queen Elizabeth | 22 | |
| 1602 | Lord deputy of Ireland | 12 | 12 |
| 1603 | Lord deputy of Ireland | 26 | 955 |
|      | King James VI & I | 929 | |

[a] Sir Thomas Coningsby, 'Journal of the Siege of Rouen, 1591', ed. J. G. Nichols, *Camden Miscellany I* (Camden Soc., old ser., 39; 1847), 71 n. 27.
*Source*: William A. Shaw, *The Knights of England*, 2 vols. (London, 1906), ii. 83–129.

It was customary for the commanders of military and naval expeditions to confer knighthoods upon the battlefield or upon the quarterdeck. In 1586, as governor-general of the Netherlands, the earl of Leicester had created thirty-seven knights, six more in 1587, and three in 1588. Some of the knights created by Leicester played an important role in helping to raise companies of volunteers in England. When the duke of Parma abandoned his attempt to take Bergen-op-Zoom by siege in the autumn of 1588, Peregrine Bertie, Lord Willoughby, who had succeeded Leicester as governor and lord general in the Netherlands, held a military review within sight of the enemy at which he conferred the order of knighthood on five English and Dutch officers.[41] Willoughby made a total of eleven knights in 1588. The lord admiral also created a total of seven knights in 1587 and 1588—although some of these newly dubbed knights were peers or sons of peers such as Edmund, Lord Sheffield, and Lord Thomas Howard, and the others included important naval commanders such

[41] *The Triumphs of Nassau*, trans. W. Shute (London, 1613) [STC 17677], 108–9; Simon Adams, 'A Puritan Crusade? The Composition of the Earl of Leicester's Expedition to the Netherlands, 1585–6', in his *Leicester and the Court: Essays in Elizabethan Politics* (Manchester, 2002), 187.

TABLE 3.2 *Creation of English knights bachelors, 1605–1700*

| Year | Knights bachelors<br>Created by | Number | Total |
|------|----------------------------------|--------|-------|
| 1605 | Lord deputy of Ireland | 27 | 94 |
|      | King James I | 67 | |
| 1610 | Lord deputy of Ireland | 2 | 24 |
|      | King James I, or by letters patent | 22 | |
| 1615 | Lord deputy of Ireland | 6 | 69 |
|      | King James I, or by letters patent | 63 | |
| 1620 | Lord deputy of Ireland | 5 | 33 |
|      | King James I | 28 | |
| 1625 | Lord deputy of Ireland | 6 | 76 |
|      | King Charles I | 70 | |
| 1630 | Lords justices of Ireland | 2 | 39 |
|      | King Charles I | 37 | |
| 1635 | Lord deputy of Ireland | 8 | 23 |
|      | Earl of Lindsey, admiral of fleet | 6 | |
|      | King Charles I | 9 | |
| 1640 | Lord deputy and lords justices of Ireland | 3 | 18 |
|      | King Charles I | 15 | |
| 1645 | King Charles I | 38 | 38 |
| 1650 | King Charles II | 6 | 6 |
|      | in exile in Holland and in Scotland | | |
| 1655 | Lord Protector Cromwell | 3 | 3 |
| 1660 | King Charles II | 223 | 223 |
| 1665 | [Lord Deputy? | 2] | 44 |
|      | King Charles II | 42 | |
| 1670 | [Lord Deputy? | 5] | 36 |
|      | King Charles II | 31 | |
| 1675 | King Charles II | 26 | 26 |
| 1680 | Lord lieutenant of Ireland | 2 | 31 |
|      | King Charles II | 29 | |
| 1685 | Lord lieutenant of Ireland | 1 | 34 |
|      | duke of Monmouth | 1 | |
|      | King James VII & II | 32 | |
| 1690 | King William III, | 10 | 16 |
|      | King James VII & I | 6 | |
| 1695 | King William III | 7 | 7 |
| 1700 | Lords justices of Ireland | 2 | 10 |
|      | King William III | 8 | |

*Source*: William A. Shaw, *The Knights of England*, 2 vols. (London, 1906), ii. 136–272.

as Sir John Hawkins and Sir Martin Frobisher.[42] Elizabeth did not object to any of these knighthoods, so far as we know. Elizabeth's objection to the knighthoods made by Essex was that he cheapened knighthood by handing out too many battlefield honours. It also appears that Essex was building a party of martialists who would be obliged to him. In 1598, Thomas, fifteenth Lord Grey of Wilton, a contentious person, complained that Essex had attempted to compel him to declare his loyalty for either Essex or Sir Robert Cecil. This falling-out between Grey, on the one hand, and Essex and the third earl of Southampton, on the other, did not prevent Grey from accepting a knighthood from Essex the next year. Ever the opportunist, Grey hoped that his accepting a knighthood from Essex would not offend the queen.[43]

During his very first command, when he led an expedition into Normandy in 1591 to assist the king of Navarre against the Catholic Leaguers, Essex took it upon himself to create twenty-six knights— twenty-two of them during the Siege of Rouen.[44] What distinguishes Essex's action in dubbing so many knights on the battlefield from the actions of earlier military and naval commanders is that Essex reached further down in the military hierarchy to gentlemen who were only captains or volunteers without commissioned rank—although four of them were sons or grandsons of peers, and five of them subsequently became peers. While Essex was waiting to begin the siege of Rouen, a letter arrived ordering Essex back to England. Essex began making arrangements to appoint deputies to assume command, but in the meantime sent Sir Robert Cary with a letter for the queen. Cary, whom Essex knighted on the beach at Dieppe after his return from court, had persuaded Elizabeth to rescind her command ordering Essex to return by telling her that, if Essex withdrew from Rouen, where he was to join forces with the king of Navarre, the whole world would attribute his action to cowardice, which would damage his honour and reputation.[45] Elizabeth relented and ordered Essex to

[42] See Table 3.1; Robert Cary, earl of Monmouth, *Memoirs* (London, 1759) [ESTCT 147779], pp. xvii–xxii, 40.

[43] HMC, *Salisbury MSS* viii. 26; A. L. Rowse, *Shakespeare's Southampton: Patron of Virginia* (New York, 1965), 140, 143; GEC vi. 187.

[44] Sir Thomas Coningsby, 'Journal of the Siege of Rouen, 1591', ed. J. G. Nichols, in *Camden Miscellany I* (CS, old ser., 39; London, 1847), 71 n. 27.

Shaw is in error where he states that Essex made only two knights during the Rouen campaign (see Table 3.1).

[45] Cary, earl of Monmouth, *Memoirs*, 32–40.

resume his duties before Rouen. This episode, and the other times when Elizabeth subsequently tried to countermand Essex's orders or undercut his authority, suggest that the queen might have benefited from the presence of more military men on her Privy Council, or, at least, the use of a subordinate council of war. That distinctive point of view was lacking in the advice that she did receive from the gownsmen on her Council, and the tendency of swordsmen to shun the court did their cause no good.[46]

The earl of Essex's generosity in bestowing knighthoods caused many other volunteers to flock about him when it became known that he was to go Ireland with the title of lord lieutenant. There was clearly a great hunger among the aristocracy and gentry for battlefield honours, and it should cause no surprise that Elizabeth and some of her advisers anticipated trouble over this question. Essex had already offended the lord admiral, Charles Howard, first earl of Nottingham, in a dispute about military patronage in the Netherlands and had also butted heads with Sir Walter Raleigh on the Azores Voyage of 1597. Essex's conflict with the queen concerning the distribution of knighthoods over which she wished to retain absolute control hampered his ability to command effectively in the field.[47] Elizabeth had ordered Essex before his departure for Ireland to make no knights without her leave, but there were many precedents for arguing that the lord lieutenant created knights 'by right of his office'.[48] After Essex had created eighty-one knights during the four-month campaigning season of 1599, Elizabeth ordered a proclamation drawn up declaring those knights to be degraded (apparently on the advice of Sir Francis Bacon), but Sir Robert Cecil intervened and told the queen that knights could not be unmade in this manner and that consequently such a proclamation would be 'null and void'.[49] Among those knighted by Essex in

[46] Elizabeth's field commanders, it must be said, sometimes conspired to defeat her commands, as was the case on the expedition to Spain and Portugal in 1589, when the highest priority was to destroy the ships that had survived the 1588 Armada expedition and were riding at anchor in the harbours of Santander and La Coruña, but Sir Francis Drake and Sir John Norris decided instead to try and start a land war in Portugal in hopes of provoking an uprising by the Portuguese (Wernham, *After the Armada*, chs. V and VI).

[47] *The Letters of John Chamberlain*, i. 51, 65–6, 84; Richard C. McCoy, *The Rites of Knighthood: The Literature and Politics of Elizabethan Chivalry* (Berkeley, Calif., 1989), 87.

[48] Shaw, *The Knights of England*, i, p, ei.

[49] *The Letters of John Chamberlain*, i. 104–5; Shaw, *The Knights of England*, i, p, li; Thomas Birch, *Memoirs of the Reign of Queen Elizabeth*, 2 vols. (1745; repr. New York, 1970), ii. 455–6.

Ireland was the queen's godson, Sir John Harington, who held the rank of captain of foot. Harington felt obliged to apologize to the queen for accepting the honour, and the queen told him that he would do well 'to get home', because it was 'no season to fool it' in Ireland.[50] Although the evidence is often vague concerning the specific reasons for conferring knighthoods on particular individuals, it does seem that Essex's motivation in distributing honours was a desire to build up a party of followers rather than to reward specific instances of valour on the battlefield. Elizabeth's own motivation in creating knighthoods was always complex, highly political, and not at all concerned with recognizing martial virtue. Sir Philip Sidney's knighthood, despite all the later mythology depicting him as an exemplar of cavalier culture, was conferred on him in 1583, not as a recognition of valour on the battlefield (for he was a martial virgin at the time), but rather to allow him to act as proxy for John Casimir, Count Palatine, when he received the Order of the Garter. Elizabeth chose to knight the *Pfalzgraf* rather than give him the money he had requested to lead a Protestant crusade in the Netherlands. Sidney's knighthood merely made him worthy enough to enter the Garter Chapel at Windsor: it certainly was not a recognition of Sidney's loyalty.[51]

The lords deputy and the lords justices of Ireland continued to confer knighthoods throughout the seventeenth century, albeit on a more modest scale than Essex and Falkland. Nor can we assume that all Irish knights were swordsmen: Sir John Davies was dubbed by the lord deputy in 1603 after he had taken up his duties as solicitor general of Ireland.[52] Sir John Digby, brother of the more famous Sir Kenelm Digby, served his apprenticeship in arms in the navy under the lord admiral, Robert Bertie, earl of Lindsey, on a punitive expedition dispatched to suppress pirates in 1636. At the conclusion of the voyage, Digby was one of those knighted on the lord admiral's quarterdeck, but Lindsey depended upon a special commission that he received from the king authorizing him to bestow 'that mark of honour and preeminence upon those deserving it'.[53] Despite Elizabeth's

---

[50] Sir John Harington, *Nugae Antiquae: Being a Miscellaneous Collection of Original Papers*, ed. Thomas Park, 2 vols. (London, 1804), i. 317–18.

[51] Blair Worden, *The Sound of Virtue: Philip Sidney's* Arcadia *and Elizabethan Politics* (New Haven, 1996), pp. xxii–xxiii.

[52] See Table 3.2; Sir John Davies, *A Discovery of the True Causes Why Ireland Was Never Entirely Subdued* (1612), ed. James P. Meyers (repr. Washington, 1988), 9; Shaw, *The Knights of England*, ii. 129.

[53] [Edward Walsingham,] 'Life of Sir John Digby (1605–1645)', ed. Georges Bernard, in *Camden Miscellany XII* (CS, 3rd ser., 18; London, 1910), 63, 73.

attempt to control the creation of Irish knights, those who governed
Ireland in the seventeenth century continued to assume that this prerogative belonged to the government of Ireland. When Roger Boyle,
first earl of Orrery, served as one of the three lords justices of Ireland
following the Restoration, he took it upon himself to create a number
of knights. This is one of the ways that old Cromwellians became
entrenched in Restoration Ireland.[54]

Contemporaneous observers all agree that James VI and I cheapened
the honour of knighthood by his prodigality and lack of discrimina-
tion in conferring the rank. He further diminished the value of
knighthood by creating the order of baronets and selling those titles
without regard to merit in order to raise money for his army in Ulster.
All knights and esquires with lands worth £1,000 p.a. were to purchase baronetcies for £1,080, and some 200 took advantage of the
offer. Although James did not actually sell knighthoods, he allowed
favourites and courtiers to do so for a fee paid to the Crown. If the
number of knighthoods created per year was restricted after 1603, it
was only in order to keep the price at a sufficient level. Sir Edward
Walker, who was Garter King-of-Arms under Charles I, thought that
this venality in the distribution of titles of honour had weakened the
prestige not only of knighthood but of the monarchy as well.[55]

Neither Charles I nor Charles II was as lavish as James I in bestowing
peerages and knighthoods. Nor were they particularly generous in
awarding knighthoods and peerages for military service, although
they had few other means of acknowledging such loyalty during the
Civil Wars. Of the 1,630 English royalist officers of field-grade and
general-officer rank during the Civil Wars who can be identified, 1,485
(or 89 per cent) were without peerages or knighthoods when first
commissioned. Those holding titles of honour numbered 172, including 44 peers, 56 baronets, and 72 knights. Subsequently, Charles I and
Charles II distributed a further 236 titles of honour over a period of
sixteen years (including those conferred at the Restoration), compris-
ing 27 peerages, 45 baronetcies, and 164 knighthoods. Hardly very

[54] Thomas Morrice, *The State Letters of . . . Roger Boyle, 1st Earl of Orrery*
(London, 1742) [ESTCT 14784], 35.

[55] Stone, *Crisis of the Aristocracy*, 74–85; C. H. Firth, 'The Ballad History of the
Reign of James I', *Trans. R. Hist. Soc.*, 3rd ser., 5 (1911), 25; Sir Edward Walker,
'Observations upon the Inconveniencies that have Attended the Frequent Promotions
to Titles of Honour and Dignity, since King James Came to the Crown of England', in
*Historical Discourses* (London, 1705) [ESTCT 97417], 292.

generous when compared to James I or (in the matter of knighthoods) to the second earl of Essex, and it would appear that some, at least, of these titles had to be purchased.[56] If Charles I was stinting in his distribution of titles of honour in England—especially after the assassination of the duke of Buckingham—he was more generous in rewarding his English subjects with Irish titles and probably created nearly as many new peerages in Ireland as he did in England. Sir Edward Walker stated that the new Irish peers threatened to flood the Irish House of Lords before 1641, and after that date 'many of the new noblemen acted against the king'.[57]

Despite the consolidation of royal power in early modern England, the exercise of the royal prerogative in granting titles of honour and dignity continued to be disputed by high-ranking members of the military nobility and other members of the community of honour. This was not only recognized by the royal heralds, but was also conceded by some of the Stuart monarchs themselves in unguarded moments. The question whether the king was the fount of honour, or merely recognized the manifestation of inherent virtue, was never really settled. The regulation of honourable and aristocratic status caused tension on every front: the jurisdiction of heralds in granting arms and conducting visitations was resented because everyone knew that they sold coats of arms; the Court of Chivalry was perceived as another prerogative court resting upon dubious legal authority. Yet the members of the community of honour believed that something needed to be done to put 'mushroom gentlemen' in their place. Wishing to regulate honourable status themselves, many gentlemen (and not just martial men) preferred to do so by maintaining a code of honour through the cult of duelling. Royal efforts to curb this practice were feeble, judges and juries often refused to condemn the victors in fatal encounters, and Parliament refused to outlaw this pernicious practice.

No one challenged the Crown's attempt to regulate aristocratic status and monopolize the distribution of titles and honours quite so directly as the second earl of Essex. The abandonment of the long Elizabethan peace and the intervention of England in the Dutch

---

[56] P. R. Newman, 'The Royalist Officer Corps, 1642–1660: Army Command as a Reflexion of Social Structure', *HJ* 26.4 (1983), 950.

[57] Walker, 'Observations upon the Inconveniencies', 307.

war of independence precipitated a crisis of aristocratic honour, because Elizabeth did not respond to the justifiable demand for the recognition of valour demonstrated on the battlefield or the high seas. Essex challenged Elizabeth's stinginess in the recognition of and regulation of honour by going after the office of earl marshal and by creating knights on the battlefield in order to build up a following of swordsmen.

The Chivalric Revival had fed the desire on the part of would-be swordsmen to validate their honour on the field of battle, and they expected their own prince to recognize the existence of that honour. Except for the Wars of the Three Kingdoms and the various wars in Ireland, the opportunities for military service remained meagre at home in the British Isles during the late sixteenth and seventeenth centuries, and consequently numerous gentlemen from the Three Kingdoms were driven to seek service overseas in order to pursue an apprenticeship in arms and, in many cases, a career in the armies of foreign princes and states. When swordsmen from the British Isles failed to achieve recognition from their own monarch of the titles of nobility, knighthoods, and other honours that they had received from the princes and states of mainland Europe, they were not disposed to acquiesce in the Crown's claim to monopolize the recognition of virtue and nobility.

CHAPTER FOUR

# Gentlemen Volunteers: The Military Education of the Aristocracy

The French have a virtue proper to them that not a gentleman
thinks himself anything until he has seen the wars and learned at
least good and perfect use of his arms . . .

> (*The Advice of that Worthy Commander, Sir Edward*
> *Harwood, Colonel. Written by King Charles's*
> *Command* (1642), in *The Harleian Miscellany*,
> ed. William Oldys and Thomas Park, 10 vols.
> (London, 1808–13), iv. 273)

The earl of Essex, perceiving how little he was beholding to
Venus, is now resolved to address himself to the court of Mars,
and to this purpose he descendeth into the Netherlands, which
at that time was the school of war for the nobility of England
in their exercise of arms. There he had no sooner arrived but
with magnificent joy he was entertained by Grave Maurice who
saw both in his carriage and his courage the lively image of
his father. He at first trailed a pike and refused no service in the
field, which every gentleman is accustomed to perform. This did
much endear him to his soldiers . . .

> (Robert Codrington, *The Life and Death of*
> *the Illustrious Robert Earle of Essex*
> (London, 1646) [Wing C4877], 7)

In early modern Europe, military academies were few in number
and often short-lived. Their function was mostly limited to teaching
swordsmanship, equitation, and dancing as well as keeping gentlemen
thugs off the streets. Institutions that provided professional officer
training for young cadets were, in any case, not introduced into the

British Isles until the middle of the eighteenth century.[1] During the period from the official English intervention in the Dutch war of independence in 1585 until the end of the seventeenth century, noblemen and gentlemen from the Three Kingdoms learned the exercise of arms and the art of war by serving in the ranks as gentlemen volunteers before being commissioned as officers. Since this apprenticeship in arms was usually served in continental European Armies—especially before the outbreak of the Wars of the Three Kingdoms in 1639—these young gentlemen became immersed in a European military culture. Learning their craft under some of the leading practitioners and innovators of the military revolution, such as Maurice of Nassau and Gustavus Adolphus, they became, in turn, it is generally supposed, the instruments by which the new methods of warfare were introduced into the British Isles.[2] However, the influx of amateur gallants from the British Isles into mainland European armies was especially heavy in the late-Elizabethan and Caroline periods, and the antique chivalric notions that they carried with them tended to dilute the more professional and innovative aspects of the apprenticeship in arms that they experienced.

A dictionary of military terms, published in 1702, defined the term 'volunteers' as 'gentlemen, who without having any certain post or employment in the forces under command, put themselves upon warlike expeditions and run into dangers only to gain honour and preferment'. This may have been true for the wealthier English aristocracy and gentry, but others turned to martial pursuits as an honourable way of earning a living—especially the Irish and Scots. In some armies the volunteer served without remuneration, but such volunteers, who were sometimes called cadets because they were often

---

[1] See J. R. Hale, 'The Military Education of the Officer Class in Early Modern Europe', in his *Renaissance War Studies* (London, 1983), 225–46; id., *War and Society in Renaissance Europe, 1450–1620* (New York, 1985), 98, 143–4; Christopher Storrs and H. M. Scott, 'The Military Revolution and the European Nobility, c.1600–1800', *War in History*, 3 (1996), 24–9; Geoffrey Parker, *The Military Revolution: Military Innovation and the Rise of the West, 1500–1800* (2nd edn.; Cambridge, 1996), 21, 184.

The first military academy in England was the Royal Military College, Woolwich, established in 1744. Its function was limited to training military engineers and artillery officers. Comparable academic training for prospective officers in the cavalry and infantry did not become available until the founding of the present military college at Sandhurst early in the nineteenth century.

[2] See Barbara Donagan, 'Halcyon Days and the Literature of War: England's Military Education before 1642', *P&P* 147 (May 1995), 65–100, esp. 67–8; Pádraig Lenihan (ed.), *Conquest and Resistance: War in Seventeenth-Century Ireland* (Leiden, 2001), 353–65; Charles Carlton, *Going to the Wars: The Experience of the British Civil Wars, 1638–1651* (London, 1992), 8.

younger sons of noble and gentry families, did enjoy other privileges that were commensurate with their social rank.[3] Although less structured than the course of studies later devised for the military academies, the apprenticeship in arms of the gentleman volunteer emphasized the acquisition of discipline by the young man, so that as a junior officer he could in turn maintain discipline during the heat of battle among soldiers who were trained in the close-order drill and tactics of the use of the musket and pike. The main function of the subaltern was to present an example of bravery in the face of the enemy to men whose courage could not be taken for granted.[4]

The custom of gentlemen volunteers serving an apprenticeship in the ranks continued as long as the social hierarchy remained more permanent than the military hierarchy in martial culture. In the seventeenth century, social rank was more important than military rank, and the differences between soldier and civilian remained less important as long as the distinctions between swordsmen and gownsmen or between battlefield knighthoods and carpet knighthoods persisted. Although one should distinguish between those volunteers who liked military life and sought to make a profession of it and the amateur gallants who were content to appear on the battlefield to display a bit of bravado under fire for one or two campaigning seasons, the custom of all martial gentlemen and peers undergoing the apprenticeship in arms under the tutelage and patronage of seasoned commanders promoted shared values and standards among both professionals and amateurs, and facilitated the movement of such individuals from the armies and camps of one country to another.

Roger Boyle, earl of Orrery, thought that the spread of the system of purchasing military commissions in Restoration England and Ireland weakened the custom of serving an apprenticeship in arms in the ranks before accepting a commission. The purchase system had existed in the Irish standing army since at least the time when Thomas

---

[3] *A Military Dictionary Explaining all Difficult Terms in Martial Discipline, Fortification and Gunnery . . . by an Officer* (London, 1702) [ESTCT 145661], unpaginated, *sub* 'Volunteers' *and* 'Cadet'; André Corvisier, *Armies and Societies in Europe, 1494–1789*, trans. A. T. Siddall (Bloomington, Ind., 1979), 10–11; S. P. Huntington, *The Soldier and the State: The Theory and Practice of Civil–Military Relations* (Cambridge, Mass., 1957), 20–1.

[4] Hale, 'The Military Education of the Officer Class', 226–7; *Aphorisms of Sir Philip Sidney*, 2 vols. (London, 1807), i. 71; *A Myrrour for English Souldiers: Or, an Anatomy of an Accomplished Man at Armes* (London, 1595) [STC 10418], sigs. C2ᵛ–C3ʳ, E1ᵛ; [Thomas Proctor,] *Of the Knowledge and Conduct of Warres* (n.p., 1578) [STC 20403], fos. 37ᵛ–39ᵛ; George Whetstone, *The Honourable Reputation of a Souldier* (London, 1585), sig. B1ʳ.

3. Oil portrait of James Butler, 1st duke of Ormonde (1610–88), when marquis of Ormonde, by Sir Peter Lely. Philadelphia Museum of Art, bequest of Arthur H. Lea. Ormonde was the Royalist lord lieutenant of Ireland during the civil wars and at the beginning of the Restoration period.

Wentworth, earl of Strafford, had served as lord deputy and lord general of Ireland in the 1630s. James Butler, first duke of Ormonde, lord lieutenant of Ireland during the reign of Charles II, also recognized and lamented the situation: 'Good officers who wanted dexterity, money or favour were never advanced, nor could volunteers, who carry pikes in the regiment, ever come to be ensigns, to the discouragement of all those who have a mind to learn the trade.' Ormonde claimed that he had hoped to reform the system of awarding military commissions by purchase, but by the time James VII and II had replaced Ormonde with the earl of Tyrconnell, all the Protestant officers who had acquired commissions under Ormonde had purchased them, so there is reason to be sceptical about Ormonde's intentions.[5]

By the beginning of the eighteenth century, the needs of military discipline and the difficulty of the amateur volunteer conforming to an increasingly professional military organization led to a decline in the use of gentlemen volunteers, although the practice did not disappear entirely. By the late seventeenth century, those gentlemen volunteers in mainland European armies who wished to make a career of the military life were spending longer and longer periods in the ranks, and without patronage or influence they might serve many years before becoming a middle-aged lieutenant or an elderly captain. With the rise of professional and disciplined armies, more limited warfare, and the widespread use of the purchase system of commissions in the eighteenth century, the opportunities for advancement from the ranks diminished. There was undoubtedly more warfare in the first half of the seventeenth century, and the low survival rate of those who experienced camp life and battle provided abundant opportunities for advancement and promoted a greater degree of egalitarianism than was to be found among the more rigidly aristocratic officers corps of eighteenth-century armies.

Denoting something above the status of a page in a warrior's household or entourage, the rank and status of gentleman volunteer was used in the French and Spanish armies in the sixteenth century and in the Dutch army by the beginning of the seventeenth century. Having long fought in the Italian and Low Countries conflicts of the sixteenth

[5] Roger Boyle, earl of Orrery, *A Treatise of the Art of War* (London, 1677) [Wing O495], 15; HMC, *Report on the Manuscripts of the Marquess of Ormonde . . . Preseved at Kilkenny Castle*, ed. J. T. Gilbert, 2 vols. (old ser.; London, 1895, 1899), ii. 265; P. H. Hardacre, 'Patronage and Purchase in the Irish Standing Army under Thomas Wentworth, earl of Strafford, 1632–1640', *Journal of the Society for Army Historical Research*, 67 (1989), 44, 105; T. C. Barnard, 'Aristocratic Values in the Careers of the Dukes of Ormonde', in Toby Barnard and Jane Fenelon (eds.), *The Dukes of Ormonde, 1610–1745* (Woodbridge, 2000), 167–9.

century with their characteristic siege warfare and infantry battles, the *hidalgos* of Spain came to accept the new conditions of war more readily and did not consider it demeaning to fight on foot as infantry officers and volunteers. Thus the Spanish army may be said to have begun the practice of young gentlemen serving as volunteers before accepting commissions. Service in the Spanish army was voluntary and was considered honourable. It was not unusual for *hidalgos* to serve in the ranks, and even persons with the shakiest claims to gentility might, after ten years or so, win a captaincy, because the Spanish army was open to careers of talent, and distinguished military service could assist social ascent. Gentlemen volunteers in the Spanish Army of Flanders were called *particulares* or *entretenidos*, and many of them came from the British Isles.[6]

In France, the apprenticeship in arms could begin as early as the age of 4 or 5 as a page and continued until the age of 15 to 17 years, when the volunteer entered regiments reserved exclusively for gentlemen. Among the earliest of such units were the *compagnies d'ordonnance*. However, the intrusion of seigneurial social hierarchies often disrupted the military hierarchies of these units in which aristocratic cavalrymen were mixed in with their servants and retainers serving as footmen.[7] Blaise de Monluc offered a better example upon which many younger sons and poor noblemen throughout mainland Europe and the British

---

[6] Felipe Fernández-Armesto, *The Spanish Armada: The Experience of War in 1588* (Oxford, 1988), 27–8; Fernando Gonzáles de León, ' "Doctors of the Military Discipline": Technical Expertise and the Paradigm of the Spanish Soldier in the Early Modern Period', *Sixteenth Century Journal*, 27.1 (1996), 61–85; John Keegan, *A History of Warfare* (New York, 1993), 334.
When Sir William Stanley's Regiment defected from Dutch service to the Spanish at the surrender of Zutphen in 1587, the regiment contained 200 English Catholic gentlemen, who made up one-fifth of the strength of the regiment. After the end of the Irish Rebellion (or Nine Years War) in 1601, the same regiment recruited a number of Irish Catholic gentlemen from the province of Munster, who went into exile with their Gaelic lords (Gràinne Henry, *The Irish Military Community in Flanders, 1586–1621* (Dublin, 1992), 55, 109). Among the gentlemen volunteers who served in the English units of the Spanish Army of Flanders were members of such recusant families as the Treshams and Catesbys. Guy Fawkes and a number of his fellow Gunpowder Treason conspirators were veterans of the Spanish Army of Flanders, where they learned how to handle explosives (Geoffrey Parker, *The Army of Flanders and the Spanish Road, 1567–1659: The Logistics of Spanish Victory and Defeat in the Low Countries War* (Cambridge, 1972), 41 and *n.*).
[7] François de La Noue, *The Politicke and Military Discourses of the Lord De La Nowe*, trans Edward Aggas (London, 1587) [STC 15215], 78–9; Mark Motley, *Becoming a French Aristocrat: The Education of the Court Nobility, 1580–1715* (Princeton, 1990), 176–8; Sir Roger Williams, *A Briefe Discourse of Warre* (London, 1590) [STC 25732], 27–9.

Isles could model their lives and military careers. He began his military career as an archer before accepting a commission, because he believed that nobility derived from valour displayed on the battlefield.[8]

France, with its prestigious martial culture, had long attracted swordsmen from the British Isles as both tourists and volunteers. Sir Nicholas Malby and Sir Richard Bingham, who later fought in the Elizabethan wars in Ireland, both began their military careers as volunteers in an English troop of light cavalry in the French royal army in the 1550s, whence they were attracted by the prospect of both honour and booty.[9] Sir Walter Raleigh, after studying briefly at Oxford and the Inns of Court, craved adventure. He served in Henry Champernoun's English troop of gentlemen volunteers in France during the Wars of Religion.[10]

In order to avoid confusion, it is necessary to distinguish between several varieties of gentlemen-rankers who served in European armies. 'Gentlemen volunteers' were distinguished by that style on company and troop muster rolls in the Dutch army. In English regiments of the States' Army, gentleman volunteers served as file leaders where it was assumed that their example would stiffen the courage of men of more humble birth. Gentlemen volunteers also mounted the guard and led advance patrols (*sentinelles perdues*) to scout enemy lines.[11] A related rank in the Anglo-Dutch Brigade of the States' Army and, later, in the English Parliamentary armies was the 'gentleman of the arms', who was the eldest gentleman-ranker of a company or a regiment. He acted as a kind of storekeeper for the pikes and muskets, and was responsible for making sure that they were kept clean and repaired. The rank seems to have disappeared after the late 1650s.[12] Seventeenth-century armies also contained another kind of gentleman volunteer called a reformado, or reformed officer. A reformado was an

---

[8] Blaise de Lasseran-Massencome, seigneur de Monluc, marshal of France, *The Commentaries of Messire Blaize de Montluc, Mareschal of France*, trans Charles Cotton (London, 1674) [Wing M2506], 2.

[9] Thomas Churchyard, *A Generall Rehearsal of Warres, Called Churchyarde's Choise* (London, 1579) [STC 5235], sigs. A1$^{r-v}$, A3$^v$; *DNB, sub* Sir Richard Bingham (1528–99) *and* Sir Nicholas Malby (1530?–1584).

[10] [Benjamin Shirley,] *The Life of the Valiant & Learned Sir Walter Raleigh, Knight* (London, 1677) [Wing S3495], 14–15; Sir Robert Naunton, *Fragmenta Regalia, or Observations on Queen Elizabeth, her Times and Favorites*, ed. J. S. Cervoski (1641; repr. Washington, 1985), 71–4.

[11] Henry Hexham, *The Principles of the Art Militarie Practiced in the Warrs of the United Netherlands* (London, 1637) [STC 13264], sig. B$^{r-v}$, pp. 4–5.

[12] Ibid. 4–5; C. H. Firth, *Cromwell's Army: A History of the English Soldier during the Civil Wars, Commonwealth and Protectorate* (repr. London, 1962), 45 and *n*.

officer whose company or regiment had been disbanded, leaving him without command. He retained his rank and seniority by courtesy while carrying arms in the ranks on whole or half-pay until he could find another command.[13]

The apprenticeship in arms in part derived from the grand tour, which was coming to be practised among the aristocracies of the Three Kingdoms from the early seventeenth century. Sir Robert Dallington advocated travel abroad, particularly in France and Italy, and he was also a propagandist of the martial values of the court of Henry, prince of Wales, which were in marked contrast to the pacifism of his father, James VI and I. Dallington admired the French nobility's reputation for valour, while Sir Edward Harwood praised the custom of the French *noblesse d'épée* of serving a time in the wars; Harwood assumed that they were skilled in horsemanship and added that knowledge of the use of firearms was as widespread among them as good equestrian skills, and such training often began as early as the age of 14. The French aristocracy were careful about educating their sons, but book-learning was of secondary importance to military aristocrats, who were more anxious to secure an apprenticeship in arms for those sons who chose the military life. James Cleland, another writer on the fringe of the court circle of the prince of Wales, advised young men touring Europe to seek out military camps in the Netherlands and to visit Hungary to witness and, perhaps, to participate in the Imperialist crusade to drive the Turks out of Christian Europe.[14]

---

[13] *A Military Dictionary*, *sub* 'Reformed Officer'; Francis Grose, *Military Antiquities Respecting a History of the British Army*, 2 vols. (London, 1786–7) [ESTCT 83275], i. 312.

[14] Sir Robert Dallington, *This View of France* (1604; repr. Oxford, 1936), sigs. S3–4; J. W. Stoye, *English Travellers Abroad, 1604–1667: Their Influence in English Society and Politics* (London, 1952; repr. 1968), 262–3; Felicity Heal and Clive Holmes, *The Gentry in England and Wales, 1500–1700* (Stanford, Calif., 1994), 379; *The Advice of . . . Sir Edward Harwood*, in *The Harleian Miscellany*, ed. William Oldys and Thomas Park, 10 vols. (London, 1808–13), iv. 273; Jonathan Dewald, *Aristocratic Experience and the Origins of Modern Culture: France, 1590–1715* (Berkeley, Calif., 1993), 83; James Cleland, *The Institution of a Young Nobleman* (1611), ed. Max Molyneux, 2 vols. (repr. New York, 1948), i. 267–8; Fritz Redlich, *The German Military Enterpriser and his Work Force*, 2 vols. (Vierteljahrschrift für Sozial- und Wirtschaftsgeschichte, 47–8; Wiesbaden, 1964–5), i. 163–5.

By the early seventeenth century, the French gentleman had replaced the Italian as the model upon which the English gallant patterned his behaviour in dress, manners and swordsmanship ([Ralph Knevet,] *ΣTPATΩTIKON [STRATIOTIKON], or a Discourse of Militarie Discipline* ([London,] 1628), sig. F2ʳ; G. B. Parks, 'The Decline and Fall of the English Renaissance Admiration of Italy', *Huntington Library Quarterly*, 31 (1968), 341–57.

4. Oil portrait of James Graham, 1st marquis of Montrose (1612–50), after Gerard van Honthorst. Scottish National Portrait Gallery. Montrose held command in the Scottish Covenanting Army, and later, after he had changed sides, in the Royalist army in Scotland.

The custom of undergoing an apprenticeship in arms was shared by the aristocracies of the Three Kingdoms. The first earl of Cork in 1635 entrusted his two younger sons, Lord Broghill and Viscount Kilmeaky, to a Huguenot and former soldier who, serving as the boys' tutor, governor, and travelling companion, escorted them on a tour of France, Switzerland, and Italy where they studied mathematics, horsemanship, dancing, and fencing, and viewed modern fortifications in the style of the *trace italienne*. In their leisure time they met important personages and diverted themselves with hunting. When they came home in 1639, their father thought they should serve their king against the Scottish Covenanting Army in the Bishops' Wars. They joined their elder brother, Viscount Dungarvan, as volunteers and, later, officers in a troop of cavalry that he had raised in Ireland. James Graham, fifth earl and first marquis of Montrose, also undertook a three-year grand tour of France and Italy at about the same time and spent a year of that time at the French military academy at Angers. The younger sons of John Erskine, second earl of Mar, spent the better part of their grand tour between 1617 and 1620 at the Calvinist military academy at Saumur in the company of their governor.[15] Robert Monro, the Scots mercenary, firmly believed that young gentlemen should serve an apprenticeship as volunteers before they were given commands. His own apprenticeship was served in France in the King's Regiment of Guards. He recalled his punishment for sleeping late one morning, when he should have been at his military exercises: 'I was made [to] stand from eleven before noon to eight of the clock in the night [as a] sentry armed with a corslet, head-piece, [and] bracelets, being iron to the teeth, in a hot summer's day, till I was weary of my life, which ever afterward made me the more strict in punishing those under my command.'[16] The anonymous author of *Advice to a Soldier* (1680) reiterated the same sentiments and insisted that no amount of reading in the art of war could substitute for the skill learned under fire. To accept a commission before he was ready could bring a young gentleman's reputation into peril. If, through

---

[15] K. M. Lynch, *Roger Boyle, First Earl of Orrery* (Knoxville, Ten., 1965), 11–20; E. J. Cowan, *Montrose: For Covenant and King* (London, 1977), 21–2; HMC, *Manuscripts of the Earl of Mar and Kellie*, 2 vols. (London, 1904), ii. 81–4, 87.

[16] Robert Monro, *Monro his Expedition with the Worthy Scots Regiment (called Mac-keyes Regiment) Levied in August 1626 by Sir Donald Mac-key Lord Rhees*, 2 vols. (London, 1637) [STC 18022], i. 45; See also Matthew Sutcliffe, *The Practice, Proceedings and Lawes of Armes* (London, 1593) [STC 23468], 301.

ignorance, a young man accepted a commission before he had been seasoned in the ranks, then he could not 'lay it down without disparagement'. He must be prepared to acquire those martial skills in which he was deficient and not be ashamed to learn from 'inferiors'. Even in the late seventeenth century this same writer thought that the best apprenticeship in arms was still to be had in the French or Dutch armies.[17] In 1585, Sir Francis Drake was making preparations for an expedition to the West Indies, and Sir Philip Sidney's part in the voyage was kept secret because Sidney was thought not to have served his apprenticeship in 'martial actions'. In the event, Sidney was prohibited from sailing with Drake, and was instead offered employment with his uncle Leicester's expedition to the Netherlands.[18]

The military ethos was developed in young Scottish noblemen by training in the exercise of arms and was exalted by a legacy of chivalry that celebrated valorous noble lineages. If their fathers could afford it, they were encouraged to travel in mainland Europe to further their knowledge of the latest military theory and practice as well as to put polish on the other attainments expected of Renaissance gentlemen. It is unfair to regard all Scots noblemen and gentlemen who took service in foreign armies as mercenaries, but there can be no doubt that many heads of noble houses, who were customarily generous in providing settlements for younger sons and daughters, were increasingly driven to send their sons into military service abroad in the seventeenth century for reasons of financial exigency after the availability of confiscated ecclesiastical lands had diminished at the end of the sixteenth century.[19] The Ruthvens, on the other hand, sought service in mainland European armies, because the Ruthvens of Gowrie were attainted in 1603 for treason, and the surname of the various branches of the family was proscribed. Patrick Ruthven of Ballandean, a grandson of the attainted William, first Lord Ruthven of Gowrie, took service with the Swedish army and steadily rose through the ranks, commanding many regiments, garrisons, and towns in the Russian and German wars. He lived long enough to become

---

[17] Anon., *Advice to a Soldier (1680)*, in *Harleian Miscellany*, ed. Oldys and Park, i. 477–83.

[18] Sir Fulke Greville, Lord Brooke, *Life of Sir Philip Sidney* (1652), ed. Nowell Smith (Oxford, 1907; repr. 1971), 147–9.

[19] [George Lauder,] *The Scottish Souldier, by Lawder* (Edinburgh, 1629) [STC 15312], sig. A2ᵛ; Keith M. Brown, *Noble Society in Scotland: Wealth, Family and Culture, from Reformation to Revolution* (Edinburgh, 2000), 2–3, 90.

a major-general and the eldest Scottish officer in Swedish service. He was knighted by Gustavus Adolphus on the battlefield. By the early seventeenth century, an extensive network of kinship had arisen among Scottish soldiers abroad. Because the family fortunes were depleted, James Somerville of Drum, armed with a letter from his cousin, the earl of Winton, to his uncle Sir John Seton, a captain in the French Royal Regiment of Guards, took service as a gentleman volunteer. He did not become a commissioned officer until he came home to fight as a lieutenant in the Midlothian (or College of Justice) Regiment in the Covenanting Army some twenty-five years later.[20]

The Montgomerys of Ards furnish a well-documented example of how one Scots–Irish family pursued an education in military affairs and acquired practical experience by serving in the Dutch army. Their experiences fighting in both the Eighty Years War and the Irish civil wars also illustrate at a personal level the process of the transfer of military technology and martial culture from mainland Europe to Ireland. Sir Hugh Montgomery began his career as sixth laird of Braidstone in south-western Scotland. He was educated at Glasgow University, travelled in France, and spent some time at court before proceeding to the Netherlands, where he eventually became a captain of foot in a Scots regiment sometime in the 1580s. He emigrated to Ireland in 1605, where he was granted part of the estates formerly belonging to Conn O'Neill, lord of Upper Clandeboye and the Great Ards, and he was raised to the peerage as first Viscount Montgomery of the Ards.[21]

The first Viscount Montgomery was able to send two of his sons, James and George, on tours abroad. George went to the Netherlands, where he was a gentleman volunteer. He was the first of the sons born in Ireland, and, before he sailed for Holland from Leith, he visited Braidstone to meet his Scottish kinsmen. He was welcomed into the Dutch army by his fellow Scots volunteers because he had ready cash. Although his schoolmaster in Newtown decided that he would never

---

[20] *Ruthven Correspondence: Letters and Papers of Patrick Ruthven, Earl of Forth and Brentford*, ed. W. D. Macray (Roxburghe Club, 6; London, 1868), pp. ii–xii; James [by right 11th Lord] Somerville, *Memorie of the Somervilles*[, ed. Sir Walter Scott], 2 vols. (Edinburgh, 1815), ii. 127–95.

[21] William Montgomery of Rosemount, *The Montgomery Manuscripts (1603–1706)*, ed. George Hill (Belfast, 1869), 10; Jane H. Ohlmeyer, ' "Civilizing of those Rude Parts": Colonization within Britain and Ireland, 1580s–1640s', in Nicholas Canny (ed.), *The Origins of Empire: British Overseas Enterprise to the Close of the Seventeenth Century* (Oxford, 1998), 138.

become a scholar, he learned to 'drink, smoke', and speak Dutch 'like a Dutchman' and rose to the rank of captain. He later served as a captain of horse in his elder brother's cavalry regiment during the Irish civil wars. James, the other son, was designated to handle the family's legal business in London and at court. He was educated at St Andrew's University and the Inns of Court in London and made the grand tour through France, Italy, and Germany, ending up in the Netherlands, where he was a gentleman volunteer. During the civil wars he raised a troop of horse, and a regiment of seven companies of foot, and fortified and defended Downpatrick. A grandson, Hugh, later third viscount, was also sent on the grand tour in the 1630s; he seems to have attended a French military academy, where he acquired a knowledge of military practice, fortification, and mathematics. He returned to Ireland in 1642 and assumed command of the troop of horse and regiment of foot that his father had raised for King Charles.[22]

The English authorities in Dublin Castle considered Murrough O'Brien, sixth baron (and later first earl) of Inchiquin, to be a particularly reliable Protestant among the mostly Catholic Old English. His grandfather, the fourth Lord Inchiquin, had died in 1597 at the Battle of the Erne Ford, near Beleek, fighting for Queen Elizabeth. As he was a minor, his lands were administered by William St Leger, president of Munster, who belonged to his mother's family. When he approached his majority, he went to Italy, where he served his apprenticeship in arms in the Spanish army. During the civil wars in Ireland he was a skilful general, although he changed sides rather too frequently in the opinion of some people. In 1650, he retired to France, became a Catholic, and was later appointed high steward of Queen Henrietta Maria's household. It was with good reason that Sir Robert Gordon of Gordonstoun told the fourteenth earl of Sutherland that young noblemen on the grand tour should never travel south of the Alps without a good 'conductor'.[23]

The custom of serving as gentlemen volunteers in the wars had become an integral part of European military culture by the sixteenth century, and even persons of royal blood were not free to ignore this usage unless they were reigning princes. In 1637, Prince Rupert of the Rhine, whose family had been granted refuge at the court

[22] *Montgomery Manuscripts*, ed. Hill, 87, 151–4, 348–9.
[23] *DNB*, *sub* Murrough O'Brien, 6th baron and 1st earl of Inchiquin (1614–74); Nicholas Canny, *Making Ireland British, 1580–1650* (Oxford, 2001), 571–2; Sir William Fraser, *The Sutherland Book*, 3 vols. (Edinburgh, 1892), ii. 344–5.

of Frederick Henry, prince of Orange, after being driven out of the Rhenish Palatinate by Imperialist forces, began his military career in the prince of Orange's Life Guards,[24] 'rejecting all distinction of rank, discharging all duties and sharing hardships of the private soldier'. While his elder brother, the Elector Charles Louis, was trying to raise money and troops for another expedition to recover the Palatinate, Rupert and his younger brother Maurice went off to campaign with the prince of Orange at the Siege of Breda in 1637. It was here that Rupert and Maurice met Col. George Goring, later Lord Goring, and his lieutenant, George Monck, and other future cavaliers such as Henry, Lord Wilmot (a captain of horse in Dutch service and later first earl of Rochester), and Sir Jacob Astley (the future royalist major-general and later Baron Astley). The prince of Orange had intended to keep Prince Rupert out of action, but Rupert had already rushed off into battle before he could be stopped, and was conspicuous for his bravery.[25] James, duke of York, 'being very desirous of making himself fit . . . to serve the king his brother in a useful capacity', entered the French army in 1652 during the Interregnum and served as a volunteer under Marshal Turenne. James had to borrow money to equip his very large entourage and baggage train. In a battle between the French king's forces, commanded by Turenne, and the rebel forces, led by the prince of Condé, James saw one of Condé's officers perform a feat of courage that James particularly admired. He saw the officer repeatedly try to persuade his soldiers to follow him through a breach in the fortification three times, marching with a pike in his hands, to the bastion, until he shamed his men into following him through the breach. By the Restoration, the custom of the nobility and gentry volunteering to fight in the wars—whether for their own monarch or overseas—was well established.[26] During the Interregnum, the absence of the monarch

[24] Life guards were elite corps—usually cavalry—raised to protect the person of a prince or an important military commander. They were usually commanded by noblemen and the troopers were gentlemen.
[25] Elliot Warburton, *Memorials of Prince Rupert and the Cavaliers*, 3 vols. (London, 1849), i. 56, 450; [Thomas Malthus,] *Historical Memoires of the Life and Death of that Wise and Valiant Prince Rupert, Prince Palatine of the Rhine* (London, 1683) [Wing H2104], 4–5; Patrick Morah, *Prince Rupert of the Rhine* (London, 1976); 24–5; *DNB*, *sub* Henry Wilmot, 1st earl of Rochester (1612?–1658) *and* Sir Jacob Astley, Baron Astley (1579–1652).
[26] *The Memoirs of James II: His Campaigns as Duke of York, 1652–1660*, ed. and trans A. Lytton Sells (London, 1962), 57–9, 68; Steven Saunders Webb, 'Brave Men and Servants to his Royal Highness: The Household of James Stuart in the Evolution of English Imperialism', *Perspectives in American History*, 8 (1974), 65.

and the royal court from London had weakened the influence of courtly culture and given other cultural milieux such as London, the universities, and the European military world the opportunity to exert their influence on swordsmen from the British Isles. Therefore, the king was no longer the arbiter of good manners, as the books of poetry and essays of Dudley, third Lord North, make clear.[27]

Gentlemen served as volunteers in King William's campaigns in Flanders as part of their grand tours as late as the 1690s. The practice of gentlemen 'of good family' enlisting in the ranks as volunteers continued well into the eighteenth century. If they belonged to cadet branches of greater gentry families or enjoyed the patronage and friendship of important personages, they might hope to rise to high place in the army. However, Humphrey Bland, who was an advocate of the custom of serving in the ranks and learning the duties of all non-commissioned officers before accepting a commission, inferred that the practice was being undermined by the tendency of wealthy aristocratic families to purchase commissions in the army before their sons had learned their duties: 'It is from this way of thinking that so many of them do so little credit to their posts.'[28]

Gentleman volunteers were also to be found in the navy. Permanent grades of rank, as distinct from commissions and warrants conferring an office aboard a particular ship or for a particular expedition, were not established until as late as 1860. Before that time naval 'officers' held posts or offices that were retained for a limited duration and in no sense constituted permanent naval rank.[29] This makes the vagueness of the status of gentleman volunteer somewhat more comprehensible. Except on the deck of a ship or a battlefield, social rank continued to count for more than military or naval rank. When John Holles, later first earl of Clare, fought against the Spanish Armada in 1588, he did so as a gentleman volunteer without command, but was summoned to all councils of war as though he did hold command.[30]

---

[27] [Dudley North, 3rd Lord North,] *A Forest Promiscuous of Several Productions* (London, 1659) [Wing N1284], 17–18, 20, 28, and esp. 82–91.

[28] John Childs, *The British Army of William III, 1689–1702* (Manchester, 1987), 38; J. A. Houlding, *Fit for Service: The Training of the British Army, 1715–1795* (Oxford, 1981), 103–4; Humphrey Bland, *A Treatise of Military Discipline* (London, 1727) [ESTCT 160420], 115.

[29] Michael Lewis, *England's Sea Officers: The Story of the Naval Profession* (London, 1939), 42–4, 76.

[30] Gervase Holles, *Memorials of the Holles Family, 1493–1656*, ed. A. C. Wood (CS, 3rd ser., 60; London, 1937), 89.

There was always a certain vagueness about the chain of command and assignment of duties in a naval or military expedition where social status signified more than office or position of authority, and a naval or military commander needed to be assertive. A well-known example of this problem is that of Thomas Doughty, previously a friend of Sir Francis Drake, who sailed with Drake on the Circumnavigation Voyage of 1577. Doughty, a gentleman volunteer, sought to undermine Drake's authority, which derived from the queen's commission, and Drake constituted a court martial and had Doughty executed on the spot. Drake warned other members of the expedition: 'I must have the gentleman to haul and draw with the mariner, and the mariner with the gentleman.'[31]

In the late sixteenth and seventeenth centuries, a young gentleman who wished to 'follow the sea' usually began his training as a captain's servant. Depending on his own social rank, a ship's captain might take on board as part of his retinue a certain number of personal servants. Other ship's officers were also allowed to take servants with them, but this was probably the course of apprenticeship followed by tarpaulins,[32] while gentlemen cadets seem always to have been captain's servants. The captain drew pay for his servants and assigned them duties. He customarily fed them, usually at his own table, but was not obliged to pay them, and many captains appear to have pocketed the pay officially allowed for their servants. The captain's servants comprised those who were going to sea to prepare for a career; from the Restoration period they served a seven-year apprenticeship. The gentleman volunteer who did not intend to prepare for a career might go to sea for only one campaign to show that he was 'gallant'. The choice of such men—captain's servants or volunteers—was made by the captain himself rather than by the Navy Board or Admiralty.[33]

While Samuel Pepys was secretary to the Admiralty, he created in 1676 a new type of naval cadet called a 'volunteer-per-order'. The captain of a ship could be obliged to accept persons appointed in this manner in preference to his own nominees. Pepys's intention was for such cadets to serve one year as midshipmen and two years as

---

[31] Ibid. 44–5; James A. Williamson, *The Age of Drake* (Cleveland, 1965), 166, 174–81.

[32] Tarpaulins were professional naval officers of more humble birth promoted from the lower decks who had not been born and bred gentlemen.

[33] J. D. Davies, *Gentlemen and Tarpaulins: The Officers and Men of the Restoration Navy* (Oxford, 1991), 15; Lewis, *England's Sea Officers*, 78–9. For examples, see 'Life of Sir John Digby (1605–1645)', ed. Georges Bernard, *Camden Miscellany XII* (CS, 3rd ser., 18; London, 1910), 72; John Charnock, *Biographia Navalis*, 4 vols. (London, 1795) [ESTCT 73785], iii. 314.

volunteers-per-order before becoming eligible for commissions. The introduction of the volunteer-per-order system increased the social diversity of the navy by bringing in larger numbers of gentlemen to balance the tarpaulin and old Cromwellian officers who continued to constitute a strong presence in the Royal Navy of the early Restoration period. The system was diluted by the influx of large numbers of aristocratic volunteers during the Second and Third Anglo-Dutch Wars. Probably only a small number of officers actually entered naval service as volunteers-per-order; most continued to train as captain's servants right through the eighteenth century.[34]

The volunteer movement, which sent thousands of English, Scots, and Irish peers, gentlemen, and younger sons abroad in the seventeenth century to serve in all the armies of continental Europe, was a complex phenomenon. It involved both Protestants and Catholics who bestowed their allegiances in ways that were not always dictated by religious belief. We know more about why English Protestant swordsmen undertook this service than we do about the ideals and motivation of English Catholics or the martialists of Ireland and Scotland. Certainly, for many English gentlemen volunteers, the wars against the Habsburgs constituted a Protestant crusade. The English government began the war against Spain in 1585 because it feared invasion by Spain using the Low Countries as a base. It appeared to the militant followers of the war party that the peace party, led by Lord Burghley and Sir Robert Cecil, pursued the Anglo-Spanish war in a half-hearted manner; after the deaths of Leicester in 1588 and Sir Francis Walsingham in 1590, who were the leaders of the war party, the peace party dominated the making of policy in the 1590s. Hindsight allows us to see that a war fought on so many fronts with inadequate financial resources presented Elizabeth's government with few alternatives in the way of policy or strategy. However, the younger generation, led by Sir Philip Sidney and the second earl of Essex, wished to pursue a more aggressive war against Spain, and thus were driven to take service abroad or to outfit privateering expeditions.[35]

Sir Philip Sidney, before he accompanied his uncle to the Netherlands, had attempted to join a privateering expedition against the Spanish in the New World, but was frustrated by the queen. During a period of enforced idleness, he composed the (Old) *Arcadia* as a

---

[34] Lewis, *England's Sea Officers*, 83–4; Davies, *Gentlemen and Tarpaulins*, 29–30.
[35] Anthony Esler, *The Aspiring Mind of the Elizabethan Younger Generation* (Durham, NC, 1966), 99.

veiled attack on Elizabeth's failure to provide sufficient aid to fight the military and political manifestations of reformed Catholicism. Faced with the hostility of Elizabeth, Sidney turned elsewhere and discovered through service in the Netherlands that authority and antique virtue in William of Orange that he had found so lacking in his own prince. The military attribute of virtue was a neostoic concept associated with the teachings of the Flemish scholar Justus Lipsius whom Sidney came to know while in the Netherlands.[36]

Most of the ideas associated with neostoicism derived from the writings of the Roman historian Cornelius Tacitus, through a new and more accessible Latin edition prepared by Lipsius and published in 1574. The philosophy of Roman neostoicism, as reinterpreted by Lipsius, was intended to help the virtuous young nobleman, living through tumultuous times, overcome his fears and confusion, acquire discipline, and impart that discipline to his soldiers.[37] Sir Henry Savile, who was associated with the circle of the second earl of Essex, provided an English edition of Tacitus in 1591, which was read by Essex and a number of his followers. From Tacitus, the Essexians learned that long periods of peace promoted vice, luxury, effeminacy, and the loss of virtue in the ancient Roman sense. Tacitus' account of post-Augustan politics in Rome also reinforced the Essexian distrust of courtiers and base-born gownsmen and gave them a paranoid and conspiratorial view of English court politics in the late 1590s. Thus Essex's reading of Tacitus ignored much good and prudent advice from Savile, Bacon, and others that might have helped him to avoid the confrontation with Elizabeth that ultimately led to his execution for treason in 1601. Many believed that Essex's crimes did not merit a traitor's death, and, despite Savile's brief imprisonment for complicity with Essex, scholars and writers such as William Camden and Ben Jonson continued to promote a Tacitean view of history that advocated a belief in virtuous action and war against the Habsburgs.[38]

---

[36] Blair Worden, *The Sound of Virtue: Philip Sidney's* Arcadia *and Elizabethan Politics* (New Haven, 1996), 3–8, 31–3.

[37] Anthony Grafton, 'Portrait of Justus Lipsius', *American Scholar*, 56 (1986–7), 382, 386.

[38] Malcolm Smuts, 'Court-Centred Politics and the Uses of Roman Historians, c.1590–1630', in Kevin Sharpe and Peter Lake (eds.), *Culture and Politics in Early Stuart England* (Stanford, Calif., 1993), 24–5, 27, 29; John Nichols, *The Progresses and Public Processions of Queen Elizabeth*, 3 vols. (London, 1823; repr. New York, 1966), iii. 161–2; Blair Worden, 'Ben Jonson among the Historians', in Sharpe and Lake (eds.), *Culture and Politics in Early Stuart England*, 83–4.

The Lipsian reading of the Roman way of war was that offensive tactics were always to be preferred to the defensive.[39] One anonymous volunteer, when presented with the choice of joining an English regiment in the States' Army or participating in the Portugal Expedition of 1589, chose the latter because, in seeking revenge for the 'unsupportable wrongs' offered by the king of Spain, he thought that it would be accounted more honourable to pursue an offensive war in a raid upon Spain and Portugal than to serve in an essentially defensive war in the Netherlands.[40] Many gallants continued to regard the style of war as practised in the Low Countries to be expensive and devoid of glamour, while privateering voyages not only offered scope for individual glory, but held out a better prospect for plunder and profit.[41] Francis Markham, whose own military career must have proved disappointing, stripped bare the motivation of those who participated in the raid on Cadiz in 1596: 'some [were] led by their own ambition, some by their wives, and some . . . only for company, without either noble end or tolerable purpose, for as they were led by vainglory, so commonly they were followed by want and finished with disgrace and dishonour . . .'[42] When British swordsmen discuss their motives for becoming gentlemen volunteers, one needs to be aware that they are fashioning suitable persona for public consumption.

Whether through travel or service in foreign armies, nobles and gentry from the Three Kingdoms learned languages and acquired knowledge and experience of modern warfare. At the same time such shared experiences promoted a European consciousness not only in military matters but in political awareness and scientific knowledge as well. The prospect of a career in a continental standing army was for some sons an alternative to an apprenticeship in London. Although ordinary men sought to avoid being pressed for soldiers, gentlemen

[39] Sir James Turner, *Pallas Armata: Military Essayes of the Ancient Grecian, Roman, and Modern Art of War* (London, 1683; repr. New York, 1968), 353–61.
[40] *A True Coppie of a Discourse by a Gentleman employed in the Late Voyage of Spain and Portingale* (1589), ed. Alexander B. Grosart (repr. Manchester, 1886), 40.
[41] Michael West, 'Spenser's Art of War: Chivalric Allegory, Military Technology, and the Elizabethan Mock-Heroic Sensibility', *Renaissance Quarterly*, 41 (1988), 654–5, 659; Paul A. Jorgenson, *Shakespeare's Military World* (Berkeley, Calif., 1956), 37; Sir Charles Oman, *A History of the Art of War in the Sixteenth Century* (London, 1937), 285–7. See also Malcolm Vale, *War and Chivalry: Warfare and Aristocratic Culture in England, France and Burgundy at the End of the Middle Ages* (London and Athens, Ga., 1981), 171–4.
[42] Francis Markham, *Five Decades of Epistles of Warre* (London, 1622) [STC 17332], 27.

volunteers hoped that they might recoup their fortunes in Ireland or the Low Countries.[43] Sydenham Poyntz came from a gentry family of ancient stock who were related to the Poyntzes of Iron Acton, Gloucestershire. As a consequence of the improvidence of his father, Poyntz was apprenticed in London, where his experiences were unhappy in the extreme. By the age of 16 Poyntz decided that 'to be bound an apprentice . . . I deemed little better than a dog's life and base. At last I resolved . . . [that] to live and die a soldier would be as noble in death as life . . .' He joined Edward, fourth Lord Vaux's Regiment in the Spanish Army of Flanders in 1625, paying his own expenses.[44] When a relative offered to help set up the Irish Jacobite, Peter Drake, as a West Indies merchant in 1699, he replied that he was inclined to the military life.[45] With the death of his father, Thomas Raymond was placed in the care of his uncle, Sir William Boswell, who became the English resident at The Hague. Enjoying neither money nor 'countenance' from his uncle, Raymond joined an English regiment in the service of the States General as a volunteer and 'trailed a pike'. He enlisted as a servant to the colonel, Sir Philip Pakenham, in the colonel's own company where gentlemen volunteers usually served, and conceived a great admiration for Pakenham, who had raised himself to his present position through merit and long experience in the wars. Raymond's first taste of battle came at the Siege of Rhineberg in 1633.[46]

At the beginning of the Elizabethan period, aristocratic and armigerous gentry households still contained numerous servants of small-gentry and yeomanry background, who shared the taste of their masters for hunting and other field sports, and were often disorderly and lacking in the useful skills necessary for employment in a civil society. At the instigation of their masters, they were often drawn into feuding and poaching forays against rival households

[43] Sir George Clark, *War and Society in the Seventeenth Century* (Cambridge, 1958), 97–8; Richard Bagwell, *Ireland under the Tudors*, 3 vols. (1885–90), iii. 250–1.

[44] *The Relation of Sydenham Poyntz, 1624–1636*, ed. A. T. S. Goodrick (CS, 3rd ser., 14; London, 1908), 45–7.

Thomas Digges thought that 'To play the merchant was only for gentlemen of Florence, Venice and the like that are indeed but the better sort of citizens . . .' (Thomas and Dudley Digges, *Foure Paradoxes and Politique Discourses concerning Militarie Discipline* (London, 1604) [STC 6872], 77).

[45] *The Memoirs of Capt. Peter Drake* (Dublin, 1755) [ESTCT 145643], 29–30.

[46] *Autobiography of Thomas Raymond*, ed. G. Davies (CS, 3rd ser., 28; London, 1917), 35–7.

and retinues. By the end of the Elizabethan era, high cost, the queen's disapproval, and the appearance of alternative opportunities led to a decline in the size of such households. Opportunities for military adventure had been scarce earlier, but England's intervention in the Dutch war of independence changed that and created new opportunities for lesser gentry and younger sons to elevate their social status by military service, which was more prestigious than wearing livery in an aristocratic household or becoming an apprentice.[47]

As a consequence of the end of the Anglo-Spanish War in 1604 and a period of truce in the Eighty Years War in the Netherlands between 1609 and 1618, such opportunities diminished during the period of the Jacobean peace. Francis Holles, a younger son of Sir Gervase Holles, was sent by his father to 'trail a pike' in the colonel's company of Sir Francis Vere's Regiment in the Netherlands. He also accompanied Vere as a gentleman volunteer on the Islands Voyage of 1597. Holles next went to Ireland, where he was commissioned as a cornet in Lord Mountjoy's own troop of horse, and fought in the Battle of Kinsale in 1601. He was promoted captain, but never had the opportunity to serve at that rank because the campaign against the Irish rebels ended in 1602, and he found himself without employment under James I. Lacking the kind of experience needed to gain a commission in a European army, he could not face going back to serving as a gentleman private in the Dutch army after having commanded 'in the service of his own prince', so he returned to civilian life in England. He found employment for a time as a tutor, but had to endure a long period of unemployment before his grandfather purchased for him the office of muster-master of Nottinghamshire, which required him to train the militia in the latest techniques of warfare that he had learned in the Dutch army.[48]

In Scotland, opportunities were always meagre, and the Cromwellian conquest further diminished the need for swordsmen. Patrick Gordon found that, as a Catholic, he could not attend any of the Scottish universities. His 'patrimony being but small as the younger son of a younger brother of a younger house', he 'resolved . . . to go to some foreign country'. Like many of his compatriots, he headed for the Baltic

---

[47] Roger B. Manning, *Hunters and Poachers: A Cultural and Social History of Unlawful Hunting in England, 1485–1640* (Oxford, 1993), 18, 145–7, 178–81, 194, 226–8; Lawrence Stone, *The Crisis of the Aristocracy, 1558–1641* (Oxford, 1965), 208–14.

[48] Holles, *Memorials*, 184–5.

countries. Gordon studied for a time at a Jesuit college near Königsberg, but he yearned for a more active life. By 1655 he had made his way to Hamburg, where he encountered Swedish recruiting officers eager to sign on Scots. After serving in the Swedish, Polish, and Russian armies, Gordon became a general in the service of Peter the Great.[49]

Cromwellian rule made all the British Isles a more peaceful place, and for swordsmen, a duller one. Rodolphus, the hero of Charles Croke's semi-autobiographical picaresque novel, *Fortune's Uncertainty*, found the life of a student at Oxford tedious, and he longed to play the gallant. While seeking solace in the Mermaid Tavern, he spied a troop of horse marching up the High Street,

bravely accoutred and well mounted, advancing with their officers at the head of them, and their naked swords in . . . so noble a posture that it hugely delighted our young gentleman . . . who being ravished with martial resolution, immediately began to incite and encourage the minds of his associates with a desire of completing the company with their own persons and endeavours . . . they . . . without delay pawned their gowns in the tavern, and merrily drank the health of their new admirers as far as the worth of their gowns would permit them; and afterwards solemnly protested that in exchange of such monkish habit, they would put on the buff coat with the iron hat and doublet, and never wear gown more in Oxford.[50]

Besides serving as a rite of passage or a means of climbing to a higher social station, military service could also wipe away the stain of criminality, which was not uncommon among boisterous aristocrats and gentlemen of the early modern period. After being imprisoned in the Tower of London for abducting a young lady, the 18-year-old earl of Rochester, probably with the king's encouragement, joined the earl of Sandwich's expedition to Bergen, Norway, as a volunteer and was accommodated in a cabin aboard Sandwich's flagship. Rochester found it a sobering experience to lose his friend Edward Montagu, who was cut down by a cannon ball while standing next to him. Similarly, great sieges such as those at Vienna, Budapest, Breda, or Namur attracted flocks of gentlemen seeking to redeem themselves.[51]

[49] *The Diary of General Sir Patrick Gordon of Auchleuchries, 1635–1699*, ed. Joseph Robertson (Spalding Club Publications, 31; Aberdeen, 1859), 5–8, 17–19; Dimitry Fedosov, *The Caledonian Connection: Scotland–Russia Ties, Middle Ages to Early Twentieth Century* (Aberdeen, 1996), 45.

[50] [Charles Croke,] *Fortune's Uncertainty, or Youth's Unconstancy* (London, 1667; Luttrell Soc. Reprints, 19; Oxford, 1959), 25–6.

[51] *The Letters of John Wilmot, Earl of Rochester*, ed. Jeremy Treglown (Chicago, 1980), 16, 43–8; Gregory Hanlon, *The Twilight of a Military Tradition: Italian Aristocrats and European Conflicts, 1560–1800* (New York, 1998), 263–4.

Outside the martial community, opinion varied widely concerning how useful or appropriate the service of volunteers was. The Puritan divine Richard Bernard thought that it was lawful for men to go to war as volunteers because it was a practice sanctioned by the reformed churches of Europe. Before volunteering, however, the young gentleman needed to consider the religion of the participants in the war, and must be prepared to accept military discipline.[52] The poet and courtier Sir Thomas Overbury was more cynical: he thought younger brothers were best suited to martial pursuits, and elder brothers ought to be thankful for the means of getting rid of them.[53] Clarendon, writing in exile in 1670, disapproved of volunteers as men who will 'kill one another for something to do'.[54] John Earle, bishop of Salisbury, thought that a younger son's 'last refuge' was to serve as a volunteer in the Netherlands, 'where rags and lice are no scandal, where he lives a poor gentleman of a company, and dies without a shirt'.[55] Although he was an old soldier himself (and later died of battle wounds), La Noue condemned those who took delight in war or would make it a perpetual profession. To be a mercenary soldier was not compatible with family life and raising children.[56]

Besides gaining experience that would later allow them to command as officers, gentlemen volunteers serving in the ranks were thought to have special attributes. In the dirty siege warfare of the Low Countries, where infantrymen were expected to assault the new-style fortresses with low profiles and thick earthenwork ramparts heavily defended by artillery, the presence of gentlemen volunteers in the ranks was thought to stiffen the courage of lesser breeds of men, who, it was assumed, fought for money and plunder rather than honour. The Dutch army found that English and Scots soldiers performed very

---

[52] Richard Bernard, *The Bible-Battells, or the Sacred Art Military* (London, 1629) [STC 1926a], 63–9.

[53] *The Miscellaneous Works in Prose and Verse of Sir Thomas Overbury*, ed. Edward F. Rimbault (London, 1856), 76–7.

[54] Edward Hyde, 1st earl of Clarendon, 'Of War', in *A Collection of Various Tracts* (1727), repr. in *A Book of English Essays (1600–1900)*, ed. S. V. Makower and B. H. Blackwell (London, 1917), 26.

[55] John Earle, *Microcosmography*, ed. Harold Osborne (1633; repr. London, 1971), 23–4.

Sir Thomas Wilford, an old soldier who was reduced in his latter years to serving as a provost-marshal rounding up vagrants, complained to Sir Robert Cecil that his son had served as volunteer in four separate expeditions with the earl of Essex, and never received any recompense except his wounds. He had spent £1,000 of his own money to sustain himself in that service (HMC, *Salisbury MSS*, viii. 343).

[56] La Noue, *The Politicke and Militarie Discourses*, 116–18.

well in hand-to-hand combat when reinforced by gentlemen rankers, and used them extensively. Although official English intervention in the Dutch war of independence did not come until 1585, the first English band, consisting of 300 men, of whom more than 100 were gentlemen, was sent to the Netherlands in 1572 under the command of the Welsh soldier Thomas Morgan of Pencarn.[57] Gervase Markham, himself an English veteran of the Low Countries wars, stated that the Dutch Republic, although characterized by bourgeois values, had developed a system of training that could turn any man, who was not a natural-born coward, into a well-disciplined and effective soldier. But Markham still insisted that gentlemen made better soldiers than 'boors'.[58]

There existed a distinctive martial culture in the Three Kingdoms in the seventeenth century just as there was a recognizable courtier culture and an urban culture, but one should not assume that they were mutually exclusive. Individuals moved between these different milieux. Circumstances might dictate that a young man gravitated towards the one rather than another, but there were distinct advantages in serving an apprenticeship in arms as a rite of passage in a world where honour weighed so heavily—not to mention the prospect of plunder from the wars. Sir Henry Rich, later Lord Kensington and earl of Holland, was the younger son of a noble house, but, since this gave him no particular advantage at court, he spent two or three campaigns in the Netherlands and intended to make war his profession. As was usual with gentlemen volunteers, he returned to England during the winter months and discovered that 'his winning presence and gentle conversation' gained attention at court, and he ingratiated himself with the king and became a 'creature' of the duke of Buckingham. He abandoned his military career, but returned to it with the outbreak of the English Civil War.[59] Ben Jonson, at the age

---

[57] A Breefe Declaration of that which happened within as without Oostende sithence the vij of Januarie 1602 (Middelburg, 1602) [STC 18891], 3; William Camden, The History of the Most Renowned and Victorious Princess Elizabeth (4th edn.; London, 1688; repr. New York, 1970), 507.

Williams was one of the gentlemen volunteers in Morgan's company, and he has left an eye-witness account of the English involvement in the late Elizabethan phase of the Eighty Years War (Sir Roger Williams, The Actions of the Low Countries, ed. D. W. Davies (1618; repr. Ithaca, NY, 1964)).

[58] Gervase Markham, 'The Muster-Master', ed. C. L. Hamilton, in Camden Miscellany XXVI (CS, 4th ser., 14; London, 1975), 68–70.

[59] Edward Hyde, 1st earl of Clarendon, The History of the Rebellion and Civil Wars in England, ed. W. D. Mackray, 6 vols. (Oxford, 1888; repr. 1958), i. 78–9.

of 18, spent at least one campaigning season as a volunteer in the States' Army, and believed that he had earned a measure of honour. Jonson admired Sir Horace Vere, Lord Tilbury, as 'a valiant man' of 'Roman virtue', and celebrated Edward, first Lord Herbert of Cherbury, as 'all-virtuous Herbert'.[60] Thomas Raymond, like Ben Jonson, thought that one summer of campaigning in the Dutch army constituted an initiation into the profession of soldiering. At the same time he 'observed how brisk and fine some gallants were at the beginning of a campaign, but at the latter end their briskness and gallantry so faded and cloudy that I could not but be minded of the vanity of this world . . .' In his first experience of battle, Raymond admits that he momentarily doubted his courage, but soon conquered his fear. Raymond concluded that he could not abide the cruelty of war, and, after his father procured a place for him in Basil, Lord Feilding's embassy to Venice, Raymond was able to obtain his discharge from the Dutch army.[61] The diarist John Evelyn also briefly served as a volunteer in the Netherlands. Although he was a Royalist in sentiment, Evelyn wished to remain aloof from English politics, and, drawn by his interest in modern fortifications, he joined an English regiment of the States' Army in 1641 and was issued a horse and a pike. However, the August heat and the damp evening mists at his camp were not to Evelyn's taste, and his military career ended after one week.[62]

While many gentlemen volunteers were looking for career opportunities as military officers, some were simply observing the widely accepted maxim that aristocratic honour had to be validated in each generation by the exercise of arms and dangerous undertakings. In the leaguers of the Low Countries or camps elsewhere swordsmen from many countries became acquainted with one another and shared the same dangers and experiences. This later became the basis of a cavalier culture among the swordsmen of the British Isles. Famous and protracted sieges usually served to bring gallants together. In 1610, hearing that war had broken out over the disputed Duchy of Cleves, located on the border between the Netherlands and Germany, Edward,

---

[60] *The Works of Ben Jonson*, ed. Francis Cunningham, 3 vols. (London, 1910–12), iii, pp. i–xi, epigrams 108 (iii. 250), 91 (iii. 243), and 249 (iii. 249).

Another playwright, Philip Massinger, moved on the fringe of a group of swordsmen who served in military expeditions and fought duels (*The Plays and Poems of Philip Massinger*, ed. P. Edwards and C. Gibson, 3 vols. (Oxford, 1976), i. pp. xxxv–xxxvi).

[61] *Autobiography of Thomas Raymond*, 38, 43–4.

[62] Stoye, *English Travellers*, 245–6, 259–60.

first Lord Herbert, who had been on a grand tour, and Grey Brydges, fifth Lord Chandos, went to join the camp of Maurice of Nassau, who was besieging Juliers. Here they were joined by other volunteers, such as Theophilus, Lord Howard de Walden and later second earl of Suffolk, and Sir John Paulet, son of the marquis of Winchester. Four thousand English soldiers were present under the command of Sir Edward Cecil, Lord Wimbledon, and Herbert built a hut next to Wimbledon. Herbert described Wimbledon as a 'very active general', who was in the habit of going, sword in hand, beyond his own front trenches to chase the enemy's forward sentinels back into their own lines. Here Lord Herbert encountered the renowned French cavalier, the seigneur de Balagni, who was a colonel in the French forces, which had joined the Dutch in opposing the Spanish and Imperialist forces at Juliers. Balagni told Herbert that the latter's reputation for daring had preceded him and challenged Herbert to accompany Balagni in a raid on the enemy's front lines, while artillery batteries and several hundred musketeers poured their fire on the two of them. When the barrage became too heavy, Herbert boasted that he retreated 'leisurely and upright'. In 1614, Herbert was back in Juliers—still under siege—where he performed similar acts of bravado.[63]

In 1637, the gathering place for English gallants was the siege of Breda. Charles Louis, the Elector Palatine, and his brothers, Prince Rupert and Prince Maurice, led 'a great train of English noblemen and gentlemen' there. Among the members of this entourage, some of whom had begun as personal followers of Elizabeth of Bohemia, daughter of King James VI and I—called the 'queen of hearts' for the devotion that she inspired—were Richard Rich, second earl of Warwick, Spencer Compton, second earl of Northampton, William Villiers, first Viscount Grandison, and William, first earl of Craven, who subsidized Elizabeth and her brother, King Charles I, on many occasions.[64] Gentlemen

---

[63] *The Life of Edward, First Lord Herbert of Cherbury, Written by Himself*, ed. J. M. Shuttleworth (London, 1976), 52–4; Sir Ralph Winwood, *Memorials of Affairs of State of the Reigns of Queen Elizabeth and King James*, comp. Edmund Sawyer, 3 vols. (London, 1725) [ESTCT 149866], iii. 211–12; Stoye, *English Travellers*, 259–60.

[64] Henry Hexham, *A True and Briefe Relation of the Famous Siege of Breda* (Delft, 1637) [STC 13265], 7, 14, 35, 48. Most of the English volunteers served in the colonel's company of Goring's Regiment, commanded by George Goring, later Lord Goring, but some were to be found in Thomas Culpeper's Regiment, where the 3rd earl of Essex was lieutenant colonel. Among those present at the Siege of Breda were two captains in the Dutch army who later became generals during the English civil wars—Philip Skippon and George Monck, later duke of Albemarle (F. J. S. ten Raa and F. de Bas, *Het Staatsche Leger*, 8 vols. (Breda, 1911–80), iv. 240–4.

volunteers were accorded special status in all armies, but Maurice of Nassau, prince of Orange, and his brother and successor, Frederick Henry, had a reputation for particularly welcoming volunteers into the States' Army. The volunteers of highest social rank were usually commanded by the general and had the privilege of dining at his table. During the late Elizabethan period, gentlemen volunteers serving in English regiments of the States' Army had been paid one shilling *per diem*, the same rate of pay as a corporal, but Maurice expected volunteers to pay their own expenses—whether they served in the horse or the foot. They received no pay, were not expected to pass musters, and were assigned no particular duties, 'but as free and noble gentlemen may bestow their hours in any honourable fashion'. Despite the freedom to come and go as they pleased, Francis Markham thought that they discharged their duties, which they voluntarily assumed, more conscientiously than mercenaries.[65] The *entretenidos* of the Spanish Army of Flanders received an extra allowance beyond their private's pay, but such supplements were unreliable. Daniel O'Farrel, a gentleman volunteer in Henry O'Neill's Regiment early in the seventeenth century, had his supplementary allowance reduced from 40 to 10 *escudos* a month, and was obliged to ask for a licence to beg.[66]

Most gentlemen volunteers served their apprenticeship in arms in special companies commanded by the colonel or lieutenant colonel of the regiment. Such companies were larger than other companies because they had places set aside for cadets, and access to these places was gained through networks of patronage and kinship. Thomas Holles was educated at Cambridge and Gray's Inn by his elder brother, John, first earl of Clare. While visiting an older brother, Sir George, who was already serving in the States' Army, Thomas Holles took 'a liking to the soldier's life' and became a volunteer in the company commanded by his kinsman, Sir Edward Vere. Sir George Holles had already enlisted in the same company because his temperament was inclined 'more to the active trade of a soldier than the sedentary life of a scholar'. Thomas remained in the same regiment, commanded by Robert, nineteenth earl of Oxford, and was promoted through the various ranks from ensign to lieutenant colonel, replacing Sir Edward

[65] Markham, *Five Decades of Epistles of Warre*, 25–8; C. G. Cruickshank, 'Dead Pays in the Elizabethan Army', *EHR* 53 (1938), 93–7; Stoye, *English Travellers*, 259–60.
[66] Henry, *The Irish Military Community in Flanders*, 11, 48.

Vere after he was killed in battle. He afterwards held the same rank in Goring's Regiment. Like many of the poorer English officers in the States' Army, Thomas married a Dutch lady, who was well connected with members of the States General and the States of Gelderland. His elder brother, Sir George, became lieutenant to Sir Edward Cecil, whom he disliked, and was later sergeant major of Sir Francis Knollys's Regiment. Sir George participated in the Siege of Ostend, where he lost an eye. He never married, and was more troubled by his failure to accumulate wealth than the loss of his eye.[67]

The first earl of Clare was also instrumental in placing Sir Thomas Fairfax (the future parliamentary general and later third Lord Fairfax) in the company commanded by Horatio Vere, Lord Tilbury, at Dordrecht, where Lord Houghton, Clare's son and heir, promised to look after him. In 1620, when the English Privy Council complained about Clare's late payment of a contribution towards the cost of the Palatinate Expedition, he reminded the Council that he had already sent his son Francis as a volunteer on the expedition and continued to pay his expenses, and was thus making a double contribution. Lord Tilbury's company functioned much like a military academy; besides military exercises, the young cadets also received instruction in mathematics, fencing, and dancing. Thomas Fairfax's grandfather, Thomas, first Lord Fairfax, had fought in the Netherlands under Leicester; Lord Fairfax told Clare that he pinned all his hopes on his grandson because of his disappointment with his son Ferdinando (later second Lord Fairfax). The grandfather remarked that he had sent Ferdinando 'into the Netherlands to train him up as a soldier; and he makes a tolerable country justice, but a mere coward at fighting'. His grandson, aged 17, did not stay long in the Netherlands because, in 1628, there was not enough action to occupy him, and his return home further disappointed the grandfather.[68] Sir Edmund Verney the younger's father, the knight marshal, found him a place as a volunteer in the army raised to fight the Scots in 1639. Following the Pacification of Berwick, he joined the Dutch army and was enlisted as a volunteer in Sir Thomas Culpeper's company. When the army went into winter quarters at Utrecht, the younger Sir Edmund

    [67] Holles, *Memorials*, 73–5, 86–7.
    [68] *Letters of John Holles, 1587–1637*, ed. P. R. Seddon, 3 vols. (Thoroton Soc., 31, 35, 36; Nottingham, 1975–86), ii. 248–9; *The Fairfax Correspondence*, ed. G. W. Johnston, 2 vols. (London, 1848), i. 160; BL, Add. MS 18,979 (Fairfax Correspondence), fos. 15^{r–v}; Stoye, *English Travellers*, 262–3.

began studying Latin and French with a dedication that was in marked contrast to the earlier neglect of his studies at Oxford. Sir Edmund's younger brother appears to have joined the States' Army somewhat earlier. Both were commissioned in the States' Army, and subsequently served as colonels in the English Royalist army. Henry pursued a military career more out of a sense of family tradition, duty, and honour. What he was really fond of was horse racing, but, since there were plenty of opportunities to participate in that sport in his garrison, he was content.[69]

Edward Davies, a veteran of the Spanish Army of Flanders and also a firm believer that gentlemen should learn the profession of arms from the bottom up, said that many gentlemen who aspired to be commissioned officers were prevented from achieving that ambition by the disbandment of military units and the fortunes of war. In order to keep body and soul together and in hopes of obtaining preferment, they were compelled to remain in the ranks as volunteers, although some armies created for them the nebulous rank of voluntary lieutenant. Davies thought it was desirable for volunteers to be close to a captain or a colonel who could supervise their demeanour, see to their training, observe their conduct under fire, and help advance their careers when they had proved their valour and competence. Davies thought that it was acceptable for the gentleman volunteer to serve in either a paid or an unpaid capacity. Volunteers who served in the cavalry were expected to provide themselves with well-apparelled servants to carry their arms and hold their horses. In the Spanish Army of Flanders, it was apparently the practice not to require the gentleman volunteer to stand sentinel, but rather to act as a kind of sergeant of the guard who set and supervised the watch. They also acted as file or squadron leaders and assisted the lieutenant. Those who were fortunate enough to serve as cadets in colonels' companies were allowed to dine at the colonel's table.[70]

After the beginning of the Wars of the Three Kingdoms in 1639, the English armies, following the continental European practice, began

---

[69] F. P. and M. M. Verney, *Memoirs of the Verney Family during the Seventeenth Century*, 2 vols. (London, 1907), i. 98, 105–12.

[70] Edward Davies, *The Art of War and England's Traynings* (London, 1619; repr. Amsterdam, 1968), 101–3, 127–8. Henry Hexham's experiences in the late-sixteenth-century Dutch army were very similar, except that gentlemen volunteers were expected to stand sentinel for a month as part of their initiation into military life (*Principles of the Art Militarie*, 4–5).

experimenting with special units for training cadets. Edmund Ludlow, the future parliamentary general in Ireland, began as a trooper in the third earl of Essex's Life Guard.[71] Following the Restoration of Charles II, this practice became more regularized, and the Royal Life Guards usually consisted of between 500 and 600 gentlemen troopers training for commands and old reformados needing employment. At the rate of 4s. *per diem*, they were paid considerably more than privates in the infantry and enjoyed higher social status. The Nine Years War (1688–97) required an expansion of the English army, and by 1692 the size of the Life Guards had risen to 800 volunteers and reformados divided between four troops. With the return of peace after the War of Spanish Succession, the Life Guards lost their distinctive status as a kind of informal military academy.[72]

The Life Guards never provided enough opportunities for young gentlemen who wished to serve an apprenticeship in arms. After Sir John Reresby had failed to obtain a commission for his younger brother Edmund, the latter enlisted in 1665 in the ranks and 'went to trail a pike in the King's Regiment of [Foot] Guards'. Edmund fought as a volunteer in several naval battles during the Third Anglo-Dutch War of 1672 before obtaining an ensign's commission in the same regiment.[73] Like many aspiring swordsmen during the Restoration period, George Carleton served as a naval volunteer in the Third Dutch War, because 'it was looked upon among the nobility and gentry as a blemish not to attend the duke of York aboard the fleet'. Carleton participated in the Battle of Solebay in late May 1672, and came away filled with admiration for the duke of York's bravery under fire. Being disappointed of a military career at home, Carleton enlisted in the prince of Orange's Company of Guards, where he served as a volunteer with John Graham of Claverhouse (later first Viscount Dundee) and David Colyear (subsequently first earl of Portmore). Even obtaining a place in this company required patronage; Carleton's position was secured by a letter from Major General Walter Vane

---

[71] *Memoirs of Edmund Ludlow . . . 1625–1672*, ed. C. H. Firth, 2 vols. (Oxford, 1894), i. 44.

[72] Edward Chamberlayne, *Anglia Notitia: Or, the Present State of England* (2nd edn.; London, 1669) [Wing C1820], 284; (14th edn., 1682), i. 200; (17th edn., 1692), 152; John Childs, *Armies and Warfare in Europe, 1648–1789* (New York, 1982), 94–5.

[73] *Memoirs of Sir John Reresby*, ed. Andrew Browning (Glasgow, 1936; repr. 1991), 54, 72, 88. By 1685, Edmund Reresby had risen to the rank of captain in the Duke of Grafton's Regiment of Guards (ibid. 382).

of the States' Army to Count Solms, who commanded the Prince of Orange's Foot Guards.[74]

The military career of Charles, second earl of Middleton, also began during the Third Dutch War. He had intended to join the 300 volunteers led by James, duke of Monmouth, and Robert Constable, third Viscount Dunbar, who were sent by Charles II to serve in the French army, but he missed their departure, and, instead, went aboard the *Royal Katherine* and fought as a naval volunteer at Solebay. Middleton's performance in that battle earned him notice, and his father purchased a commission for him in the earl of Mulgrave's Regiment.[75] James Touchet, second earl of Castlehaven, already a veteran of wars in Ireland and continental Europe, found himself unemployed after the Peace of the Pyrenees of 1659, and returned home at the Restoration. He served in the Second Dutch War as a naval volunteer.[76] John Sheffield, earl of Mulgrave, first entered upon his military career at the age of 17 during the Second Dutch War. He served first on the flagship commanded jointly by Prince Rupert and the duke of Albemarle, where he shared a cabin with other volunteers such as Sir Thomas Clifford, later lord treasurer, Henry, fifth Lord Blayney, and Henry Savile, who later pursued a diplomatic career. Mulgrave ended the Second Dutch War as captain of a troop of horse garrisoned at Dover Castle, which was disbanded with the coming of peace. He was returned to Parliament at the age of 18, but was not allowed to take his seat because he was under age. Mulgrave was not unhappy, because at that stage of his life he preferred to pursue a military career. With the outbreak of the Third Dutch War, the earl of Ossory invited him aboard the *Victory* as a volunteer.[77] During the

[74] *The Military Memoirs of Capt. George Carleton from the Dutch War, 1672, in which he served, to the Conclusion of the Peace of Utrecht, 1713* (London, 1728) [ESTCT 70326], 1–4, 10–13; *DNB, sub* John Graham of Claverhouse, 1st Viscount Dundee (1649?–1689) *and* David Colyear, 1st earl of Portmore (d. 1730).

Carleton's *Memoirs* were considered for a long time to be a work of fiction authored by Daniel Defoe on the rather specious grounds that they sounded too authentic to be true, but their authenticity is now generally accepted (*DNB, sub* George Carleton (fl. 1728); Stieg Hargevik, *The Disputed Assignment of Memoirs of an English Officer to Daniel Defoe* (Stockholm, 1974); Paul Hopkins, *Glencoe and the End of the Highland War* (Edinburgh, 1986), 224 n. 49).

[75] George Hilton Jones, *Charles Middleton: The Life and Times of a Restoration Politician* (Chicago, 1967), 18–19.

[76] *The Earl of Castlehaven's Review: Or his Memoirs . . . of the Irish Wars* (London, 1684) [Wing C1237], app., 19–21.

[77] John Sheffield, 3rd earl of Mulgrave and 1st duke of Buckingham and Normanby, 'Memoirs', in *Works*, 2 vols. (London, 1740) [ESTCT 86931], ii. 4.

Restoration, martial values had become strong enough in courtier culture that even Roger Palmer, earl of Castlemaine, who made a career of politics and diplomacy, served at sea with the duke of York, and later wrote a book about the Second Dutch War.[78]

The presence of so many aristocratic volunteers in the military and naval forces of European states not only retarded the emergence of professional officer corps, but hindered the technological development of weapons and tactics as well. Despite the new methods of warfare associated with the military revolution, the 'face-to-face tradition' of fighting persisted strongly among members of the military aristocracies in many European countries and provoked what John Keegan calls 'the warrior crisis of the sixteenth century'. The distaste of the knightly class for missile weapons—that is, longbows, crossbows, and firearms, which gave ordinary foot soldiers an advantage over those skilled in the use of cavalry tactics—called into question the military and social pre-eminence of the knightly class.[79] The preference of the European knightly class for fighting face to face with edged weapons was deeply ingrained culturally and recalled the methods of warfare of Greek and Roman antiquity. It persisted despite the influence of the military revolution, and provides another example of 'irrational technology'.[80]

[78] Roger Palmer, earl of Castlemaine, *A Short and True Account of the Material Passages in the Late War between the English and the Dutch* (London, 1671) [Wing C1247], sig. A3.

Among the volunteers serving with James, duke of York, at the Battle of Sole Bay was Col. Richard Nicholls. Nicholls had served in the French army with James, had been his lieutenant on several occasions, and had recently returned from New York, where he had been governor. Like others of James's followers, Nicholls and other volunteers felt obliged 'to show themselves brave men and servants to his royal highness'. Nicholls was killed at James's side on board the *Prince* (Webb, 'Brave Men and Servants', 65). Volunteers from other navies, caught between commands, sometimes served in the Royal Navy. Among them were Gustavus, Count Horne, later vice-admiral in the Swedish navy, and George and Eric Sjöblad, who fought aboard the *Revenge* during the Second Dutch War. Eric became an admiral in Sweden's war with Denmark (*The Journal of Edward Montagu, First Earl of Sandwich, 1659–1665*, ed. R. C. Anderson (NRS, 64; London, 1929), 143 n.; Davies, *Gentlemen and Tarpaulins*, 30–1).

[79] Keegan, *A History of Warfare*, 333–4.

[80] Martin van Creveld, *Technology and War from 2000 BC to the Present* (New York, 1989), 72–3; Lindsay Boynton, *The Elizabethan Militia, 1558–1638* (London, 1967), 107.

Shakespeare assumed that 'trailing a pike' was a mark of genteel status in the ranks:

> PISTOL. Discuss unto me; art thou officer?
>     Or art thou base, common, and popular?
> KING (in disguise). I am a gentleman of a company.
> PISTOL. Trails't thou the puissant pike?
> KING. Even so . . .
>
>                 (*Henry V*, IV. i)

Gradually, gentlemen came to perceive that fighting on foot could be honourable, but still preferred edged weapons, such as pikes and swords, to firearms. Therefore, gentlemen volunteers almost invariably served as pikemen in the infantry or as cavalry troopers. Robert, third earl of Essex, was one of many gentlemen volunteers in the Dutch army trailing a pike.[81]

Donald Lupton, himself a veteran of the Dutch wars, wrote a treatise on the pike published in 1642. Lupton thought that the experience of the mainland European wars had led many to view the pike as a less flexible, less useful, and, indeed, archaic weapon. Musketeers viewed pikemen as privileged and less exposed to the dangers of 'sallies, convoys, skirmishes, onslaughts' and 'all dangerous and tedious enterprises'. This produced 'heart-burnings' among the musketeers. Lupton would have preferred to abolish pikes, but, recognizing the widespread prejudice in favour of retaining them, he thought pikemen, at least, should also be able to function as musketeers.[82] Because pikemen were socially superior, it was assumed that they must be more 'gently used' than musketeers. An English drill manual of 1690 stated that, when an infantry battalion marched off the parade ground by companies, pikemen must always precede the musketeers.[83] Richard Elton, the writer of a widely used military manual, thought that 'the pike is the most honourable of arms . . . in respect of its antiquity, for there hath been the use of the pike and the spear many hundreds of years before there was any knowledge of the musket'.[84]

[81] Robert Codrington, *The Life and Death of the Illustrious Robert Earle of Essex* (London, 1646) [Wing C4877], 7. See also *A Collection of Original Letters and Papers . . . Found among the Duke of Ormonde's Papers*, ed. Thomas Carte, 2 vols. (London, 1739) [ESTCT 101387], i. 38; P. R. Newman, *The Old Service: Royalist Regimental Colonels and the Civil Wars, 1642–46* (Manchester, 1993), 137.

[82] Donald Lupton, *A Warre-like Treatise of the Pike* (London, 1642) [Wing L3496], sig. A4, pp. 75, 100.

[83] Thomas Styward, *The Pathwaie to Martiall Discipline* (London, 1581) [STC 23413], 18; [anon.,] *The Exercise of the Foot: With the Evolutions according to the Words of Command* (London, 1690) [Wing E3863], 222.

[84] Richard Elton, *The Complete Body of the Art Military* (London, 1650) [Wing E653], 2.

Roger Boyle, 1st earl of Orrery, was against reducing the number of pikemen in proportion to musketeers, and doubted that gentlemen volunteers would be attracted to firing a musket rather than wielding a pike (*A Treatise of the Art of War*, 24–5). The pike was still in use in some regiments of the Spanish Army of Flanders at the beginning of the War of Spanish Succession (*Memoirs of Capt. Peter Drake*, 50–1). Although the socket bayonet generally replaced the pike in European armies at this time, the armies of Revolutionary France revived the use of the pike during a temporary shortage of muskets. Even when muskets and bayonets became available for all infantrymen, the belief persisted in France that martial élan was best expressed with the cold steel of the

Lupton's treatise gives us a rare view from the bottom up: private soldiers who carried muskets viewed pikemen as privileged shirkers. But that perception may not be entirely fair, because gentlemen volunteers were expected to take greater risks. Earlier in the century, Sir Edward Cecil, Lord Wimbledon, wrote that gentlemen volunteers were especially chosen to fill the very exposed forward position of 'perdue sentinel' (*sentinelle perdue*):

The perdue sentinels were drawn from the gentlemen of companies of whom we make account as our principal seminary for officers. For after they have gotten experience, they provide for the most part the best officers and best captains, because they stand in awe of shame, and have a more natural feeling of reputation than men of obscure birth; and are stirred up to do well by the greater expectation of advancement.[85]

Wimbledon adds that having undergone the experience of serving as a perdue sentinel makes a volunteer more sympathetic to the ordinary private soldier: 'For besides the better perfecting of knowledge it is impossible an officer can judge of the patience and misery a sentinel suffereth without having suffered it.' If, on the other hand, a gentleman volunteer was found lacking in courage, the discovery was made before he became a commissioned officer. Just as some gentlemen volunteers did not prove to be good candidates for commissioned rank, Cecil thought that there were soldiers of humble birth who, because of 'merit in their own persons . . . proved very sufficient captains—but not generally'.[86]

---

bayonet, an official tactical doctrine that was not unconnected with the earlier cult of the pike (John A. Lynn, 'En Avant! The Origins of the Revolutionary Attack', in John A. Lynn (ed.), *Tools of War: Instruments, Ideas, and Institutions of Warfare* (Urbana, Ill., 1990), 161, 170; id., 'French Opinion and the Military Resurrection of the Pike, 1792–1794', *Military Affairs*, 41.1 (1977), 1–7).

[85] BL, Harley MS 3638 ['The Duty of a Private Soldier', by Sir Edward Cecil, Lord Wimbledon], fo. 159ᵛ.

[86] Ibid.

There can be no doubt that many gentlemen recklessly and unnecessarily exposed themselves to danger in battle. Clarendon recalled that Lucius Cary, second Viscount Falkland, who had unsuccessfully attempted to establish a military career serving as a volunteer in the Low Countries and Ireland, and, later in life, serving once again as a volunteer in the English Civil War, was such a man. Clarendon thought that Falkland effectively committed suicide by throwing away his life at the Battle of Newbury in 1643 after he had become despondent over the diminishing prospects for peace (Hyde, 1st earl of Clarendon, *History of the Rebellion*, iii. 178–9; *DNB*, *sub* Lucius Cary, 2nd Viscount Falkland (1610–43); Michael MacDonald and Terrence Murphy, *Sleepless Souls: Suicide in Early Modern England* (Oxford, 1990), 97–8).

Personal honour and reputation were everything to the aristocrat, and contemporary opinion during the Renaissance held that honour derived not only from ancient lineage, but also from personal accomplishments. More to the point, it was understood that honour had to be validated in each generation. This had long been accepted by sword families and, as we have seen, was part of European martial culture. The practice of gentlemen volunteers from the Three Kingdoms serving in continental European armies during the late sixteenth and seventeenth centuries reinforced the validity of this custom, and seems also to have exerted a compelling influence upon those, such as Henry Rich, earl of Holland, and Roger Palmer, earl of Castlemain, who served as volunteers, but who might more usually be identified with courtier circles, for courtier and martial cultures were never mutually exclusive. Renaissance manuals of education devoted as much space to how to educate young gentlemen for military service as to the task of how to breed up courtiers, councillors, and magistrates. Besides gaining skill in the exercise of arms, horsemanship, mathematics, and the like, the education of a young nobleman required considerable self-fashioning, since the most important qualities of a military officer were honour and reputation, without which he had no social identity. Moreover, by being placed as a gentleman volunteer in the colonel's company of an elite regiment, the young cadet hoped that he might cut a figure and attract the attention of a patron who could advance his career.[87]

Serving an apprenticeship in arms reached back to an older tradition in English military history when formal rank hardly existed. Foreign service in the age of the military revolution brought British and Irish gentlemen into contact with the more formal and structured military hierarchies of the Spanish, Dutch, and French armies as well as exposure to more modern military technology. The older English rituals of initiation into the profession of arms were modified in accordance with mainland European usage, and it became accepted practice that young swordsmen should serve their apprenticeships in the ranks as gentlemen volunteers before accepting commissions as military officers. That the great powers of Europe were engaged in religious wars sanctioned respectively by the Catholic and Reformed churches lent an urgency and respectability to such military service,

---

[87] Dewald, *Aristocratic Experience*, 53–4.

while the rediscovery of Roman historians and military writers taught that peace breeds effeminacy while war sharpens virtue. This shared experience placed much emphasis upon acquiring those same qualities and attributes that are associated with that social and cultural phenomenon that we call the rechivalrization of the British Isles.

PART II

# Martial Culture and the Discourse of Violence, 1585–1702

CHAPTER FIVE

# Private Warfare and the Language of the Sword

Generally, all warlike people are a little idle, and love danger better than travail. Neither must they be too much broken of it, if they shall be preserved in vigour . . .

('Of the Greatness of Kingdoms and Estates', *Essays*, no. 24, in *The Works of Francis Bacon*, ed. James Spedding, 14 vols. (London, 1857–74; repr. Stuttgart, 1963), vi. 448)

No quarrel of any subject can be lawful except in defense of their prince or country; the revenging of all private wrongs only belongs to us (under God) into whose hand he hath put the sword for that purpose.

(A Royal Proclamation prohibiting the publishing of any reports of duels (1613), in *Stuart Royal Proclamations*, vol. i: *Royal Proclamations of James I, 1603–1625*, ed. J. F. Larkin and P. L. Hughes (Oxford, 1973), no. 132)

War was almost universally sanctioned by divines, jurists, and political philosophers in the sixteenth and seventeenth centuries. As a consequence of the chivalric revival and the eruption of religious wars throughout Europe, more and more noblemen and gentlemen in the British Isles were becoming acquainted with a martial culture based upon honour, which was spreading throughout the camps and courts of Europe, as well as the aristocratic households and urban centres of the British Isles. Concepts of honour and virtue, which were prominent features of European martial culture, taught swordsmen and gallants to think of war and vengeance in personal and individualistic terms; only powerful centralized states could maintain the distinction between public war (*bellum*) and private war (*duellum*).[1] Historians

---

[1] Samuel Clark, *State and Status: The Rise of the State and Aristocratic Power in Western Europe* (Montreal, 1995), 340–2.

are beginning to recognize that the Tudor monarchs of England and
Ireland and the Stuart kings of Scotland never really succeeded in
gaining a monopoly on violence. Although they certainly attempted
to discourage aristocratic rebellion and feuding, the chivalric revival
and exposure to mainland European martial values resuscitated an
honour culture with an assertiveness and an accompanying code of
duelling that no European government could entirely contain. The
belief that honour needed to be demonstrated on the battlefield provided, to some extent, a useful outlet for the energies of swordsmen,
but it was difficult to prevent such violent proclivities from spilling
over into activities such as duelling, feuding, and brawling.

## Interpersonal Violence

Although Sir Francis Bacon was involved in James I's efforts to
suppress duelling and other forms of interpersonal violence, he also
recognized that the defence of the realm required martialists and that
the state needed to show a degree of indulgence towards persons of
high degree who expressed themselves better in violent deeds than in
legal pleading in order to keep them in fighting trim. Very clearly, there
developed in the English realm under the Stuart monarchs a policy of
granting pardons to first offenders among the aristocracy and gentry
who had committed murder; judges and juries were sometimes prepared
to cooperate by acquitting such felons or convicting them on lesser
charges. Intermittent periods of peace or the demobilization of military forces following the end of wars always turned loose on society
former soldiers who lacked useful skills for gainful employment or
were not prepared to return to peaceful ways. During the Restoration,
London became a place where former soldiers from the English civil
wars and other European wars gathered, together with serving officers
and soldiers of the royal guards. Some of these reformados and discharged soldiers were hired by recruiting officers from continental
European armies, who were often to be found in the taverns of the
metropolis, but others found outlets in crime and violence.
     In the absence of modern means of coercion, such as standing
armies and police forces, there was little that a government could do
without turning to the aristocracy for assistance. But the military
aristocracy, with their habits of expressing themselves through the
language of the sword, were one of the main sources of disorder.
Only the kingdom of Ireland possessed something like a standing army

before the Wars of the Three Kingdoms began in 1639; although the
Tudor and Stuart monarchs possessed other, though limited, means
of coercion, they could not tame the nobilities of their kingdoms
without the consent and active cooperation of a significant part
of that estate.[2] Rebellions in England and Scotland prior to 1639
were invariably put down by royal forces commanded by noblemen
and raised, for the most part, from among their retinue, tenants, and
clansmen. Therefore, considerable means of coercion always remained
in the hands of the nobility. On such occasions, royal authority was
used to legitimate their exercise of force.[3] The peer or magnate who
deployed that force probably did not think it was more legitimate
when he assisted the king than when he took it upon himself to punish
someone whose behaviour he regarded as insulting or inappropriate.[4]
Only lawyers and other gownsmen thought in terms of the legality
of the punishment; swordsmen were men of action who thought in
terms of legitimacy.

Violence is often generated by societies with strong aristocratic
cultures in states lacking strong centralized government. The aristocracy of England was undergoing a remilitarization at the end of
the Elizabethan period, while those of Scotland and Ireland had never
really been demilitarized.[5] Although Scotland fought no wars between
1573 and 1639, many Scots served in European armies, while individual Scots at home still possessed arms and resorted to their use
frequently. Private feuds abounded in both the Highlands and the
Lowlands.[6] Ireland was a land of perpetual warfare and rebellion,
which the migration of aggressive and acquisitive English and Scottish
swordsmen to that unhappy isle did nothing to dispel. It was ruled
by lords deputy who were invariably soldiers, and saw three major
periods of civil war and rebellion between 1592 and 1691.[7]

Putting aside any discussion of large-scale rebellions and civil wars,
it is difficult to say whether there was more or less violence in the

[2] Keith M. Brown, *Bloodfeud in Scotland, 1573–1625: Violence, Justice and Politics in an Early Modern Society* (Edinburgh, 1986), 269–70.
[3] Georges Sorel insisted that force is wielded by a government to secure obedience to legitimate authority, while violence is directed against that authority (*Reflections on Violence*, trans T. E. Hulme and J. Roth (1950; repr. 1961), 175).
[4] Susan Dwyer Amussen, 'Punishment, Discipline and Power: The Social Meanings of Violence in Early Modern England', *JBS* 34 (1995), 1–5.
[5] See Chapter 1.
[6] Brown, *Bloodfeud in Scotland*, 19–20, 269–70.
[7] T. W. Moody, F. X. Martin, and F. J. Byrnes (eds.), *Early Modern Ireland, 1534–1691*, vol. iii of *A New History of Ireland* (Oxford, 1976), esp. chs. I, III–IV.

Three Kingdoms in the late sixteenth and seventeenth centuries than there had been earlier. A partial answer is provided by Keith Brown, who argues that sixteenth-century Scotland was a more violent place than the kingdom had been in the fifteenth century because the Church had been weakened by the Reformation, and the monarchy was in a state of collapse under Mary Stuart. There was much internal strife in Scotland before James VI and I began to bring the blood feud under control in the 1590s.[8] Elsewhere, I have suggested that in England the aristocracy and gentry continued to pursue protracted and violent feuds under the guise of poaching forays.[9]

In seventeenth-century England, there existed considerable moral and judicial tolerance of the use of violence for settling disputes in both the public and the private spheres. Short of homicide, the authorities were disinclined to interfere in instances of violent assault, nor were victims likely to complain to a magistrate. Most assaults and brawls were treated as private matters, and constables were advised not to intervene unless property was seriously damaged.[10] In Restoration Kent, judges and juries routinely punished theft of property more severely than the taking of a life in a quarrel or a brawl.[11] One cannot doubt that many English people of all classes and both sexes were given to violent chastisement of those who disagreed with them after reading the pages of George Fox's *Journal*— although it should be admitted that the Quaker leader must have sorely tried their patience. Fox was frequently beaten and stoned by crowds when he invaded parish churches or began preaching in public places. Codes of civility were not well developed, and individuals showed little patience or self-control in resolving disputes.[12]

---

[8] Brown, *Bloodfeud in Scotland*, 266–8.
[9] Roger B. Manning, *Hunters and Poachers: A Cultural and Social History of Unlawful Hunting in England, 1485–1640* (Oxford, 1993), *passim*, esp. 135–48, 184–5, 230–1; see also Dan Beaver, 'The Great Deer Massacre: Animals, Honor and Communication in Early Modern England', *JBS* 38.2 (Apr. 1999), 187–216, esp. 197–8.
[10] J. M. Beattie, 'Violence and Society in Early-Modern England', in A. N. Doob and E. L. Greenspan (eds.), *Perspectives in Criminal Law* (Aurora, Ont., 1985), 36, 42.
[11] *Calendar of Assize Records: Kent Indictments, Charles II, 1676–1688*, ed. J. S. Cockburn (London, 1997), nos. 27, 84, 155, 184, 230, 266, 336, 342, 370, 481, 555, *et passim*.
[12] *The Journal of George Fox*, ed. John L. Nickalls (Cambridge, 1952), 97–9, 126–31, 146–9, 307–8; Beattie, 'Violence and Society in Early-Modern England', 45–6; Jay P. Anglin, 'The Schools of Defence in Elizabethan London', *Renaissance Quarterly*, 37 (1984), 395–6; Sydney Anglo, *The Martial Arts of Renaissance Europe* (New Haven, 2000), 35–6, 273–4.

Violence and the readiness to resort to it (providing one used the appropriate edged weapons) helped to define a person of noble or gentle status, and this assumes a continuing tolerance of violence outside the law and independent of royal authority. The medieval ancestors of aristocrats had made a trade of violence in warfare, and the interpersonal violence of aristocratic brawls and duels is not easily separated from the political violence of war. The tendency of aristocrats and even monarchs such as Charles I to view politics in terms of personal honour meant that a potential for political violence continued. Aristocratic violence and crime assumed characteristic forms such as blood feuds, unlawful deer hunting, duelling, kidnapping heiresses, and inflicting brutal and humiliating punishment upon social inferiors; when they were in straightened circumstances, gentlemen sometimes turned to highway robbery. An especially striking attribute of aristocratic and gentry crime is that public awareness of such actions did not induce a sense of shame.[13]

Vaunting words or verbal posturing usually preceded this aristocratic readiness to resort to arms and force. Verbal posturing could substitute for a resort to arms, or it could lead to combat, but it always preceded aristocratic violence, because such expressions of physical force would have been meaningless except as an exercise in self-assertion. This competitive assertiveness was a consequence of the chivalric revival that was influencing the British Isles as well as the rest of Europe. When honour and reputation were at stake, any quarrel could cause men to assume 'martial postures', because they were unused to expressing disagreement in any language except that of the sword.[14] Because swearing was associated with violence, Puritan reformers sought to suppress and punish the swearing of

[13] Kristin B. Neuschel, *Word of Honor: Interpreting Noble Culture in Sixteenth-Century France* (Ithaca, NY, 1989), 65–6; J. S. McClelland, *The Crowd and the Mob from Plato to Canetti* (London, 1989), 63–4; Caroline Hibbard, 'The Theatre of Dynasty', in R. M. Smuts (ed.), *The Stuart Court and Europe: Essays in Politics and Political Culture* (Cambridge, 1996), 161–2.
Although aristocrats and gentlemen usually displayed no sense of shame about committing violent crimes, Capt. Beau, formerly of the guards, committed suicide after another highwayman revealed that Beau was of the same occupation (Narcissus Luttrell, *A Brief Historical Relation of State Affairs from September 1678 to April 1714*, 6 vols. (Oxford, 1857; repr. Wilmington, Del., 1974), v. 104).
[14] Neuschel, *Word of Honor*, 65–6; Mervyn James, *English Politics and the Concept of Honour, 1485–1642* (P&P Supplement, 3; Oxford, 1978), 1. See also Anna Bryson, *From Courtesy to Civility: Changing Codes of Conduct in Early Modern England* (Oxford, 1998), 327.

oaths, and military codes of conduct often attempted to prohibit the practice as well in order to maintain discipline.[15]

Among all classes, quarrels were frequently inflamed by drink—especially those disagreements that began in taverns.[16] Shortly before his death, the earl of Rochester confessed to Bishop Burnet that he was never completely sober for a period of five years, during which time he was not 'cool enough to be perfectly master of himself', and said and did many 'wild and unaccountable things' and rarely missed an opportunity to mix wit and malice in composing eclogues and satires about other men.[17] George Fox recounts the story of a justice of the peace in Cheshire named Sir Geoffrey Shakerley, who attacked a young Quaker with his cane, but was disarmed. Shakerley, who was drunk, repeated his attacks with pistols and rapier, but was disarmed each time by the young man, whose father had frequently attacked him while drunk, and so he had become expert in disarming such people. Shakerley wished to charge the young man, but was dissuaded from doing so by the constable and an Anglican minister.[18]

In seventeenth-century England, it was assumed that the maintenance of constitutional liberties ultimately rested not upon law and legal institutions, but upon the possession of arms in the hands of householders. In the absence of standing armies and modern police forces, this took the form of an obligation to heed the 'hue and cry', and join the *posse comitatus* if called upon to do so by a magistrate, and it was assumed that the householder would be armed. While attempts were made to keep weapons out of the hands of servants and artificers, this was prompted as much by the fear that the possession of such weapons might facilitate poaching as it was by the fear of popular rebellion.[19] Except for Catholic recusants, there was never any attempt to curtail the possession of weapons by peers and the greater gentry, who always wore swords at their sides and were prepared to use them. Even as late as the early eighteenth century, the armouries of peers might contain considerable store of arms

---

[15] David Underdown, *Fire from Heaven: Life in an English Town in the Seventeenth Century* (New Haven, 1992), 77.

[16] Beattie, 'Violence and Society in Early-Modern England', 45–6.

[17] Gilbert Burnet, 'Some Passages of the Life and Death of . . . John, Earl of Rochester (1680)', repr. in Vivian de Sola Pinto (ed.), *English Biography of the Seventeenth Century* (London, 1951), 101–2.

[18] *Journal of George Fox*, ed. Nickalls, 534–5.

[19] Joyce Malcolm, *To Keep and Bear Arms: The Origins of an Anglo-American Right* (Cambridge, Mass., 1994), pp. x–xi, 2–4; Manning, *Hunters and Poachers*, 97–8.

and munitions. The duke of Beaufort's armoury contained sufficient weapons to equip a couple of companies of foot, half a battery of artillery, and a small detachment of cavalry.[20] Even in London, which still remained a lawless place during the late seventeenth century, many citizens continued to equip themselves with weapons; some possessed small armouries containing weapons remaining from the civil wars or used for periodic musters of the trained bands.[21]

London was the scene of a disproportionate amount of violence, because it was a place of confluence for aristocrats from the Three Kingdoms, and their bloody antics were highly visible to the letter writers and memoirists who also gathered there. The many skilled swordsmen who frequented the capital could not resist testing their prowess and settling old scores. On one occasion, Sir John Suckling the poet and sixteen followers ambushed Sir John Digby at the Blackfriars in revenge for an earlier incident in which Digby had publicly caned Suckling for forcing his attentions on a young lady. Although Digby was accompanied by only a servant and two companions, he routed the lot of them and would have run Suckling through with his sword if the latter had not been wearing a coat of mail under his doublet.[22]

In December 1670, another gang of aristocratic henchmen, procured by Charles II's bastard son, James, duke of Monmouth, and led by a guards officer, Sir Thomas Sands, attacked and slit the nose of Sir John Coventry, MP for Weymouth, for reflecting unfavourably upon the king and his mistresses on the floor of the House of Commons during the debate on a bill to levy a tax upon playhouses. As a consequence of this incident, Parliament framed a bill, which became known as the Coventry or Maiming Act, which made it capital felony without benefit of clergy to mutilate a person.[23] In 1612, Robert, eighth Lord Crichton of Sanquhar, enraged by a taunt from King Louis XIII of France asking him if the man who put out his eye still lived, returned to London and had the fencing master who had accidentally done the deed murdered. At his execution in Palace Yard, Westminster,

[20] HMC, *Fourth Report, Part I* [Fitzhardinge MSS] (1874), 336a.
[21] Peter Earle, *The Making of the English Middle Class: Business, Society and Family Life in London, 1660–1730* (London, 1989), 243, 296.
[22] [Edward Walsingham,] 'The Life of Sir John Digby (1605–1645)', ed. Georges Bernard, in *Camden Miscellany XII* (CS, 3rd ser., 18; London, 1910), 72–3; See also *The Memoirs of Sir Hugh Cholmley* (1777; repr. 1870), 5–8, for a similar incident involving an armed ambush in London.
[23] HMC, *Fourteenth Report*, Appendix, Part IV [Kenyon MSS] (1894), 87; *Memoirs of Sir John Reresby*, ed. Andrew Browning (Glasgow, 1936; repr. 1991), 81 and n.

Sanquhar attributed his moral lapse to his apostasy from the Catholic faith in which he had been raised, and insisted that he never would have consented to such a deed if he had remained faithful.[24]

The drunken and disorderly conduct of gentlemen and their servants, including numerous volunteers and military officers on leave or returned from military expeditions, frequently disturbed the peace of London. Much of this rowdiness occurred in the western suburbs of London, where there was a concentration of playhouses and taverns and where the Inns of Court harboured many sons of the aristocracy. In July 1629, a riot erupted near the Temple, in which some soldiers led by Capt. John Stamford, a follower of the duke of Buckingham, attempted to rescue one of their fellows who had been arrested by the watch. Sixty gentlemen participated in this battle with constables and the City trained bands, and one military officer was killed when a sergeant of the watch ran him through with his halberd. Another captain, named Asheham or Ashenhurst, was convicted and condemned for murder together with Stamford, who was charged as an accessory. Stamford's wife and father appealed to the king for a pardon, but the king refused, explaining that Stamford had already enjoyed one pardon for murdering a watchman. Asheham and Stamford were both hanged for murder.[25]

---

[24] Brown, *Bloodfeud in Scotland*, 24; James, *English Politics and the Concept of Honour*, 14; Michael C. Questier, *Conversion, Politics and Religion in England, 1580–1625* (Cambridge, 1996), 72.

[25] V. G. Kiernan, *The Duel in European History: Honour and the Reign of Aristocracy* (Oxford, 1988), 120–1; Thomas Birch, *The Court and Times of Charles I*, ed. R. F. Williams, 2 vols. (London, 1848), ii. 24–5.

John Holles, 1st earl of Clare, who was usually well informed, states that 240 people were killed in this riot, including London apprentices. Clare also states that Stamford and Asheham, when captured, were tried in a 'privy sessions' before the chief justice, found guilty, and hanged the next morning after the king had refused to stay their execution even two days. Clare, with bitterness, remarks that the Crown insisted that the authority of the City magistrates and constables was upheld because 'the City must not be displeased, whose purse is to be preferred before the best of our lives' (*Letters of John Holles, 1587–1637*, ed. P. R. Seddon, 3 vols. (Thoroton Soc., 31, 35, 36; Nottingham, 1975–86), iii. 392–3).

For a similar case, cf. Keith Lindley, 'Riot Prevention and Control in Early Stuart London', *Trans. R. Hist. Soc.*, 5th ser., 33 (1983), 115.

An anonymous play, entitled *A Warning for Fair Women* (1599), which concerns a murder committed by an officer who had served in the Irish wars, attempts to depict the young 'gallant', who was hanged for the crime, as a 'goodly man' who had been corrupted by the fleshpots of London. The play is discussed at length by Peter Lake ('From Troynouvant to Heliogabulus's Rome and Back: "Order" and its Others in the London of John Stow', in J. F. Merritt (ed.), *Imagining Early Modern London: Perceptions and Portrayals of the City from Stow to Strype, 1598–1720* (Cambridge, 2001), 232–3.

Another riotous rescue was effected in March 1638 by numerous gentlemen servants of James, third marquis of Hamilton, who broke into and destroyed a house near Charing Cross, where one of their number had been confined temporarily by the watch. During the riot, Hamilton's servants had killed a sergeant of the watch and threatened to blow up the house with gunpowder. Charles I found it necessary to intervene in this matter and issue a proclamation for the apprehension of the leaders of the riot who had gone into hiding.[26] On the evening of 6 January 1641, the noise caused by 'roistering' courtiers in a tavern in Covent Garden set in motion a rumour that there was a royalist plot to seize the City of London. This came two days after the king had invaded the House of Commons.[27] After thirty bailiffs had attempted to seize the goods of some gentlemen living in Fuller's Rents, Gray's Inn, in 1673, they were attacked by over 100 gentlemen armed with swords. Twenty-one of the bailiffs were wounded, and at least one of them died. Much violence was perpetrated by soldiers spoiling for a good fight who entered the tumult on both sides.[28]

A surprising amount of the violence caused by gentlemen in London was casual and unprovoked. In August 1691, a young gentleman strolling through Gray's Inn Lane passed a shoemaker with a clay pipe in his mouth, which he gratuitously broke with his hand. When the shoemaker protested, the gentleman drew his sword and ran the shoemaker through. After being tried, convicted, and condemned, the gentleman rode to his execution at Tyburn in a coach and was given a 'great funeral' the next day. Apparently, a number of younger members of the aristocracy and gentry indulged in the pastime of assaulting in the street harmless and inoffensive persons, but particularly enjoyed attacking members of the watch.[29]

[26] *The Earl of Strafford's Letters and Dispatches*, comp. W. Knowler, 2 vols. (Dublin, 1740) [ESTCT 110679], ii. 165; *Stuart Royal Proclamations*, vol. ii: *Royal Proclamations of King Charles I, 1625–1646*, ed. J. F. Larkin (Oxford, 1983), no. 258.

[27] Lawson Nagel, ' "A Great Bouncing at Everyman's Door": The Struggle for London's Militia in 1642', in Stephen Porter (ed.), *London and the Civil War* (London, 1996), 71.

[28] *Letters Addressed from London to Sir Joseph Williamson*, ed. W. D. Christie, 2 vols. (CS, NS 8, 9; London, 1874), i. 52.

[29] *The Portledge Papers, Being Extracts from the Letters of Richard Lapthorne*, ed. R. J. Kerr and I. C. Duncan (London, 1928), 119–22; Max Beloff, *Public Order and Popular Disturbance, 1660–1714* (London, 1938), 32–3. For a similar case where two gentlemen attacked an alehouse keeper, see *Portledge Papers*, ed. Kerr and Duncan, 165.

Sir John Reresby thought that the hostility of Londoners towards the aristocracy had increased during the republican period: 'The citizens and common people of London had then so far imbibed the custom and manners of a commonwealth that they could scarce endure the sight of a gentleman . . .' When Reresby returned from his continental tour in May 1658, dressed presumably in the French fashion, he and his servant were accosted by working men repairing the street, who called them 'French dogs' and threw sand upon them. When he and his servant drew their swords, a riot ensued and they barely escaped with their lives into a nearby house.[30] Such hostility between gentry and citizens continued to seethe during the Restoration period and into the early eighteenth century. In September 1690, a group of young noblemen and gentlemen accompanied by female companions attending Bartholomew Fair went into the cloisters of St Bartholomew's Hospital to dance , 'where the [*populum*] *mobile*, pressing to be spectators', offended the gentlemen, who 'descended from words to blows and drawn swords'. Nine of the crowd were seriously wounded and one or two killed.[31]

Gentlemen and army officers frequently quarrelled when they went to London. An affront offered to Edward Ravenscroft, a playwright of deservedly minor reputation, led him to seek his revenge six months later in another playhouse. His attack precipitated a brawl that drew in a peer, a knight, a colonel, and a captain, and injured three of them.[32] Sir John Reresby recalled going into a coffee house after dinner with six other gentlemen, two of whom fell to quarrelling. Reresby tried to reconcile the two, one a major in the guards and the other an MP, and broke one of their swords doing so. They could not be pacified and insisted on fighting a duel that very afternoon. After stopping to buy a new sword, they went to Hyde Park and proceeded to fight a duel, with Reresby acting as second for both of them. Reresby finally succeeded in reconciling them after each had drawn blood. Afterwards, they 'all went to supper and parted good friends'.[33]

Towards the end of Queen Anne's reign, gangs of gentlemen thugs calling themselves 'Mohocks', a faction of the Whig Calf's Head Club, roamed the streets of London slashing people with swords and

---

[30] *Memoirs of Sir John Reresby*, ed. Browning, 21–2.
[31] *Portledge Papers*, ed. Kerr and Duncan, 84; Luttrell, *Brief Historical Relation*, ii. 99.
[32] *Letters Addressed from London to Sir Joseph Williamson*, ed. Christie, i. 87.
[33] *Memoirs of Sir John Reresby*, ed. Browning (1991 ed.), 325–6.

knives. A particularly vicious trick that they perpetrated was to put an old woman in a hogshead and roll her down a hill. One member of the gang was identified as Lord Hinchingbrooke, the heir of the earl of Sandwich and a captain of dragoons. At least six of the dozen or so members of this particular gang had been or were officers in the army. Another victim was a gentleman who drew his sword to defend himself; he captured one of the Mohocks and committed him to the house of correction, but the young man bribed a guard and escaped. Ned Ward reported that the escapades of the Mohocks came to an end when a gang of them, after assaulting a young lady in a sedan chair, were stoutly resisted by the chairmen employing their poles as weapons. 'Their leader, whom the rest called their "emperor" . . . received a fracture in his skull, which proved his bane, though it was given out that he died of the pox.'[34] In 1726, a Swiss visitor, appalled by such behaviour, stated that fraternities of young gentlemen at the end of an evening's 'debauch' would go out into the streets and swear to kill the first person whom they met. On one occasion, two young gentlemen, having failed to encounter anyone at 2 o'clock in the morning, knocked on a door and killed the man who opened the door. They were hanged for their crime, but other culprits often succeeded in gaining pardons for comparable offences.[35]

Gangs of idle and mischievous gallants, called 'roaring boys', 'roisterers', 'hectors', and 'bravadoes', who were loosely organized into gangs and fraternities, had existed in London since at least late-Elizabethan times. They frequented taverns, engaged in duelling, which could be distinguished from brawling only with difficulty, and wantonly assaulted passers-by in the late hours of the evening. Their ranks often included reformados and volunteers, who, for want of honest employment, often turned to activities such as extortion, confidence schemes, and highway robbery. They presented the dark underside of martial culture. In the 1620s and 1630s, these fraternities went by such names as 'the Order of the Bugle' and the 'Tityre-tues' (the last so called after the first two words of Virgil's First Eclogue:

[34] The Wentworth Papers, 1705–1739, ed. J. J. Cartwright (London, 1883), 277 and n.; [Edward Ward,] The Whigs Unmask'd: Being the Secret History of the Calf's-Head Club (London, 1713) [ESTCT 147726], 128–9; Daniel Statt, 'The Case of the Mohocks: Rake Violence in Augustan London', Social History, 20 (1995), 182, 186–9, 197–9.
[35] [Beat Louis de Muralt,] Letters Describing the Character and Customs of the English and French Nations (London, 1726) [ESTCN 19973], 33–4.

'Titere tu . . .') Some of these fraternities wore tawny-orange ribbons —possibly because of an association with the Orangist cause in the Netherlands where they seem to have originated—but one fraternity was composed of Catholic veterans of Lord Vaux's Regiment in the Spanish Army of Flanders. Following the end of the English civil wars, reformados and discharged soldiers gathered in London and formed themselves into gangs called 'Hectors' and 'Knights of the Blade'. One trick practised by the hectors was to extort money from wealthy citizens rather than be compelled to fight a duel. Other members of the fraternity were thought to live by highway robbery. Acts of vandalism were perpetrated by Hectors, who may have been driven by ideology; John Milton's windows were smashed by Royalists.[36] These rowdy veterans had their imitators in the 'town gallant', who was regarded as the generic form of the Mohock and was given over to duelling, brawling, and gratuitous violence.[37]

However outrageous the violent acts of aristocrats were, the Stuart monarchs and their judges were prepared to indulge them up to a point. In 1636, a courtier named Peter Apsley was reprimanded by the king and confined to his chamber for fighting within the verge of the court—an offence that in Tudor times would have resulted in the offender losing his right hand. Peers were likely to escape altogether the penalties that were appropriate for their violent misdeeds, and this was true even during Cromwell's rule. In 1657, Henry Grey, first earl of Stamford, a parliamentary general who had already been impeached in 1645 for assaulting Sir Arthur Haselrig, was condemned at the assizes for murdering, with two of his servants, a man on a highway. He managed to obtain a reprieve of fifteen days to go to London and beg for a pardon. He was obviously successful, because he survived until 1673, and showed his gratitude to the lord protector by declaring for Charles II in 1659 and participating

---

[36] T. S. Graves, 'Some Pre-Mohock Clansmen', *Studies in Philology*, 20 (1923), 395–421; Samuel Butler, 'An Hector', in Butler, *Characters*, ed. C. W. Davies (Cleveland, Oh., 1970), 278–9.

[37] Anon., *The Character of a Town-Gallant: Exposing the Extravagant Fopperies of the Some Vain, Self-Conceited Pretenders to Gentility and Good Breeding* (London, 1675), repr. in *The Old Book Collector's Miscellany*, ii, ed. Charles Hindley (London, 1872), 3, 8–9. Markku Peltonen (*The Duel in Early Modern England: Civility, Politeness and Honour* (Cambridge, 2003), 180–90) has an extended discussion of town gallants and beaux and the anti-French and anti-Jacobite ideologies that went with these sentiments. Anna Bryson discusses the rakes and libertines who chose to reject the code of civility in ch. 7 of *From Courtesy to Civility*.

in Booth's Rising. In 1681, Alexander Montgomerie, eighth earl of Eglintoun, killed the postmaster of Doncaster in a drunken rage. His uncle, John Leslie, duke of Rothes and lord chancellor of England, was able to procure a pardon for him.[38] The son of Sir Edward Turner, the deceased former speaker of the House of Commons and some-time chief baron of the Exchequer, was tried in 1693 for killing his manservant. The lord chief justice interceded on his behalf, and the defendant was convicted on the lesser charge of manslaughter.[39] The jury at the Old Bailey, which tried a man named Walters in 1688 for killing Sir Charles Pym in a tavern brawl, wanted to convict him of murder, but the presiding judges instructed the jury to convict him of manslaughter.[40] Juries were sometimes equally indulgent: a cornet in a cavalry regiment was found not guilty of killing a man in a brawl in a victualling house in Maidstone.[41]

Those who had killed once and were pardoned or allowed to plead benefit of clergy often killed again.[42] Since such culprits were burned in the hand, they carried a permanent criminal record on their persons. This probably was the case with Capt. Charles Walsingham, who was accused of murdering two men with his sword in a brawl. In his last speech just before he was hanged at Tyburn in June 1689, he said that he had been a soldier all of his life and admitted that he was given to 'too much passion and rashness'.[43]

Perhaps no gallant caused so much havoc in late-seventeenth-century England as Charles, fourth Lord Mohun. He had served as a volunteer with the Brest Expedition of 1694, and in the same year was commissioned a captain in a cavalry regiment with which

---

[38] Sir John Lauder of Fountainhall, *Historical Observations, 1680–1686*, ed. A. Urquhart and D. Laing (BC 66; Edinburgh, 1837), 27.
[39] *Portledge Papers*, ed. Kerr and Duncan, 164.
[40] Ibid. 31, 34.
Manslaughter was also a capital felony. Ben Jonson, the playwright, was indicted for killing an actor, Gabriel Spencer, in an encounter in Hoxton Fields in 1598. The jury returned a verdict of manslaughter. Jonson pleaded benefit of clergy and was branded with the Letter 'M'. Another part of the penalty was confiscation of his chattels. Before his conviction, Jonson was imprisoned for a month on remand awaiting general gaol delivery, and he also had to pay certain fees to his gaoler (J. D. Aylward, *The English Master of Arms from the the Twelfth to the Twentieth Century* (London, 1956), 54).
[41] *Calendar of Assize Records: Kent Indictments, Charles II, 1676–1688*, ed. Cockburn, no. 1341.
[42] *Portledge Papers*, ed. Kerr and Duncan, 90.
[43] *An Account of the Penitent Behaviour, Last Speech and Confession of Captain Charles Walsingham* (London, 1689) [Wing A335A], 1–2.

he saw action in Flanders. In December 1692, he was accused of killing an actor in a duel. The incident came about because his friend, Capt. Richard Hill of the Foot Guards, was infatuated with Anne Bracegirdle, a well-known actress, and wished to marry her. Mrs Bracegirdle spurned the captain's attentions; Hill imagined that she was carrying on a liaison with William Mountfort, another actor. At first Hill and Mohun, with the assistance of a number of soldiers, attempted to kidnap the actress and force her into a coach, but that scheme failed. Hill swore that he would be revenged, and he and Mohun waited in Howard Street outside Mrs Bracegirdle's lodgings with drawn swords and several bottles of wine, hoping to intercept her lover. When William Mountfort appeared, Hill ran him through with a sword while Mohun either held him or stood by—the evidence is unclear. Mountfort had no time to draw his sword, as witnesses later testified.[44]

Mohun was able to defy the law with impunity. Earlier, while parading up and down the street with drawn swords outside Bracegirdle's lodgings, Mohun had refused an order from the watch to disperse, saying that he was a peer of the realm and they dared not touch him. In duels, all participants were considered to be principals, but, when Mohun was committed to Hicks Hall, the Middlesex house of correction, following the murder of Mountfort, he was immediately bailed by friends. The coroner's inquest ruled that death of Mountfort was murder. Hill fled and Mohun's mother was unsuccessful in obtaining a pardon from King William III, who told her 'it was a barbarous act, and he would leave it to the law'. Mohun was committed to the Tower of London to await trial by the House of Lords. In February 1693, the House of Lords chose to ignore the evidence that the murder of Mountfort occurred during an ambush and not a duel, and voted 69 to 14 to acquit Mohun.[45]

Mohun continued to fight in brawls and duels—the difference between the two seemed to escape him. In 1694, Mohun attempted to murder a coachman in Pall Mall, but was prevented from doing

[44] Luttrell, *Brief Historical Relation*, ii. 637–8, iii. 11, 27, 29; T. B. Howell (ed.), *A Complete Collection of State Trials and Proceedings for High Treason*, 33 vols. (London, 1809–26), vol. xii, columns 949–1050; *DNB, sub* Anne Bracegirdle (1663?–1748) and William Mountfort (1664?–1692); Victor Stater, *Duke Hamilton is Dead! A Story of Aristocratic Life and Death in Stuart Britain* (New York, 1999), 42–61.

[45] Howell, *State Trials*, vol. xii, columns 949–1050; Luttrell, *Brief Historical Relation*, ii. 637–8, iii. 11, 27, 29.

so by a Cornish MP, whom Mohun wounded as he was being disarmed. Afterwards, he sent a challenge to the MP.[46] In 1697, following a debauch at the Rummer Tavern in Charing Cross, Mohun stabbed to death Capt. William Hill of the Coldstream Guards. The coroner's inquest found manslaughter; the Middlesex grand jury indicted Mohun for murder, but once again the House of Lords acquitted him.[47] Their lordships tried Mohun for murder a third time in 1699, after Mohun had killed Capt. Richard Coote in another tavern brawl. Again, he was acquitted. By this time Mohun was old enough to have taken his seat in the House of Lords. The Whig majority in the upper house was slender at this time, and Victor Stater suggests that William III and the Whigs had probably decided that Mohun's vote could not be spared. His wretched life came to an end on 15 November 1712, when he and James Douglas, fourth duke of Hamilton, killed one another in a duel in Hyde Park. Mohun was the son of a father who had also been killed in a duel in the year he was born, and with the son's death the Mohun line came to an end.[48]

As the case of Lord Mohun demonstrates, military officers sometimes procured their subordinates to assist them in the perpetration of violent deeds. After being entertained at dinner by Sir Robert Viner, one Cornet Wroth 'drew a pistol on his host', and, with the assistance of seven or eight of his troopers, kidnapped Viner's ward. Before Wroth could cross the Thames at Putney Ferry, he was intercepted, but escaped. His intended bride was so frightened that she was unable to speak when rescued.[49] In August 1688, a senior officer of Kirke's Regiment (known sardonically as 'Kirke's Lambs') was being conveyed across the Thames to his lodgings in Southwark where his unit was quartered when the waterman splashed water on his uniform coat. The officer was enraged, and killed the waterman. A crowd of people saw what happened, and attempted to carry the officer to a magistrate, but he was rescued by soldiers from his regiment.[50]

---

[46] Ibid. iii. 381.

[47] Ibid. iv. 207, 278, 280, 296, 303, 312, 318, 321, 329. A fascinating account of the background of this notorious duel is found in Stater, *Duke Hamilton is Dead!*

[48] *DNB, sub* Charles Mohun, 4th Baron Mohun (1675?–1712).

[49] F. P. and M. M. Verney, *Memoirs of the Verney Family during the Seventeenth Century*, 2 vols. (London, 1907), ii. 321.

[50] *Portledge Papers*, ed. Kerr and Duncan, 43.

Although soldiers serving at home were supposed to be subject to the civil courts,[51] and to military courts when serving overseas, military officers sometimes handed out punishments of their own devising in fits of rage. George Lindsay, fourteenth earl of Crawford, was murdered by a lieutenant in his own regiment in the Swedish army after provoking the subaltern by caning him in public. A Swedish court martial refused to convict the lieutenant of murder because cudgelling an officer was contrary to Swedish military discipline. Crawford was buried in Stettin, and, when the governor of that city, Major-General Sir Alexander Leslie, heard about the incident, he had the lieutenant shot by his own authority.[52] In 1673, the countess of Shrewsbury came upon two gentlemen troopers of the Royal Horse Guards quarrelling. She told her coachman to try and separate them with his whip, and the guardsmen killed him. When the guardsmen were brought before their commander, George Villiers, second duke of Buckingham, he beat one of the soldiers severely. Although the Court of the Verge found the crime to be only manslaughter (presumably with the possibility of a pardon), Buckingham declared that he was determined to see the man hanged.[53] While serving in the Tangier Regiment and Garrison, a captain, Sir John Mordaunt, abused a lady and quarrelled with his fellow officers. His behaviour was so disruptive that his fellow officers tried him before a court martial for treason and sentenced him to be shot. Although he was reprieved by the governor, the earl of Middleton, and allowed to write to his kinsman, the earl of Peterborough, for a pardon, the sentence was ultimately carried out.[54] Another officer in the Tangier Regiment with a quick temper was Capt. Richard Dudley, who had been given a commission because his father had lost his estates in the service of the king during the civil wars. One day when the regiment was drawn up in parade order,

[51] *Case of Soldiers* (1601), in Sir Edward Coke, *Reports*, 13 parts (4th edn.; London, 1738) [ESTCN 12827], vol. vi, fo. 27.
    For an example of the trial at the Kent Assizes of a gentleman volunteer who stabbed and killed another gentleman volunteer aboard the *Rupert* while anchored in the R. Medway at Chatham, see *Calendar of Assize Records: Kent Indictments, Charles II, 1676–1688*, ed. Cockburn, no. 1334 (1687).
[52] [Daniel Defoe,] *The Scots Nation and Union Vindicated* (London, 1714) [ESTCT 56966], 28.
[53] *Letters Addressed from London to Sir Joseph Williamson*, ed. Christie, i. 86.
[54] *Tangier at High Tide: The Journal of John Luke, 1670–1673*, ed. H. A. Kaufman (Geneva and Paris, 1958), 30, 58, 93, 96, 104. The usual president of the military court at Tangier, John Luke, a civilian, did not preside at the trial and disapproved of the sentence.

Dudley noticed that one of his men was standing out of alignment. He ordered his sergeant to knock the man down, but, when the sergeant did not do so with sufficient force, he grabbed the sergeant's halberd and split the offending soldier's skull in half. The soldier died immediately, but Dudley escaped with his life and lived long enough to be hanged as a highwayman in 1681.[55]

Some gallants sought to escape prosecution for murder and other violent deeds by fleeing overseas. The Danvers brothers, Sir Charles and Sir Henry, having been outlawed for the death of a man in 1594, 'took refuge in France and distinguished themselves in the French army'. Through the intercession of Henry IV, they obtained pardons from the queen in 1598. Charles died a traitor's death for his complicity in the Essex Rebellion of 1601; Henry subsequently became earl of Danby.[56] In the 1680s, a gentleman named Parsons fled to the Netherlands after murdering a man in Essex. He became a major in the Dutch army, and accompanied William of Orange in the descent on England in 1688. After his return to England, he 'debauched' a citizen's wife, and she, in revenge, caused him to be indicted for the murder he had committed seven years earlier.[57]

When going abroad, the wary traveller knew that soldiers were to be avoided at all costs. Colin Lindsay, third earl of Balcarres, was robbed, stripped of his clothes, and very roughly treated near Aachen by soldiers from garrisons at Maastricht or Liège. James Drummond, fourth earl of Perth, while dining at an English nunnery near Antwerp, learned that soldiers from the Three Kingdoms, even when they were practising Catholics, were not welcome at religious houses in the Spanish Netherlands.[58]

Travellers in the British Isles also needed to keep an eye out for highwaymen. Highway robbery came to be regarded as a distinctly

[55] *The Complete Newgate Calendar*, ed. J. L. Rayner and G. T. Crook, 5 vols. (London, 1926), i. 275–9. Dudley's career as a highwayman was extensive, and Charles II refused to pardon him because when he was tried at the Old Bailey there were some eighty indictments brought against him in the county of Middlesex alone. Among his victims were General Monck and the keeper of Newgate Prison.

[56] *The Letters of John Chamberlain*, ed. N. E. McClure, 2 vols. (Philadelphia, 1939), i. 43 n.; *Aubrey's Brief Lives*, ed. Oliver Lawson Dick (London, 1950), 77–8; *DNB*, *sub* Sir Charles Danvers (1568?–1601) *and* Sir Henry Danvers, earl of Danby (1573–1644).

[57] *Portledge Papers*, ed. Kerr and Duncan, 111–12.

[58] *Letters from James Earl of Perth . . . to his Sister, the Countess of Errol*, ed. William Jerdan (CS, old ser., 33; London, 1845), 31, 35, 38.

aristocratic crime. Bishop Earle noted that the last resort of younger sons, before becoming gentlemen volunteers in the Low Countries, was to take to 'the king's highway, where at length their vizard is plucked off, and they strike fair for Tyburn; but their brother's pride, not love, gets them a pardon'.[59] From the time of the civil wars, most highwaymen were drawn from the ranks of demobilized soldiers, especially former officers and cavalry troopers, because they usually possessed the necessary tools of the trade—a horse and a brace of pistols. The numerous ballads published during this time about highwaymen suggest that a certain roguish glamour attached to their escapades, but, by the end of the civil wars and during the Restoration, highwaymen became a plague upon the land and few well-dressed travellers escaped their ministrations.[60]

A well-known gentry family that earned their livelihood in this profession was headed by Sir George Sandys, who was first indicted at the Middlesex Sessions in 1616 on four counts of highway robbery. He was acquitted on this occasion, but another source reported that he had robbed a dozen persons near Kensington in one evening. The following year he was residing near Enfield and had shifted his operations to the eastern environs of London, where he was hanged 'at Wapping for taking purses on the highway, having been formerly pardoned for the like offences . . .' His wife, Susannah, Lady Sandys, and his son George were gaoled as accomplices; they appear to have been subsequently pardoned. It fell to George to support the family, and he was again indicted in 1619, but acquitted. However, in 1626 he murdered one of his victims. The evidence that convicted him of this crime was provided by a woman to whom he had confessed the crime while raping her. He and two accomplices were condemned and hanged at Tyburn on 6 September 1626.[61]

In May 1647, following the end of the First English Civil War, the sheriff of Oxfordshire reported that gangs of discharged royalist cavalry troopers, including Irishmen, had taken to the highways in considerable numbers and robbed travellers. He raised a *posse*

[59] John Earle, *Microcosmography*, ed. Harold Osborne (1633; repr. London, 1971), 23–4.
[60] Malcolm, *To Keep and Bear Arms*, 82–3.
[61] 'The Life and Death of Mr George Sandys', in *A Pepysian Garland: Black-Letter Broadside Ballads of the Years 1595–1639 Chiefly from the Collection of Samuel Pepys*, ed. Hyder E. Rollins (Cambridge, 1922), 248–55.

*comitatus* and captured 100 of them.[62] Anthony Wood told of two former Royalist officers, without employment and reduced to poverty, who turned to highway robbery and were caught and executed at Oxford. 'They were exceedingly pitied by all men', and Royalist sympathizers cut down their bodies and buried them in the parish church of St Peter Le Bailey.[63] In the north of England, Capt. Edward Holt, a former member of the Pontefract Royalist garrison, murdered an inhabitant of the town and preyed upon those travelling between Lancashire and the West Riding.[64] Another former Royalist captain turned highwayman was Philip Stafford. He served throughout the civil wars, but sequestration of his estates near Newbury, Berks., led him to try to recoup his losses by robbing Parliamentarians. He was hanged at Reading.[65] The notorious 'Capt.' James Hind's military rank was actually a highwayman's honorific. Although he fought with the Royalist forces and was a corporal in the marquis of Ormonde's Life Guard, he had been a highwayman before the war. Charles II commended his bravery to his commander, the second duke of Buckingham, after the Battle of Worcester, and pardoned him from a sentence of death passed upon him for manslaughter. The stories that he preyed upon regicides such as Cromwell, John Bradshaw, and the Puritan cleric Hugh Peters are apparently mythical. Nonetheless, the Parliamentarians executed him for treason at Worcester in 1652. Royalists insisted that Hind's only crime was his loyalty to the king.[66]

Another Royalist highwayman who boasted of his high-ranking parliamentarian victims was Capt. Zachary Howard. He had inherited an estate in Gloucestershire worth £1,400 p.a. When the Civil War broke out in 1642, he mortgaged his estate for £20,000 to raise a troop of cavalry for the king. He went into exile after the First Civil

[62] Bulstrode Whitelocke, *Memorials of the English Affairs*, 4 vols. (1682; repr. Oxford, 1853), ii. 138; *The Diary of Bulstrode Whitelocke, 1605–1675*, ed. Ruth Spalding (British Academy, Records of Social and Economic History, NS 13; London, 1990), 192.
[63] *The Life of Anthony à Wood . . . 1632–1672, Written by Himself* (Oxford, 1772) [ESTCT 33548], 78–9.
[64] Ronan Bennett, 'War and Disorder: Policing the Soldiery in Civil War Yorkshire', in M. C. Fissel (ed.), *War and Government in Britain, 1598–1650* (Manchester, 1991), 262.
[65] *Complete Newgate Calendar*, ed. Rayner and Crook, i. 105–16.
[66] Ibid. i. 95–105; *DNB, sub* James Hind (d. 1652); James Fraser, *Chronicles of the Frasers*, ed. William Mackay (SHS, 1st ser., 47; Edinburgh, 1905), 393–4.

War and returned with Charles II and participated in the Battle of Worcester. Howard remained in England after the Royalist defeat and swore to be revenged upon the king's enemies, and took up the life of a highwayman. Among the victims whom he claimed were the third earl of Essex, the wife and daughter of the Lord General Fairfax, and the lord protector himself. Soon after his robbery of Cromwell, Howard was captured near Maidstone, tried at the Kent Assizes, and hanged in 1652 at the age of 32 years.[67]

The Scots and the Irish also turned to banditry as a result of the dislocations caused by the Wars of the Three Kingdoms, but more is known about the former than the very numerous Irish tories, who were not romanticized by the ballad-mongers of London.[68] The Scots highwayman Sawny Douglas came from Portpatrick, Galloway, and, being an enthusiastic presbyterian, he joined the Covenanting Army. At the Restoration, he had been a soldier for nearly twenty years and had risen to the rank of sergeant. Upon his discharge, he went to England, and, being destitute, he became a highwayman. Among those he claimed to have robbed were the duchess of Albemarle and the earl of Sandwich. The last refused to be intimidated and shot Sawny's horse from under him, which allowed Sandwich's servants to seize and carry him to Newgate Prison. He was hanged at Tyburn in September 1664. Instead of carrying a Bible to his execution, as was customary, he carried a copy of the ballad *Chevy Chase*.[69] Andrew Melville achieved the rank of major in the Scottish Royalist forces, and served under the duke of Hamilton and the earl of Derby in the Third Civil War. With the defeat of Charles II at Worcester, Melville escaped to the Continent, but was unable to find military employment. He fell into bad company with some unemployed officers from the duke of Lorraine's mercenary army, and was accused of participating in the robbery of a French army payroll convoy. He was imprisoned and interrogated, but eventually released.[70]

---

[67] *Complete Newgate Calendar*, ed. Rayner and Crook, i. 84–9.

[68] For references to tories, or outlaws drawn from those dispossessed of their lands and livings during the civil wars in Ireland, see [Roger Boyle, earl of Orrery,] *A Letter from the Lord Broghill . . . to William Lenthall, Speaker of the Parliament* (London, 1651) [BL, Thomason Tracts E.640], 1; Thomas Morrice (comp.), *The State Letters of . . . Roger Boyle, 1st Earl of Orrery* (London, 1742) [ESTCN 14784], 316; and John Prendergast, *The Cromwellian Settlement of Ireland* (3rd edn.; Dublin, 1922), 340–6.

[69] *Complete Newgate Calendar*, ed. Rayner and Crook, i. 179–81.

[70] *Memoirs of Sir Andrew Melville*, trans. & ed. Torick Ameer-Ali (London, 1918), 119, 121, 137–44; *DNB*, *sub* Andrew Melville (1624–1706).

Aristocratic families were often remarkably indulgent towards their criminous kinsfolk. Richard Hals was a black-sheep cousin of the Verneys who was born in Ireland and sent to England for an education. From the beginning, he was disinclined to take up a useful occupation, and ended up in Newgate Prison as early as 1656, when he wrote Sir Ralph Verney pleading for help. Eventually, Edmund Verney found him a place aboard the *Revenge* in 1666 as a volunteer with Prince Rupert and the duke of York during the Second Anglo-Dutch War. He had hoped to obtain something more permanent in the way of a civil or military office, but he lacked the capital to purchase a place, and Edmund Verney was disinclined to lend him anything more than small sums. By 1669, Hals had fallen in with highwaymen. He continually pestered the Verneys for money, writing, for example, from Exeter Gaol in 1671 and asking for the price of a winding sheet so that he might be decently buried after he was hanged. Yet, by obtaining reprieves and escaping from various prisons, he avoided being hanged until as late as 1685. His name was struck out of a general pardon by the king in 1672. After escaping from Newgate, he fled with the help of his Verney relatives, with the intention of enlisting in the French army, but he was recaptured and put in Chelmsford Gaol. Throughout his career as a highwayman, he visited his Verney relatives, and was invited to family weddings.[71]

Charles II was prepared to pardon worse crimes for reasons of state. A case in point is that of Col. Thomas Blood, a former military officer, who, as a popular ballad put it, committed 'more villainies than ever England knew'. Blood was born in Co. Meath, Ireland, the son of a prosperous Protestant blacksmith, and he may have served under Prince Rupert. After the end of the civil wars he entered the Parliamentary forces with the rank of lieutenant. He enjoyed the patronage of Henry Cromwell, who made him a justice of the peace. While on a visit to Lancashire, he married a daughter of the Holcrofts, a prominent county family. With the Restoration, Blood lost his lands in Ireland, and, in an attempt to regain them, he fell to plotting with old Cromwellians. He entered into a conspiracy to seize Dublin Castle and the lord lieutenant, James Butler, duke of Ormonde. After the failure of this plot, Blood fled to the Netherlands, where he joined Fifth Monarchy men and other dissidents. He plotted

---

[71] F. P. and M. M. Verney, *Memoirs of the Verney Family during the Seventeenth Century*, 2 vols. (London, 1907), ii. 121, 348–63.

with them to seize Limerick and restore the Long Parliament, and he actually participated in the Pentland Rising of 1666 in Scotland. In 1667, Blood and fellow conspirators attacked a cavalry detachment escorting a friend, Capt. Mason, to York to stand trial. On this occasion, Blood shot several soldiers and was wounded himself.[72]

Blood never forgot his feud with the duke of Ormonde, and, in December 1670, he and five others kidnapped Ormonde as he was returning to Clarendon House, his residence near St James's Palace. Ormonde, it appears, was to be taken to Tyburn Hill, where the kidnappers intended to hang him. Despite his age, the duke fought back and escaped. Ormonde's son publicly attributed this kidnapping plot to the second duke of Buckingham, one of Ormonde's political opponents.[73] Alan Marshal thinks that this was likely to have been the case. Buckingham had connections with various radicals and republicans, and he may also have had a hand in removing Ormonde from office in Ireland in 1669. Dr Marshall further thinks that Buckingham had hand-picked Blood for the assassination of Ormonde because of his reputation as a skilful operator. Even more startling is the possibility that the king and his mistress, Buckingham's cousin Barbara Villiers, countess of Castlemaine, were involved in the plot against Ormonde.[74]

A few months later, in May 1671, Blood carried out his most daring exploit—the theft of the royal crown and sceptre of England from the Tower of London. Blood contrived this escapade by impersonating a clergyman and pretending to arrange a marriage between his nephew and the daughter of the keeper of the king's regalia. Blood requested that the keeper show him the crown jewels, and then he and his nephew (actually his son, who was a highwayman by trade) took the crown and sceptre, stabbed the keeper, and escaped. They were soon caught, and, when examined, Blood declared that he would

---

[72] DNB, sub Thomas Blood (1618?–1680); [H.R.,] Remarks on the Life of the Fam'd Mr. Blood (2nd edn.; London, 1680) [Wing H113], 5–6; W. C. Abbott, Colonel Thomas Blood, Crown Stealer, 1618–1680 (New Haven, 1911), 20–5. The most complete account of Blood is found in Alan Marshall, Intelligence and Espionage in the Reign of Charles II, 1660–1685 (Cambridge, 1994), 186–223.

[73] [H.R.,] Remarks on the Life of . . . Blood, 8–9; Abbott, Colonel Thomas Blood, 10–20; Conway Letters: The Correspondence of Anne, Viscountess Conway, Henry Moore and their Friends, 1642–1684, ed. Marjorie Hope Nicholson (New Haven, 1930), 325–6.

[74] Alan Marshall, 'Colonel Thomas Blood and the Restoration Political Scene', HJ 32.3 (1989), 561–82, esp. 565–7.

speak only with the king. After being examined by the duke of York, Blood was granted an interview with the king, who, for reasons that are far from clear, pardoned Blood of all his numerous felonies, returned his Irish estates, and gave him a pension and a court office. One possible explanation is that the king admired Blood's audacity, and Buckingham intervened to secure a pardon. The more likely explanation is that Blood was already retained in the government's pay by Sir Joseph Williamson from the early 1670s to spy on those Puritans and old Cromwellians who were thought to be conspiring with the Dutch. Blood's ability to detach leading members of these conspiracies was simply too valuable to allow him to hang.[75]

This was not the only instance where Charles II overlooked notorious crimes and subverted justice for reasons of state. The murder of Thomas Thynne, esq., a Whig member of Parliament, provides anther example. Thynne was murdered by two foreign mercenary officers and a servant as he rode in his carriage through a London street near Charing Cross on 12 February 1681/2. The assassination of Thynne was procured by Count Karl-Johann von Königsmarck, the 24-year-old scion of a prominent Brandenburg–Swedish family,[76] who had been a suitor to Elizabeth Percy, Lady Ogle, the only daughter of the heiress of the earl of Northumberland.[77] Lady Ogle had chosen instead to marry Thynne, which sent Königsmarck into a jealous rage. The three persons who carried out the assassination included

[75] [H.R.,] *Remarks on the Life of . . . Blood*, 11–12; Abbott, *Colonel Thomas Blood*, 67–81; Marshall, 'Colonel Thomas Blood and the Restoration Political Scene', 567–9; K. H. D. Haley, *William of Orange and the English Opposition, 1672–4* (Oxford, 1953), 65–6.
Andrew Marvell the poet, never a lover of the Restoration Anglican Church, in his satyrical 'Epigram upon Blood's Attempt to Steal the Crown', made much of the fact that Blood disguised himself as a parson (*Complete Poetry*, ed. George de F. Lord (New York, 1968), 193).
Blood also seems to have obtained a commission for his son, who was a captain in John Foulkes's Regiment in 1692, when he became implicated in the robbery of a mail coach by a group of highwaymen, who stole £500 being dispatched to Portsmouth to pay the regiment before it was to sail for the West Indies (Luttrell, *Brief Historical Relation*, iii. 1). Another son, Holcroft Blood, was acquitted after being tried for robbing the mail on another occasion. He later became a noted military engineer and was promoted to the rank of brigadier general (*DNB*, *sub* Holcroft Blood (1660–1707)).
[76] The Königsmarcks were descended from Count Hans-Christoph von Königsmarck, who had commanded the left wing of the Swedish forces at the Battle of Breitenfeld in 1642.
[77] *Memoirs of Sir John Reresby*, ed. Browning, 249–57; Luttrell, *Brief Historical Relation*, i. 167–8.

Capt. Christopher Vratz, a German mercenary from Pomerania and sometime highwayman in Poland, who had once been a servant of Königsmarck and his uncle and had led the forlorn hope at the Siege of Mons in 1678, where the prince of Orange commended his bravery and made him a lieutenant in his guards. The king of Sweden afterwards gave him command of a troop of horse. John Stern, the second culprit, was a Swedish lieutenant who had met Königsmarck while serving in the army of Louis XIV, and George Boroski was Vratz's Polish servant, who actually fired the blunderbuss into Thynne's coach and killed him.[78]

Charles II was concerned about how this matter was handled, not only because of the diplomatic implications, but also because Thynne had been an adherent of the duke of Monmouth, and Charles feared that the anti-court faction would attempt to stir up trouble over this incident. Sir John Reresby was a newly appointed justice of the peace for Middlesex and Westminster, and the king sent him, together with Monmouth and Charles, Lord Mordaunt, to apprehend the murderers. The Swedish lieutenant led them to Vratz's lodgings, and he, in turn, identified Königsmarck, who was caught a week later in Gravesend while attempting to flee overseas. He was the brought before the Privy Council and examined. Königsmarck denied complicity in the murder.[79] Königsmarck's uncle Otto-Wilhelm, the governor of Swedish Pomerania, was about to marry the aunt of the king of Sweden, and Charles I and Reresby conspired to get Königsmarck indicted as an accessary to the murder rather than a principal. Solomon de Foubert or Faubert, the Huguenot proprietor of a French academy for gentlemen in London, where Königsmarck's younger brother, Philipp-Christoph, was a pupil, appears to have exerted diplomatic pressure on Reresby on behalf of the Swedish king. Thynne's friends and relatives had undertaken 'a very strict prosecution' against the defendants. At the latter's request they were tried before a jury composed of six Englishmen and six strangers

[78] *A True Account of the Last Speeches, Confessions and Execution of Christopher Vrats, George Boriskie and John Stern* (London, 1682) [Wing T2380A], 1–4; *An Account of the Trial and Examination of Count Conningsmark* (London, 1682) [Wing A412A], 1–2; Marshall, *Intelligence and Espionage in the Reign of Charles II,* 279–80, 286–7.

[79] *A True Account of the Discovering and Apprehending of Count Conningsmark* (London, 1682) [Wing T2364], 1–2; *A True Account of the Apprehending and Taking of Count Koningsmark* (London, 1682) [Wing T2341], 1–2.

at the Old Bailey; Königsmarck was acquitted and the other three defendants sentenced to hang.[80]

At his trial, Capt. Vratz stated that, having been a servant to the Königsmarcks, he 'thought himself bound in point of honour to take the quarrel upon himself'. He had intended to challenge Thynne to a duel, but apparently the latter refused the challenge. Later, Vratz stated that it was the custom in his country 'to pistol anyone who refuses a challenge'. John Evelyn, along with many other notables, talked with Vratz before his execution; Vratz told Evelyn that 'dying' was something that he 'did not value a rush, and [he] hoped and believed that God would deal with him like a gentleman'.[81] Understandably, the friends of Thynne among the adherents of the duke of Monmouth were dismayed that the count had escaped justice. Lords Cavendish and Mordaunt sent a challenge to Königsmarck, but the two were prevented by the secretary of state from meeting Königsmarck. The count was in Paris in August 1682 when Colonel MacCarty, Lord Cavendish's second, again told Königsmarck that Cavendish was prepared 'to meet him anywhere', but the count pleaded that he was an officer in the French army and 'the laws were very severe against duelling in France'.[82]

Like many spectators at the execution of Königsmarck's henchmen, John Evelyn thought that Capt. Vratz went to his execution 'like an undaunted hero', but he regarded Königsmarck as a 'base coward'.[83] Reresby thought Vratz's 'whole carriage, from his first being apprehended till his last, relished more of gallantry than religion'.[84] Lieut. Stern's confession was taken down by Bishop Burnet while the former was still in prison. Stern said that he was the bastard son of a Swedish count and had been a soldier throughout Europe for twenty-three of his forty-two years. At the time unemployed, he had come to London hoping to enlist in the guards.[85]

---

[80] *A True Account of the Last Speeches, Confession and Execution of Christopher Vrats, George Boriskie and John Stern*, 1–4.
For a discussion of 'Monsieur Faubert's Academy', see Aylward, *English Master of Arms*, ch. viii, esp. 101–2.

[81] *The Diary of John Evelyn*, ed. E. S. de Beer, 6 vols. (Oxford, 1955), iv. 273; *An Account of the Trial and Examination of Count Conningsmark*, 1–2; *The Last Confession . . . of Lieutenant John Stern* (London, 1682), repr. in *The Harleian Miscellany*, ed. W. Oldys and T. Park, 10 vols. (London, 1808–13), ix. 9–45.

[82] Luttrell, *Brief Historical Relation*, i. 174, 210.

[83] *Diary of John Evelyn*, ed. de Beer, iv. 273.

[84] *Memoirs of Sir John Reresby*, ed. Browning, 257.

[85] *The Last Confession . . . of Lieutenant John Stern*, in *Harleian Miscellany*, ix. 10.

When one considers the tendency of martialists to employ the language of the sword, to hold courts, lawyers, and negotiated settlements in contempt, to assert themselves in a highly competitive manner, and to fashion larger-than-life images of themselves, it is little wonder that the rechivalrization of aristocratic culture and, to a certain extent, popular culture spawned numerous acts of violence. One of the characteristics of martial culture in the seventeenth century was a strong tendency to view war in personal and individualistic terms, thus obscuring the boundary between wars undertaken by authority of the prince or the state and the pursuit of private quarrels to vindicate honour or to seek revenge. The adherence of British and Irish swordsmen to a European martial culture and their service in foreign armies and distant garrisons isolated them from the mainstream of life at home, and many of them assumed that English or Scots law did not apply to them when punishing inferiors or persons whose behaviour they found offensive. They had their code of conduct, which was based solely on honour, and, even in persons who had committed what magistrates regarded as criminal acts, their courage in the face of death on the gallows could stir admiration in those who condemned their violence and lawlessness. Moreover, officers and soldiers who had fought in the civil wars or foreign wars sometimes acquired a taste for plunder, and, when unemployed, might be tempted to turn to crimes such as highway robbery.

The monarchs of Europe realized that they needed the assistance of aristocracies with martial spirit to raise, command, and officer their armies, and for that reason they understood that they must indulge the violent proclivities of this class as long as such acts did not threaten political disloyalty. In the British Isles, this degree of indulgence varied among the monarchs of the seventeenth century. Elizabeth I and James I professed not to tolerate such expressions of violence, but, in fact, tacitly accepted limited expressions of violence if suitably masqued and contained. Persons committing murder under the Stuart monarchs were routinely pardoned for the first offence unless the circumstances of the crime were especially outrageous. Charles II, the most indulgent of all the Stuart rulers, was quite prepared to subvert justice for reasons of state or to avoid offending friendly sovereign powers. William III was the least indulgent of the Stuart monarchs towards this sort of crime and maintained rigourous discipline within his armies. Otherwise, it is hard to avoid the conclusion that the toleration of aristocratic crime by the Stuart monarchs together with the leniency of judges and juries towards aristocratic swordplay contributed to these manifestations of violence—most notably in Restoration London. In Parliament, the House of Lords could never agree on any legislation that would curtail the cult of duelling, and, as the case of Lord Mohun demonstrates, their Lordships, when sitting in judgment upon a criminous peer, were quite prepared to ignore evidence that Mohun was a psychopath in order to preserve the aristocratic privilege of vindicating honour.

## Feuding

In Ireland and Scotland, societies that were driven by an honour culture and a martial ethos retained their habits of pursuing private warfare on a collective basis. The lords and chiefs of Ireland outside the Pale, the Anglo-Scottish Border, and the Highlands and the Isles of Scotland were able to raise sizeable private armies until the end of the sixteenth century and these areas continued to be disturbed by blood feuds, reiving, cattle raiding, and the like (not to mention rebellion) throughout the seventeenth century. The acquisitiveness of the New English planters in Ireland and the growing intolerance of Lowland Scots for this kind of disorder, when backed by James VI and I's policy of imposing civility upon persons and societies, gradually closed the frontiers of the British Isles and limited the scale and incidence of private warfare during the seventeenth century, but it did not disappear. The displacement of tenants and landless persons in these areas, especially during the Wars of the Three Kingdoms, led to the persistence of banditry and feuding (which we can often recognize as a kind of guerrilla warfare) by bands of woodkernes in Ireland (later called tories and rapparees), cateran bands of 'broken men' in the Highlands, and reivers (later 'mosstroopers') on the Borders. All these forms of disorder and private war arose from the importance that lords and chieftains and their followers attached to being able to raise private armies, to seek revenge in quarrels, to display good lordship, and to offer seemingly limitless hospitality.[86]

---

[86] Jane H. Ohlmeyer, ' "Civilizing of those Rude Parts": Colonization within Britain and Ireland, 1580s–1640s', in Nicholas Canny (ed.), *The Origins of Empire: British Overseas Enterprise to the Close of the Seventeenth Century* (Oxford, 1998), 128–9, 143–4.

To speak of these activities as private war in no way implies that this was submilitary combat or primitive war, and the comparison of Celtic clans and kinship groups to aboriginal peoples is of limited usefulness. Primitive warfare does not employ tactical operations, and is regarded by Turney-High as being beneath the 'military horizon'. Although the Celtic and Border clans may have temporarily lagged behind some of the technological innovations of the military revolution, they did employ tactics that were well adapted to the terrain and the lack of good overland communications. There existed more than sufficient social control to sustain organized and cohesive military operations over extended periods of time, and these Celtic warriors and Borderers knew how to feed themselves when fighting.[87] What they were unable to do was to secure clear-cut victories, but their societies were so oriented towards making war that such an end was probably inconceivable.

Writing during the Scottish Enlightenment, when the Scots had learned to harness their energies to more productive and less destructive pursuits, Adam Ferguson observed that man is by nature competitive and 'his sports are frequently an image of war'. The Scots had long been addicted to violent and highly competitive sports such as football, archery, and feats of strength such as tossing the caber. Hunting and similar activities—especially in the Highlands—when joined with hosting, or a summoning of a chief's armed followers in full battle array, encouraged the military ethos. Attitudes towards cattle raiding were one of the main causes of contention between Highlanders, who viewed it as a game with a set of rules and a spirit of redistributive justice, and Lowlanders, who regarded it as plain theft of individual property. Highlanders felt justified in raiding Lowlanders' cattle because they viewed lowlanders as deficient in courage and believed that this gave them a right to plunder Lowlanders. In contemplating the connection between war and sport, Adam Ferguson observed that man 'was not meant to live forever, and even his love of amusement has opened a path that leads to the grave'.[88]

[87] H. H. Turney-High, *Primitive War: Its Practice and Concepts* (2nd edn.; Columbia, SC, 1971), 21–2, 30; Keith M. Brown, *Noble Society in Scotland: Wealth, Family and Culture, from Reformation to Revolution* (Edinburgh, 2000), 226; Jane Dawson, 'The Gaidhealtachd and the Emergence of the Scottish Highlands', in Breadan Bradshaw and Peter Roberts (eds.), *British Consciousness and Identity: The Making of Britain, 1537–1707* (Cambridge, 1998), 286–7.

[88] Adam Ferguson, *An Essay on the History of Civil Society* (Edinburgh, 1767; repr. New York, 1971), 35–6; Brown, *Noble Society in Scotland*, 226; Dawson, 'The Gaidhealtachd and the Emergence of the Scottish Highlands', 286–7.

Aristocratic feuding had by no means disappeared from England at the beginning of the seventeenth century, although it was usually masked as something less naughty that would incur lesser legal penalties than those prescribed for high treason or felony. In the fielden areas of England, the gentry often procured anti-enclosure riots against their neighbours in pursuit of feuds. In sylvan regions, poaching affrays were a usual means of visiting retribution upon a rival, which is undoubtedly one of the reasons why the Jacobean Court of Star Chamber devoted a seemingly disproportionate amount of time to prosecuting unlawful hunting. Hunting and warfare were regarded as being 'symbolically interchangeable', and aristocratic poaching wars in England were pursued with much military ritual, as Star Chamber records vividly indicate. A poaching raid upon a rival's deer park was often used as a challenge to a duel, and to refuse such a challenge was regarded as cowardly and subjected one to the scorn of neighbours.[89]

One of the more noteworthy feuds in early modern England was that between the Lisles and the Berkeleys, which arose over a disputed inheritance during the Wars of the Roses and was inherited by Robert Dudley, earl of Leicester, and Henry, eleventh Lord Berkeley. In the time of Queen Elizabeth I, this feud, which was part of what has been described as the longest lawsuit in English history, was prosecuted in the Vale of Berkeley by means of poaching wars. On one occasion in 1572, Queen Elizabeth and Leicester 'havocked' Berkeley's deer park at Berkeley Castle because he was not at home to offer hospitality. This feud finally petered out in 1610.[90] Another important feud of late Elizabethan England was that between the Talbots, earls of Shrewsbury, and the Stanhopes of Shelford, Notts., which comprehended armed confrontations between parties of up to 150 retainers, poaching wars, and single combats. It seems to have originated in a broken marriage contract, and it subsumed a number of lesser quarrels in the East Midlands.[91] Except for the depredations

[89] R. B. Manning, *Village Revolts: Social Protest and Popular Disturbances in England, 1509–1640* (Oxford, 1988), 93; id., *Hunters and Poachers*, ch. 2; Walter Burkert, *Homo Necans: The Anthropology of Ancient Greek Sacrificial Ritual and Myth*, trans. P. Bing (Berkeley, Calif., 1983), 47.

[90] Manning, *Hunters and Poachers*, 136.

[91] W. T. MacCaffrey, 'Talbot and Stanhope: An Episode in Elizabethan Politics', *BIHR* 33 (1960), 79–85; Gervase Holles, *Memorials of the Holles Family, 1493–1656*, ed. A. C. Wood (CS, 3rd ser., 60; London, 1937), 90–2; J. P. Cooper, 'Retainers in Tudor England', in G. E. Aylmer and J. S. Morrill (eds.), *Land, Men and Beliefs: Studies in Early Modern History* (London, 1983), 95.

of poaching gangs, which continued for another century and more, private warfare in England at the beginning of the seventeenth century, it must be said, was but a shadow of the baronial anarchy of the fifteenth century. England had become a civil society, and that underlined the difference between England and Lowland Scotland, on the one hand, and the Scottish Borders and Highlands and Ireland beyond the Pale, on the other.

In the late Middle Ages and continuing into the sixteenth century, Irish and Scottish Gaeldom had shared a common classical language in which bardic poets depicted and praised the epic heroes and warrior traditions of their lords and chiefs. The English regarded the Gaelic or Old Irish as a barbarian rather than a civil society— one characterized by perpetual warfare. Irish society, they further concluded, was supported by a largely pastoral economy, which the English, who were experiencing an agricultural revolution, thought bred idleness and contentiousness. Land was of little value to the Irish, since they were pastoralists who practised transhumance; cattle were the commodities they valued the most, and private warfare in Ireland usually centred around making off with someone else's herds. If successful, cattle raiding was always followed by prolonged feasting. In war, the Irish chieftains and lords were more interested in acquiring followers than land or towns (of which there were few in Ireland). The remedy, argued the New English, was to destroy the Irish chieftains, their bards, and armed retainers, and bend their tenants to the plough.[92]

Irish society was based upon lineage and organized into clans. So powerful was this corporate identity that newcomers, such as the Vikings and the Anglo-Normans or Old English, were rapidly assimilated into Gaelic culture and clan-based society, which was political in nature and looked to the lord or chief for justice or vengeance and protection. However, the clan system excluded humble folk who did not belong to any social group other than their own families. The lesser folk were squeezed out by the sons of the chiefs and warriors (including the numerous bastard sons in what more closely resembled polygamous rather than monogamous marriage institutions). The

---

[92] Dawson, 'Gaidhealtachd and the Emergence of the Scottish Highlands', 260; J. M. Hill, *Celtic Warfare, 1595–1763* (Edinburgh, 1986), 17–18; Katherine Simms, 'Warfare in the Medieval Gaelic Lordships', *IS* 12 (1975–6), 98–9; Ohlmeyer, ' "Civilizing of those Rude Parts" ', 124–5.

Irish chieftains were warlords and never sought to become feudal lords. These warlords were numerous and there was little effective restraint upon their ability to make war until the beginning of the English reconquest of Ireland in the sixteenth century. The lack of a settled system of inheritance promoted much violent conflict, since any grandson of a chief was theoretically eligible for that position if he possessed the might to claim it. Moreover, native Irish law lacked any concept of criminality, and every injury was treated as a kind of tort that could be compensated by payments to the injured party rather than by punishments. Irish law did not have a category of felonies and did not impose the death penalty except on outlaws.[93]

The nature of the terrain did much to shape war in Ireland. The methods of warfare of northern Europe, emphasizing cavalry tactics, were more suitable for fighting on champion fields and plains; the Irish way of war was better adapted to the bogs, mountains, and forests that covered much of Ireland. Here the foot soldier had to bear the brunt of the fighting. Although the Gaels were skilled in the use of the bow, it was a weapon that was always secondary to the sword and the axe. The Irish and the Highland Scots thus had no chivalric tradition, and cavalry played a minor role in Irish warfare. Late medieval Irish chieftains avoided pitched battles until they knew that their enemy was weakened, and instead took advantage of the cover provided by the terrain to ambush their enemies. Thus, the Irish employed a kind of irregular warfare that observers who were used to more conventional forms of fighting regarded as barbaric. Although pitched battles and cavalry charges may have been more typical of armed conflict on the Great Northern European Plain, in fact, where centralized government was lacking and terrain was difficult, most armed conflict took the form of small-scale private wars between local lords. In Ireland, cattle raiding was the most typical form of conflict, and it more closely resembled the feuds or small-scale private warfare

---

[93] Kenneth Nicholls, *Gaelic and Gaelicized Ireland in the Middle Ages* (Dublin 1972), 8–11, 21–6, 53–4.

In his appeal to the king of Spain to drive the English out of Ireland, Philip O'Sullivan Beare, who served as an officer in the Spanish armed forces, blamed Irish descent into incivility on the 'wars . . . of the English which for more than four hundred years have reduced the sacred island to a rude and uncultivated place' (*Historiae Catholicae Iberiae compendium* (Lisbon, 1621), quoted in Claire Carroll, 'Irish and Spanish Cultural and Political Relations in the Work of Philip O'Sullivan Beare', in Hiram Morgan (ed.), *Political Ideology in Ireland, 1541–1641* (Dublin, 1999), 234.

of the mountainous areas of southern Europe than the more developed kind of warfare found in England or northern Europe.[94]

The cattle raid usually provoked a counter-attack by the victims, who would seek revenge. Thus the raiders had to expect to fight a rearguard action, which is where the Irish lords and chieftains and their retainers might be found mounted on light horses. These horsemen wore chain mail and round helmets and carried a thin lance 12 feet long. Their appearance, method of fighting, and war cry reminded foreign visitors of Saracens. Irish cattle raids were typically carried out by bands numbering fewer than 150 warriors and a few horsemen. The Irish did not kill women and children, and the numbers killed in their wars were small. The Gaelic warrior was driven by personal honour, and was not amenable to discipline. This kind of private war, which aimed only at capturing cattle and forcing the enemy to submit (when he would be allowed to buy some of his cattle back), persisted as late as 1692.[95]

The martial ethos was dominant in Gaelic aristocratic culture and was sustained by the bardic poet, who validated the rule of the lords and chiefs by recording the semi-mythological history of the warrior-chief (who was also his patron) and his descent. This was done by demonstrating that his deeds had been prophesied or foreshadowed by the actions of other great warriors. A perpetual state of war was generated by the belief that the chieftainship of a clan belonged to the most powerful and that a particularly valiant and victorious leader of a clan was entitled to subdue and possess all Ireland. The right to rule was based upon conquest, and, although some poets recognized that in the past foreigners had invaded and partially conquered Ireland, they assumed that such foreigners had always been assimilated and Gaelicized like the Vikings and Anglo-Normans. Michelle O Riordan has argued that this tendency to take the long view of the impact of foreign incursions failed mentally to prepare the Irish lords and chieftains and the Gaelic literati for the determination of the English to complete their conquest and to extirpate Gaelic culture and Catholicism that came in the sixteenth and seventeenth

[94] Simms, 'Warfare in the Medieval Gaelic Lordships', 98–108; James Michael Hill, 'The Distinctiveness of Gaelic Warfare, 1400–1750', *European History Quarterly*, 22.3 (1992), 327–8; John Larner, *The Lords of the Romagna: Romagnol Society and the Origins of the Signorie* (Ithaca, NY, 1965), 30–1, 67–74.

[95] Simms, 'Warfare in the Medieval Gaelic Lordships', 98–108; Hill, 'Distinctiveness of Gaelic Warfare', 327–8.

centuries.[96] Marc Caball disputes this argument and insists that many Gaelic poets simply ignored the successive waves of conquerors and continued to justify the political hegemony of the Gaelic lords. Poets were accorded a sacred status inherited from the pagan past—a position in Irish society comparable to that of the priest. Although the professional poet's world collapsed in the seventeenth century, the spread of literacy among the aristocracy and the appearance of amateur vernacular Gaelic poets continued the traditions of Gaelic poetry, and, when combined with the intellectual energy of the Catholic Reformation, articulated a more modern sense of Irish identity.[97]

In any case, the English authorities of Dublin Castle regarded Gaelic poets, together with bards and minstrels, as subversive, and proscribed them along with vagrants. For their part, the poets were hostile to English culture and the use of the English language. Laoiseach Mac anBhaird attacked Gaelic Irish noblemen who abandoned the traditional garb of men of their rank for the dress of English courtiers with coifed hair and rapiers at their side. The Gaelic swordsman wore an Irish sword at his side and was always prepared to engage in battle, according to Mac anBhaird's idealized stereotype. Other poets criticized the Gaelic Irish nobility for accepting English titles or not offering enough resistance to preserve spiritual and political autonomy in Ireland. In a rare moment of candour for a Gaelic poet, Aonghus Ó Dálaigh, while inviting the Irish to rebel against the English, admitted that the Irish had been defeated because God was punishing them for their sins. In another poem by Eochaidh Ó hEódhusa, we find a bardic poet admitting that war had always been endemic in Ireland because the mutual hatred between the Saxons and the Gaels made conflict inevitable. Yet he accepts the inevitability of conflict without attempting to explain it or proposing a remedy. The purpose of traditional bardic poetry was simply to keep Gaelic martial culture alive among the Old Irish and Anglo-Norman aristocracies, which helps to explain official hostility to them.[98]

---

[96] Michelle O Riordan, *The Gaelic Mind and the Collapse of the Gaelic World* (Cork, 1990), 4–9; David Edwards, 'Ideology and Experience: Spenser's *View* and Martial Law in Ireland', in Morgan (ed.), *Political Ideology in Ireland, 1541–1641*, 127–30.

[97] Marc Caball, *Poets and Politics: Continuity and Reaction in Irish Poetry, 1585–1625* (Notre Dame, Ind., 1998), 1–9; Nicholls, *Gaelic and Gaelicized Ireland in the Middle Ages*, 82–3.

[98] Caball, *Poets and Politics*, 40–2, 47, 54–5, 70–3.

The Old English nobility had once functioned as mediators between the English government and the Gaelic Irish. However, in the late sixteenth century they were influenced by the ideas of the Catholic Reformation, and James Eustace, third Viscount Baltinglass, and Gerald Fitzgerald, fourteenth earl of Desmond, led a rebellion against the New English between 1579 and Desmond's death in 1583. This fall from 'civility' destroyed the privileged position of the Old English lords, who were no longer trusted to summon the 'general hosting' of their armed tenants and retainers in order to maintain order among the Gaelic Irish. It was now assumed that only the New English could be trusted to defend Ireland. The Old Irish lords and chiefs and their warriors were driven into the woods and bogs and came to be regarded as nothing more than 'common outlaws and woodkernes'.[99] The Gaelic Irish who were dispossessed by the New English plantations and who organized themselves into bands to fight the expansion of English rule were called 'tories'. The label was later applied to the guerrilla fighters of the Catholic Confederacy during the Irish civil wars whom the Cromwellian forces refused to treat as anything but outlaws. These irregular forces never wholly disappeared during the Restoration, and, reinforced by the remnants and deserters of the Jacobite armies during the Williamite wars, came to be called rapparees. Because the rapparees provisioned themselves by cattle raiding, it was assumed that they were nothing but common bandits.[100]

The Anglo-Scottish Border may not have been part of the Celtic world, but the English and Scottish Borderers shared many characteristics with the Gaelic Irish and the Highland Scots. The inhabitants of the Scottish frontier were bound to their chiefs, lords, and lairds by strong loyalties and ties of kinship that resembled those of the Highland clans. These allegiances were based not only upon sharing the same surname, but also (in Scotland) on bonds of manrent, which obliged members of the same kinship group to support their lords

---

[99] Nicholas Canny, *Making Ireland British, 1580–1650* (Oxford, 2001), 124–7; Victor Treadwell, *Buckingham and Ireland, 1616–1628* (Dublin, 1998), 32; Caball, *Poets and Politics*, 54–5.

[100] Allan I. Macinnes, *Clanship, Commerce and the House of Stuart, 1603–1788* (East Linton, East Lothian, 1996), 120 n.–121 n.; Éamonn Ó Ciardha, 'Tories and Mosstroopers in Scotland and Ireland in the Interregnum: A Political Dimension', in J. R. Young (ed.), *Celtic Dimensions of the British Civil Wars*, (Edinburgh, 1997), 142–9; *The Journal of John Stevens Containing a Brief Account of the War in Ireland, 1689–1691*, ed. R. H. Murray (Oxford, 1912), 61–2.

and chiefs in military or legal actions against all except the king. It was in the nature of a lineage society that the Borderers were prone to disorder and hostile to government centralization. National allegiances were undeveloped. Contemporary observers saw little difference between the English and Scots Borderers. They were both skilled horsemen, hardened by perpetual warfare, and remained attached to old feudal families. Most tenants in northern England held their lands by military tenures. The English and Scots Borderers were addicted to blood feuds among themselves as well as cross-border skirmishes. The chiefs and lords kept alive the traditional martial spirit and enhanced the bonds of kinship by hunting and hawking with their followers. Living as they did on a perpetual wartime footing, those who lived close to the Borders were disinclined to invest time and effort in tilling the soil, because such effort would be wasted if they were driven off their lands. Many of those who had been dispossessed turned to cattle raiding and robbery, and these injuries could lead to prolonged blood feuds. Although they appear to have had no moral compunction about murder, they normally did not wantonly kill because they feared the consequences in time of war.[101]

The Borderers, especially those who lived at the higher elevations, were semi-nomadic; they followed their horses and cattle, which were often stolen from Lowlanders, into summer pastures. Although careless in regard to other peoples' property, they had a highly developed sense of honour and thought it shameful to break one's word—except in dealing with one's enemy. John Leslie, the Catholic bishop of Ross, said the Borderers did not believe in private property: 'They have a persuasion that all property is common by the law of nature, and is therefore liable to be appropriated by them in their necessity.' Bishop Leslie, who wrote at the beginning of the Scottish Reformation, also noted that the Borderers were slow to accept the reformed religion and always offered thanksgiving prayers when they returned from a successful raid. Like the Gaelic Irish and the Highland Scots, they also indulged in extravagant feasting on such occasions. Border reiving, or banditry, reached its zenith in the sixteenth century, when

---

[101] Thomas I. Rae, *The Administration of the Scottish Frontier, 1513–1603* (Edinburgh, 1966), 8–9; D. L. W. Tough, *The Last Years of a Frontier: A History of the Borders during the Reign of Elizabeth* (Oxford, 1928), 31–6; C. J. Neville, 'Local Sentiment and the "National Enemy" in Northern England in the Later Middle Ages', *JBS* 35 (Oct. 1996), 420–1, 437; M. E. James, *Change and Continuity in the Tudor North: The Rise of Thomas, Lord Wharton* (Borthwick Papers, 27; York, 1965), 3, 6, 7–8.

bands of English and Scots Borderers lived by cattle raiding and feuding across the Border and amongst one another, practising extortion and arson, kidnapping for ransom, and even murder. This was a classic kind of private warfare and had little to do with declared wars between the rulers of England and Scotland. The Anglo-Scottish Border had an indistinct boundary and its inhabitants frequently evaded royal justice until the end of the sixteenth century.[102]

Although the smallhold tenants suffered the most from reiving, aristocratic feuds underlay most of this banditry. Bands of reivers engaging in cross-border raids usually comprised 100 or more men and were often procured by Border lairds and lords if not actually led by them. At the beginning of the seventeenth century, a survey conducted by the Scottish Parliament of 1587 discovered that tenants of the estates of twenty-two Border lairds and lords had been involved in reiving or had been raided by reivers. The Somervilles were an old Border family who were given to pursuing blood feuds about several disputed inheritances. Their declining fortunes drove some of them into reiving. James, fifth Baron Somerville of Cambusnethen, was declared a fugitive from justice and a rebel because he spent an extended period of time away from home in his youth associating with Border riders. As private war receded on the Borders in the early seventeenth century, the Somervilles gradually recovered their social and economic position by serving in the French and Venetian armies.[103]

The season for reiving was concentrated in the autumn and spring, when longer nights afforded cover for cattle raids. Late September to early November was the best time, because the fells were dry and the cattle well fed; the depths of winter brought severe weather and the animals would have grown weaker. The smaller raids were carried out by night, and the skill with which the captain of a band of reivers navigated the hidden byways and dales of the Cheviot Hills under cover of darkness and mist and returned with his purloined herds shaped his reputation. William Camden remarked upon the eloquence of reivers on the rare occasions when they were

---

[102] G. M. Fraser, *The Steel Bonnets: The Story of the Anglo-Scottish Border Reivers* (London, 1971), 3–7, 44–9; John Leslie, bishop of Ross, *The Historie of Scotland*, trans John Dalrymple, 2 vols. (Scottish Text Society, nos. 5, 14, 19, 34; Edinburgh, 1888–95; repr. New York, 1968), 97–8.

[103] James [by right 11th Lord] Somerville, *Memorie of the Somervilles* [ed. Sir Walter Scott], 2 vols. (Edinburgh, 1815), ii. 91–2; *DNB, sub* James Somerville (1632–90).

caught and brought to justice.[104] Border outlaws could be captured only by large-scale campaigns led by nobles with their retinues. The problem was that, in the absence of professional military forces, the marcher lords and wardens often had to employ thieves to catch thieves. These punitive expeditions differed from the usual cross-border reiving in that they were carried out in broad daylight and conducted like formal military campaigns with careful attention given to planning, strategy, and the need to maintain reserves. Musters for punitive expeditions on the Scottish side of the Border were ordered ten times between 1580 and 1599. Frequently, the cooperation of the English Border officials was requested to prevent reivers from fleeing south. In August 1598, four Scottish lairds, in a scenario reminiscent of the Border ballad *Chevy Chase*, led a party of 200 riders in a hunting foray across the Border to present a challenge to fight. Sir Robert Carey (later first earl of Monmouth) gathered together 400 English Borderers to confront them, but he had trouble controlling his men as they fell to pursuing private feuds, and four or five Scots were killed.[105]

Conferences between the English and Scots wardens of the Border marches were often tense, because their retinues were made up of reivers spoiling for a fight. These parleys were usually called to demand that the other warden deliver up notorious bandits, and the members of each warden's retinue would be fearful that they might be among the ones named. On one such occasion in July 1575, Sir John Foster, warden of the English Middle March and governor of Berwick, met with one J. Carmichael, the warden of Liddesdale in Scotland, at Redsquire Hill. After an exchange of hot words about delivering up 'rank-riders' for justice, order broke down and the two bands fell to settling individual quarrels and plundering nearby pedlars. The Scots were reinforced by another band from Jedburgh, and the English put to flight. Sir George Heron, warden of Tynedale and Reddesdale, and others were slain, and Foster, Francis Russell,

---

[104] G. M. Fraser, *Steel Bonnets*, 91–3; Tough, *Last Years of a Frontier*, 48–9; Alan I. Macinnes, 'Crown, Clans and Fine: The Civilising of Scottish Gaeldom, 1587–1638', *Northern Scotland*, 13 (1983), 31.

[105] Rae, *Administration of the Scottish Frontier*, 123, 130, 134–6, 148–9; James, *Change and Continuity in the Tudor North*, 3–4; Manning, *Hunters and Poachers*, 49 and n.; *The Border Papers: Calendar of the Letters and Papers relating to the Affairs of the Borders of England and Scotland . . . 1560–1603*, ed. Joseph Bain, 2 vols. (Edinburgh, 1894–6), ii. 557, 559–61.

son of the earl of Bedford, and many other English were carried away
as prisoners by the Scots.[106]

One of the boldest raids ever carried out across the Border was
that led by Sir Walter Scott, the 'Bold Buccleuch' (later first Lord
Scott of Buccleuch), who was keeper of Liddesdale and a reiver himself. In 1596, William Armstrong of Kinmont, the most notorious
of the Border reivers, who was later to be romanticized in the ballad
'Kinmont Willie', was attending a truce parley when a band of English
raiders captured and imprisoned him in Carlisle Castle—a violation
of Border protocol. This brought a protest from Buccleuch, who took
it as a personal affront to his honour and demanded Armstrong's
release in a letter addressed to Thomas, tenth Lord Scrope, warden
of the English West March. Scrope refused to release Armstrong
and, with some justice but little prudence, regarded Buccleuch as no
better than a bandit. Buccleuch also appealed to Sir Robert Bowes,
the English ambassador to Scotland, who advised Scrope to release
Armstrong, but to no avail. It was then that Buccleuch planned and
carried out his daring raid on the formidable Carlisle Castle to rescue
Armstrong with the help of sympathizers on the English side of
the Border such as the Grahams of Eske, the Carletons, and soldiers
within the castle garrison. The raiding party was assembled under
cover of attending the Langholm Races, and the assault on the castle
was carried out that evening by a band of several hundred equipped
with scaling ladders. Buccleuch had shown himself to be a master
of guerrilla tactics, and he was later to become a superb soldier in
the Netherlands. The diplomatic consequences of the raid were
embarrassing to James VI, and Buccleuch accepted voluntary exile in
England in 1597. In 1603, as part of a scheme for Border pacification,
Buccleuch was allowed to raise a regiment of 2,000 Borderers for
service in the States' Army. After he had returned home from the wars
*circa* 1608, he helped to hunt down Border reivers, burnt their houses
and peel towers, and, after being granted immunity, conducted mass
executions of bandits.[107]

[106] William Camden, *The History of the Most Renowned and Victorious Princess
Elizabeth* (4th edn.; London, 1688; repr. New York, 1970), 210–11.

[107] G. M. Fraser, *Steel Bonnets*, 53, 102–3, 116–18, 329–45; *DNB, sub* Sir Walter
Scott, 1st Baron Scott of Buccleuch (1565–1611); GEC ii. 364; Steve Murdoch and
Alexia Grosjean, 'Scotland, Scandinavia and Northern Europe, 1580–1707' (database
@ www.abdn.ac.uk/history/datasets/ssne), no. 5010.

The Scottish Privy Council had determined that exile and service in foreign armies was a good solution to the problem of bandits and aggressive swordsmen. Among those who joined Sir Andrew Gray's Regiment for service in the Palatinate and Bohemia in 1620 were 120 'mosstropers' who were removed from the Scottish marches by order of the Privy Council. Sir James King, an Orkney Scot (later Baron Eythin in Scotland and Baron Sandshult in Sweden), was compelled to leave Scotland after he had killed a man in a feud. He later became a general in the Swedish army under Gustavus Adolphus. François de La Noue, the famous Huguenot soldier, commanded a force of five troops of Scottish cavalry in the Dutch army. Most of the gentlemen troopers who served under La Noue were in exile because they had engaged in feuds or duels having to do with personal reputation or disputed inheritances. Sir Roger Williams thought that they were 'resolute, faithful men of war, that fought either for religion or reputation, to maintain their words after the old Roman fashion'.[108]

It was necessary to pacify the Anglo-Scottish Borders not only because they had provided 'lurking places' for bandits and rebels such as James Hepburn, fourth earl of Bothwell, but also because they were perceived to be places where foreign powers could stir up mischief. The Elizabethan government thought some of the followers of Mary, queen of Scots, had conspired with the Spanish to cause incursions into Redesdale 'to divert Queen Elizabeth from the Low Country war'. The personal union of the Crowns of Scotland and England in 1603 lessened the likelihood of intervention by hostile foreign powers, but Border turbulence never completely disappeared. The English and Scottish governments simply ignored the problem after 1603.[109]

Scotland had been at peace with England since 1573, but was a more violent society in the late sixteenth century than had been the case since the fifteenth century. The moral authority of the Kirk had been weakened by the Reformation, and the monarchy was in a state of collapse under Mary Stuart. The number of Scots who had served in the French royal army had probably declined since the end of the 'auld alliance', and opportunities for service in the Scandinavian and

[108] James Grant, *Memoirs and Adventures of Sir John Hepburn* (Edinburgh, 1851), 8, 167; Murdoch and Grosjean, 'Scotland, Scandinavia and Northern Europe', no. 2814; Sir Roger Williams, *A Briefe Discourse of Warre* (London, 1590) [STC 25732], 32–3.
[109] Camden, *History* (1970 edn.), 302; Rae, *Administration of the Scottish Frontier*, 220.

Dutch armies were just beginning to open up. At the same time, individual Scots still possessed arms and resorted to their use frequently to settle private feuds until James VI began to bring the blood feud under control in the 1590s. The blood feud had been as prevalent in the Lowlands as in the Highlands in the sixteenth century, but it began to disappear in the former by the beginning of the seventeenth century.[110]

The eradication of the blood feud in Scotland was as intractable a problem as was the suppression of duelling in England. There is good reason for believing that the exile of swordsmen (or, if one prefers, the export of mercenary soldiers) from Scotland in the seventeenth century did more to curtail feuding than the exercise of royal justice. Moreover, those Scottish soldiers who survived the wars to come home seem to have brought back with them a taste for the Italian and French cult of the individual duel. Before then the feud was the usual way of settling questions of honour in Scotland. Revenge had always been considered honourable in itself, and it did not much matter whether revenge was obtained by open confrontation, ambush, or assassination. This was because revenge was a form of justice, and was associated with divine retribution. Thus, the Scottish blood feud never had formal rules like the Italian *duello*. Scottish law permitted the relatives of the person being avenged to accept compensation, but sometimes they could be satisfied only by blood vengeance. In seeking blood vengeance, it was preferable to draw the blood of the perpetrator of the evil deed being avenged, but if that was not possible the blood of a blood relative would do instead. This was because of the widely accepted belief that honour and dishonour were transmitted by blood. Violence directed against property could also accompany the blood feud, although blood vengeance was always preferred. Hence, in the Border and Highland regions, cattle raiding frequently accompanied feuding. While it was sometimes possible to settle a dispute by peaceful arbitration, the Scottish Crown lacked the means at hand to compel arbitration or acceptance of a judgment except by turning to some powerful member of the nobility. Whether the dispute was resolved by giving a nobleman with a private feudal jurisdiction a commission of 'fire and sword' to punish the perpetrator of the evil deed, or whether private vengeance was sought, violence was the outcome.[111]

[110] Brown, *Bloodfeud in Scotland*, 21–2, 266–8.
[111] Ibid. 26–33; Ohlmeyer, ' "Civilizing of those Rude Parts" ', 133.

Outside Edinburgh, justice, such as it was, was dispensed by territorial magnates and clan chieftains such as the earls and marquises of Argyll, the earls of Sutherland, and the earls of Seaforth, who possessed heritable jurisdictions as justiciars or sheriffs. There was no appeal from these private feudal courts to the Crown, and heritable jurisdictions were not abolished until 1747. During the seventeenth century, the Scottish Crown was little concerned with the quality of justice dispensed, but rather was mostly interested in insuring that the costs of justice were borne by the nobility and that the Crown received its share of the revenue from these courts. When a particular kindred or cateran band caused trouble by their feuding or banditry, the Crown could issue a commission of fire and sword to the chief or lord of the injured party, authorizing him to dispense summary justice. The possessor of such a commission and retinue would also be indemnified against any legal penalties for murder or destruction of property involved in carrying out the commission of fire and sword. Where depredations upon landed property were involved, such commissions almost invariably favoured landed magnates. These commissions of fire and sword were open to abuse of powers, but Professor Macinnes says they were more usually carried out with restraint.[112]

The blood feud had been part of the fabric of society in the ancient and medieval worlds, but it survived longer in Scotland than any other part of northern Europe. The power of the monarchy had decayed in late-medieval times when most of the Crown's resources were directed towards fighting the English rather than keeping order and dispensing justice or had been given away as rewards to followers among the nobility, so that the Scots nobility had gained the ascendancy and came to possess, as Patrick Abercrombie remarked, the 'nerves of war'. Consequently, their tenants were more subject to them than to the king. Although blood feuds were as prevalent in the Lowlands as in the Highlands, it proved more difficult to re-establish royal authority in the Highlands, and, consequently, feuding and banditry persisted longer there. Blood feuds also persisted longer in Scotland because of the survival of kindreds that were based on male descent to a greater degree than upon marital ties. The former tended to enhance motives of blood vengeance, while the latter usually diluted such motives. The kinship groups or clans were reinforced by

---

[112] Macinnes, *Clanship, Commerce and the House of Stuart*, 46–50.

182    THE DISCOURSE OF VIOLENCE

the feudal power of the nobility. Vengeance was always at hand as long as lords and clan chiefs retained private armies and could call upon their kindred. Keith Brown has identified 365 feuds between 1573 and 1625, with most of them occurring before 1610. While some feuds grew out of court politics, most were local and many occurred within kinship groups as well as between them. At their worst, as in the Huntly–Moray feud of the 1580s and 1590s, they could comprehend not only private vengeance, but also rebellion against the Crown, and the possibility of Spanish intervention in order to promote a Scottish Counter-Reformation as well as conspiracies to kidnap the king and assassinate the chancellor.[113]

The blood feud may have been in retreat in early modern Scotland, but banditry and cattle raiding continued to be a problem in the Highlands for the remainder of the sixteenth century. The Scottish Parliament of 1587 had determined that cateran bands had operated from or preyed upon the estates of 107 Highland lords and chiefs. Feuding—especially when it took the form of cattle raiding—was regarded as a kind of a game with mutually understood rules and 'was not reputed robbery'. However, such values and customs had been abandoned even in the Highlands by the end of the seventeenth century except among such notorious clans as the MacGregors. Since the judicial system remained decentralized and privatized, the Crown's policy was to compel the *fine*, or clan gentry, to become responsible for the behaviour of their tenants and dependents and to settle disputes by arbitration in the sheriffs' or burgh courts. In dealing with serious breaches of order such as murder, the arbitration might result in the payment of a 'blood price' in exchange for granting indemnity to the culprit. The condition of a grant of indemnity might be the requirement that the offending and aggrieved parties be obliged to enter into bands of friendship, that were legally recognized contracts that restored peace and required the parties to submit future disputes to arbitration. The gradual restoration of peace was not a manifestation

---

[113] Patrick Abercrombie, *The Martial Achievements of the Scots Nation*, 2 vols. (Edinburgh, 1711) [ESTCT 86819], i. 218; Brown, *Bloodfeud in Scotland*, 3–8, 16–19, 43, 143–73, 276–7; Jenny Wormald, 'Bloodfeud, Kindred and Government in Early Modern Scotland', *P&P* 87 (May 1980), 54–97; David Stevenson, *Alasdair MacColla and the Highland Problem in the Seventeenth Century* (Edinburgh, 1980), 8–9; R. A. Dodgshon, ' "Pretense of Blude" and "Place of thair Duelling": The Nature of Scottish Clans, 1500–1745', in R. A. Houston and I. D. Whyte (eds.), *Scottish Society, 1500–1800* (Cambridge, 1989), 173.

of the power of the Crown, but rather a desire on the part of the nobility to give up feuding.[114]

The Scottish Crown sought to alter some of the Highland customs that had given rise to feuding and disorder by the promulgation of the Statutes of Iona of 1609. These laws continued the royal policy of making the clan *fine* responsible for the good behaviour of their clansmen, and the carrying of arms was restricted to the clan gentry except when the whole clan was summoned for royal service in war or for a punitive expedition. Schooling in English and the preaching of Protestantism in the Highlands were intended to integrate the clan *fine* into Scottish landed society. This attempt to demilitarize clansmen occurred at the same time that archery skills were supposedly in decline, and the more costly firearms were being introduced. The Statutes of Iona recognized the responsibility of the clan *fine* to protect their clansmen, but by disarming the latter it degraded their status and enhanced that of the gentry. This may have compensated somewhat for the laws aimed at curtailing the hospitality of chiefs, and reducing the consumption of drink. Households were to be reduced in size in order to discourage the keeping of armed retainers and the maintenance of bardic poets, who were regarded as a source of seditious verses. The establishment of inns would provide alternative accommodation for travellers to the households of chiefs. Behind much of this legislation was a determination to undermine the idea that the size of a chief's military retinue determined his social status. The statutes also attempted to dilute the Gaelic elements in Scottish culture and especially destroy the status of those pillars of the Gaelic world, the bardic poets. In other words, James VI wished to turn a martial society into a civil society in the Highlands.[115]

James's government had no means by which to enforce the Statutes of Iona except punitive expeditions raised under the authority of commissions of fire and sword, which, in the eyes of the clansmen being punished, must have resembled nothing so much as clan warfare. Andrew Stewart, third Lord Ochiltree, had led a punitive expedition into the West Highlands and Isles in 1608; he kidnapped a number

[114] Ibid. 196; Macinnes, 'Crown, Clans and Fine', 31–2; id., *Clanship, Commerce and the House of Stuart*, 6–7, 10; Brown, *Bloodfeud in Scotland*, 269–70.
[115] Macinnes, *Clanship, Commerce and the House of Stuart*, 65–8; id., 'Crown, Clans and Fine', 38–9; Edward J. Cowan, *Montrose: For Covenant and King* (London, 1977), 51–2.

of chiefs and their heirs and clapped them in prison for the winter. Archibald Campbell, seventh earl of Argyll, was never backward in advancing his claims against the MacDonalds, and he was granted the MacDonald lands in Jura and Kintyre in 1607. He also continued the campaign to exterminate the MacGregors in Glenorchy, who were regarded as incorrigible bandits. The king had ordered the kidnapping of the chiefs or their sons in order to educate them in English, to inculcate Protestant ideas, and generally to teach them to live like Lowlanders. With the backing of the Crown, Argyll kept the chiefs of Clan Donald South on the defensive between 1608 and 1614, but the household retainers of chiefs in the Western Isle and on the western seaboard did not adapt well to tilling the soil and peaceful habits, and in 1614–15 the Clan Ian Mor, the sept of the MacDonalds that was the most closely associated with the redshank trade with Ireland, rose up in rebellion. Between 1625 and 1636, the ClanRanald returned to their old bad habits of piracy, and in the 1620s Gaelic-speaking Irish Franciscans began a mission to the Western Isles that promoted a revival of Catholicism. Although the seventh earl of Argyll had himself converted to Catholicism and actually served in the Spanish army, he was perhaps perceived as being more Campbell than Catholic; the resistance of the MacDonalds was particularly aimed at Campbell power, and this animosity would again resurface during the civil wars.[116]

The clans of the West Highlands and the Isles were willing to fight to preserve their language and way of life, but some landlords on the Lowland peripheries supported the Statutes of Iona. In a letter of advice written in about 1630 by Sir Robert Gordon of Gordonstoun to his young nephew, John Gordon, fourteenth earl of Sutherland, Gordonstoun urged the boy to use his power as a landlord to discourage his tenants from speaking Gaelic and wearing Highland garb:

Use your diligence to take away the relics of Irish barbarity which as yet remain in your country, to wit, the Irish language and habit. Purge your country piece and piece from that uncivil kind of clothes, such as plaids, mantles, trews and blue bonnets. Make severe acts against those that shall wear them. Cause the inhabitants of the country to clothe themselves as the most civil provinces of the kingdom do . . . The Irish language cannot so

---

[116] Hill, *Celtic Warfare*, 45–6; Stevenson, *Alasdair MacColla*, 29–30; Macinnes, 'Crown, Clans and Fine', 41; Cowan, *Montrose*, 51–3.

[i.e., too] soon be extinguished. To help this, plant schools in every corner in the country to instruct the youth to speak English. Let your chief schools of learning be in Dornoch, and persuade the gentlemen of your country to bestow largely upon their children to make them scholars, for so shall they be fittest for your service. Press to civilize your country and the inhabitants thereof, not only in this point, but likewise in all things which you shall observe abroad in your travels among other nations.[117]

How widespread these views were among Highland chiefs and lords is questionable. The example of another north-eastern clan, the Frasers of Lovat, suggests that many other Highland lords continued to expect their tenants to be ready for battle to defend their lands against encroachment. In the late 1580s, Thomas Fraser, tutor of Lovat, required the tacksmen, or clan gentry, as part of their seven-year leases, to ensure that every tenant kept both a bow and a gun and participated in musters where they exercised arms. They were also obliged to maintain watches to keep out the Rosses and the Macintoshes, who were apt to encroach. When the tutor of Lovat travelled about the lordship, he was accompanied by 100 bowmen. The late Lord Fraser had encouraged archery by both precept and example, and every able-bodied man within the lordship was expected to be an expert with the bow. Lord Fraser had gone 'on circuit' to make sure that the clansmen maintained high standards of archery and to encourage wrestling, swimming, and jumping. This tradition was carried on in the 1630s and 1640s by Hugh Fraser, seventh Lord Lovat, who continued encourage all sorts of 'martial manly exercises'. Archery was the sport that Lovat particularly favoured, but he maintained an armoury stored with pikes, firearms, and munitions, and was ready to raise a regiment for royal service. Lord Lovat also sent out the master of Lovat, aged 15, to list all 'fencible' men. The master of Lovat was later a lieutenant colonel under Sir Alexander Leslie in the Covenanting Army. 'In his time, the country was thronged with pretty [i.e. brave or gallant] men of all sorts . . .'[118]

The Statutes of Iona notwithstanding, many Highland chiefs continued to mobilize their clansmen for hunting, marriages, and funerals throughout the seventeenth century. The clansmen often possessed little more than swords and bows, clearly lacking sufficient weapons

[117] Sir William Fraser, *The Sutherland Book*, 3 vols. (Edinburgh, 1892), ii. 359.
[118] James Fraser, *Chronicles of the Frasers*, ed. William Mackay (SHS, 1st ser., 47; Edinburgh, 1905), 150, 184, 257, 309.

to protect themselves from cateran bands, but the practice of hosting continued because the chiefs and the clan *fine* wanted to display clan solidarity and strength and to put rival clans on notice that they were prepared to use force to resolve disputes. But, most of all, they wished to proclaim their status. The funeral of Simon Fraser, sixth Lord Lovat, in 1632 drew more than 5,000 men from eight different clans. That of Hugh, eighth Lord Lovat, in 1672 could still draw as many as 2,700 clansmen from ten clans. Even in the latter part of the seventeenth century, it was thought that a nobleman demeaned his status if he appeared on such occasions with a meagre entourage.[119]

The fact that the Statutes of Iona were aimed at the idiosyncracies of Highland Society is indicative of the divergence of the Gaelic and Lowland Scots cultures at the beginning of the seventeenth century. Although Highlanders and Lowlanders had shared many similarities during the previous century and a half, contemporary commentators chose to emphasize the differences of language, custom, and culture that divided the two. More recent observers have tended to see clanship as the most distinctive feature of Highland society, but, in fact, both Lowlanders and Highlanders developed a strong attachment to kinship groups based upon surnames during the turmoil of the previous century and more. Feudalism and its bonds of loyalty were strong in the Highlands, while kinship had come to play a more prominent role in Lowland society. The growth of clanship in the Highlands was a response to lawlessness and disorder, not a cause of it, although Lowlanders had come to perceive clanship as a positive evil. In aristocratic circles of Highland Scotland, the praise of Gaelic vernacular poets for the warrior elite of the clan represented martial ideals that were different from the more individualistic chivalric virtue admired by the Lowland nobility. The custom of the grand tour, foreign travel, and military service abroad by the latter had probably contributed to this divergence of cultural values. At the same time, the massive secularization of church lands, a growing permeation of the land market with the spirit of commercialism, the increasing importance of urban life, and the emergence of professional groups diminished the importance of the Lowland nobility. Because there were few towns in the Highlands, these developments had little effect

---

[119] Martin Martin, *A Description of the Western Isles of Scotland* (2nd edn.; London, 1716) [ESTCT 31703], 107; Macinnes, *Clanship, Commerce and the House of Stuart*, 22–3, 31.

upon the Gaels. However, the Scottish Gaelic chiefs had always acknowledged the kings of Scotland as their feudal chiefs. Thus, a strong Scottish Gaelic identity emerged during the seventeenth century, and it was permeated by an equally strong allegiance on the part of the Highland chiefs to the Stuart kings.[120]

The Highlands in the seventeenth century were governed by an incompatible marriage of clanship and feudalism in which the proprietary claims of the individual lordships belonging to the clan *fine* and the chiefs competed with the collective clan exploitation of land resources. Ancient clan feuds and hatreds, which frequently arose from conflicts in land use, were usually resolved by the tendency of the Crown and Edinburgh lawyers to favour individual registered proprietary claims over long collective possession by the clans and to award commissions of fire and sword allowing the winners to dispossess the losers with little regard to justice. This created a considerable amount of lawlessness in Highland society, and there were limited opportunities for the employment of the landless in the Highlands. These dispossessed tenants, cottars, and unemployed servants were known as 'broken men', and were drawn into the ubiquitous cateran bands that preyed upon the Highlands and the peripheries.[121]

The depredations of cateran bands or reivers constituted the most widespread form of lawlessness in the Highlands in the seventeenth century. Made up of masterless men for the most part, they extorted money from Lowland farmers or engaged in the theft of cattle, burglary, and murder in the Highlands. The *creach*, or the ritual of the cattle raid—once the rite of passage for adolescents of the clan *fine*—was in decline as opportunities for service as mercenary soldiers overseas opened up, and cattle raiding was coming to be perceived as robbery except among notorious clans such as the MacGregors, the Lochaber MacDonalds, and the Gunns. However, opportunities for professional soldiers dried up all over Europe in the 1650s as armies demobilized. Like the rapparees and the tories of Ireland, Highland cateran bands became more numerous as a result of the dislocations associated with the civil wars or the terrible famine of the 1690s, but banditry

---

[120] Dawson, 'The Gaidhealtachd and the Emergence of the Scottish Highlands', 289–90, 296–7; Stevenson, *Alasdair MacColla*, 15–16.

[121] Macinnes, *Clanship, Commerce and the House of Stuart*, 22–3, 32–3, 39–41; id., 'Crown, Clans and Fine', 41.

remained a problem as long as the Highlands produced surplus labour. The Highland bandits operated in gangs of between forty and sixty, and were sometimes led by younger sons of the clan gentry. While they were not particularly welcome in the Highlands, they could not have continued without the connivance of the clan *fine*, and they were often hired by landed families such as the Gordons, earls of Huntly. The victims of this cattle thieving sometimes employed a watch consisting of armed bands to recover their stolen property or to protect their herds and homes, but such protection was expensive, and there was little to choose between the characters of the reivers and the watch. In the late 1650s, one band of reivers, consisting for the most part of former Royalist soldiers, singled out the estates and tenants of James Ogilvie, first earl of Airlie. The procurers of this cateran band were lesser gentry from the MacDonalds of Glencoe and the ClanChattan confederation who resented Airlie's collaboration with the commander of the Cromwellian garrison at Inverlochy in order to identify the culprits. The location of the strife was in the Braes of Angus, a territory that was disputed between the Gordons and the Campbells and that had also been the scene of fierce fighting between the Royalists and the Covenanters in the 1640s. This particular band of reivers continued to raid the Airlie estates as late as 1667 under the leadership of John MacCombie, who had fought under Montrose.[122]

The inability to distinguish between public and private war was especially evident in the West Highlands and the Isles. Although Highland soldiers from the north-east had served in the wars of northern Europe prior the British civil wars, most swordsmen from the West Highlands were familiar only with clan warfare. When they were recruited for the Royalist Army by James Graham, first marquis of Montrose, and his lieutenant general, Alasdair MacColla, their fighting spirit was encouraged by the Gaelic poet, Iain Lom (*alias* John MacDonald of Keppoch), who employed the imagery of past blood feuds and clan traditions. This is why MacColla's men, mostly from the Clan Donald South, which was located on both the Scottish and Irish sides of the North Channel, spent so much time laying waste the lands of their ancient enemies the Campbells before they could be persuaded to move against the other Covenanters. Feuding had always been used to promote clan solidarity. It was only after 1626

---

[122] Martin, *Description of the Western Isles of Scotland*, 101–2; Brown, *Bloodfeud in Scotland*, 19–20; Macinnes, *Clanship, Commerce and the House of Stuart*, 32–5.

that the clan *fine* of the MacDonalds began shipping surplus red-shank mercenaries to the European mainland. Until then, they could have known little of the European military world.[123]

Highland feuds were fuelled by population pressure on land resources, but the proximate causes might include disputed inheritances, confusion over the collective claims to land put forth by clans that conflicted with individual possession, together with an assertion of the status that attached to the possession of land. Feuding was also fed by complex family alliances, and the bardic poets traditionally glorified such feuds as heroic struggles. During the civil wars of the 1640s, the vernacular Gaelic poets continued this tradition by stressing the theme of clan feuding rather than emphasizing the political, religious, or ideological dimensions of the conflict. Although it remained true that most conflicts were settled by arbitration rather than by a resort to violence, it was difficult for a Highland chief to avoid feuds without abdicating his responsibility to his clansmen. In terms of human life, the toll of feuding could be fearful. At the least, the aggressor clan or faction would attempt to destroy the food resources of an opposing clan or faction, which could bring starvation to communities whose agriculture was marginal to start with. The feud amongst the MacLeods of Assynt, which ended in 1609, lasted a little more than half a century and resulted in the deaths of fourteen of the twenty-eight male descendants of Angus Moir MacLeod. The feud began when Angus was murdered by his brother John. Although bloody, the MacLeod feud was short in comparison to the feud between the Macintoshes, who dominated ClanChattan, and the Camerons. That dispute, which persisted for 360 years, came to an end only in 1665 with the symbolic exchange of swords between the two clan chiefs, Lachlan Macintosh of Torcastle and Sir Ewen Cameron of Lochiel. However, Lochiel refused to abide by the terms of the settlement until there was a confrontation between 1,500 clansmen of ClanChattan and a band of 1,200 cobbled together from the Camerons and their allies the MacGregors and the MacDonalds of Glencoe and an intervention by John Campbell of Glenorchy (later first earl of Caithness, Breadalbane, and Holland), backed up by the authority of Archibald, ninth earl of Argyle.

---

[123] A. I. Macinnes, 'Gaelic Culture in the Seventeenth Century: Polarization and Assimilation', in S. G. Ellis and S. Barber (eds.), *Conquest and Union: Fashioning a British State, 1485–1725* (London, 1995), 173–5; id., *Clanship, Commerce and the House of Stuart*, 68; Hill, *Celtic Warfare*, 16–17.

The tendency of the Scottish Crown and magnates such as the ninth earl of Argyll to favour the proprietary interests of clan elites over the collective possession of lands by whole clans gave Torcastle the excuse to go after the MacDonalds of Keppoch, whom he accused of possessing their lands 'by mere force and banditry', and to expel them from Lochaber. In 1671, Torcastle had Archibald MacDonald and other MacDonald gentry declared rebels. The dispute smouldered another nineteen years until 1681, when Torcastle was granted a commission of fire and sword. However, the MacDonalds of Keppoch managed to survive by an astute exploitation of clan and national politics; because of their Royalist and Catholic affinities, they were viewed by Charles II's government as potential supporters of James, duke of York, against any attempt by the ninth earl of Argyll to prevent the succession of the duke of York to the throne. When Argyll did indeed rebel in 1685, the MacDonalds were only too happy to pull him down. Other members of the nobility also resented Torcastle's jurisdiction as steward of the lordship of Lochaber by inheritance, and Torcastle had forfeited the sympathy of his own clansmen and could host only 300 men in 1679, when he attempted to punish the MacDonalds, whereas he had been able to summon 1,500 in 1665 to expel the Camerons. Torcastle actually had to call upon government troops for assistance. At the Battle of Mulroy in 1688, the last of the great clan battles, Torcastle was able to muster only 500 members of the ClanChattan confederation, whereas the MacDonalds and their allies could host 800. The latter inflicted a severe defeat upon Torcastle, who was captured, but the government sent a punitive expedition to drive the MacDonalds out, but not before the MacDonalds had laid waste the land of the Macintoshes and their ClanChattan allies. The Williamite conquest of Scotland and Ireland, the famine of the 1690s, and a certain amount of sympathy for the MacDonalds as underdogs delayed Torcastle's attempt to be revenged upon the MacDonalds, and this last of the clan feuds was not finally concluded until 1700.[124]

Private warfare had once been pervasive in many parts of late-medieval Europe but had been suppressed in England and Wales

---

[124] Macinnes, *Clanship, Commerce and the House of Stuart*, 37–46, 123, 247–9; id., 'Gaelic Culture in the Seventeenth Century: Polarization and Assimilation', in Steven G. Ellis and Sarah Barber (eds.), *Conquest and Union: Fashioning a British State* (London, 1995), 172–3; Brown, *Bloodfeud in Scotland*, 77–8, 284.

by the end of the fifteenth century except where rudimentary forms of feuding persisted and were disguised as poaching or less obvious forms of conflict. The Tudor monarchs and some of their Norman and Plantagenet predecessors had made it their business to extinguish baronial anarchy, and the relative ease of communications and geographical configuration of England south of the Humber facilitated this task. Obviously, the remoteness and difficult terrain that characterized the Celtic parts of the British Isles made it more difficult for the monarchs of England to consolidate their rule and impose justice and civility upon Ireland; in any case, until the loss of Calais they remained more interested in expanding their European possessions than in completing the conquest of Ireland. The failure of the Stuart kings of Scotland to subdue the Borderers and the Highlanders can be attributed to the distractions of the religious changes, the Marian Civil Wars, the minority of her son and heir, but also to a lack of political will equal to this formidable task. At the time when James VI was beginning to deal effectively with the task of suppressing blood feuds and reining in unruly Borderers, he assumed the added responsibility of attempting to govern the whole of the British Isles. Outside Edinburgh and parts of the Lowlands, royal justice in Scotland remained undeveloped when compared to the system of royal assizes and quarter sessions in England. The English Crown had long since asserted the jurisdiction of royal courts at the expense of private feudal jurisdictions and imposed a highly developed sense of what constituted criminal behaviour—even if that criminal law was not always administered in an even-handed manner by the Stuart monarchs. All this is well known and generally accepted by historians.

At the same time, the Gaelic Irish, the Borderers, and the Highland Scots possessed strong resources for resistance. Their strong ties of kinship and loyalty to their chiefs reinforced communities that were organized for war and driven by a martial ethos that had never subsided. Their economies were primarily pastoral rather than arable, towns hardly existed until alien garrisons were planted, and their contacts with other parts of Europe were limited before the beginning of the seventeenth century. Loyalty to the kindred based upon male descent and dependence upon cattle grazing encouraged blood feuds and cattle raiding, the two most prevalent forms of private warfare in these regions. When New English planters and Lowland Scots set about to 'civilize' these regions, the swordsmen were offered very few alternatives other than extermination or permanent exile. They were not without military resourcefulness and imagination; besides adapting mainland European military technology, they developed their own distinctive styles of warfare that were well suited to the terrain and limited resources. They were, in fact, among the earliest practitioners of what later came to be called guerrilla warfare. Ireland and Scotland could not be incorporated into a United Kingdom until the problems of Gaelic resistance to assimilation into English and Lowland Scots cultures began to be addressed at the beginning of the eighteenth century. The solution to the problem of Gaelic swordsmen, which was never fully realized, was a military rather than a political one: to force the irreconcilables into exile in foreign armies, and to employ those who were willing to make a few compromises with English hegemony as soldiers in foreign and colonial wars.[125]

[125]   Linda Colley (*Britons: Forging the Nation, 1707–1837* (New Haven, 1992)) and Bruce Lenman (*England's Colonial Wars, 1550–1688: Conflict, Empire and Identity* (Harlow, 2001) and *Britain's Colonial Wars, 1688–1783* (Harlow, 2001)) provide an excellent introduction to this theme, with a discussion of recent literature.

CHAPTER SIX

# Duelling and Martial Culture

They that are glorious, must needs be factious; for all bravery
stands upon comparisons. They must needs be violent to make
good their own vaunts.

(Sir Francis Bacon, 'Of Vain-Glory', in *The Essayes or
Counsels, Civill and Morall*, ed. Michael Kieran
(Cambridge, Mass., 1985), 161)

A valiant man will not refuse an honourable duel; nor a wise
man fight upon a fool's quarrel.

(The duke of Newcastle, quoted in Margaret Cavendish,
duchess of Newcastle, *The Life of William Cavendish, Duke
of Newcastle* (1667), ed. C. H. Firth (London, 1906), 132)

An English royal proclamation of 1613 complained that many
gentlemen, with the connivance of magistrates, assumed that defending one's reputation with the sword was a 'birth-right', despite the
prohibitions contained in royal proclamations. This was a legacy of
the medieval belief that noble status conferred both the right to bear
arms and the right to fight a duel. These rights derived, in turn, from
'the *droit de guerre*, the right to make war'.[1] Although he does not
condone frivolous quarrels and combats, there runs throughout the
book about fencing and the code of the duel written by Vincentio
Saviolo, the second earl of Essex's Italian fencing master, the assumption that honour was above religion and morality, and a duel needed
no other justification than the vindication of honour.[2] Margaret
Cavendish, duchess of Newcastle, recalled that her father, Sir Thomas

---

[1] *A Publication of His Ma[jes]ties Edict and Severe Censure against Private
Combats and Combatants* (London, 1613) [STC 8498.5], 1; M. H. Keen, *The Laws of
War in the Late Middle Ages* (London, 1965), 19.
[2] *Vincentio Saviola his Practice: In Two Books, the First Intreating Use of the
Rapier and Dagger, the Second, of Honor and Honorable Quarrels* (London, 1595)
[STC 21788], sig. B2ᵛ *et passim*.

Lucas, 'as soon as he came to man's estate', killed another man in a duel, and, for this crime, he had been exiled by Queen Elizabeth. Upon his accession, James VI and I had pardoned Lucas and allowed him to return home. Ignoring the laws against murder and the prohibitions against duelling, his daughter could not see, by the laws of honour, how her father could have done otherwise.[3]

The experience of violence and the exposure to danger and death, whether in war or duelling, gave the swordsman a special knowledge and status that distinguished him from other men. For these reasons, he came to inhabit a separate and distinct mental world and to claim special privileges. Thus, the man of honour was both violent and assertive, and belonged to a culture with its own peculiar rules.[4] Peers and gentlemen from the British Isles served extensively in the armies of other European states during the seventeenth century, and the assumptions, traditions, and customs that they acquired during their service abroad were those of a European martial culture. Part of the cultural baggage that they brought home with them consisted of Italian and French fashions in duelling. So deeply did the cult of duelling put down roots among the aristocracies of the British Isles that no monarch or government of the seventeenth century possessed the power or political will to suppress such practices.

By defending their right to fight duels, the nobility and gentry defied the moral authority of both the Catholic and Protestant churches as well as the jurisdiction of the royal courts. There also existed within this culture based upon honour the belief that fate, rather that Divine Providence, guided the outcome of duels, and any injuries or deaths that resulted were purely accidental and served no moral purpose except the maintenance of honour. Honour was not touched by success or failure, death or survival; nor could there be any culpability for deaths or injuries resulting, provided that the duelling code was observed and seconds supervised the encounter. The practice of duelling was widely perceived as being, if not strictly legal, at least legitimate.[5]

---

[3] Margaret Cavendish, duchess of Newcastle, *The Life of William Cavendish, Duke of Newcastle* (1667), ed. Sir Charles Firth (London, 1906), 155–6.

[4] Jonathan Dewald, *Aristocratic Experience and the Origins of Modern Culture: France, 1590–1715* (Berkeley, Calif., 1993), 65–7; M. E. James, *English Politics and the Concept of Honour, 1485–1642* (P&P Supplement, 3; Oxford, 1978), 6–7.

[5] James Kelly, *'That Damn'd Thing Called Honour': Duelling in Ireland, 1570–1860* (Cork, 1995), 13–14; Ute Frevert, *Men of Honour: A Social and Cultural History of the Duel*, trans. Anthony Williams (Cambridge, 1995), 10; James, *English Politics and the Concept of Honour*, 6–7; Gregory Hanlon, *The Twilight of a Military Tradition: Italian Aristocrats and European Conflicts, 1560–1800* (New York, 1998), 242–3.

François Billacois was surely wrong when he noted the absence of political aims or discourse in the duel; the emergence of duelling in sixteenth-century Europe represented a reassertion of aristocratic values at a time when the utility of nobility was being questioned and undermined by the changes in warfare associated with the military revolution and the emergence of sovereign states ruled by absolutist monarchs. Norbert Elias viewed duelling as a form of revolt against state centralization. Looked at from another angle, the eruption of duelling was also a manifestation of the rechivalrization of Europe and the British Isles.[6] It provided a means by which the community of honour, rather than the monarch, could regulate aristocratic status.

The introduction of the modern duel into sixteenth-century Italy represented an attempt to transform and regulate the seemingly endless and savage medieval vendettas or feuds by substituting a conventionalized and limited form of combat involving only individuals rather than kindred and clan. The proprieties of duelling required a delay between the challenge and the actual combat, which was supervised by seconds. This small degree of self-restraint was supposed to differentiate the duel from the common variety of brawling. However, since the rechivalrization of aristocratic culture heightened the sense of honour and virtue, and the readiness to challenge or be challenged helped to define one's status as a gentleman, it is questionable how much the proprieties of the duelling code lessened conflict among swordsmen or contributed to a civil society.[7]

In France after *circa* 1550, the king ceased to regulate duels within his jurisdiction as an official procedure. In other countries, generally speaking, the duel always lacked official sanction, unlike the earlier medieval judicial combat. In France, after 1602, duelling became a criminal offence, and Queen Elizabeth and King James VI and I also discouraged duels. Private duels, usually fought in the rural countryside, became more frequent as public duels were discountenanced. As

    [6] François Billacois, *The Duel: Its Rise and Fall in Early Modern France*, trans. Trista Selous (New Haven, 1990), 333; Kelly, 'That Damn'd Thing Called Honour', 11; Arthur B. Ferguson, *The Chivalric Tradition in Renaissance England* (Cranbury, NJ, 1986), 111–12; V. G. Kiernan, *The Duel in European History: Honour and the Reign of Aristocracy* (Oxford, 1988), 53; Norbert Elias, *The Court Society*, trans. Edmund Jephcott (paperback edn.; New York, 1983), 240.

    [7] Hanlon, *Twilight of a Military Tradition*, 342–4; Donna T. Andrew, 'The Code of Honour and its Critics: The Opposition to Duelling in England, 1700–1850', *Social History*, 5.3 (Oct. 1980), 411–13; Anna Bryson, *From Courtesy to Civility: Changing Codes of Conduct in Early Modern England* (Oxford, 1998), 247–8.

the formalities that accompanied earlier duels were dropped, the time that elapsed between challenge and combat was sometimes reduced to minutes. Thereafter, it often became difficult to distinguish duels from brawls. This was especially the case where there were multiple combats, with the seconds participating in the duel instead of enforcing the proprieties of the duelling code. A certain amount of brawling, or what appears to be brawling, may actually have resulted from agreements between rivals to have 'chance encounters', so that crown prosecutors could not argue premeditated murder. The aristocracy remained uncomfortable with the need to fight duels in private because they had been declared illegal; they would have preferred to make the duelling field a more highly visible theatre of honour.[8]

One of the most persistent causes of duelling was the widespread tendency to equate justice with revenge. Aristocrats believed that 'revenge is necessary to keep the world in good order', and this tempted many of them to take the law into their own hands. Cicero's *De officiis* not only provided a justification for revenge, but made it a duty. Duelling was kept alive as an adjunct of martial culture by an exaggerated emphasis on the point of honour to the extent that a martialist could not suffer any indignity or aspersion on his honour for fear that it might diminish his reputation. Young men especially, in an attempt to fashion a reputation for valour, would seize upon every quarrel as an opportunity to demonstrate, by engaging in a duel, that they did not fear death. For those on the periphery of aristocratic society, it could also help them ascend the social hierarchy. It did not add to one's honour to fight a duel, but it certainly diminished that honour to refuse a challenge.[9]

---

[8] Billacois, *The Duel*, 65, 121; Charles Moore, *A Full Inquiry into the Subject of Suicide, to which are Added . . . Two Treatises on Duelling and Gaming*, 2 vols. (London, 1790) [ESTCT 111258], ii. 242; Ute Frevert, 'The Taming of the Noble Ruffian: Male Violence and Dueling in Early Modern Germany', in Pieter Spierenburg (ed.), *Men and Violence: Gender, Honor, and Rituals in Modern Europe and America* (Columbus, Oh., 1998), 38; Samuel Butler, 'A Dueller', in *Butler, Characters*, ed. C. W. Davies (Cleveland, 1970), 270.

[9] John Hales, *Golden Remains* (London, 1659) [Wing H269], 74–5; Sir George Clark, *War and Society in the Seventeenth Century* (Cambridge, 1958), 47–8; Moore, *Two Treatises on Duelling and Gaming*, ii. 251; Markku Peltonen, *The Duel in Early Modern England: Civility, Politeness and Honour* (Cambridge, 2003), 42–3, 49–50. The quotation comes from the earl of Northampton's pamphlet against duelling, 'Duello Foiled, or the Whole Proceedings in the Orderly Disposing of a Design for a Single Fight between Two Valliant Gentlemen', in Thomas Hearne (ed.), *A Collection of Curious Discourses*, 2 vols. (London, 1771), ii. 223–42, quoted in James, *English Politics and the Concept of Honour*, 14.

While it could be argued that the duel settled nothing in the opinion of spectators, this did not signify to gentlemen who believed that the laws of honour were more important than any divine, natural, or positive law. The laws of honour represented the best means of punishing vice and exalting virtue. Lost honour could not be restored by arbitration in the courts, and aristocratic dignity would not permit magistrates to determine affairs of honour; only the exercise of virtue could preserve a gentleman's honour. Moreover, some defenders of the duel went as far as to argue that a single combat provided a better means of demonstrating valour than the exploits of the battlefield. This led to a situation where duelling and war overlapped and the distinction between *duellum* and *bellum* remained imprecise. Yet, while duelling provided an outlet for the aggression of military adventurers, it was not analogous to war, because most divines and political philosophers agreed that war, when declared by the authority of the prince, was morally justifiable, but, at the same time, condemned duelling.[10]

The worst insult to a gentleman's honour and a frequent cause of duelling was to have another gentleman give him 'the lie'. The early Stuart monarchs and their councillors recognized that no gentleman could endure the supreme insult of being called a liar, and that the traditional remedy was to offer a challenge. Hoping to avoid occasions for such duels, they provided severe punishments for those who defamed or insulted others through the jurisdictions of the Court of Star Chamber and the Earl Marshal's Court. The former was intended to punish those, who, being regarded as 'churls' or 'peasants', had no right to challenge a gentleman, and were judged guilty of libel or *scandalum magnatum*. The latter court attempted to arbitrate points of honour. Lodowick Bryskett, an Italian-born scholar who was for seven years clerk of the Council, knowing that gentlemen resorted to the duel because it was regarded as ancient and traditional, tried to demonstrate that the duel was of quite recent origin and, in any case,

---

[10] Ruth Kelso, *The Doctrine of the English Gentleman in the Sixteenth Century* (Univ. of Illinois Studies in Language and Literature, 14.1–2; Urbana, Ill., 1929), 103–4; James Thomas Johnson, *Just War Tradition and the Restraint of War: A Moral and Historical Inquiry* (Princeton, 1981), 44–5; Clark, *War and Society in the Seventeenth Century*, 50–1; Abraham Gibson, *Christiana Polemica, or a Preparative to Warre . . . A Sermon Preached at the Wooll-Church in London before the Captaines and Gentlemen that exercise in the Artillerie-Garden . . . April 14. 1618* (London, 1619) [STC 11828], 23–4.

the practice was inconsistent with a civil society.[11] However, Bryskett had to contend with the influence of writers such as Castiglione, whose *Book of the Courtier* (1561) was widely read in English translation. Castiglione stated that 'the principal and true profession of a courtier ought to be feats of arms . . . The fame of a gentleman that carrieth weapon, if it be once tarnished with cowardice, or any other reproach, doth evermore continue shameful.'[12] Jean Gailhard pointed out that it was one thing to suffer religious persecution for the sake of conscience, but quite another to suffer an affront. Gailhard mentions fighting off highwaymen as one example of defending oneself, but he also clearly states that one must also defend one's reputation in order to avoid the imputation of cowardice. Such actions were justified by the 'custom and laws of all nations'.[13]

The Renaissance code of courtesy and civility dictated that the courtier and gentleman was supposed to rein in his emotions, make himself pleasing to others and not utter everything that came into his head. The practice of duelling with rapiers, so the argument goes, effectively enforced a code of civil courtesy among courtiers because the outcome was often deadly. Duelling is thought to have reduced the incidence of aristocratic violence by imposing an elaborate code of courtesy to restrain violence. However, the practical difficulties of distinguishing duelling, fought according to rules and properly supervised by seconds who were not supposed to participate in the combat, from plain brawling obscure the connection between duelling and civility. Markku Peltonen challenges this view that duelling could be a means of enforcing a culture of politeness. He argues instead that the cult of duelling was part and parcel of the 'Italian Renaissance notion of the gentleman and courtier', which was transmitted to England by English translations of Castiglione's *The Book of the Courtier* and Giovanni Della Casa's *Galateo* (1576).[14] It is well to emphasize that

[11] Robert Ward, *Animadversions of Warre* (London, 1639) [STC 25025], 189; Matthew Carter, *Honor Redivivius, or An Analysis of Honor and Armory* (London, 1660) [Wing C659], 20–1; Lodowick Bryskett, *A Discourse of Civill Life* (London, 1606) [STC 3959], 64–8.
[12] Count Baldasare Castiglione, *The Book of the Courtier*, trans. Sir Thomas Hoby (1561; repr. New York, 1967), 48; see also Sydney Anglo, 'How to Kill a Man at Your Ease: Fencing Books and the Duelling Ethic', in S. Anglo (ed.), *Chivalry and the Renaissance* (Woodbridge, 1990), 3.
[13] Jean Gailhard, *The Compleat Gentleman*, 1 vol. in 2 pts. (London, 1678) [Wing G118], ii. 126.
[14] Peltonen, *The Duel in Early Modern England*, 5–6, 65–7. See also Norbert Elias, *Power and Civility, ii: The Civilizing Process*, trans. Edmund Jephcott (New York, 1982), 8, 271, 281; id., *The Court Society*, trans. Edmund Jephcott, 240.

the code of civil courtesy was associated with courtier and London culture and displayed very different values from martial culture. The code of civil courtesy reasserted hierarchy and 'vertical honour', and required that the courtier abase himself and curry favour with his social superiors. 'Horizontal honour' is more characteristic of the world of the professional soldier, which tended towards a system of merit, and had a levelling effect within the community of honour.[15]

Although most duels were fought between individuals, challenges could arise from long-standing feuds. Francis, second Lord Norris (later first earl of Berkshire), had a long festering dispute with the Berties, which began with a duel in 1610 with Robert Bertie, Lord Willoughby de Eresby, and concluded in 1613 with a single combat in 1613 with Lord Willoughby's brother Peregrine. On one occasion, Lord Norris took offence at Lord Willoughby's 'niggardly salutation' upon meeting the latter in a church in Bath and attacked him with a sword thrust to breast—without, it seems, doing him any harm. Another man named Piggot came to Lord Willoughby's defence, and Lord Norris killed him. Norris was convicted of manslaughter, but was pardoned.[16]

Besides the difficulty that monarchs encountered in trying to provide a legal remedy for injured honour that would be acceptable to all parties to a dispute, it was also difficult to discourage a practice that was widely regarded by young gallants as an entrée to manhood. In Charles Croke's semi-autobiographical picaresque novel, his hero Rudolphus, while a student at Oxford aged 15, becomes sufficiently proficient in fencing 'to think himself a man' and 'to gain some applause with his military master'.[17] The opportunity to engage in a single combat was not something that one could passively await, because it was accounted more honourable to be a challenger than a respondent.[18] Roger Boyle, later first earl of Orrery, when he was 19 years old, challenged Thomas Howard, son of the earl of Berkshire, to a duel in a dispute over the hand of a young lady. Orrery's father,

[15] Peltonen, *The Duel in Early Modern England*, 68–9, 73, 149–50, 166–7.

[16] *Letters of John Holles, 1587–1637*, ed. P. R. Seddon, 3 vols. (Thoroton Soc., 31, 35, 36; Nottingham, 1975–86), i. 82–3 and n.; *Calendar of State Papers, Domestic, 1603–1625*, 4 vols. (London, 1857–9), 308.

[17] [Charles Croke,] *Fortune's Uncertainty or Youth's Unconstancy* (1667) (Luttrell Soc. Reprints, 19; Oxford, 1959), 14. See also *The Memoirs of Capt. Peter Drake* (Dublin, 1755) [ESTCT 145643], 29–30.

[18] 'Anthony Wingfield's Discourse', in R. B. Wernham (ed.), *The Expeditions of Sir John Norris and Sir Francis Drake to Spain and Portugal, 1598*, ed. (NRS 127; Aldershot, 1988), 247–8.

Richard Boyle, first earl of Cork, approved of neither the duel nor the young lady.[19] Lord Herbert of Cherbury took up duelling on his first trip to France in 1612. Here he made the acquaintance of Damien de Montluc, seigneur de Balagni, the nephew of Bussy d'Amboise, who, having killed eight or nine men in duels, was accounted, said Herbert, 'one of the gallantest men in the world', and highly regarded by the ladies for that reason. As James I's ambassador to France some years later, Lord Herbert was much concerned with punctilio, and was recalled after he had challenged the duc de Luynes, the ultra-Catholic leader, to a duel.[20]

Even gentlemen who were not aggressive found it difficult to avoid encounters on the duelling field. Sir Thomas Compton was regarded as a 'slow-spirited' and easy-going person, and men of bravado frequently took advantage of his good nature, with the consequence that he was reputed a coward. 'One Bird, a roaring captain', repeatedly tried to provoke Compton. The latter's friends told him that 'it were better to die nobly once than to live infamously ever', and attempted to screw up Compton's courage sufficiently to get him to issue a challenge. After the duel had been agreed upon, Capt. Bird insisted on fighting in a sawpit, so that Compton could not run away. Bird, thinking that he was about to slaughter a lamb, held his sword above his head in a 'disdainful' way. Compton dashed under Bird's sword and ran the captain through.[21] Sir Richard Atkins, colonel of a regiment of foot, was a man who seemed to provoke duels compulsively. Within the space of one month, he issued three challenges: two of his designated opponents he accused of laying with his wife. The first refused to draw and Atkins caned him in front of a coffee house; the second, Lord Thomas Howard, denied the accusation, but fought Atkins anyway. The third was a Catholic recusant, Sir Edward Longueville; 'they have obtained a pass for both of them to go beyond sea'.[22]

[19] Kathleen M. Lynch, *Roger Boyle, First Earl of Orrery* (Knoxsville, Tenn., 1965), 28–9.

[20] When he got home, Herbert went so far as to request that James I send a trumpeter-herald into France to demand a combat with de Luynes (*The Life of Edward, First Lord Herbert of Cherbury, Written by Himself*, ed. J. M. Shuttleworth (London, 1976), 42, 45, 98–100, 110).

[21] Arthur Wilson, *The Life and Reign of James, the First King of Great Britain* (1653), repr. in [White Kennett,] *Complete History of England*, 3 vols. (1706) [ESTCT 145258], ii. 727a, b.

[22] Narcissus Luttrell, *A Brief Historical Relation of State Affairs from September 1678 to April 1714*, 6 vols. (Oxford, 1857; repr. Wilmington, Del., 1974), iii. 494, 506 (4 July–1 Aug. 1695).

Sir John Reresby was also a quarrelsome person, much addicted to violent confrontations. Even when he was nearly 50 years of age, Reresby remained a prickly character, and was disinclined to overlook any slight, real or imagined. Twice within one week, he called two gentlemen out, offering to put aside his dignity as governor of York and fight as a private person. The first was an ensign in the York garrison who had complained of Reresby's porter 'with some sharpness'; the second was Sir John Brooks, bt, of York, who presumed to move Reresby's cushion in York Minster into his own pew. Neither was willing to accept Reresby's challenge. Reresby's father had also been a person who was quick to take offence and issue challenges. The elder Reresby, while serving as a major in a Royalist militia regiment during the civil wars, had once killed a man in a tavern brawl. He was tried for murder, but acquitted after a sympathetic surgeon testified that the elder Reresby's victim died of the pox rather than a head wound.[23] In Scotland, a challenge to a duel resulted from rough play during a football match involving Francis Stewart Hepburn, fifth earl of Bothwell, and the master of Marischal. King James VI intervened and 'with some difficulty' effected a reconciliation.[24]

In the late eighteenth century, Charles Moore undertook a thorough and systematic investigation of why the practice of duelling persisted for so very long. Above all, he concluded, the duel had become a test of courage during the seventeenth and eighteenth centuries. The possessors of courage 'will always meet with admiration' and 'the destroyers of men have always been more celebrated than their benefactors' by poets and historians. Moreover, the man who refused a duel was 'ever thereafter deemed incapable of performing one honourable action', and not 'deserving the attention of his equals in life'.[25] Sir William Hope, the Scottish author of a fencing manual that was frankly aimed at those who fought duels, asserted that those who followed the sword were distinguished by something extraordinary, while those who held swordsmanship in contempt and neglected that art did 'ungentleman themselves'.[26] At the time of the Third

[23] *Memoirs of Sir John Reresby*, ed. Andrew Browning (Glasgow, 1936); repr. (1991), pp. xli–xliii, 316–18.

[24] *The Correspondence of Robert Bowes of Aske, Esq., the Ambassador of Queen Elizabeth to the Court of Scotland* (Surtees Soc., 14; London, 1842), 448–9.

[25] Moore, *Two Treatises on Duelling and Gaming*, ii. 262.

[26] Sir William Hope, *The Sword-Man's Vade Mecum* (London, 1694) [Wing H2717], 94–5.

Anglo-Dutch War, John Sheffield, earl of Mulgrave, took offence at something the earl of Rochester said about him, 'which according to his custom was very malicious'. They arranged to fight a duel near Knightsbridge that apparently was to be a multiple combat on horseback involving seconds as well as principals. When Rochester showed up with a fully equipped trooper of the Life Guards instead of his previously approved second, Mulgrave objected and insisted that they fight on foot. Rochester, whose courage failed him on this occasion, pleaded that he was too ill to fight on foot, and withdrew. Mulgrave was willing to agree to this, but his second, Col. Aston, wrote an account of this affair and circulated it throughout London.[27] The earl of Sandwich's first cousin, Edward Montagu, who was master of the horse in Queen Catherine of Braganza's household, fought a duel in 1662 in which he fell backwards into a ditch and lost his sword. His opponent refused to take advantage of him. Usually, there was no dishonour in losing a duel, but Pepys thought that Montagu 'did carry himself very poorly in the business and hath lost his honour forever with all people'.[28]

In Scotland, the duel in the Italian fashion never gained much of a hold on aristocratic society, and the blood feud remained the more usual way of settling affairs of honour until the end of the reign of James VI and I, although the Scottish Privy Council did sometimes issue cartels for single combats.[29] In the time of the Covenanting Movement in the 1640s, the atmosphere of Edinburgh became very tense as both Covenanting and Royalist noblemen got into the habit of travelling about with large numbers of armed retainers. Nevertheless, the Scottish Estates tried to keep a lid on the situation. When Lord Henry Ker, the alcoholic younger son of the earl of Roxburgh, sent a challenge to the marquis of Hamilton in 1641, the Scottish Parliament compelled him to apologize to Hamilton.[30]

---

[27] John Sheffield, 3rd earl of Mulgrave and 1st duke of Buckingham and Normanby, 'Memoirs', in Works, 2 vols. (London, 1740) [ESTCT 86931], ii. 8–11.

[28] The Diary of Samuel Pepys, ed. R. C. Latham and W. Matthews, 11 vols. (Berkeley, Calif., 1970–83), iii. 157.

[29] Keith M. Brown, Bloodfeud in Scotland, 1573–1625: Violence, Justice and Politics in an Early Modern Society (Edinburgh, 1986), 25.

[30] H. L. Rubinstein, Captain Luckless: James, First Duke of Hamilton, 1606–1649 (Edinburgh, 1975), 131.

For a discussion of local customs concerning the means by which challenges were issued for duels on the Anglo-Scottish Border, see D. L. W. Tough, The Last Years of a Frontier: A History of the Borders during the Reign of Elizabeth (Oxford, 1928), 104–5.

Within the community of honour, it was assumed that gentlemen and peers were equal, and that a gentleman or a knight could challenge any peer to combat. During the Middle Ages, it was widely held that on the battlefield or in other military matters soldiers enjoyed a rough equality one with another so long as they bore the same weapons. This rested upon the further assumption, which persisted in martial culture, that there was no essential difference between public wars and private combats. Sir William Segar, the Garter king-of-arms, considered any gentleman who could claim three generations of gentry descent to be noble, but he accepted the idea that service in the wars could speed up the process: 'a soldier basely born, having lived in continual exercise of arms by the space of ten years, without committing any disobedience or reproachful act, ought to be admitted to fight with any gentleman born.'[31]

Among the various objections to duelling was the perception that the practice was socially subversive and potentially seditious. John Selden insisted that a gentleman might challenge a duke to a duel, and the latter would be obliged to accept if he had done that gentleman an injury. Thus, the practice of duelling had a levelling effect among the gentry and aristocracy, which some observers found troubling. Sir Francis Bacon blamed the craze for duelling on 'the confusion of degrees' whereby every man assumed the 'attribute of honour'. For this reason, it was thought prudent by some to avoid duelling altogether and to be especially careful not to insult or injure an inferior, for, if one did so, he descended to that level and made that person an equal to himself.[32] After Sir Philip Sidney's famous encounter with Edward de Vere, seventeenth earl of Oxford, on the tennis court, when Oxford called Sidney a 'puppy', and Sidney gave him the lie, a challenge was issued as a prelude to a duel. Queen Elizabeth would not countenance such a confrontation because of the disparity of social rank. The queen insisted that Sidney's lack of respect towards an earl would set a bad example for peasants and might lessen their respect for their betters. Sidney asserted the principle that peers and gentry were all

[31] Keen, *Laws of War in the Late Middle Ages*, 254–5; Sir William Segar, *Honor, Military and Civil* (London, 1602) [STC 22164], iii. 121–3.

[32] [Richard Milward,] *The Table-Talk of John Selden*, ed. S. W. Singer (1855; repr. Freeport, NY, 1972), 47–8; *The Charge of Sir Francis Bacon . . . Touching Duells* (London, 1614) [STC 1125], 55–6; Thomas Pestell, *Sermons and Devotions Old and New* (London, 1659) [Wing P1675], 325; William Higford, *The Institution of a Gentleman* (1660), in *Harleian Miscellany*, ed. William Oldys and Thomas Park, 10 vols. (London, 1808–13), ix. 596.

free men and Oxford was not his lord. He further reminded the queen that her father, Henry VIII, had thought it wise to give the gentry leave to protest the power and oppression of grandees.[33]

John Selden's pregnant imagination saw an even more politically charged analogy to the case of a duke being bound in honour to grant a combat to a plain gentleman if he had injured that person. A prince must also accept the right of his subjects to resort to arms to redress their grievances:

> This will give you some light to understand the quarrel betwixt a prince and his subjects. Though there be a vast distance between him and them, and they are to obey him according to their contract, yet he hath no power to do them an injury; then they think themselves as much bound to vindicate their right as they are to obey his lawful commands; nor is there any measure of justice left on earth but arms.[34]

This linking of a belief in the legitimacy of duelling to the right of resistance possessed by the king's subjects may help to explain Parliament's reluctance during the early modern period to ban the practice of duelling by statute law.

Whatever Selden thought about the connection between duelling and theories of aristocratic resistance, the rise of the duelling phenomenon remained the 'darker side of the chivalric revival'; it was 'chivalric honour gone rotten'.[35] Unlike the earlier code of chivalry, the craze for duelling was, for most gallants, justified by no idealism; it was concerned solely with revenge and the vindication of personal honour. The difficulty in distinguishing between duelling and plain brawling is symptomatic of a surge of ruffianly behaviour among martial men and courtiers alike and the difficulty of preserving a code of honour in practice. Sir Thomas Overbury assumed that strong drink lay behind displays of valour in swordplay: 'a soldier is the husbandman of valour; his sword is his plough, which honour and *aqua vitae*, two fiery metalled jades, are forever drawing.'[36] Duelling

---

[33] Arthur Collins (ed.), *Letters and Memorials of State*, 2 vols. (London, 1746; repr. New York, 1973), i. 101–2.

[34] [Milward,] *Table-Talk of John Selden*, ed. Singer, 47–8. The contents of Selden's *Table-Talk* were collected by his secretary, Richard Milward, during the last twenty years of Selden's life. Selden died in 1654.

[35] Ferguson, *The Chivalric Tradition*, 96; Sidney Anglo, 'Introduction', in S. Anglo (ed.), *Chivalry and the Renaissance* (Woodbridge, 1990), pp. xiii–xiv.

[36] André Corvisier, *Armies and Societies in Europe, 1494–1789*, trans. A. T. Siddall (Bloomington, Ind., 1979), 183–4; *The Miscellaneous Works in Prose and Verse of Sir Thomas Overbury*, ed. Edward F. Rimbault (London, 1856), 76–7.

frequently arose out of drunken orgies. In 1641, Sir Kenelm Digby was at dinner at a French nobleman's house when a French gallant evidently called the king of England a coward. Digby had been too far into his cups to remember the incident, but, when reminded, he challenged the Frenchman to single combat. The duel lasted four hours before Digby finally killed his opponent. Digby immediately went to the French royal court and revealed everything to the king, who pardoned him and gave him a guard of 200 men to carry him safely to Flanders.[37] Jean Bodin, writing at the end of the sixteenth century, thought that duelling among the nobility provided an alternative outlet for aggressive behaviour that helped to avoid civil war, but later observers believed that the spread of martial culture among the aristocracies of the British Isles kept the practice alive.[38]

The chivalric revival prolonged the medieval jousting tournament and may even have pumped some new life into that quaint martial exercise. Although some of the antecedents of modern duelling may be discerned in medieval jousting tournaments and officially supervised judicial trials by combat, one cannot demonstrate an uninterrupted continuity between the two. Unlike the judicial combat, the duel usually lacked official sanction. The duel also differed from the jousting tournament in that it was not a game, but a serious combat where the participants intentionally gambled with their lives.[39]

In medieval times, the court tournament had been regarded as a rehearsal for war, but, with the decline in the use of heavy cavalry from the fifteenth century on, it lost whatever military relevance it had ever possessed and became a 'courtly spectacle'.[40] Running at the ring and similar exercises were more useful because they emulated light-cavalry tactics, but the many equestrian exercises at tournaments had degenerated into little more than horse ballet. Under Elizabeth, the purpose of the Accession Day tilts was to keep alive martial exercises

[37] *Sir Kenelm Digby's Honour Maintained: By a Most Couragious Combat which he Fought with the Lord Mount le Ros, who by Base and Slanderous Words Reviled him* (London, 1641) [BL, Thomason Tracts, E. 175(9), sigs. A2–3.

[38] Kelso, *The Doctrine of the English Gentleman*, 103–4; Robert R. Harding, *Anatomy of a Power Elite: The Provincial Governors of Early Modern France* (New Haven, 1978), 78–9; John Cockburn, *The History and Examination of Duels* (London, 1720) [ESTCT 118651], 229–30, 232.

[39] Kelly, 'That Damn'd Thing Called Honour', 9; Frevert, 'The Taming of the Noble Ruffian', 38; Billacois, *The Duel*, 16.

[40] J. R. Hale, 'The Military Education of the Officer Class in Early Modern Europe', in his *Renaissance War Studies* (London, 1983), 234–5; Anglo (ed.), *Chivalry and the Renaissance*, p. xiii.

206 THE DISCOURSE OF VIOLENCE

during a period of prolonged peace without actual blood letting. Sir Henry Lee, the queen's champion and organizer of these events, wanted to enhance the image of the English aristocracy as chivalrous knights in the service of Protestantism in order to wean the people away from saints' days.[41] The ceremonies of the Elizabethan tiltyard were artificial and provided an inadequate outlet for aristocratic aggression. While Sir Henry Lee merely pranced through the tilts as a demonstration of chivalric ritual, Sir John Perrott, who had soldiered in Ireland, charged his opponent with such ferocity that the queen was obliged to intervene and stop the combat. Coming as they did on the anniversary of Elizabeth's accession to the throne, these spectacles were also supposed to provide the occasion for unqualified adulation of the queen. However, Richard McCoy argues that Elizabethan chivalry remained 'contentious', and the earls of Leicester and Essex as well as Sir Philip Sidney used the tiltyard as a theatre in which to display aristocratic power and to act out a kind of symbolic rebellion against the Crown.[42] Eventually, these exercises proved unsatisfactory for such proud aristocrats, and they turned instead to the wars in the Netherlands and Ireland to demonstrate their honour and virtue, or, in the case of Essex, who was unable to reconcile honour and obedience, to actual rebellion.

James VI and I praised jousting in the *Basilikon Doron*, the book that he wrote for his son, but he kept his own participation in royal tournaments to a minimum, doing no more than running at the ring. Although James was fond of hunting and spent many hours in the saddle, he disassociated himself from the chivalric culture and martial exercises of tournaments and forfeited much goodwill by his very visible distaste for crowds. Disappointment with James made Henry, prince of Wales, who was devoted to such pursuits, more popular with swordsmen, and he gave promise of growing into a soldier-king. Although not old enough for jousting, in 1610 Prince Henry fought a combat on foot with six others across a barrier at a tournament held in the Banqueting Hall in Whitehall. Following Henry's death in

---

[41] Frances Yates, *Astraea: The Imperial Theme in the Sixteenth Century* (London, 1975), 88, 90, 92, 101; Richard C. McCoy, *The Rites of Knighthood: The Literature and Politics of Elizabethan Chivalry* (Berkeley, Calif., 1989), 244–7; David Cressy, *Bonfires and Bells: National Memory and the Protestant Calendar in Elizabethan and Stuart England* (Berkeley, Calif., 1989), 5–6.
[42] McCoy, *Rites of Knighthood*, 2–3, 14; id., 'From the Tower to the Tiltyard: Robert Dudley's Return to Glory', *HJ* 27.2 (1984), 431–2.

1612, the annual Accession Day tilts went into decline and ceased to be held after Charles I became king. The Caroline court, embarrassed by the disastrous military and naval expeditions of the 1620s, cast aside all association with a martial culture and, instead, made a virtue of the Caroline peace of the 1630s, which was celebrated in the stilted tableaux of the court masque.[43]

Although the elaborate rituals of the *duello*, as supervised by seconds, were supposed to distinguish the duel from feuds and common brawls, the participation of seconds along with principals in multiple combats blurred such distinctions. One of the earliest known English examples of a challenge to a multiple combat was written in Italian in 1622 by one Colonel Norris. The duel was to begin on horseback with swords and pistols.[44] The practice of engaging in multiple combats was introduced into England from France. Even in France, opinion was divided on this kind of encounter. Henri de Campion liked to participate in multiple combats because they afforded a better opportunity for displaying his valour and being noticed than was the case in war. Montaigne, on the other hand, insisted that multiple combats grew out of cowardice, or the fear of fighting alone.[45]

Multiple combats became quite common in court circles during the Restoration period. The second duke of Buckingham and Francis Talbot, eleventh earl of Shrewsbury, engaged in a combat in January 1668 involving six persons. Shrewsbury and one of the seconds died and the rest were all wounded. Pepys thought that the affair brought the Privy Council into disrepute, since Buckingham was a member, and he raised questions about Buckingham's sobriety, since the cause of the quarrel concerned a woman who was a known whore.[46] While serving as lieutenant colonel in the Holland Regiment, Charles, second earl of Middleton, formed a close friendship with the colonel, John

---

[43] Alan Young, *Tudor and Jacobean Tournaments* (London, 1987), 37–40; J. S. A. Adamson, 'Chivalry and Political Culture in Caroline England', in Kevin Sharpe and Peter Lake (eds.), *Culture and Politics in Early Stuart England* (Stanford, Calif., 1993), 161–97, esp. 165.

[44] PRO SP 84/111, fos. 11, 31. Since this challenge came to the attention of the Privy Council, the encounter may not have taken place.

[45] Roger Chartier (ed.), *A History of Private Life*, iii: *Passions of the Renaissance*, trans. Arthur Goldhammer (Cambridge, Mass., 1989), 27; *The Complete Essays of Montaigne*, trans. D. M. Frame (Stanford, Calif., 1958), 525 (bk. ii, ch. 27).

[46] *The Diary of Samuel Pepys*, ed. Latham and Matthews, ix. 26–7; John Childs, *The Army, James II and the Glorious Revolution* (New York, 1980), 118 n. Buckingham was pardoned for the death of Shrewsbury by Charles II in Feb. 1668 (*DNB*, *sub* George Villiers, 2nd duke of Buckingham (1628)).

Sheffield, earl of Mulgrave. As an opponent of the duke of Monmouth's faction, Mulgrave was frequently drawn into multiple combats, and Middleton was expected to fight as his second. Middleton was seriously wounded on one occasion. The earl of Rochester's friends were similarly addicted to duelling and he also fought frequently as a second in multiple combats.[47]

Further blurring the distinction between public war and private combat was the practice among some of the more archaic swordsmen of the chivalric revival of challenging a representative of the enemy of equal social rank to engage in a single encounter to determine the outcome of a battle or siege. Peregrine Bertie, Lord Willoughby of Eresby, while he was governor of Bergen-op-Zoom, sent a personal challenge to the marquis of Guasto, who was reputed to be the bravest of the prince of Parma's soldiers in the Spanish Army of Flanders, to engage in a personal combat.[48] At the Siege of Zutphen of 1591, Prince Maurice permitted a single combat between a young Dutch gentleman volunteer named Rihouen and an Italian 'giant'. The Dutch gentleman won the encounter in a spectacular display of swordsmanship and was 'bountifully rewarded' by Prince Maurice.[49] While standing before the gates of Lisbon in 1589, the second earl of Essex, 'preferring the honour of the cause, which was his country's, before his own safety', sent a challenge to a single combat to the commander of the Spanish garrison 'if they had any of his quality'. If not, then he proposed a 'duello' between 'six, eight or ten or as many as they would appoint' with a like number from the English army. The Spanish commander threatened to hang Essex's trumpeter for bringing such a message.[50]

---

[47] George Hilton Jones, *Charles Middleton: The Life and Times of a Restoration Politician* (Chicago, 1967), 27–9; *The Letters of John Wilmot, Earl of Rochester*, ed. Jeremy Treglown (Chicago, 1980), 22–3. See also Luttrell, *Brief Historical Relation*, i. 113, 50, 191, for other examples of multiple combats fought during the Restoration period.

[48] Emmanuel van Meteren, *A True Discourse Historicall of the Succeeding Governors in the Netherlands and the Civill Warres there Begun in the Yeere 1565*, trans. Thomas Churchyard (London, 1602) [STC 17846], 105.

[49] *True Newes from one of Sir Fraunces Vere's Companie* (London, 1591) [STC 24652], sigs. A3–B2.

[50] *A True Coppie of a Discourse by a Gentleman Employed in the Late Voyage of Spaine and Portingale* (1589), ed. Alexander B. Grosart (repr. Manchester, 1881), 84. Bertrand de Loque, in his *Discourses of Warre and Single Combat*, trans. John Eliot (London, 1591) [STC 16810], 55–8, condemned single combats undertaken by two representatives of opposing armies to determine the outcome of a battle. Since the English edition of this book was dedicated to Robert, 2nd earl of Essex, this raises the question whether Essex, or anyone in his household, read this book or approved its contents.

The tendency of grandees such as Lord Willoughby and the second and third earls of Essex to approach warfare as an occasion for individual displays of bravado was emulated by their followers. Richard Peeke accompanied the third earl of Essex on the expedition to Cadiz in 1625. He was taken prisoner and tried by a military court presided over by the duke of Medina Sidonia, who challenged Peeke to fight with a Spaniard. Peeke disarmed his opponent and the duke challenged him to fight another. Peeke claimed that he offered to fight as many as five Spaniards with a quarter-staff fashioned from a halberd. He entered the 'lists' with three opponents who were armed with rapier and poniard; he killed one and the others fled. Medina Sidonia freed Peeke and presented him to the king of Spain, who offered him employment. Peeke preferred to go home and was allowed to depart in peace with a gift of money. On his way through France, Peeke states that he met two more Spaniards who insulted his country. Peeke fought a duel with one of them. At this point two other Englishmen entered the tavern, which had hastily been converted to a field of honour, and, with their help, Peeke compelled the Spaniards to recant on their knees.[51] While tales such as Peeke's smack of the fabulous, the important point to note is the lack of a clear distinction among gallants between *bellum* and *duellum*.

Surely the prince of braggadocio among English swordsmen was Captain John Smith. While Smith was serving in an Imperialist cavalry regiment at the siege of Regal in Transylvania, the Turkish governor, complaining of a want of activity during the slow siege, invited challengers from the Habsburg forces to meet him in single combat. Smith claims that he fought and killed the pasha and cut off his head. He then met two more Turkish challengers and claimed two more heads, and thereafter blazoned his coat armour with three Turks' heads.[52] Perhaps remembering the second earl of Essex's penchant for histrionic display, Prince Rupert, following his first victory at age 22 at Powick Bridge, just prior to the Battle of Edgehill in 1642, sent

---

[51] R[ichard] Peeke, *Three to One: Being an English–Spanish Combat performed by a Western Gentleman of Tavistock . . . with an English Quarterstaff against Three Spaniards . . . at Sherries* [Jerez] *. . . the 15th day of November 1625*, in *Stuart Tracts, 1603–1693*, ed. C. H. Firth (Westminster, 1903; repr. Wilmington, Del., 1973), 279–93.

[52] *The True Travels, Adventures and Observations of Captaine John Smith in Europe, Asia, Africa and America, from 1593 to 1629* (London, 1630), in *Travels and Works of Captain John Smith*, ed. Edward Arber and A. G. Bradley, 2 vols. (Edinburgh, 1910; repr. New York, 1967), ii. 838–40.

a challenge to the third earl of Essex, as commander of the parliamentary forces, to decide by single combat the quarrel between king and Parliament. The letter of challenge accused Essex of coveting the throne, and was undoubtedly intended as a propaganda piece, but there is no reason to doubt that Rupert would have fought with Essex had the latter accepted.[53]

Duelling has always been dealt with more leniently in the soldier than in the civilian. Refusal to accept a challenge or to offer one when justified was regarded as reprehensible conduct in an officer. Indeed, well into the nineteenth century in the British Army officers continued to debate the question whether fellow officers who failed to accept or offer challenges where honour was touched should not be tried by court martial. This was because officers believed that the bravery that was required to hazard one's life on the field of honour against a private enemy was exactly the same kind of courage needed to face a public enemy on the field of battle.[54] The Whig pamphleteer John Oldmixon, who wrote a pamphlet in defence of Lord Mohun's second, Gen. Macartney, argued that a soldier who neglected his own honour could hardly be expected to defend the honour of his country. Thus, well into the eighteenth century military men continued to offer the excuse that, if they avoided duels, they would lose the respect of their fellow officers and those under their command. This would make it impossible for them to pursue the military profession, they insisted. Following this logic, if princes needed gentlemen of honour and courage to lead their standing armies, they must be prepared to tolerate duelling among military officers. It was a vicious circle, and one early eighteenth-century critic was convinced that the cult of duelling would wither if military men would lay aside the practice.[55]

Soldiers regarded duelling to be at the heart of martial culture. Vincentio Saviolo thought that swordsmanship or fencing was 'the beginning and foundation of the art military'. Besides the practical skills of self-defence, swordsmanship provided an introduction to the world of the soldier and taught the finer points of honour and the professional jargon without which a volunteer or newly commissioned

---

[53] Patrick Morah, *Prince Rupert of the Rhine* (London, 1976), 83.

[54] Clifford Walton, *A History of the British Standing Army, 1660–1700* (London, 1894), 582–3; Moore, *Two Treatises on Duelling and Gaming*, ii. 262.

[55] Cockburn, *History and Examination of Duels*, 229; Peltonen, *The Duel in Early Modern England*, 192, 289, 295–6.

officer would be regarded as green. Moreover, the practical skills of swordsmanship were also useful in small skirmishes, which occurred frequently in war.[56] Thus, duelling was especially prevalent in military camps, garrison towns, and large cities such as London, where officers and volunteers gathered when on leave or between campaigns. Ute Frevert says that the Thirty Years War fostered the practice of duelling because of official tolerance of the practice in armies made up mostly of mercenaries from different nationalities.[57]

Sir William Segar, Norroy king-at-arms in the late-Elizabethan period, laid down rules for challenges to duels that simply ignored statute law, royal proclamations, and the express wishes of his royal mistress, and were instead, so Segar claimed, derived from the practice of the ancient Greeks and Romans.[58] However, the fact remains that persons who fought duels in England risked the bother of being indicted for murder, and the attitude of monarchs such as Elizabeth and James I discouraged the practice, although royal pardons could be obtained. Martialists discovered that the courts of Maurice, prince of Orange, and Elizabeth, queen of Bohemia, in the Netherlands proved much more tolerant of gallants addicted to duelling.[59]

Rumours of war or news of current sieges caused gallants to flock to the European mainland seeking military glory. Chamberlain reported a spate of duelling at home during the Siege of Juliers in 1610: 'indeed, it were fitter they had some place abroad to vent their superfluous valour than to brabble so much as they do here at home.' Chamberlain's prescribed cure was no better than the disease, because the presence of gallants led to displays of bravado and punctiliousness in the camp before Juliers, where drinking and quarrelling in the colonels' messes between the factions of Sir Edward Cecil and Sir Horace Vere erupted into numerous duels. The same animosity also persisted for years in the Anglo-Dutch Brigade of the States' Army between the followers of Cecil and Sir Edward Vere. Since they were adherents of the Veres, the numerous martial members of the Holles clan were also drawn

[56] *Vincentio Saviola his Practice*, 2–3.
[57] Hales, *Golden Remains*, 86; Frevert, *Men of Honour*, 12–13; George Whetstone, *The Honourable Reputation of a Souldier* (London, 1585) [STC 25339], sigs. A2ᵛ–A3ʳ.
[58] Segar, *Honour, Civil and Military*, iii. 121.
[59] *Letters from George, Lord Carew to Sir Thomas Roe . . . 1615–1617*, ed. John Maclean (CS, old ser., 76; Westminster, 1860), 10, 65.

212 THE DISCOURSE OF VIOLENCE

into this faction fighting. Prince Maurice was from time to time obliged to intercede to keep peace and maintain discipline within his camp.[60]

Duelling had been slow to displace the blood feud in Scotland, but Scottish soldiers abroad readily took up the practice, and, according to Sir Thomas Urquhart, quite distinguished themselves. Following the Battle of Worcester (1651), in which he fought with an ill-disciplined Scots Royalist army, Urquhart published a book to vindicate the honour of the Scots nation.[61] Urquhart's purpose was to enumerate the more noteworthy exploits of the many Scottish soldiers who served overseas in European armies. The martialists to whom Urquhart gave pride of place were all duellists, such as Francis Sinclair, natural son of the earl of Caithness, famed for repelling assaults by gangs of adversaries or defeating in public combats martial bullies regarded as invincible. Of all the Scots 'devoted to the shrine of Mars', the greatest was James Crichton, more familiarly known as 'the admirable Crichton', who, after serving two years in the French army, attracted attention as a servingman at the court of Mantua, where he volunteered to vindicate the honour of the court by dispatching in single combat a vicious and notorious Italian duellist who had been making his way across Europe challenging all comers. Moreover, says Urquhart, Crichton dispatched his opponent with such extraordinary grace and style that the three fatal strokes, if joined together, would have formed 'a perfect Isosceles triangle'.[62] Crichton was also, so Urquhart tells us, a man of prodigious memory, rare judgement, and extraordinary learning, who mastered twelve languages and could dispute with learned doctors on any subject. Nor was there any aspect of martial or athletic prowess in which he did not excel. Such perfection could only excite envy, and 'the admirable Crichton' was murdered by a drunken gang of courtiers led by Vincentio di Gonzaga, prince of Mantua, the son and heir of the duke of Mantua, during

[60] *The Letters of John Chamberlain*, ed. N. E. McClure, 2 vols. (Philadelphia, 1939), i. 297–8; *Life of Edward, First Lord Herbert of Cherbury*, ed. Shuttleworth, 54–9; PRO SP 84/108, fos. 1–3; Gervase Holles, *Memorials of the Holles Family, 1493–1656*, ed. A. C. Wood (CS, 3rd ser., 60; London, 1937), 78–81.

[61] Sir Thomas Urquhart of Cromarty, ΕΚΣΚΥΒΑΛΑΡΟΝ *[EKSKIBALAVON]: Or The Discovery of a Most Exquisite Jewel . . . found in the Kennel of Worcester-Streets the Day after the Fight . . . anno 1651, Serving in this Place to Frontal a Vindication of the Honour of Scotland* (London, 1652), repr. *Works* (Maitland Club Publications, 30; Edinburgh, 1834).

[62] Ibid. 220–44, esp. 223.

a Shrove Tuesday brawl.[63] Another Scottish soldier of fortune who
took up duelling on the continent was Sir James Turner. He at least
recognized duelling to be 'a sin against God' and confessed that he
was always in his cups when he fought duels. By comparison to other
martialists, Turner was not a bloodthirsty man; he abhorred cruelty
and spoke out against and attempted to prevent atrocities.[64]

Gervase Holles, on the other hand, had been prevented from becoming a soldier as a young man by the head of the family, the earl of Clare,
because he was the only surviving son in his family. He became a
lawyer and an antiquarian instead, but still found an outlet for his
energies in duelling. In 1636, Clare again intervened to stop Gervase
from going to France to serve as a second because he assumed that
the encounter would take the form of a multiple combat involving
seconds.[65] Sir John Reresby had acquired his habit of duelling from
contact with former Royalist officers while he was a student at Gray's
Inn during the Interregnum. When he went on a grand tour in 1654, he
became involved in duels or quarrels nearly everywhere he went while
in France. The loss of a cousin and a close personal friend in duelling
contests in no way deterred him from engaging in these combats.[66]

Although the early proponents of duelling regarded it as an aristocratic privilege, the practice was soon imitated by members of the
professional and commercial middle classes. This was because the
influence of martial culture was never confined to the aristocracy,
and someone of marginal gentle status might feel even more compelled to defend his honour. One can hardly describe Marmaduke
Rawdon of York, a Canary merchant, as a swordsman: he spent the
whole time of the civil wars trying to avoid becoming involved or

[63] While the DNB (sub James Crichton (1560–85)) states that Urquhart embellished
his account of Crichton's life and death, it is accurate in the main details. Urquhart
himself insisted that many Scots soldiers who served on the Continent could testify to
the truthfulness of his account. More to the point, the story of 'the admirable Crichton'
reveals much about the Cavalier values of Urquhart himself.

Sir Thomas Urquhart sent a written challenge in 1658 to his kinsman, John
Urquhart of Craigfintray, who had entered upon Sir Thomas's estates and pretended
to be laird of Cromarty or Cromartie. The duel was never fought (A Challenge from Sir
Thomas Urquhart of Cromartie (Luttrell Soc., no. 4: Oxford, 1947), pp. xxvvi–xxvii.

[64] Sir James Turner, Memoirs of his Own Life and Times, 1632–1670 (BC 28;
Edinburgh, 1829), 42–3.

[65] P. R. Newman, The Old Service: Royalist Regimental Colonels and the Civil War,
1642–46 (Manchester, 1993), 155; HMC, Fourth Report, pt. I (De La Warr MSS)
(1874), 304a.

[66] Memoirs of Sir John Reresby, ed. Browning, pp. xxxvi n., 2–11, 277.

even declaring his allegiance. Yet his memoirs recount in detail four occasions on which he felt obliged to defend his honour or that of ladies of his acquaintance, and he was not backward in doing so.[67] The rapier became the usual duelling weapon in the late sixteenth century through the influence of Italian fencing masters. Rocco Bonetti is supposed to have introduced the method of fighting with rapier and dagger into England; he kept a fencing school in Blackfriars that was patronized by members of the court such as the seventeenth earl of Oxford, Sir John North, and Sir Walter Raleigh. Vincentio Saviolo and his brother Jeronimo also taught at the Blackfriars school. Samuel Butler thought that the only purpose of fencing masters was to teach gallants how to fight duels with rapiers so that they might kill their opponents. Thus there was a direct connection between fencing schools, the use of the rapier, and the introduction of the cult of duelling into England.[68]

Critics of the cult of duelling insisted that in former times swords were worn as a privilege of aristocratic status and were to be employed only 'under authority' in defence of one's country, 'to protect the weak and innocent from the violence of oppressors, [and] also to preserve their persons from outrage'. It was not formerly the practice to wear broadswords all the time because they were heavy and cumbersome, but the rapier, the weapon of choice of duellists, was light and worn everywhere and therefore always at hand. Apparently, it required greater skill to wield the more lethal rapier than the medieval broadsword or the more modern edged weapons of war, such as the cavalry sabre or the infantry hanger.[69] George Silver, the author of a fencing

[67] Hanlon, *Twilight of a Military Tradition*, 342–3; Kelly, 'That Damn'd Thing Called Honour', 13; Moore, *Two Treatises on Duelling and Gaming*, ii. 254; *The Life of Marmaduke Rawdon of York*, ed. Robert Davies (CS., old ser., 85; London, 1863), 56–63.

[68] Peltonen, *The Duel in Early Modern England*, 61–2; C. W. Wallace, *The Evolution of the English Drama up to Shakespeare* (Schriften der Deutschen Shakespeare-Gesellschaft, IV; Berlin, 1912), 186–7; Samuel Butler, 'A Fencer', in Butler, *Characters*, ed. Davies, 272–3.

[69] François de La Noue, *The Politicke and Militarie Discourses of the Lord De La Nowe*, trans. Edward Aggas (London, 1587) [STC 15215], 134; Castiglione, *Book of the Courtier*, trans. Hoby, 53; Anglo, 'How to Kill a Man at Your Ease', 3; Gailhard, *The Compleat Gentleman*, ii. 49–50.

For a discussion of Vincentio Saviolo, George Silver, and other English fencing masters, See J. D. Aylward, *The English Master of Arms from the Twelfth to the Twentieth Century* (London, 1956), chs. v and vi. Another early English fencing master who advocated use of the rapier was Joseph Swetnam, who claimed to have been the fencing teacher to Henry, prince of Wales (*The Schoole of the Noble and Worthy Science of Defence* (London, 1617) [STC 23543], sig. A2 n.).

manual dedicated to the second earl of Essex, which was meant to answer Vincentio Saviolo's book, thought that skill had little to do with combats employing rapiers, and that duelling fatalities were more often the result of accidents rather than skill. Silver condemned 'outlandish' fencing masters and insisted that the proper weapons for defence were the short sword and the half-pike, because poniards and rapiers were too long for battlefield combat. Moreover, the thin-bladed rapier often broke and had to be replaced.[70] Montaigne thought that the use of the rapier favoured the individuality of the duel over organized and disciplined warfare, but he also condemned the practice of duelling as cowardly.[71]

Thus, the skills needed for duelling in aristocratic circles as taught by fencing masters such as Saviolo were not applicable to war. Fencing with a rapier had no purpose other than to serve as an efficient weapon for killing in private combats. The purpose of the fencing master's art was to emphasize 'lethal assault' rather than defence.[72] In 1600, John Chamberlain reported a duel between two of the second earl of Essex's knights. At first, they were both thought to be dead, but after a time they revived. One sustained eight wounds from his opponent's rapier, and the second received twelve wounds. More usually, rapier wounds proved fatal, and surgeons resented the loss of business; there had been more patching up to be done when, as in former times, duellists had banged it out with broadsword and buckler. By the middle of the seventeenth century, some swordsmen, such as John Weale, a lieutenant in the Commonwealth Navy, found an outlet for their swordplay in fencing as a sport with foils rather than rapiers.[73]

[70] George Silver, *Paradoxes of Defence* (London, 1599; repr. Amsterdam, 1968), sigs. A4$^{r-v}$, A5$^{r-v}$, B2r$^r$, pp. 4, 7, 18–20; *Barrington Family Letters, 1628–1632*, ed. Arthur Searle (CS, 4th ser., 28; London, 1983), 42; Peltonen, *The Duel in Early Modern England*, 94–7.

[71] Harding, *Anatomy of a Power Elite*, 78–9.

[72] Anglo, 'How to Kill a Man at Your Ease', 4–9; id., *The Martial Arts of Renaissance Europe* (New Haven, 2000), 280–1.

Schools of defence were originally founded to serve the needs of the commonalty in a lawless society, but in the sixteenth century came to serve the needs of gentlemen. They gave instruction in the use of the long sword, rapier, and staff (Jay P. Anglin, 'The Schools of Defence in Elizabethan London', *Renaissance Quarterly*, 37 (1984), 395–6.

[73] *Letters of John Chamberlain*, ed. McClure, i. 107, 109; John Earle, *Microcosmography*, ed. Harold Osborne (1633; repr. London, 1971), 69–70; 'The Journal of John Weale, 1654–1656', ed. J. R. Powell, in *The Naval Miscellany IV*, ed. C. Lloyd (NRS 92; 1952), 86–9, 98–9.

Just as the aristocracies of the British Isles believed that the recognition and regulation of noble status properly belonged to the community of honour and not the monarch, they likewise clung to the belief that the determination of disputes involving honour and reputation was also vested in those persons of noble status as a birthright. These attitudes had not changed since the Middle Ages; monarchs such as Elizabeth I, James VI and I, and Charles I pursued peace rather than war as a public policy and no longer valued their nobility and knights as a military resource.[74] Private war was forbidden and public war could be waged only by royal authority—a distinction that was too finely drawn for some swordsmen. That the Stuart monarchs could not enforce this policy and frequently allowed exceptions by granting pardons probably lessened respect for royal authority in many quarters. On the other hand, it is difficult to imagine a monarchy in seventeenth-century Britain and Ireland strong enough to enforce a total prohibition against duelling and other forms of aristocratic violence. Considering the widespread leniency of judges and juries towards persons who had killed another in a duel where the proprieties of the duelling code had been observed, it is difficult to see how the Stuart monarchs could have enforced a more stringent prohibition against duelling lacking, as they did, strong popular support for such a policy and more effective powers of enforcement.

Duelling among aristocrats was potentially both subversive and seditious, a tendency that did not go unnoticed by Queen Elizabeth, John Selden, Francis Bacon, or Algernon Sidney, although it has largely escaped the attention of modern historians. It involved no leap of logic to perceive, as Selden did, that a prince who ignored the rights of his subjects should not be surprised if some of his more martial subjects felt obliged to vindicate their rights by a resort to arms. That this right of resistance was widely assumed may be linked to the reluctance of Parliament to enact legislation specifically condemning the practice of duelling. That most duelling encounters were probably provoked by strong drink and a vengeful spirit rather than principle did nothing to lessen the danger latent in the failure of the Stuart monarchs to curb the phenomenon of duelling among swordsmen and courtiers.

---

[74] Algernon Sidney, *Discourses Concerning Government* (1698; repr. New York, 1979), 419.

CHAPTER SEVEN

# Duelling and Authority

*BUSSY.* When I am wrong'd and the law fails to right me,
Let me be king myself (as man was made)
And do a justice that exceeds law;
If my wrong pass the power of single valour
To right and expiate, then be you my king,
And do a right exceeding law and nature.
Who to himself is law, no law doth need,
Offends no king, and is a king indeed.

(George Chapman, *Bussy d'Ambois*, ed. Nicholas
Brooke (London, 1964), II. i. 197–204 (p. 39))

Fighting becomes none but those of the military profession; nor
yet them, except in a public cause and when lawful authority
requires it.

(John Cockburn, *The History and Examination of Duels*
(London, 1720) [ESTCT 118651], p. viii)

The critics of the phenomenon of duelling agreed that, at best, the
practice ignored royal proclamations, offended divine law, and was
inconsistent with the values of a civil society. Ultimately, the practice
of duelling invaded the royal prerogative, was symbolically an act of
subversion and rebellion, and asserted the regulation of aristocratic
status by the community of honour rather than royal authority.
Theologians and ethicists condemned duelling as murder or suicide
depending on the outcome of private combats, and military commanders discovered that duelling subverted military hierarchies and
undermined military discipline, and they issued articles of war prohibiting the practice. But so strong was the influence of martial
culture, and so great the esteem evoked by the valour associated with
duelling, that the practice persisted in the British Isles and, indeed, the

218    THE DISCOURSE OF VIOLENCE

English-speaking world and beyond for more than a century and a half after the end of the seventeenth century.[1]

Sir Francis Bacon, attorney-general of England from 1613 and lord chancellor after 1618, provided the most clearly stated argument against duelling from the perspective of upholding the law and maintaining royal authority. He specified a number of ways in which the practice was injurious. The right to seek revenge by dispensing justice is given by God to the prince or magistrate for the public good, and is usurped by those who fight duels for private ends. It is a perversion of justice for a man to make law for his own benefit and to sit in judgment on his own case. Any justification of duelling must injure the law, because it would be based upon the assumption that there was one law for gownsmen and another for men of honour, who must defend their reputations. Furthermore, the law of England does not distinguish between murder and killing a man upon a challenge in a duel, nor does the law of God do so either. The attempt to make such a distinction 'was never authorized by any law or ancient examples, but is a late vanity crept in from the practice of the French, who themselves have grown so weary of it, as they have been forced to put it down with all severity'. The deaths that result from duelling deprive the king of soldiers or potential soldiers, and the toleration of such individual combats can lead to civil war.[2]

The medieval Church had always opposed private warfare, and the English medieval kings came to share this view as well. Jean d'Espagne, who was commissioned by Charles I to write a treatise against duelling, found that English monarchs had permitted combats in the past, but he could find no evidence of a monarch having done so since 1441, when Henry VI allowed Sir Richard Woodville to fight a Spanish knight. D'Espagne thought that a combat was the worst of expedients for settling a dispute.[3] Much confusion existed

[1] John Cockburn, *The History and Examination of Duels* (London, 1720) [ESTCT 118651], p. xiv; Matthew Sutcliffe, *The Practice, Proceedings and Lawes of Armes* (London, 1593) [STC 23468], 325–6.
[2] *The Charge of Sir Francis Bacon . . . Touching Duels* (London, 1614; repr. Amsterdam, 1968), 8–11, 22, 45–6.
Jean Bodin, on the other hand, thought that to deny combats to vindicate honour nourished the kind of animosity that led to civil war (*The Six Bookes of a Commonwealth*, ed. K. D. McRae (1606; repr. Cambridge, Mass., 1962), 527–8).
[3] M. H. Keen, *The Laws of War in the Late Middle Ages* (London, 1965), 73–4; Jean d'Espagne, *Anti-Duello: The Anatomie of Duells* (London, 1632) [STC 10530], 44, 63.

in the minds of jurists and antiquarians concerning the distinction between duels and the medieval trial by combat, and also concerning whether trials by combat could be authorized by the king and his judges. When the Puritan Sir Thomas Posthumous Hoby sought redress from Ralph, third Lord Eure, president of the Council in the North, concerning abusive behaviour by the Cholmleys and some of Eure's own kinsmen who had invaded Hoby's household and impugned his honour, he was dismayed to hear Eure speak of the possibility of resolving the feud by means of a trial by combat. Eure told Hoby that he must understand 'that men had not swords only to wear, but sometimes to draw them to defend their reputations'.[4] John Rushworth found evidence, as late as 1638, of a judge being compelled to allow a combat between two minor gentry about a land dispute. The demandant, Richard Claxton, actually threw down the gauntlet in the Court of Pleas of the County Palatine of Durham, and challenged Richard Lilburne (the father of John Lilburne, the future Leveller leader). However, Judge Richard Berkeley discovered an error in the court record (deliberately inserted by the clerk of court), and stopped the combat on a technicality.[5]

John Selden was prepared to admit the legality of sanctioning duels under the laws of England provided the aggrieved parties could not be reconciled by arbitration. Injured honour requires a just remedy, insisted Selden. His ingenious mind reasoned that, if war is lawful, and a Providential God will decide the outcome, then it becomes possible to construct a similar argument to justify the resort to a combat in order to decide a private quarrel.[6] John Cockburn, a Scottish divine who condemned duelling in no uncertain terms, found evidence that doubt still existed in the minds of royal judges in the Elizabethan period concerning whether they could deny parties to a suit the right to demand a trial by combat. The judges yielded to such a demand by Simon Lowe and John Kyme, plaintiffs, and Thomas Paramour, defendant, to engage in a judicial combat concerning a dispute about

⁴ The quotation is from Felicity Heal and Clive Holmes, *The Gentry in England and Wales, 1500–1700* (Stanford, Calif., 1994), 5. See also Felicity Heal, *Hospitality in Early Modern England* (Oxford, 1990), 13–14; Roger B. Manning, *Hunters and Poachers: A Cultural and Social History of Unlawful Hunting in England, 1485–1640* (Oxford, 1993), 228–9.

⁵ John Rushworth, *Historical Collections*, 8 vols. (London, 1721–2) [ESTCN 33526], II. i. 788–90.

⁶ [Richard Milward,] *The Table-Talk of John Selden*, ed. S. W. Singer (1855; repr. Freeport, NY, 1972), 47–8.

a parcel of land on the Isle of Sheppey, Kent. Apparently, the principals, their lawyers, and the justices of the Court of Common Pleas had actually assembled in Tothill Fields, Westminster, and the ceremony had proceeded to the point of combat, when the chief justice read a command from the queen forbidding the combat. The chief justice then read the judgment of the court in the case. Cockburn quotes the historian John Speed's comment upon this episode: ''Twas always judged insulting [of] authority and invading of the prerogative either to fight and give challenges without the king's leave, which no wise or good king will ever grant, nor will any ask who regards the precepts of religion, or consults reason and common sense, or wisely considers their private interest or public good.'[7]

Not all martialists believed that they possessed a right to resolve disputes of honour by combat or duel, although they did generally believe that the monarch was obliged to find an outlet for the bellicosity of noble spirits. Jousting tournaments were officially organized theatrical spectacles intended to display knightly prowess. However, they were supposed to be devoid of personal enmity and were not intended to resolve disputes. The royal tournaments in the tiltyard at Westminster provided for a time an outlet for aristocratic aggressiveness and martial prowess, but, as the case of the second earl of Essex demonstrates, such noble spirits would ultimately seek fulfilment of their ambitions through service in foreign wars, or, in Essex's case, in rebellion.[8]

Henry Howard, first earl of Northampton, accepted the concepts of honour and civil courtesy and agreed that a gentleman could be injured by insults. He understood that, because of these values, it was difficult to avoid the occasion of duelling. At the same time he argued strongly against duelling and tried to find an alternative solution to the problem of insults that injured a gentleman's reputation. Northampton advocated that friends attempt to settle the quarrel by arbitration, that they attempt to disarm the parties if a duel or a brawl threatened, or, in the last resort, that the dispute be brought

[7] Cockburn, *History and Examination of Duels*, pp. xii–xiv. See also Charles Moore, *A Full Inquiry into the Subject of Suicide, to which are Added . . . Two Treatises on Duelling and Gambling*, 2 vols. (London, 1790) [ESTCT 111258], ii. 241.

[8] Thomas Pestell, *Sermons and Devotions Old and New* (London, 1659) [Wing P1675], 325; Ute Frevert, *Men of Honour: A Social and Cultural History of the Duel*, trans Anthony Williams (Cambridge, 1995), 10–11; Richard C. McCoy, ' "A Dangerous Image": The Earl of Essex and Elizabethan Chivalry', *Journal of Medieval and Renaissance Studies*, 13.2 (1983), 316–17.

before a court of honour in the form of the revived Court of Chivalry. Northampton was well acquainted with the literature of civil courtesy and duelling, and was also one of the commissioners of the Court of the Earl Marshal, otherwise known as the Court of Chivalry. However, Northampton's policy for resolving disputes of honour did not long survive his death in 1614.[9]

Critics of duelling in England generally agreed that any attempt to deter the practice must first punish the offensive words that gave rise to challenges to duels. By the very end of the Elizabethan period, the Court of Star Chamber had developed a legal doctrine of seditious libel for punishing those who defamed ministers of the Crown, bishops, magistrates, and other great persons, but the emphasis was upon punishing social inferiors who libelled their betters, and much of the effort of the court was directed towards stifling popular political criticism and discourse. Moreover, the doctrine of sedition asserted that a true libel was worse than a false one because it was more likely to provoke a breach of the peace. The Court of Star Chamber punished those who issued or carried challenges to duels, but it never attempted to hear and determine disputes of honour, which was a jurisdiction that properly belonged to the Earl Marshal's Court. James I and VI had revived the jurisdiction of this court to settle disputes that might lead to challenges to duels, and the theory was that, once the Court of Chivalry had intervened, the quarrel was supposed to be extinguished. However, the impartiality of the Earl Marshal's Court remained suspect because, when arbitrating a dispute between an untitled gentleman and a grandee, the court was more interested in preserving the social hierarchy than rendering justice.[10] This went against the assumption, widespread amongst swordsmen, that there was a rough equality among members of the community of honour—regardless of social

[9] Markku Peltonen, *The Duel in Early Modern England: Civility, Politeness and Honour* (Cambridge, 2003), 131, 135–6, 144.

[10] Roger B. Manning, 'The Origins of the Doctrine of Sedition', *Albion*, 12.2 (1980), 99–121; Sutcliffe, *The Practice, Proceedings and Lawes of Armes*, 325–6; Sir George Clark, *War and Society in the Seventeenth Century* (Cambridge, 1958), 38; *The Charge of Sir Francis Bacon . . . Touching Duells*, 55–6; *A Publication of His Ma[jes]ties Edict and Severe Censure against Private Combats and Combatants* (London, 1613) [STC 8498.5], 21–2; *Stuart Royal Proclamations*, i: *Royal Proclamations of James I, 1603–1625*, ed. J. F. Larkin and P. L. Hughes (Oxford, 1973), 132; G. D. Squib, *The High Court of Chivalry* (Oxford, 1959), 27, 57, 101–2, 144; P. H. Hardacre, 'The Earl Marshal, the Heralds, and the House of Commons, 1604–1644', *International Review of Social History*, 2 (1957), 106–25.

rank within that community. Moreover, many martialists assumed that honour disputes could not be adjudicated by gownsmen, but only settled by trial on the field of honour where the language of the sword spoke more eloquently than lawyers' arguments.

In an age of pervasive war and widespread interpersonal violence, attempts to limit the destructiveness of war and to suppress duelling were culturally linked; these evils were different facets of the same uncontrolled urge to seek revenge. Swordsmen who were used to leading the king's armies into battle to avenge the king's honour had difficulty understanding why they could not avenge their own honour. Again, it is the same old difficulty that swordsmen had in distinguishing between public war and private war.[11] As modern writers like to put it, the problem was for the monarch to secure a monopoly on the use of violence. This is an oversimplification. Sixteenth- and seventeenth-century writers put a different emphasis on the question of when the use of violence was appropriate. Bertrand de Loque said that 'private revenge is forbidden and not public revenge, which is executed by the magistrate according to the law and by the commandment of God'. Private persons who presume to take the sword into their own hands are '*ipso facto* seditious'.[12] John Hales insisted that the main function of monarchy was to compose quarrels and dispense justice, 'for were men peaceable, were men not injurious to one another, there would be no use for government'. For a subject to take it upon himself to fight a private duel cannot but diminish the authority of a prince or magistrate.[13] James VI and I placed the blame for the phenomenon of duelling on the animosity and violence generated by the continental religious wars and asserted that the fashion for private combats was a custom 'born and bred in foreign parts, but after conveyed over into this land, as many other hurtful and unlawful wars are oftentimes in close packs'.[14]

King James VI and I spoke vehemently against duelling, but in practice he enforced that policy inconsistently. It was Henry Howard, first earl of Northampton, as a commissioner for the office of earl marshal,

[11] J. T. Johnson, *Just War Tradition and the Restraint of War: A Moral and Historical Inquiry* (Princeton, 1981), 43–4.

[12] [Bertrand de Loque,] *Discourses of Warre and Single Combat*, trans John Eliot (London, 1591) [STC 16810], 3–4.

[13] John Hales, *Golden Remains* (London, 1659) [Wing H269], 90–1.

[14] *Stuart Royal Proclamations*, vol. i, no. 136. See also André Corvisier, *Armies and Societies in Europe, 1494–1789*, trans A. T. Siddall (Bloomington, Ind., 1979), 4.

who led the campaign against duelling and wrote the proclamation against private combats published in 1613 with James's backing. James would sometimes sit in the Court of Star Chamber and pronounce the sentence of the court himself, as he did on 13 February 1617 when he punished two gentlemen of the Inns of Court with imprisonment in the Tower of London; he also fined them £1,000 apiece, forbade them to wear any weapon for seven years, and prohibited them from coming within ten miles of the royal court. But, despite the declared policy, announced in 1613, of denying pardons to persons engaging in duels and banishing them from court, James granted a pardon to Sir Edward Sackville after he had killed Edward, second Lord Bruce of Kinlosse, in a notorious encounter in the Netherlands and allowed him to return to court; he granted a similar pardon to Francis, second Lord Norris, after he had killed a servant of Lord Willoughby in a duel. By contrast, James's Scottish subjects appear to have been dealt with more strictly. Colonel Andrew Ramsay, an officer in the Swedish army, was banished from Scotland after challenging the royal favourite, Robert Carr, Viscount Rochester and later earl of Somerset, to a duel.[15]

Those contemporary commentators who were prepared to tolerate single combats to vindicate honour that had been impugned usually preferred to see such combats sanctioned and supervised by a 'tribunal of arms' or a court of chivalry.[16] John Selden assumed that the Court of the Earl Marshal still had the authority to permit duels to purge offences against martial honour. The authority that he cited was the 'law of arms'.[17] Even Sir Edward Coke agreed that the Court of the Earl Marshal had jurisdiction over military offences, and that a trial by combat remained possible in cases where an accusation of treason had been made.[18]

---

[15] *Letters from George, Lord Carew to Sir Thomas Roe . . . 1615–1617*, ed. John Maclean (CS, old ser., 76; Westminster, 1860), 10, 86; James Kelly, '*That Damn'd Thing Called Honour*': Duelling in Ireland, 1570–1860 (Cork, 1995), 21; *Stuart Royal Proclamations*, vol. i, no. 132; F. T. Bowers, 'Henry Howard, Earl of Northampton and Duelling in England', *Englische Studien*, 71 (1937), 350–5; Linda Levy Peck, *Northampton: Patronage and Policy at the Court of James I* (London, 1982), 160–1, 163–4; *Letters of John Holles, 1587–1637*, ed. P. R. Seddon, 3 vols. (Thoroton Soc., 31, 35, 36; Nottingham, 1975–86), i. 83–3 and n.; T. A. Fischer, *The Scots in Sweden* (Edinburgh, 1907), 75–83.

[16] [Count Annibale Romei,] *The Courtier's Academie*, trans John Kepers (London, 1598) [STC 21311], 165, 181.

[17] John Selden, *The Duello, or Single Combat* (London, 1610) [STC 22171], 40.

[18] Cited in Hardacre, 'The Earl Marshal, the Heralds and the House of Commons', 112–13.

In the time of Charles I, the Court of the Earl Marshal came close actually to allowing a trial by combat. Sir Donald Mackay of Far, first Lord Reay, described as 'a Western or Irish Scot', found himself in competition with James, marquis of Hamilton, in 1631 while attempting to raise soldiers for the army of Gustavus Adolphus. Lord Reay, the proprietary colonel of Mackay's Regiment and the most successful Scottish military entrepreneur of that time, resented the recruiting activities of Hamilton, who was a favourite of Charles I. Reay procured several of his friends to spread the rumour that Hamilton was raising six regiments, not to join the cause of Gustavus Adolphus, but to seize the Scottish throne. This animosity between the two Scottish peers evidently grew out of a feud between their respective families handed down from previous generations. It was James, Lord Ogilvy, and not Reay, who carried this accusation to the English Privy Council, but Hamilton's agent and witness on his behalf, David Ramsay, stated that the accusation originated with Reay. Ramsay demanded a trial by combat with Lord Reay before the Court of Chivalry in order to clear his own name of an accusation of treason by Reay. Ramsay forfeited any claim to sympathy because it was discovered that he had already arranged for a private duel, but Charles allowed arrangements for a public trial by combat to proceed, and Ramsay threw down the gauntlet. At the last moment, Charles cancelled the combat when the clergy and a number of common lawyers made known their opinion that the survivor of a trial by combat would be regarded, in law and morality, as being guilty of murder. Lord Reay and Ramsay were imprisoned briefly in the Tower for 'contempts' and 'seditions', and Ramsay was subsequently banished from the realm.[19]

Since the authority of the Court of the Earl Marshal had lapsed in 1521 and was revived some ninety years later by James I, it was difficult to specify where its authority came from, other than the proclamations of 1613, which had prohibited duels. The role that the Court of Chivalry could play in suppressing duelling was limited by

---

[19] Thomas Birch, *The Court and Times of Charles I*, ed. R. F. Williams, 2 vols. (London, 1848), ii. 14–17, 125–6, 135, 151–2; Gilbert Burnet, *The Memoirs of . . . James and William Dukes of Hamilton and Castle-Herald* (Oxford, 1852), 15–19; James Grant, *Memoirs of . . . Sir John Hepburn* (Edinburgh, 1851), 89–91; Rushworth, *Historical Collections*, II. i. 112–17; H. L. Rubinstein, *Captain Luckless: James, First Duke of Hamilton, 1606–1649* (Edinburgh, 1975), 29–30; Ian Grimble, *Chief of Mackay* (London, 1965), 1–9.

the low esteem in which the court was held at the beginning of the seventeenth century, and by the fact that almost all the cases brought before the court were the result of private prosecutions rather than public informations brought by the attorney general.[20] Thus, the Court of Chivalry, lacking clear direction, appeared to pursue a course that was more spasmodic than consistent in the suppression of duelling.

If the Court of Chivalry heard that arrangements had been made to fight a duel, it could act vigourously and provide severe punishments. This was because the court regarded making such arrangements in defiance of the court's exclusive jurisdiction over affairs of honour to be a more serious offence than speaking the opprobrious words that led to the challenge in the first place. In the reign of Charles I the punishments imposed by the court were severe and the fines heavy. Swordsmen determined to fight duels would often go overseas in order to fight a combat, but under both early Stuart monarchs the Court of Chivalry and the English Privy Council would try to stop combats being fought in other countries if the quarrel was notorious.[21] The most severe sentence that the Court of Chivalry ever handed down involved the case of a purser named Norman who challenged a fellow officer named Holmes aboard a merchantman bound for New England in 1634. They went ashore in Newfoundland to fight a duel and Holmes was killed. Upon his return to England, the Court of the Earl Marshal presided over by Robert Bertie, earl of Lindsey, tried Norman upon a complaint brought by Holmes's widow, and Lindsey pronounced a sentence of death against him.[22] On this occasion, the Court of Chivalry appears to have been functioning as a kind of court martial.

The Court of Chivalry continued to hear cases of honour as late as 1641. With the outbreak of hostilities, the exigencies of war and the necessity of maintaining military discipline caused the Earl Marshal's Court to be superseded by modern courts martial, which in the

[20] Hardacre, 'The Earl Marshal, the Heralds, and the House of Commons', 110–11, 120.
[21] Squib, *The High Court of Chivalry*, 146–7; Hardacre, 'The Earl Marshal, the Heralds, and the House of Commons', 120; Birch, *The Court and Times of Charles I*, i. 114; Sir Ralph Winwood, *Memorials of Affairs of State of the Reigns of Queen Elizabeth and King James*, ed. Edmund Sawyer, 3 vols. (London, 1725) [ESTCT 149966], iii. 95–6; *The Life of Edward, First Lord Herbert of Cherbury, Written by Himself*, ed. J. M. Shuttleworth (London, 1976), 42–4.
[22] *The Earl of Strafforde's Letters and Dispatches*, comp. William Knowler, 2 vols. (London, 1739) [ESTCT 145338], i. 208, 243. The earl of Strafford refers to this court as the Constable's Court, as does John Rushworth.

late sixteenth and early seventeenth centuries were sometimes called councils of war. The needs of discipline and the development of military hierarchies that gradually assumed more authority and prestige than social hierarchies led to an attempt to suppress duelling by prohibiting the practice in articles of war.[23]

The government of Lord Protector Cromwell attacked the problem of eradicating the 'courtly vice' of duelling with rather more determination, but ultimately discovered that they could not count upon the full cooperation of Parliament or the courts. A committee of the Long Parliament had recommended the enactment of harsh penalties against duelling in 1651, but the House of Commons rejected the proposed legislation. When grand juries indicted for murder in cases of fatal duels, trial juries or judges frequently reduced the charges to manslaughter, and the defendants were allowed to plead benefit of clergy. Following the dissolution of the Long Parliament, Cromwell and the Council of State proclaimed an ordinance against duelling in 1654, which was renewed in 1656. The penalties specified included imprisonment for six months for sending, carrying, or accepting a challenge. Anyone killing another person in a duel was to be tried for murder. Participants in non-fatal duels were to be banished for life, and, if subsequently caught in England, to suffer death as felons. Those who proceeded overseas to fight duels were to be treated as if the encounter had occurred in England. Cromwell tried to make examples of the most egregious offenders: he imprisoned Philip Stanhope, second earl of Chesterfield, for wounding another in a duel after Chesterfield had been called out for sending a young lady an obscene valentine. But even Cromwell lacked the power to regulate the code of honour that was the source of duelling.[24]

Because Charles II had shared exile with cavaliers and martialists, he became enmeshed in their culture to a greater degree than any of his predecessors during the previous century and a half. While he was living with his mother Henrietta Maria in exile at St Germain, his cousin, Prince Rupert of the Rhine, fought a duel in Charles's presence while he was still prince of Wales and wounded Lord Percy in the arm. Charles probably was present at similar encounters,

[23] Clifford Walton, *History of the British Standing Army, 1660–1700* (London, 1894), 583–4.
[24] Kelly, 'That Damn'd Thing Called Honour', 21–2; *Acts and Ordinances of the Interregnum, 1642–1660*, ed. C. H. Firth and R. S. Rait, 3 vols. (London, 1911), ii. 937–9; Robert Baldick, *The Duel: A History of Duelling* (New York, 1965), 68–9.

because his mother was not very successful in preventing combats between embittered former Royalist commanders.[25]

Following the Restoration, the cavaliers brought their quarrels into the king's presence. While Charles did impose sanctions, they were not consistently and vigourously enforced. In 1669, the earl of Rochester was banished from court for attacking Thomas Killigrew in the presence of the king. Charles soon admitted Rochester back into his favour, but the latter almost immediately became involved as a second in a multiple combat between Charles Stuart, duke of Richmond and Lennox, and James Hamilton. Rochester's closest friend was Henry Savile, younger brother of George Savile, marquis of Halifax. Savile was as irascible as Rochester and was briefly imprisoned for challenging the duke of Buckingham to a duel. In a drunken rage, Savile attacked and later fought a duel with the earl of Mulgrave. Rochester, a lifelong enemy of Mulgrave, fought alongside Savile as second. Several years later, in 1674, the quarrel between Savile and Mulgrave still raged. While at supper in the lord treasurer's house, in the presence of the king, Savile, 'being very drunk, fell so foully on Lord Mulgrave that the king commanded Savile to be gone out of his presence'. Mulgrave sent a challenge to Savile the next day. James, duke of York, a more determined opponent of duelling, prevailed upon the king to forbid Savile to come into the royal presence, but the prohibition did not last long.[26]

---

[25] *The Hamilton Papers . . . 1638–1650*, ed. S. R. Gardiner (CS, NS 27; London, 1880), 178; Ronald Hutton, *Charles II, King of England, Scotland and Ireland* (Oxford, 1991), 22.

[26] *The Letters of John Wilmot, Earl of Rochester*, ed. Jeremy Treglown (Chicago, 1980), 55 n.; *The Rochester–Savile Letters, 1671–1680*, ed. J. H. Wilson (Columbus, Oh., 1941), 6; *Essex Papers*, i: 1672–1679, ed. Osmund Airy (CS, NS 27; London, 1890), i. 281.
The background of this quarrel was that Buckingham had caricatured Sir William Coventry in a play, *The Country Gentleman*, jointly authored by him and John Howard. Learning of a plan to present the play, Coventry told Killigrew, the manager of the Theatre Royal, that any actor so foolish as to impersonate Coventry would have his nose slit. Coventry also sent a challenge to Buckingham. Buckingham was disinclined to fight a duel because the previous year he had killed the earl of Shrewsbury in a duel and he feared he might loose the king's favour if he fought another duel. The king suppressed the play, stripped Coventry of his offices, and sent him to the Tower of London, where he remained for a period of time. Coventry was accused of violating a statute of Henry VIII that had made it felony to conspire to kill a member of the Privy Council (John O'Neill, *George Villiers, Second Duke of Buckingham* (Boston, 1984), 62–4).

Charles II found it difficult to suppress duelling even among his own lieutenants and household officials. In 1671, Thomas, seventh Lord Windsor and later first earl of Plymouth, challenged John, first Lord Berkeley of Stratton, to a duel. Berkeley replied that he could not do so while he was still lord lieutenant of Ireland. Windsor retorted that he was lord lieutenant of Worcestershire and 'as good a man' as Berkeley, and that, if Berkeley did not fight, he would 'put him up for a coward and cudgel him'. After Lord Berkeley had complained to the Council, Windsor was sent to the Tower of London, but was released after less than a month.[27] Across the Atlantic, Lord Berkeley's brother, Sir William, the governor of Virginia, when confronted with armed defiance from Nathaniel Bacon, the leader of the Rebellion of 1675, proposed that they settle their dispute by a duel with swords. Although both were born into prominent aristocratic families in England, each had a different concept of honour: Bacon had already committed himself to leading the settlers on the frontier in a retaliatory raid against the Indians, so he refused to settle the issue by a duel.[28] When, in 1673, Charles II sought to prevent a cornet in the Life Guards from fighting a duel, the cornet and his rival and their seconds refused to allow the king to compose their quarrel. Charles had to threaten to banish them from all his kingdoms in order to compel them to come and accept their punishment.[29]

In 1682, Charles II actually sanctioned a duel and allowed it to proceed to combat. Early in January of that year, Henry Howard, sixth duke of Norfolk, had fought a duel in Flanders with the seneschal of Mons, the prince of Ligny's brother, in which the latter, presumably fighting as a second, was killed. The quarrel arose over 'abusive words' spoken by the seneschal against the duchess of Norfolk. The seneschal of Hainault, seeking revenge, subsequently came to England to fight Norfolk. Charles took Norfolk and the seneschal of Hainault into custody to prevent a private encounter, but authorized a multiple combat between Norfolk's heir, Henry, earl of Arundel, together with his second and the seneschal of Hainault and his second. Arundel

---

[27] Conway Letters: The Correspondence of Anne, Viscountess Conway, Henry Moore and their Friends, 1642–1684, ed. Marjorie Hope Nicolson (New Haven, 1930), 338–9 and n.; Cal. S.P., Dom., 1671, 346, 387.
[28] Kathleen Brown, Good Wives, Nasty Wenches and Anxious Patriarchs: Gender, Race and Power in Colonial Virginia (Chapel Hill, NC, 1996), 160–2.
[29] Letters Addressed to Sir Joseph Williamson, ed. W. D. Christie, 2 vols. (CS, NS 8, 9; London, 1874), i. 94.

broke his sword, and the combat was stopped after his second got the better of the seneschal's second.[30] Thus, even though Charles II had published a proclamation against duelling on 9 March 1680, he failed to enforce it consistently and granted numerous pardons. Two years earlier, Sir Pope Danvers had killed a man in an alehouse brawl that could hardly be considered a duel, and received a royal pardon, although a coroner's inquest called it wilful murder. Had he denied preferment to the many high-ranking royal officials who engaged in duelling, the practice might well have disappeared. Charles's failure to enforce the ban on duelling meant that his government effectively countenanced the practice.[31]

James II imposed more stringent standards of decorum on his court and announced that no person was to be allowed into his presence who 'either fights a duel, is drunk or keeps a woman openly'. James also attempted to suppress duelling by publishing an English translation of the king of France's decrees against sending challenges and engaging in private combats.[32] This probably had the effect of making the cult of duelling in England seem more patriotic and manly. James faced a showdown over this issue when a Whig grandee, William Cavendish, fifth earl and later first duke of Devonshire, struck Colonel Culpeper in the Withdrawing Room at Whitehall Palace after the latter had refused his challenge. Devonshire was required to appear before the Court of King's Bench, but he refused to plead, saying that he claimed parliamentary privilege. Devonshire subsequently pleaded not guilty, but he failed to persuade James II to grant him a pardon. He later changed his plea to guilty and the court sentenced him to pay a fine of £30,000 and find sureties for his good behaviour. Devonshire was also taken into custody until he could make arrangements to pay the fine. Ultimately, he was obliged to make his peace with James and kiss his hand.[33]

---

[30] Narcissus Luttrell, *A Brief Historical Relation of State Affairs from September 1678 to April 1714*, 6 vols. (Oxford, 1857; repr. Wilmington, Del., 1974), i. 156–7, 180–1.

[31] Cockburn, *History and Examination of Duels*, pp. xv–xvi; F. N. Macnamara, *Memorials of the Danvers Family* (London, 1895), 477–8.

[32] Thomas Belasyse, 1st earl of Falconberg, quoted in R. O. Bucholz, *The Augustan Court: Queen Anne and the Decline of Court Culture* (Stanford, Calif., 1993), 23; *The Laws of Honour: An Account of the Suppression of Duels in France* (London, 1685) [Wing L700], sig. A2.

[33] Luttrell, *Brief Historical Relation*, i. 401–3, 405–6, 417–18.

While the more thoughtful of jurists and legal writers condemned the practice of duelling, attempts consistently to enforce royal prohibitions against duelling were undercut by the ambivalence of lawyers and judges. Charles Moore thought that the practice of duelling was wrong because it substituted the private judgement of the parties to the dispute for that of judges and juries. Nor was it fit for a man to be both judge and executioner in his own case. Moreover, it subverted legally constituted authority by neglecting to submit private disputes to the court to be adjudicated by the laws of the state. Whereas lesser folk were severely punished for taking the law into their own hands, it was accounted an 'honourable action' if two gentlemen engaged in a pre-arranged combat.[34] Charles Moore quoted William Blackstone to the effect that killing another in a duel was murder, but judges and juries widely ignored this precept, which had also been maintained by Sir Francis Bacon. Challenges were sent and duels carried out quite openly—even to the point of advertising the same in newspapers. Any judicial inquiry into a duel was usually concerned with the question whether the duelling code was observed and whether a delay occurred between challenge and combat rather than with the legal facts of the case. At the end of the eighteenth century, Moore claimed that he could find no evidence of an execution occurring in England where evidence was presented that the duel had been 'fairly fought'.[35]

Examples of the failure to convict on charges of murder resulting from duelling abound. In 1699, Captain George Kirke killed a young fop, Conyers Seymour, in a multiple combat in St James's Park. Seymour's father brought a private prosecution against Kirke, who had fled to the Netherlands, but subsequently returned to stand trial in King's Bench. The victim's father, Sir Edward Seymour, told the court that the public ought to resent the fact that men such as Kirke, 'who took public money to secure the peace', made a practice of murdering other gentlemen 'in the open streets'. The dukes of Ormonde, Richmond, and St Albans, the earl of Oxford, and a multitude of

---

[34] Moore, *Two Treatises on Duelling and Gaming*, ii. 255; Jean Gailhard, *The Compleat Gentleman* (London, 1678) [Wing G118], ii. 127–8.

[35] Moore, *Two Treatises on Duelling and Gaming*, ii. 245–6, 248–9; *The Charge of Sir Francis Bacon Touching Duels*, 45–6; Donna T. Andrew, 'The Code of Honour and its Critics: The Opposition to Duelling in England', *Social History*, 5.3 (1980), 412–13; J. M. Beattie, *Crime and the Courts in England, 1660–1800* (Princeton, 1986), 97–8; id., 'Violence and Society in Early-Modern England', in A. N. Doob and E. L. Greenspan (eds.), *Perspectives in Criminal Law*, ed. (Aurora, Ont., 1985), 46.

high-ranking military officers appeared in court to stand bail for the accused and, presumably, to assert the contrary point. Kirke was convicted on the reduced charge of manslaughter and sentenced to be burnt in the hand.[36]

On 2 February 1686, Charles II's bastard son, Henry Fitzroy, duke of Grafton, killed the younger brother of the earl of Shrewsbury in a duel, and, on the same day, one of Philip, fourth Lord Wharton's sons killed an Irishman. A coroner's inquest found it manslaughter in the case of Grafton and self-defence in the latter case.[37] One could understand if judges and juries were sometimes cynical about bringing courtiers to book. Robert Constable, third Lord Dunbar, pleaded guilty at the Old Bailey to an indictment for murder for having killed his opponent in a duel, but he had the foresight to obtain Charles II's pardon before entering his plea. Dunbar subsequently led a party of 200 gentlemen volunteers to serve in the French army during the Third Anglo-Dutch War.[38] Charles II could be whimsical about granting pardons. He refused one to Sir Philip Lloyd, clerk of the Council, after he had killed an opponent in a duel. Lloyd was subsequently indicted for manslaughter by a grand jury impanelled for the Court of the Verge, and was found guilty of manslaughter after a trial in King's Bench for murder following a private prosecution by the victim's wife. However, he was allowed to plead benefit of clergy.[39]

Sir John Reresby, who was no stranger to duelling, drew the line at deaths that resulted from drunken brawls where no time elapsed between challenge and combat. He committed such persons to trial.[40] In a similar case, one Ensign Flower of the Foot Guards accidentally ran his captain through with a rapier in 1685 as the captain was trying to compose a quarrel between Flower and another officer as they were coming out of the Three Tuns in Windsor and after his captain had given Flower a direct order to cease quarreling. Flower was committed to Reading Gaol and condemned at the Assizes. His mother

---

[36] *The Diary of John Evelyn*, ed. E. S. de Beer, 6 vols. (Oxford, 1955), v. 331; Luttrell, *Brief Historical Relation*, iv. 532, 535, 539, 569, 584, 587, 607–8.

[37] Ibid. i. 370–1.
On Wednesday, 20 Dec. 1681, Sir John Reresby reported that no fewer than ten duels had been fought in London in the previous week (*Memoirs of Sir John Reresby*, ed. Andrew Browning (Glasgow, 1936; repr. 1991), 241).

[38] GEC iv. 513; George Hilton Jones, *Charles Middleton: The Life and Times of a Restoration Politician* (Chicago, 1967), 19.

[39] Luttrell, *Brief Historical Relation*, i. 154–5, 157, 159–60, 162, 170.

[40] *Memoirs of Sir John Reresby*, ed. Browning, 240.

sought a pardon or a commutation of the sentence to transportation, but the king refused because Flower had enjoyed the benefit of a pardon on a previous occasion.[41]

Such drunken combats were common among guards officers. In 1699, Edward Rich, earl of Warwick and Holland, Charles, fifth Lord Mohun, and four other officers fell to quarrelling as they emerged from the Greyhound Tavern in the Strand. They immediately hired sedan chairs to convey them to Leicester Fields (present-day Leicester Square), where they fought a combat involving three on three. Warwick was accused of killing Colonel Richard Coote, aided and abetted by Mohun and the three other surviving individuals. Warwick chose to be tried before the House of Lords and was acquitted of murder, but convicted of manslaughter, which was still a capital offence. He pleaded benefit of clergy and was warned that he would not enjoy that privilege a second time and should therefore amend his ways. Mohun was acquitted. The four remaining defendants were tried and convicted of manslaughter. They escaped hanging by pleading clergy, and one, having secured a pardon from the king, was not even burnt in the hand.[42]

As might be expected, Scottish subjects who killed one another in duels were dealt with more severely. In 1667, four gentlemen fought a multiple combat on Leith Links. William Douglas, younger brother of the laird of Blakiston, killed Sir James Hume of Eccles, a young cornet in Drummond's Regiment of Horse, while acting as a second. Douglas, who was only 21, was tried for murder, found guilty, and beheaded at the Mercat Cross in Edinburgh. John Law of Lauriston, who later pursued a career as a financier in France, was apparently under sentence of death for killing Ensign 'Beau' Wilson in London in 1694 when he escaped and made his way to France.[43]

---

[41] *A True Narrative of the Confession and Execution of Ensign Flower at Reading . . . 8th March. 1684* (London, 1684 [1685]) [Wing T 2777A], 1–4.

For a similar case in Ireland, see *The State Letters of Henry Earl of Clarendon, Lord Lieutenant of Ireland*, comp. S. W. Singer, 2 vols. (Oxford, 1763) [ESTCT 160420], ii. 97.

[42] T. B. Howell (ed.), *A Complete Collection of State Trials and Proceedings for High Treason*, 33 vols. (London, 1809–26), vol. xiii, cols. 952–1033.

Warwick and Coote had previously stood bail for Mohun in one of his earlier murder trials (HMC, *Fourteenth Report, Appendix, Pt. II* (Portland MSS iii), iii. 592; see also above, Chapter 5).

[43] Charles Dalton, *The Scots Army, 1661–1688* (London, 1909), p. xviii; *The Portledge Papers, Being Extracts from the Letters of Richard Lapthorne*, ed R. J. Kerr and I. C. Duncan (London, 1928), 173–5, 177, 192; *DNB, sub* John Law of Lauriston (1671–1729) and Edward Wilson (d. 1694).

If the Stuart monarchs, as well as judges and juries, were often ambivalent about culpability in deaths resulting from duelling, ethicists and theologians were more emphatically opposed. To kill an opponent in a duel was 'a kind of lawful and honourable murder'—but murder nonetheless. So perverse was the duelling code, said Thomas Pestel, that it was thought more honourable to take the life of an opponent than to spare it: 'So there is a double harvest of renown to be reaped from duels, that is, either to murder a man, or else to be able to vaunt that you gave him life.'[44] For a man to offer, carry, or accept a challenge constituted wilful murder if another person was killed, and it was self-murder if he himself died in a duel. In either case, that person had usurped the authority of the king, since the sword was given only to him.[45] It followed that a Christian prince could not, in good conscience, authorize a private combat without consenting to murder or self-murder. This would be tantamount to putting to death someone who had not been condemned by legal process. Bertrand de Loque also rejected the idea that the outcome of a duel would be decided by Divine Providence; to assert the same is to say that God sanctions 'enormous crimes'.[46]

Serious investigators into the ethics of duelling and the code of honour, while condemning the former, nonetheless made a serious effort to understand and explain the phenomenon. Robert Ward explained the compulsion of the martialist to fight duels in this vein:

reason tells a man that in a just cause there is no man but will resolve to defend his honour, and so put forth his best valour to offend his antagonist, his combat being to maintain the truth, and having a good conscience on his side, doth add vigour to his courage; whereas contrarily a guilty conscience will so detract from the worth and valour of the false accuser, that fear will undermine his heart, whereby he cannot perform in such a manly way as that party which hath right on his side.[47]

[44] Pestel, *Sermons and Devotions Old and New*, 328.
[45] [de Loque,] *Discourses of Warre and Single Combat*, 49; [Thomas Comber,] *A Discourse of Duels, Shewing the Sinful Nature and Mischievous Effects of them* (London, 1687) [Wing C5462], 16–19; John Sym, *Life's Preservative against Self-Killing* (1637), ed. Michael MacDonald (repr. London, 1988), 114–16; Cockburn, *History and Examination of Duels*, 189–90, 192.
[46] [de Loque,] *Discourses of Warre and Single Combat*, 49.
John Cleland warned swordsmen against thinking 'that God's assistance and power is ever tied unto their just cause; they tempt God in urging him every hour to work miracles for justifying their innocency and condemning others' guiltiness' (*The Institution of a Young Nobleman* (1611), ed. Max Molyneux, 2 vols. repr. New York, 1948), i. 232–3.
[47] Robert Ward, *Animadversions of Warre* (London, 1639) [STC 25025], 183.

Charles Moore thought that personal courage, which was a necessary ingredient of honour, had come to be regarded as its very essence, to the exclusion of those other good qualities that constitute honour. Soldiers impel one another to the performance of feats of valour that individuals might not otherwise undertake were it not for their awareness of the watchful presence of their comrades. Moore believed that duelling served the function of getting novice martialists used to the instruments of death, to the sight of blood being spilled, and to the havoc that ensued, and the ordeal served to deaden the sensibilities to all these horrible experiences.[48]

Gervase Holles had been a duellist in his younger days, but, after he had soldiered through the civil wars and suffered exile, he had second thoughts about the practice.

I cannot but lament the infinite mischief that this custom of duels hath brought into this world, having imposed (as it were) a kind of necessity upon all gentlemen (especially soldiers) to pursue an act (when their honour and reputation calls them to it) that in itself [is] both brutish and damnable, and which declined sticks an indelible blemish upon him that refuses through the iniquity of custom and falsehood of opinion. Indeed, this is that only which threatens to divide the union betwixt a Christian and a gentleman.[49]

Because religious beliefs had little influence on the aristocracy's approbation of the duelling code, many critics thought it wise to appeal to no higher values than the swordsman's sense of self-esteem. Sir Thomas Overbury insisted that a worthy commander bloodied his sword only in battle, while Richard Brathwait accused those who wielded their swords otherwise of 'preferring their blood before their honour, their safety before their reputation'.[50] James Cleland stated that it was a sign of poor judgement that a man would equate valour

---

[48] Moore, *Two Treatises on Duelling and Gaming*, ii. 260–1.

For a discussion of the difficulties in conditioning soldiers in more recent times to kill at close range and the psychological costs to those who have done so, see Dave Grossman, *On Killing: The Psychological Cost of Learning to Kill in War and Society* (Boston, 1996), 114–19, 249–55.

[49] Gervase Holles, *Memorials of the Holles Family, 1493–1656*, ed. A. C. Wood (CS, 3rd ser., 60; London, 1937), 81.

Sir Thomas Urquhart of Cromarty displayed a similar ambivalence about duelling (*Epigrams: Divine and Moral* (London, 1641), repr. in *Works* (Maitland Club Publications, 30; Edinburgh, 1834), 40).

[50] Rubinstein, *Captain Luckless*, 188; *The Miscellaneous Works in Prose and Verse of Sir Thomas Overbury*, ed. Edward F. Rimbault (London, 1856), 106–7; Richard Brathwait, *The English Gentleman* (London, 1630; repr. Amsterdam, 1975), 206.

with having fought duels. Seeking after duels signified swaggering, not courage. Those who spent their time in the fencing schools might learn skill with a rapier and could very well overcome persons who were valiant, but that did not confer true valour. George Carleton, a professional soldier, insisted that true courage was not to be found among duellists, but rather among those who fought for religious principles.[51]

In counselling young gentlemen to avoid the occasion of duelling, William Higford reminded his readers that anyone who wrongs an inferior descends to that level and makes that person equal to himself. Sir Thomas Urquhart thought that a 'base detractor' was like a 'scabbed sheep—not worth the marking'.[52] Even Lord Herbert of Cherbury was prepared to set limits on when duelling was justified: 'where with honour I could forgive, I never used revenge as leaving it always to God . . .'[53] Sir William Monson warned his son to shun quarrels and all occasions of duelling and reminded him that one 'who is conversant with a quarreller' will never be free from peril.[54] Among French writers, Montaigne condemned duelling because the practice taught men to think only of private ends, contrary to law and justice, while La Noue thought that duelling constituted an abuse of the privilege, peculiar to the *noblesse d'épée*, of wearing a sword, which should rather be dedicated to defending 'the weak and the innocent from the violence of oppressors'.[55] Another anonymous critic saw duelling as a sickness and a perversion: duellists were 'honour sick, for they deem their honour must die unless they drink the blood of the bravest'.[56]

[51] Cleland, *The Institution of a Young Nobleman*, i. 23–4; G. F., A Defender of Christian Valour, *Duell-Ease: A Worde with Valiant Spirits Shewing the Abuse of Duells . . . Challenges and Private Combates* (London, 1635) [STC 10637], sig. A4$^r$; *The Military Memoirs of Capt. George Carleton from the Dutch War, 1672, in which he Served, to the Conclusion of the Peace of Utrecht, 1713* (London, 1728) [ESTCT 70326], 6–7.
[52] William Higford, *The Institution of a Gentleman* (1660), in *The Harleian Miscellany*, ed. William Oldys and Thomas Park, 10 vols. (London, 1808–13), ix. 596; Urquhart, *Epigrams: Divine and Moral*, 44.
[53] *Life of Edward, First Lord Herbert of Cherbury*, ed. Shuttleworth, 25–6.
[54] *The Naval Tracts of Sir William Monson*, ed. M. Oppenheim, 5 vols. (NRS 22, 23, 43, 45, 49; London, 1902–15), i. 105.
[55] 'Cowardice, Mother of Cruelty', in *The Complete Essays of Montaigne*, trans. D. M. Frame (Stanford, Calif., 1958), bk. ii, ch. 27 (p. 527); François de La Noue, *The Politicke and Militarie Discourses of the Lord De La Nowe*, trans. Edward Aggas (London, 1587) [STC 15215], 134.
[56] G. F., A Defender of Christian Valour, *Duell-Ease*, sig. A4$^{r–v}$.

The critics of the cult of duelling were led to question the accepted notion of honour and the whole code of civil courtesy. Besides the attacks upon duelling from the point of view of morality, law, royal authority, and military discipline, the resort to duelling to enforce civility and politeness was viewed by opponents as a perversion of those concepts. The third earl of Shaftesbury, John Locke, and Jonathan Swift all associated the artificiality and insincerity of these perverted varieties of civility with the court, which was no place to learn good manners. Duelling was nothing but a deadly theatrical display demanded by fashion. It was based upon a false concept of honour, which in turn rested upon reputation. This was called 'horizontal honour' by Markku Peltonen, whereas 'true honour' or 'vertical honour' reflected virtue. Thus, genuine civility grew out of the *via activa* of classical republicanism with its associated attributes of patiotism and devotion to public service. Courtiers who advocated their peculiar kind of civil courtesy were thought more likely to fight for personal honour than for their country.[57]

Military men recognized that certain aspects of the cult of duelling, such as a high sense of honour and the willingness to perform feats of daring, bred in the soldier martial attributes such as boldness, courage, and confidence; they also perceived that duelling undercut military discipline and promoted disunity within political and military society.[58] Matthew Sutcliffe thought that those who provoked quarrels did not make resolute soldiers; he reminded his readers that the Romans had punished those who struck a fellow soldier with death, and accorded highest honours to soldiers who had killed the most enemies rather than those who destroyed their comrades.[59] As lord deputy of Ireland, Sir Thomas Wentworth, earl of Strafford, thought that the fact that Sir Thomas Dutton had killed another officer in a duel rendered him unfit for military duty.[60] In Cromwellian Ireland, Roger Boyle, Lord Broghill (later first earl of Orrery), who succeeded Henry Ireton as commander of the parliamentary forces in Munster,

---

[57] Peltonen, *The Duel in Early Modern England*, 116–20, 226–8, 248–52, 254–6.

[58] Clark, *War and Society in the Seventeenth Century*, 38–9, 46; *A Myrrour for English Souldiers: Or, an Anotomy of an Accomplished Man at Armes* (London, 1595) [STC 10418], sig. D4ʳ.

[59] Sutcliffe, *The Practice, Proceedings and Lawes of Armes*, 325–6.

[60] *Earl of Strafforde's Letters and Dispatches*, comp. Knowler, i. 144; Arthur Wilson, *The Life and Reign of James, the First King of Great Britain* (1653), repr. in [White Kennett,] *The Complete History of England*, 3 vols. (1706) [ESTCT 145258], ii. 683b–684a.

regarded duelling among his troops as mutiny and he cashiered those who defied his prohibition against the practice.[61] The quarrel between Thomas, fifteenth Lord Grey of Wilton, and Sir Francis Vere, which arose because Grey had refused to serve under the command of Vere, disrupted the chain of command in the English forces of the Dutch army and drew other leading figures into the factional struggle.[62] The English forces at the siege of Juliers in 1609 were riven with quarrelling and duelling. It was here that a captain in Sir Edward Cecil's Regiment, Sir Thomas Dutton, resigned his commission so that he could challenge his superior officer, Sir Hatton Cheek; they subsequently met on Calais Sands, where Dutton killed Cheek.[63] During the expedition to the Isle of Rhé in 1628, Sir William Courtney assaulted Sir Andrew Gray over how the duke of Buckingham's orders to make a stand at the edge of the marshes were to be interpreted.[64] During the Religious Wars in France, François de La Noue believed that more French noblemen died in duels than from war wounds.[65] Consequently, any expedient that would impose self-control or compose quarrels would appeal to responsible military commanders.[66]

   The degree to which military commanders succeeded in regulating duelling so as not to disrupt discipline together with the willingness of officers—especially those of aristocratic background—to accept such limitations constitute important advances in the professionalization of officer corps. Thomas Pestell suggested in 1659 that an officer who felt that his reputation had been impugned might satisfy his honour by demanding a court martial as an alternative to duelling.[67] A pamphlet aimed at new officers in the English army, published in 1680, advised the young subaltern to choose his friends carefully so that he would not be drawn into quarrels and factions, and to be aware that the consequences of defying royal prohibitions against duelling and killing

   [61] *The State Letters of . . . Roger Boyle, 1st Earl of Orrery*, comp. Thomas Morrice (London, 1742) [ESTCN 14784], 19.
   [62] *The Letters of John Chamberlain*, ed. N. E. McClure, 2 vols. (Philadelphia, 1939), i. 143–4.
   [63] Wilson, *The Life and Reign of James, the First King of Great Britain*, ii. 683b–684a.
   [64] Thomas Birch, *The Court and Times of Charles I*, ed. R. F. Williams, 2 vols. (London, 1848), i. 317–18.
   [65] Robert R. Harding, *Anatomy of a Power Elite: The Provincial Governors of Early Modern France* (New Haven, 1978), 77–8.
   [66] Gregory Hanlon, *The Twilight of a Military Tradition: Italian Aristocrats and European Conflicts, 1560–1800* (New York, 1998), 343–4.
   [67] Pestell, *Sermons and Devotions Old and New*, 334.

an opponent could impede the advancement of his career.[68] Sir Andrew Melvill, a Scottish officer in the Spanish Army of Flanders, found himself drawn into a duel with another captain, although such encounters were strictly forbidden. Melvill escaped punishment for the offence because a powerful friend interceded on his behalf and intimidated the colonel of his regiment, but he was eventually compelled to leave the Spanish Army of Flanders because of the continuing enmity of his commanding officer.[69]

Military commanders viewed duelling, whether an encounter resulted in fatalities or not, as indiscipline. While some articles of war provided the death penalty for breaches of these articles, they stopped short of declaring such an act as murder. Typically, the punishment for officers engaging in fatal duels did not extend beyond cashiering.[70] In the English garrison at Bergen-op-Zoom, a quarrel broke out between Captain Richard Orme, a habitual duellist, and Sir George Holles. Prince Maurice interceded to compose the quarrel and prevent a duel, but neither party would back down. Maurice decided that Holles was an indispensable officer, and so punished Orme by forbidding the duel upon 'pain of his head', and humiliated him by removing Orme's quarters to the edge of the camp.[71] Dutch articles of war recognized that in a polyglot army quarrels were bound to occur between officers and soldiers of different nationalities, and officers and non-commissioned officers were encouraged to try to compose quarrels. However, Dutch military authorities did not prohibit duelling altogether, and Frederick Henry of Nassau in 1627 stated that only the captain general could sanction a combat.[72]

The Dutch articles of war were much more severe on enlisted men in matters of duelling than on officers. Officers and volunteers who fought duels were to be cashiered and banished; men in the ranks could be punished by death for fighting within a camp or garrison or within the vicinity of the same, and the death penalty was also

---

[68] *Advice to a Soldier . . . Written by an Officer in the English Army* (London, 1680), repr. in *Harleian Miscellany*, viii. 355–6.

[69] *Memoirs of Sir Andrew Melvill*, trans and ed. Torick Ameer-Al (London, 1918), 112–13.

[70] Walton, *History of the British Standing Army*, 582–3.

[71] Holles, *Memorials*, 79–81.

[72] *Crijks-Ordonnantien ende Rechten ghemaect ende gheordonnert by . . . Robert, Grave van Leycester* (Leiden, 1586), no. 15; *Lawes and Ordinances . . . by Robert, Earle of Leycester, Lieutenant and Captaine-General . . . in the Low Countries* (London, [1586]) [STC 4208], no. 17; *Placate*, by order of Frederick Henry of Nassau, 3 July 1627, in Henry Hexham, *The Principles of the Art Militarie Practiced in the Warrs of the United Netherlands* (London, 1637) [STC 13264], appendix, 18–19.

prescribed for a corporal of the guard who allowed soldiers to leave the camp or garrison for that purpose or any soldier who sought to draw his comrades into a quarrel.[73] The Swedish Articles of War issued in the time of Gustaus Adolphus stated that causes of honour were to be decided by officers of the regiment or by special honour courts. Duelling was prohibited within camps and garrisons, and officers who failed to try to compose quarrels were to be cashiered.[74] The Royalist articles of war issued by Thomas Howard, second earl of Arundel and Surrey, were remarkably vague, but the emphasis was upon preventing or punishing quarrels among common soldiers. Algernon Percy, fourteenth earl of Northumberland's Royalist articles of 1640 prescribed the death penalty for any soldier who drew his sword without an order in camp or after the watch had been set, but the context suggests that this applied only to enlisted men and not to officers or gentlemen volunteers. Henry Rich, first earl of Holland's Royalist articles of war of 1640 prescribed the death penalty for any officer of the guard who permitted soldiers to leave camp to fight duels, but it appears that they did not prohibit officers from leaving camp for that purpose.[75] Robert, third earl of Essex's articles of war for his Parliamentary army are very similar and provide the death penalty for soldiers who draw their swords without an order in camp or after the watch has been set. They also made the officer of the guard as well as the corporal subject to the death penalty for permitting soldiers (but apparently not officers) to leave the camp to fight a duel. Robert Rich, second earl of Warwick, issued articles in 1642 to his Parliamentary forces that are nearly identical and, again, were designed to preserve the authority of officers. Like all the other articles of war previously discussed, they are silent about duelling among officers outside camp.[76]

[73] Ibid.

[74] *The Swedish Discipline, Religious, Civile and Military* (London, 1632) [STC 23520], 3–29.

[75] *Lawes and Ordinances of Warre . . . of His Majestie's Army Royall . . . under the Conduct of . . . Thomas, Earl of Arundel and Surrey* (Newcastle-upon-Tyne, 1639) [STC 9335], 13; *Lawes and Ordinances of Warre . . . by . . . the Earle of Northumberland* (London, 1640) [STC9336], sigs. B4ʳ–C4ᵛ; *Lawes and Ordinances of Warre Established for . . . the Armie in the Northern Parts by . . . the Earle of Holland* (London, 1640) [Wing H2420], sigs. B4ᵛ–C1ʳ.

[76] *Lawes and Ordinances of Warre . . . by the . . . Earle of Warwick, Lord General of the Forces raised by Authority of Parliament* (London, 1642) [Wing L695A], sigs. B1ʳ–C3ᵛ.

The parliamentary articles of war issued by Col. Michael Jones for the Province of Leinster in Ireland are identical to those issued by the earl of Warwick (*Lawes and Ordinances of Warre . . . by . . . Colonel Michael Jones* (Dublin, 1647) [Wing L695a]).

Reflecting the influence of the Kirk, the articles of war of the Scots Covenanting Army made a more determined effort to curtail the practice of duelling among soldiers. The Scottish articles provided for the establishment of special courts to arbitrate quarrels between officers and their men or any others. Anyone who continued to pursue a quarrel while the court was sitting was to die. Any officer who suffered a 'soldier to go forth to single combat' was to be condemned to death if convicted. The Scots Army of the Restoration period continued to specify the death penalty for any officer or private soldier who drew his sword within a camp or garrison in pursuit of a quarrel. If an officer did not attempt to compose a dispute, he was to be cashiered; but if a sergeant or corporal neglected to do so, he was to suffer death.[77]

The articles of war of the later Stuart English Army tended to become more specific, reflecting the more precise language of professional judge advocates, but the focus of the articles continued to be upon banishing the practice from camps and garrisons in order to preserve discipline. A double standard of punishments for officers and common soldiers was perpetuated, and officers found plenty of opportunities to continue their duelling habits outside camps and garrisons. The articles dealing with duelling are identical in wording between 1662 and 1692. Officers who engaged in duelling were to be cashiered; private soldiers were to be punished by riding the wooden horse.[78] The death penalty was reserved for soldiers who fought within cannon shot of camp and corporals of the guard who knowingly permitted soldiers to leave camp for the purpose of engaging in a duel.[79]

It is questionable how successful these efforts to prevent duelling from eroding military discipline were. During the Second Anglo-Dutch War, the factionalism arising from disputes about precedence among officers in the garrison at Kinsale in Ireland led to fighting between the officers and soldiers of the companies belonging to Col. St Leger and

---

[77] *Articles and Ordinances of War . . . of the Army of the Kingdom of Scotland* (Edinburgh, 1643), repr. in *Harleian Miscellany*, v. 422–8; Dalton, *Scots Army*, appendices, 86–9.

[78] An instrument of military punishment consisting of a beam upon which the soldier being disciplined was seated with heavy weights tied to his legs. The punishment lasted a considerable number of hours.

[79] *Rules and Articles for the Better Government of their Majesties' Land-Forces in the Low Countries and Parts beyond the Seas* (London, 1692), repr. in Walton, *History of the British Standing Army*, 813–14; Nathaniel Boteler, *War Practically Reformed: Shewing all the Requisites Belonging to a Land-Army* (London, 1663) [Wing B6288B], 215.

Richard Barry, second earl of Barrymore. The president of Munster, Roger Boyle, first earl of Orrery, intervened and sent Barrymore home because he was the less valuable and experienced officer of the two. The Tollemache brothers were both inveterate duellers. Thomas Tollemache lost his commission in the Coldstream Guards for duelling and was reduced to serving in the Tangier garrison as a gentleman volunteer. His younger brother William was in jeopardy of his life for killing Lord William Carnegie in Paris in 1681, and had to purchase a pardon from the French Crown. He later joined his brother at Tangier as a gentleman volunteer. While serving in the navy at Barbados, William Tollemache killed another officer and was tried by commission of oyer and determiner, found guilty of manslaughter, and, after pleading clergy, was burnt in the hand. William was subsequently commissioned a captain in the Royal Navy and Thomas later became the colonel of the Coldstream Guards and a lieutenant general.[80]

The duelling culture was especially strong at the court of William III and among the officers of his various armies. On his visit to England in 1670, his entourage was full of swordsmen who caused the prince much embarrassment—especially when one of his Dutch officers killed a French colonel in a duel in Tothill Fields, Westminster. The gentlemen troopers of the earl of Oxford's Regiment, who frequently provided escorts for William after he had became king of England, did not hesitate to fight while actually on duty, and fatalities were not uncommon.[81] Officers of William's armies also fought duels in the presence of the enemy. In 1689, two officers from a French Huguenot Regiment, quartered in the duke of Schomberg's camp at Dundalk, Ireland, fought a duel within sight of the Jacobite army's encampment because they feared a court martial if they fought near the Williamite camp. When both were wounded in the encounter, they blamed their wounds on a skirmish with the enemy.[82] A group of officers in Colonel Samuel Venner's Marine Regiment in Portsmouth challenged his authority in 1692 and prosecuted him in a court martial. Subsequently,

---

[80] *State Letters of . . . Roger Boyle, 1st Earl of Orrery,* comp. Morrice, 274; E. D. H. Tollemache, *The Tollemaches of Helmingham and Ham* (Ipswich, 1948), 75, 83–91; *DNB, sub* Thomas Tollemache (1651?–1694).

[81] HMC, *Fourteenth Report,* appendix, pt. IV (Kenyon MSS) (1894), 86; *Twelfth Report,* appendix, pt. VII (Le Fleming MSS) (1890), 74; Luttrell, *Brief Historical Relation,* iii. 388, iv. 65.

[82] [George Story,] *A True and Impartial History of . . . the Kingdom of Ireland during the Last Two Years with the Present State of Both Armies* (London, 1691) [Wing S5748], 28.

three of Venner's supporters fought a multiple combat with three of the dissident officers.[83] Such duels and multiple combats occurred frequently in Flanders during the Nine Years War.[84]

Those officials charged with enforcing the articles of war against duelling—both civil and military—routinely ignored stated policy and regulations. In 1691, William Blathwayt, secretary-at-war for England, wrote to the secretary-at-war in Ireland giving details of a duel between the colonels of the 3rd Dragoons and the 22nd Regiment of Foot. Blathwayt condoned the duel, stating that it proceeded 'according to form'. That appears to have been Blathwayt's principal concern, but he did like to be kept informed about such incidents. In May 1692, Colonel Charles O'Hara reported to Blathwayt from Flanders that an officer accused of horse stealing by his fellow officers drew his sword on one of his accusers, who happened to be on duty as adjutant. The adjutant ran the other officer through with his sword and killed him. O'Hara confined the adjutant until the king's pleasure was known. In a similar case in March 1692, Major Giles Spicer wrote to Blathwayt that he had killed another officer in self-defence after that officer had drawn his sword on Spicer following dinner at their garrison in Louvain. He assured Blathwayt that he would send him depositions concerning the course of events after his court martial had concluded.[85] Of course, neither of these two incidents can be considered proper duels, but in each case the reaction of the officer attacked was not to arrest or disarm his attacker, but to use maximum force. This lends credence to John Cockburn's insistence that the custom of duelling would have withered if courts martial and commanding officers had enforced existing regulations against the practice. The persistence of duelling, Cockburn thought, was a sad reflection on the state of discipline in the British army at the beginning of the eighteenth century.[86]

The inability of the Stuart monarchs to summon the political will to curtail the practice of duelling reveals both an essential weakness in the Stuart monarchy and the strength and persistence of martial culture

---

[83] Luttrell, *Brief Historical Relation*, ii. 513; John Childs, *The British Army of William III, 1689–1702* (Manchester, 1989), 176.

[84] Luttrell, *Brief Historical Relation*, ii. 388–9, 417, 604, iii. 489, iv. 721; HMC, *Fourteenth Report*, appendix, pt. III (Marchmont MSS) (1894), 124–5.

[85] Walton, *History of the British Standing Army*, 584; BL, Add. MSS 9723 (Blathwayt Papers), fos. 41, 115–16.

[86] Cockburn, *History and Examination of Duels*, 229–30.

in the aristocratic societies that still sustained the practice at the end of the seventeenth century.[87] The idea that the duel limited the unrestrained violence of the medieval feud by extinguishing the quarrel following combat does not seem to be applicable to British martial culture; the many instances of multiple combats fought in the latter part of the seventeenth century suggest that such vendettas had merely taken on a baroque formality. Just as the early Stuart monarchs had failed to share the martial values of the rechivalrized aristocracies of the Three Kingdoms, Charles II and William III displayed an insensitivity to the condemnations of duelling by divines, moralists, and even military writers who insisted that the practice was injurious to military discipline.[88] Of all the rulers of the British and Irish kingdoms of the seventeenth century only Cromwell and James VII and II took strong stands against the practice, but they did so without support from the English Parliament and with limited success. Although Cromwell and James VII and II recognized that the suppression of duelling was the right thing to do, many of their English and Irish subjects did not share their desire to prohibit duelling, and far too many judges and juries as well as civil and military officers accepted the practice and cared only whether the proprieties had been observed in such encounters. At the same time, the limited evidence for the northern kingdom suggests that Scots law took a more severe view of duelling.

If the various seventeenth-century articles of war are any indication, European martial culture did not conceive of killing someone in a duel as a moral wrong or a breach of divine or positive law. Military law was designed to preserve discipline, which justified prohibiting duelling among common soldiers, but the duelling proclivities of officers and gentlemen were merely banished from camps and garrisons rather than being prohibited. For a soldier to strike or kill an officer showed both a lack of discipline and a want of deference, and it is debatable which the aristocratic officer found more offensive. But officers and

---

[87] Louis XIV tried very hard to suppress duelling in France at the same time, but did not enjoy much success (John A. Lynn, *Giant of the Grand Siècle: The French Army, 1610–1715* (Cambridge, 1997), 256–7; François Billacois, *The Duel: Its Rise and Fall in Early Modern France*, trans T. Selous (New Haven, 1990), 175–80.

[88] Edward Davies, *The Art of War and England's Traynings* (London, 1619; repr. Amsterdam, 1968), 122; Thomas Venn, *Military and Maritime Discipline* (London, 1672) [Wing V192], 3–4.

The belief that feuding declined as duelling increased still persists. See Anna Bryson, *From Courtesy to Civility: Changing Codes of Conduct in Early Modern England* (Oxford, 1998), 247–8.

gentlemen killed one another with something approaching impunity and in such considerable numbers that it raises the question whether the fatalities of British and Irish military officers and gentlemen volunteers were not as numerous on the field of honour as on the field of battle. Finally, the failure of military courts to eradicate the practice of duelling among both officers and enlisted men provides evidence of less than perfect military discipline in the British army at the beginning of the eighteenth century.

The Scots divine John Cockburn thought that it was the advent of party politics that gave rise to an increase in duelling in later-Stuart and Augustan England because of the scurrilous discourse employed in party disputes. Those who attempted to settle their disputes by complaints to magistrates found that such officials were responsive only if they were of the same party. Moreover, the parliamentary reluctance to prohibit duelling was also ideological. There developed among those of Whig persuasion a belief that duelling, purged of its corrupting French notions of politeness and civility, was preferable to legislative efforts to prohibit duelling, which were associated with French absolutism and Jacobitism. Seen in this light, the mischief that resulted from duelling was a lesser evil than arbitrary government, and this choice seems to have persuaded opponents of duelling in Parliament to give up efforts to enact legislation specifically outlawing the practice. John Oldmixon, the Whig pamphleteer, presented this point of view in his defence of General George Macartney, the second to Charles, fourth Lord Mohun, in the fatal duel between Mohun and the duke of Hamilton, when he reminded readers that attempts to ban duelling had been part and parcel of the arbitrary government of Protector Cromwell (and also James VII and II). Oldmixon also attempted to tie the code of duelling to the medieval English judicial trial by combat and thus to represent it as an integral part of the ancient constitution. In contrast to James VII and II, William III approved of duelling. Thus, the belief that the practice of duelling encouraged true British valour and honour became part of Whig ideology. Nor was this merely an English notion; Scottish writers such as John Mackqueen asserted that British victories in the War of Spanish Succession could be attributed to the British Isles being 'nurseries of brave men'.[89]

---

[89] Peltonen, *The Duel in Early Modern England*, 193–5, 216. The quotation from John Mackqueen, *A Divine and Moral Essay on Courage, its Rise and Progress: With some Reflections on the Causes of British Valour* (London, 1707), 43–4, is found on p. 195.

CHAPTER EIGHT

# Conclusion

Though it be most unfit for a good commander to be prodigal of his own life or that of his soldiers upon an undue hazard, yet their condition being such as to have sold themselves to moral adventure, he will be ambitious of nothing more than to meet with a fair occasion of dying in the bed of honour, and who feareth death will never be fitting for that profession, and therefore will maintain himself prepared for it . . .

([Dudley, third Lord North,] 'A Soldier', *A Forest of Varieties, First Part* (London, 1645) [Wing N1283], 100–1)

As the end of the sixteenth century approached, the English aristocracy had become demilitarized for lack of opportunity—not for want of inclination; the Irish and Scottish aristocracies retained their medieval martial traditions, but engaged in feuding and cattle raiding, where the principal motive was personal revenge rather than the more rational military and political objectives of a modern state. Queen Elizabeth's decision to intervene in the Netherlands to keep the Spanish menace at bay engaged the aristocracies of the British Isles once again in the cockpit of mainland European politics as well as the ideological conflicts of the Protestant and Catholic Reformations. The swordsmen and gallants of the Three Kingdoms volunteered in their numbers to fight in the armies of Catholic and Protestant princes and states, as the whole of Europe became engulfed in endemic religious and dynastic warfare, which spread to the British Isles after 1638. By the end of the seventeenth century, the Three Kingdoms, under the leadership of William III, had become fully engaged in continental European and colonial wars and naval and commercial rivalries that had spread across the globe.

Military historians have emphasized the rapidly changing nature of modern warfare as the Three Kingdoms imported the innovations associated with the military revolution, and during this period of changing modes of war the Three Kingdoms also exported military manpower to fight in the wars of northern Europe. In a story of uninterrupted technological progress, the military historians have demonstrated how the modern state was invented to make war, and its financial resources exploited to raise, equip, and sustain ever larger armies armed with more formidable missile weapons systems. Cultural adaptation, however, does not always keep pace with technological innovation. Seventeenth-century swordsmen had not entirely broken with the warrior traditions of their medieval ancestors, and they retained an obsessive preoccupation with personal honour, reputation, and face-to-face combat fought with edged weapons, and did not readily accept corporate discipline and endeavour and the subordination of individual displays of prowess and motives of personal revenge to political and military objectives. Revenge got in the way of public warfare and 'was a nuisance to its practitioners'.[1] The transition from private war to public war was not easy for amateur gallants from the British Isles. This was especially true for those who sought out the leaguers, camps, and courts of mainland Europe to learn about the modern mode of warfare and encountered there a flourishing cult of duelling in the French and Italian manner to which many experienced professional soldiers remained addicted. Responsible military commanders recognized that duelling subverted military hierarchies and discipline and wasted nearly as many lives of officers as public war. It further slowed the process by which military hierarchies came to displace social hierarchies—an important aspect of the professionalization of officer corps. Yet, military officers from the British Isles and some mainland European armies clung to the practice of duelling as a way of testing the courage of a young gentleman and conditioning him to the bloody havoc and horror of the battlefield. While it is true that the apprenticeship in arms performed in the ranks by gentlemen volunteers serving as pikemen and cavalry troopers was regarded by professional soldiers as the most appropriate preparation for war and test of courage for a military career as a commissioned officer, after the system of purchasing military commissions had become more widespread in the second half of the seventeenth century an increasing number of wealthy aristocrats skipped the apprenticeship in arms served in the ranks. Had the monarchs and military commanders possessed the determination

---

[1] Henry Holbert Turney-High, *Primitive War: Its Practice and Concepts* (Columbia, SC, 1971), 150.

to suppress duelling, the practice would have withered long before it did. One falls back on the explanation that the field of honour continued as a test of courage for young gallants because it was the one test to which even the wealthy and the privileged remained subject. Unflinching courage on the battlefield was a quality that all swordsmen and military writers deemed necessary. Some commanders, such as Gustavus Adolphus, believed in leading from the front, and paid with their lives. Others were less prodigal with their lives and those of their soldiers, but they also understood that one could not always command from the rear, and even kings must appear on the battlefield from time to time. The subaltern officer, especially, was expected to present his men with an example of valour. The courage of the common soldier was thought to be derivative, and only the example of his officers could inspire it. The study of classical authors revealed how Greek and Roman commanders used their rhetorical skills to exhort their soldiers to stand and fight the enemy, and this led them to understand that brave soldiers needed to be recognized and rewarded. The study of Roman and Greek historians also led to the discovery that honour was more widely shared in republics than monarchies.

The study of classical authors of the ancient world and the experience of military service abroad—perhaps fighting for a religious cause—were bound to enlarge the worlds of swordsmen from the Three Kingdoms. In some cases these experiences reinforced old allegiances, but in other instances prolonged service by swordsmen in the United Provinces or the Venetian Republic probably helped infect them with a republican virus. Certainly soldiers of the Three Kingdoms displayed shifting allegiances and changing identities during the civil wars as well as preceding and during the Glorious Revolution and the Williamite wars. Military service abroad not only enriched the education of the aristocracies of the British Isles; it also stimulated the political imagination and provided a yardstick by which to measure their rulers and the religious and political institutions at home. This undoubtedly contributed to the turmoil encountered when these veterans returned home on the eve of the British and Irish civil wars.[2] Certain aspects of the Glorious Revolution in England and the

[2] Steve Murdoch, 'The House of Stuart and the Scottish Professional Soldier', in Bertrand Taithe and Tim Thornton (eds.), *Identities in Conflict, 1300–2000* (Stroud, 1998), 46–50; John Childs, *Nobles, Gentlemen and the Profession of Arms in Restoration Britain, 1660–1688: A Biographical Dictionary of British Officers in Foreign Service* (Soc. for Army Hist. Research, Special Publication 13; London, 1987), pp. vii–viii.

Williamite wars in Ireland and Scotland also display the characteristics of intestine war. Much of William III's invasion force that landed at Torbay in 1688 consisted of English and Scottish regiments of the Dutch army, and it would be worth investigating how many of the 10,000 Danish mercenaries whom William III employed in the conquest of Ireland came from the British Isles. The database of Scots and other persons from the British Isles who migrated to Scandinavia compiled by Steve Murdoch and Alexia Grosjean suggests that much of the officer corps of the army of the Kingdom of Denmark and Norway came from Scotland, England, and Ireland.[3]

It is well known that the rapidly evolving and competitive politics of the Renaissance state obliged aristocrats to acquire a good education based upon humanist principles. Martial prowess and ancient lineage would no longer suffice to admit a nobleman to his prince's court and council. He needed also to demonstrate his usefulness in civil affairs, but knowledge and experience of war in the modern mode was also requisite, as James Butler, first duke of Ormonde, well understood when he considered what was desirable for the education of his sons. In the upper reaches of the aristocracy wealth was also necessary, together with the ability to recruit, equip, deploy, and lead men, preferably raised from among an aristocrat's own tenants, in the king's service.[4] The best way to acquire such wealth was through the possession of inherited lands, but the kind of loyalty that Scottish and Irish lords and chieftains could call upon in recruiting tenants and followers to accompany them overseas was an acceptable substitute for great wealth. Wealth could still sometimes be acquired from the profits and plunder of war, but the best hope for poorer noblemen and gentlemen was to find employment in the new standing armies of mainland Europe or in the Three Kingdoms after 1689.

Those swordsmen who served in the Dutch army during the Eighty Years War had learned that military officers should subordinate

[3] 'Scotland, Scandinavia and Northern Europe, 1580–1707', database @ www.abdn.ac.uk/history/datasets/ssne. John Childs's *Nobles, Gentlemen and the Profession of Arms in Restoration Britain* supplements the work of Murdoch and Grosjean; his biographical dictionary is limited to 757 biographical entries of officers of English, Irish, and Scots officers who served both in the armies of the Three Kingdoms during the Restoration period and in the armies other than those of Scandinavia and Russia. They included primarily the armies of the Netherlands, Spain, France, and Portugal.

[4] T. C. Barnard, 'Aristocratic Values in the Careers of the Dukes of Ormonde', in Toby Barnard and Jane Fenlon (eds.), *The Dukes of Ormonde, 1610–1745* (Woodbridge, 2000), 164.

themselves to authorities in the civilian government. This lesson seems not to have been grasped by those who later fought in the Wars of the Three Kingdoms, perhaps because the religious conflict had a way of politicizing every aspect of life in those times. In the Dutch Republic after the end of the Eighty Years War, the Orangist party tended to politicize military life, and the English and Scots officers who had served under William III as stadtholder and captain general felt very strong ties of loyalty to him, which carried over into William's descent on England. At the same time, those Catholic officers who had been granted commissions in English and Irish armies by James II were forced once again into foreign service abroad by the Williamite victories.

Thus, those who served in the standing armies of the Three Kingdoms during the Restoration were highly politicized. The aristocracies of the Three Kingdoms during the course of the seventeenth century had become militarized, and the martial men were also highly politicized. One needed a patron in the royal administration to purchase a commission. The office of colonel of a regiment was particularly politicized. A patron was also needed to purchase a regiment, and, under William III and Queen Anne, many used the office as a stepping stone to a seat in Parliament. Many colonels did not command in the field but concerned themselves largely with raising, clothing, and equipping their regiments, and the methods of recruiting soldiers and buying votes were not wholly dissimilar.[5] Military officers who went into parliamentary politics were often experienced in the use of the sword in individual combats, and carried with them into politics military notions of honour, reputation, and retribution. In 1712, a notorious encounter between Charles, fourth Lord Mohun, and James, fourth duke of Hamilton, both generals and experienced military officers who were active in the House of Lords as well as being political rivals and contending heirs of a disputed inheritance, left both dead and their seconds, another general and a colonel, accused of murder.[6] Both peers had killed before—Mohun on several occasions—and had been pardoned; their presence in the world of parliamentary politics constituted a particularly vicious influence.

[5] [Edward Ward,] *Mars Stript of his Armour; Or, the Army displayed in all its true Colours* (London, 1709) [ESTCT 34919], 7.
[6] Victor Stater, *Duke Hamilton is Dead! A Story of Aristocratic Life and Death in Stuart Britain* (New York, 1999), 285.

There are also more positive aspects of the remilitarization of the English aristocracy and the exposure of the peers and gentlemen of the Three Kingdoms to travel and military service abroad. The acquisition of practical military knowledge and experience also exposed swordsmen to new ideas in the scientific world as well as new currents and tastes in literature, art, and architecture. Despite the rivalry between the English Lord Mohun and the Scottish duke of Hamilton, English and Scottish swordsmen served together in English armies at home during the civil wars and the Restoration period as well as in foreign armies abroad fighting for the same religious causes. That shared experience must surely have promoted a degree of integration and fellow feeling as a British army emerged after the Act of Union of 1707. Their travel abroad and shared experiences in mainland European armies, which involved cooperation with and obedience to commanders and officers in a wide variety of armies, probably made it easier to accept and enter into cooperation with the allied forces in the wars against Louis XIV's expansionism. Because many swordsmen had travelled and studied in France and not a few had served in the armies of France, Imperial Austria, and Spain, they could accept the soldiers of these countries as worthy opponents, which made it easier to abide by limitations on the destructiveness of warfare. This helped to set the wars of the eighteenth century apart from those of the age of religious wars. As swordsmen of the British Isles submitted to discipline, obedience to orders, and conformity to an emerging international body of rules of warfare, they in turn imposed such restraints on their own men.[7] Although the spread of the purchase system of commissions in the late-seventeenth-century English army and the eighteenth-century British army reasserted aristocratic privilege among the officer corps and thus retarded the development of some aspects of professionalization, this reactionary influence was largely limited to the home army and the battlefields of Europe. Because aristocratic officers did not like serving in the colonies, regiments that were posted overseas provided scope for an informal merit system, and it became possible once again for officers to be commissioned from the ranks.[8]

[7] I hope to explore some of these themes more fully in a companion volume devoted to English, Irish, and Scottish military experiences during the seventeenth century, which is tentatively entitled 'War, Society, and Martial Culture in the Three Kingdoms, 1585–1702'.

[8] J. A. Houlding, *Fit for Service: The Training of the British Army, 1715–1795* (Oxford, 1981), 103.

# Bibliography

This bibliography includes only those printed works cited more than once in the footnotes. The place of publication is understood to be London unless otherwise indicated.

## I. Manuscript Sources

British Library
  Additional MSS 9723 (Blathwayt Papers).
  Additional MS 18,979 (Fairfax Correspondence).
  Harley MS 3638 (Sir Edward Cecil, Lord Wimbledon, 'The Duty of a Private Soldier').

## II. Printed Primary Sources

*Acts of the Privy Council of England*, ed. J. R. Dasent, 46 vols. (1890–1964).
*Calendar of Assize Records: Kent Indictments, Charles II, 1676–1688*, ed. J. S. Cockburn (1997).
*Calendar of State Papers, Domestic Series, 1603–1625*, 4 vols. (1857–9).
*Calendar of State Papers, Domestic Series, Charles II*, ed. M. A. E. Green, 24 vols. (1860–1947).
*The Charge of Sir Francis Bacon . . . Touching Duels* (1614; repr. Amsterdam, 1968).
*The Complete Newgate Calendar*, ed. J. L. Rayner and G. T. Crook, 5 vols. (1926).
*Conway Letters: The Correspondence of Anne, Viscountess Conway, Henry Moore and their Friends, 1642–1684*, ed. M. H. Nicolson (New Haven, 1930).
*The Correspondence of Sir Philip Sidney and Hubert Languet*, ed. S. A. Pears (1845).
*The Earl of Strafforde's Letters and Dispatches*, comp. William Knowler, 2 vols. (1739) [ESTCT 145338].
*The Fairfax Correspondence*, ed. G. W. Johnson, 2 vols. (1848).
Howell, T. B. (ed.), *A Complete Collection of State Trials and Proceedings for High Treason*, 33 vols. (1809–26).

HMC, *Calendar of the Manuscripts of the . . . Marquis of Salisbury . . . Preserved at Hatfield House*, 24 vols. (1883–1976).
—— *Manuscripts of the Earl of Mar and Kellie*, 2 vols. (1904).
—— *Report on the Manuscripts of the Marquess of Ormonde . . . Preserved at Kilkenny Castle*, ed. J. T. Gilbert, 2 vols. (old ser.; 1895, 1899).
*The Last Confession . . . of Lieutenant John Stern* (1682), repr. in *The Harleian Miscellany*, ed. W. Oldys and T. Park, 10 vols. (1808–13), ix. 9–45.
*Letters Addressed from London to Sir Joseph Williamson*, ed. W. D. Christie, 2 vols. (CS, NS 8, 9; 1874).
*The Letters of John Chamberlain*, ed. N. E. McClure, 2 vols. (Philadelphia, 1939).
*Letters of John Holles, 1587–1637*, ed. P. R. Seddon, 3 vols. (Thoroton Soc., 31, 35, 36; Nottingham, 1975–86).
*The Letters of John Wilmot, Earl of Rochester*, ed. J. Treglown (Chicago, 1980).
Montgomery, W., of Rosemount, *The Montgomery Manuscripts (1603–1706)*, ed. G. Hill (Belfast, 1869).
*The Portledge Papers, Being Extracts from the Letters of Richard Lapthorne*, ed. R. J. Kerr and I. C. Duncan (1928).
Rushworth, John, *Historical Collections*, 8 vols. (1721–2) [ESTCN 33526].
*The State Letters of . . . Roger Boyle, 1st Earl of Orrery*, comp. Thomas Morrice (1742) [ESTCN 14784].
*Stuart Royal Proclamations*, ed. J. F. Larkin and P. L. Hughes, 2 vols. (Oxford, 1973, 1983).
*A True Copy of a Speech Made by an English Colonel to his Regiment, Immediately before their Late Transportation for Flanders at Harwich* (1691) [Wing T2633].

*III. Books Written or Printed before 1800*

Abercrombie, Patrick, *The Martial Achievements of the Scots Nation*, 2 vols. (Edinburgh, 1711) [ESTCT 86819].
*An Account of the Trial and Examination of Count Conningsmark* (1682) [Wing A412A].
*The Advice of . . . Sir Edward Harwood*, in *The Harleian Miscellany*, ed. W. Oldys and T. Park, 10 vols. (1808–13).
*Aphorisms of Sir Philip Sidney*, 2 vols. (1807).
*The Autobiography of Sir John Bramston* (CS, old ser., 32; 1845).
*Autobiography of Thomas Raymond*, ed. G. Davies (CS, 3rd ser., 28; 1917).
Bacon, Sir Francis, Viscount St Albans, *The Essayes or Counsels, Civill and Moral*, ed. Michael Kieran (Cambridge, Mass., 1985).
—— *The Works of Francis Bacon*, ed. J. Spedding, R. L. Ellis, and D. D. Heath, 14 vols. (1857–74; repr. Stuttgart, 1963).

Barret, Robert, *The Theoricke and Practicke of Moderne Warres* (1598) [STC 1500].

Birch, Thomas, *The Court and Times of Charles I*, ed. R. F. Williams, 2 vols. (1848).

Bland, Humphry, *A Treatise of Military Discipline* (1727) [ESTCT 160420].

Blandy, William, *The Castle, or Picture of Policy* (1581) [STC 3128].

Bodin, Jean, *The Six Bookes of a Commonwealth*, ed. K. D. McRae (1606; repr. Cambridge, Mass., 1962).

Boyle, Roger, earl of Orrery, *A Treatise of the Art of War* (1677) [Wing O495].

Burnet, Gilbert, *Some Passages of the Life and Death of . . . John, Earl of Rochester* (1680), repr. in V. de Sola Pinto (ed.), *English Biography of the Seventeenth Century* (1951).

Butler, Samuel, *Characters*, ed. C. W. Davies (Cleveland, Oh., 1970).

Callières, Jacques de, *The Courtier's Calling* (1675) [Wing C301].

Camden, William, *Annales: Or the History of the Most Renowned and Victorious Princesse Elizabeth* (3rd edn.; 1635) [STC 4501].

—— *The History of the Most Renowned and Victorious Princess Elizabeth* (3rd edn.; 1675) [Wing C362].

—— *The History of the Most Renowned and Victorious Princess Elizabeth* (4th edn.; London, 1688; repr. New York, 1970).

Campbell, Archibald, 1st marquis of Argyll, *Instructions to a Son* (1661) [Wing A3657].

Carter, Matthew, *Honor Redivivius, or An Analysis of Honor and Armory* (1660) [Wing C659].

Cary, Robert, earl of Monmouth, *Memoirs* (1759) [ESTCT 147779].

Castiglione, Baldasare, Count, *The Book of the Courtier*, trans. Sir Thomas Hoby (1561; repr. New York, 1967).

Cavendish, Margaret, duchess of Newcastle, *The Life of William Cavendish, Duke of Newcastle* (1667), ed. C. H. Firth (1906).

Churchyard, Thomas, *A Generall Rehearsal of Warres, Called Churchyarde's Choise* (1579) [STC 5235].

Cleland, James, *The Institution of a Young Nobleman* (1611), ed. M. Molyneux, 2 vols. (repr. New York, 1948).

Cockburn, John, *The History and Examination of Duels* (1720) [ESTCT 118651].

Codrington, Robert, *The Life and Death of the Illustrious Robert Earle of Essex* (1646) [Wing C4877].

*The Commentaries of Sir Francis Vere* (1657), in *Stuart Tracts, 1603–1693* (Westminster, 1903; repr. Wilmington, Del., 1973).

[Croke, Charles,] *Fortune's Uncertainty or Youth's Unconstancy* (1667; Luttrell Soc. Reprints, 19; Oxford, 1959).

Dallington, Sir Robert, *A Survey of the Great Duke's State of Tuscany . . . in 1590* (1605) [STC 6201].

—— *This View of France* (1604; repr. Oxford, 1936).

Davies, Edward, *The Art of War and England's Traynings* (1619; repr. Amsterdam, 1968).

*The Diary of Bulstrode Whitelocke, 1605–1675*, ed. R. Spalding (British Academy, Records of Social and Economic History, NS 13; 1990).

*The Diary of General Sir Patrick Gordon of Auchleuchries, 1635–1699*, ed. J. Robertson (Spalding Club Publications, 31; Aberdeen, 1859).

*The Diary of John Evelyn*, ed. E. S. de Beer, 6 vols. (Oxford, 1955).

*The Diary of Samuel Pepys*, ed. R. C. Latham and W. Matthews, 11 vols. (Berkeley, Calif., 1970–83).

Digges, Thomas, and Digges, Dudley, *Foure Paradoxes and Politique Discourses concerning Militarie Discipline* (1604) [STC 6872].

Douglas, Gawin, bishop of Dunkeld, *The Palis of Honoure* (1553?) [STC 7073].

Earle, John, *Microcosmography*, ed. H. Osborne (1633; repr. 1971).

*Elizabeth of England: Certain Observations concerning the Life and Reign of Queen Elizabeth by John Clapham*, ed. E. P. and C. Read (Philadelphia, 1951).

Elton, Richard, *The Complete Body of the Art Military* (1650) [Wing E653].

Ferguson, Adam, *An Essay on the History of Civil Society* (Edinburgh, 1767; repr. New York, 1971).

Ferne, Sir John, *The Blazon of Gentrie* (1586) [STC 10824].

*The Four Bookes of Flavius Vegetius Renatus . . . of Martiall Policye, Feates of Chivalrie, and Whatsoever Pertayneth to Warre* trans. J. Sadler (1572; repr. Amsterdam, 1968).

Gailhard, Jean, *The Compleat Gentleman*, 1 vol. in 2 pts. (London, 1678) [Wing G118].

Gates, Geoffrey, *The Defence of Militarie Profession* (1579) [STC 11683].

[G.F., A Defender of Christian Valour,] *Duell-Ease: A Worde with Valiant Spirits Shewing the Abuse of Duells . . . Challenges and Private Combates* (1635) [STC 10637].

Greville, Sir Fulke, Lord Brooke, *Life of Sir Philip Sidney* (1652), ed. N. Smith (Oxford, 1907; repr. 1971).

Hales, John, *Golden Remains* (1659) [Wing H269].

Hexham, Henry, *The Second Part of the Principles of the Art Militarie Practiced in the Warrs of the United Provinces* (1638)[STC 13264.2].

—— *The Principles of the Art Militarie Practiced in the Warrs of the United Netherlands* (1637) [STC 13264].

Holinshed, Raphael, *Chronicles*, 3 vols. in 2 parts (1587) [STC 13569].

—— *Chronicles of England, Scotland and Ireland*, 6 vols. (1807–8).

Holles, Gervase, *Memorials of the Holles Family, 1493–1656*, ed. A. C. Wood (CS, 3rd ser., 60; 1937).

Hume, David, of Godscroft, *The History of the House of Douglas and Angus* (Edinburgh, 1648) [Wing H3659].

Hutchinson, Lucy, *Memoirs of the Life of Colonel Hutchison*, ed. C. H. Firth (1906).

Hyde, Edward, 1st earl of Clarendon, *The History of the Rebellion and Civil Wars in England*, ed. W. D. Macray, 6 vols. (Oxford, 1888; repr. 1958).

*The Journal of Edward Montagu, First Earl of Sandwich, 1659–1665*, ed. R. C. Anderson (NRS 64; 1929).

*The Journal of George Fox*, ed. J. L. Nickalls (Cambridge, 1952).

*The Journal of John Stevens Containing a Brief Account of the War in Ireland, 1689–1691*, ed. R. H. Murray (Oxford, 1912).

Kellie, Sir Thomas, *Pallas Armata, or Militarie Instructions for the Learned* (Edinburgh, 1627; repr. Amsterdam, 1971).

La Noue, François de, *Discours politiques et militaire*, ed. F. E. Sutcliffe (1587; repr. Geneva, 1967).

—— *The Politicke and Military Discourses of the Lord De La Nowe*, trans. Edward Aggas (1587) [STC 15215].

La Rochefoucauld, François, duc de, *Maximes* (1778; repr. Paris, 1959).

Lasseran-Massencome, Blaise de, seigneur de Monluc, marshal of France, *The Commentaries of Messire Blaize de Montluc, Mareschal of France*, trans. Charles Cotton (1674) [Wing M2506].

[Lauder, George,] *The Scottish Souldier, by Lawder* (Edinburgh, 1629) [STC 15312].

*The Life of Edward, First Lord Herbert of Cherbury, Written by Himself*, ed. J. M. Shuttleworth (1976).

[Loque, Bertrand de,] *Discourses of Warre and Single Combat*, trans. John Eliot (1591) [STC 16810].

Lupton, Donald, *A Warre-like Treatise of the Pike* (1642) [Wing L3496].

Luttrell, Narcissus, *A Brief Historical Relation of State Affairs from September 1678 to April 1714*, 6 vols. (Oxford, 1857; repr. Wilmington, Del., 1974).

[Mandeville, Bernard,] *The Fable of the Bees: or, Private Vices, Publick Benefits* (1714) [ESTCT 77573].

Markham, Francis, *Five Decades of Epistles of Warre* (1622) [STC 17332].

Markham, Gervase, *Honour in his Perfection* (1624) [STC 17361].

Martin, M., *A Description of the Western Isles of Scotland* (2nd edn.; 1716) [ESTCT 31703].

*The Memoirs of Capt. Peter Drake* (Dublin, 1755) [ESTCT 145643].

*Memoirs of Edmund Ludlow . . . 1625–1672*, ed. C. H. Firth, 2 vols. (Oxford, 1894).

*Memoirs of Sir Andrew Melville*, trans. and ed. T. Ameer-Ali (1918).

*Memoirs of Sir John Reresby*, ed. A. Browning (Glasgow, 1936; repr. 1991).

Meteren, Emmanuel van, *A True Discourse Historicall of the Succeeding Governors in the Netherlands and the Civill Warres there Begun in the Yeere 1565*, trans. Thomas Churchyard (1602) [STC 17846].

*A Military Dictionary Explaining all Difficult Terms in Martial Discipline, Fortification and Gunnery . . . by an Officer* (1702) [ESTCT 145661].

*The Military Memoirs of Capt. George Carleton from the Dutch War, 1672, in which he Served, to the Conclusion of the Peace of Utrecht, 1713* (1728) [ESTCT 70326].

[Milward, Richard,] *The Table-Talk of John Selden*, ed. S. W. Singer (1855; repr. Freeport, NY, 1972).

*The Miscellaneous Works in Prose and Verse of Sir Thomas Overbury*, ed. E. F. Rimbault (1856).

Moffet, Thomas, *Nobilis, or a View of the Life and Death of Sidney*, trans. V. B. Heltzel and H. H. Hudson (San Marino, Calif., 1940).

Monck, George, 1st duke of Albemarle, *Observations upon Military and Political Affairs* (1671) [Wing A864].

Monro, Robert, *Monro, his Expedition with the Worthy Scots Regiment called Mac-keys*, ed. W. S. Brockington (1637; repr. Westport, Conn., 1999).

Moore, Charles, *A Full Inquiry into the Subject of Suicide, to which are Added . . . Two Treatises on Duelling and Gaming*, 2 vols. (1790) [ESTCT 111258].

*A Myrrour for English Souldiers: Or, an Anatomy of an Accomplished Man at Armes* (1595) [STC 10418].

Naunton, Sir Robert, *Fragmenta Regalia, or Observations on Queen Elizabeth, her Times and Favorites*, ed. J. S. Cervoski (1641; repr. Washington, 1985).

*The Naval Tracts of Sir William Monson*, ed. M. Oppenheim, 5 vols. (NRS 22, 23, 43, 45, 49; 1902–15).

[North, Dudley, 3rd Lord North,] *A Forest Promiscuous of Several Productions* (1659) [Wing N1284]. An earlier, unexpurgated edition appeared in 1645 under the title *A Forest of Varieties* [Wing N1283].

Peacham, Henry, *The Compleat Gentleman* (1622; repr. Amsterdam, 1968).

*A Pepysian Garland: Black-Letter Broadside Ballads of the Years 1595–1639, Chiefly from the Collection of Samuel Pepys*, ed. H. E. Rollins (Cambridge, 1922).

Pestell, Thomas, *Sermons and Devotions Old and New* (1659) [Wing P1675].

[Proctor, Thomas,] *Of the Knowledge and Conducte of Warres* (n.p., 1578) [STC 20403].

*The Relation of Sydenham Poyntz, 1624–1636*, ed. A. T. S. Goodrick (CS, 3rd ser., 14; 1908).

[R., H.,] *Remarks on the Life and Death of the Fam'd Mr. Blood* (2nd edn.; Wing H113].

[Romei, Annibale, Count,] *The Courtier's Academie*, trans. John Keepers (1598) [STC 21311].

Secondat, Charles Louis de, baron de La Brède et Montesquieu, *The Spirit of the Laws* (1748), trans. and ed. A. M. Cohler, B. C. Miller, and H. S. Stone (Cambridge, 1989).

Segar, Sir William, *Honor, Military and Civil* (1602) [STC 22164].

Selden, John, *Titles of Honour* (2nd edn.; 1631) [STC 22178].

Sheffield, John, 3rd earl of Mulgrave and 1st duke of Buckingham and Normanby, 'Memoirs', in *Works*, 2 vols. (1740) [ESTCT 86931].

Sidney, Algernon, *Court Maxims*, ed. H. W. Blom, E. H. Mulier, and R. Janse (Cambridge, 1996).

Sidney, Sir Philip, *An Apology for Poetry, or The Defence of Poesy* (1595), ed. Geoffrey Shepherd (Manchester, 1965).

Somerville, James [by right 11th Lord Somerville], *Memorie of the Somervilles* [, ed. Sir Walter Scott], 2 vols. (Edinburgh, 1815).

Styward, Thomas, *The Pathwaie to Martiall Discipline* (1581) [STC 23413].

Sutcliffe, Matthew, *The Practice, Proceedings and Lawes of Armes* (1593) [STC 23468].

Touchet, James, second earl of Castlehaven, *The Earl of Castlehaven's Review: Or his Memoirs . . . of the Irish Wars* (1684) [Wing C1237].

*Travels and Works of Captain John Smith*, ed. E. Arber and A. G. Bradley, 2 vols. (Edinburgh, 1910; repr. New York, 1967).

*The Triumphs of Nassau*, trans. W. Shute (1613) [STC 17677].

*A True Account of the Last Speeches, Confessions and Execution of Christopher Vrats, George Boriskie and John Stern* (1682) [Wing T2380A].

Turner, Sir James, *Memoirs of his Own Life and Times (1632–1670)* (BC 28; Edinburgh, 1829).

—— *Pallas Armata: Military Essayes of the Ancient Grecian, Roman, and Modern Art of War, Written in the Years 1670 and 1671* (1683) [Wing T3292].

*Vincentio Saviola his Practice: In Two Bookes, the First Intreating Use of the Rapier and Dagger, the Second of Honor and Honorable Quarrels* (1595) [STC 21788].

Urquhart, Sir Thomas, of Cromarty, *ΕΚΣΚΥΒΑΛΑΡΟΝ [EKSKIBALAVON]: Or the Discovery of a Most Exquisite Jewel . . . Found in the Kennel of Worcester-Streets the Day after the Fight . . . Anno 1651, Serving in this Place to Frontal a Vindication of the Honour of Scotland* (1652), repr. in *Works* (Maitland Club, 30; Edinburgh, 1834).

—— *Epigrams: Divine and Moral* (1641), repr. in *Works* (Maitland Club Publications, 30; Edinburgh, 1834).

Walker, Sir Edward, 'Observations upon the Inconveniencies that have Attended the Frequent Promotions to Titles of Honour and Dignity, since King James Came to the Crown of England', in *Historical Discourses* (1705) [ESTCT 97417].

[Walsingham, Edward,] 'Life of Sir John Digby (1605–1645)', ed. G. Bernard, in *Camden Miscellany XII* (CS, 3rd ser., 18; 1910).

Ward, Robert, *Animadversions of Warre* (1639) [STC 25025].

Whetstone, George, *The Honourable Reputation of a Souldier* (1585) [STC 25339].

Whitelocke, Bulstrode, *Memorials of English Affairs*, 4 vols. (1685; repr. Oxford, 1853).

Williams, Sir Roger, *The Actions of the Low Countries*, ed. Sir John Hayward (1618) [STC 25731].

—— *A Brief Discourse of Warre* (1590) [STC 25732].

Wilson, Arthur, *The Life and Reign of James I, the First King of Great Britain* (1653), repr. in [White Kennett,] *The Complete History of England*, 3 vols. (1706) [ESTCT 145258].


*IV. Printed Secondary Works (after 1801)*

Abbott, W. C., *Colonel Thomas Blood: Crown Stealer, 1618–1680* (New Haven, 1911).

Adamson, J. S. A., 'The Baronial Context of the English Civil War', *Trans. R. Hist. Soc.*, 5th ser., 40 (1990).

—— 'Chivalry and Political Culture in Caroline England', in K. Sharpe and P. Lake (eds.) *Culture and Politics in Early Stuart England* (Stanford, Calif., 1993).

Anderson, P., *Lineages of the Absolutist State* (repr. 1979).

Anglin, J. P., 'The Schools of Defence in Elizabethan London', *Renaissance Quarterly*, 37 (1984).

Anglo, S. (ed.), *Chivalry and the Renaissance* (Woodbridge, 1990).

—— 'How to Kill a Man at your Ease: Fencing Books and the Duelling Ethic', in S. Anglo (ed.), *Chivalry and the Renaissance* (Woodbridge, 1990).

Aylward, J. D., *The English Master of Arms from the Twelfth to the Twentieth Century* (1956).

Beattie, J. M., 'Violence and Society in Early Modern England', in A. N. Doob and E. L. Greenspan (eds.), *Perspectives in Criminal Law* (Aurora, Ont., 1985).

Berry, E., *The Making of Sir Philip Sidney* (Toronto, Ont., 1998).

Bertie, G., *Five Generations of a Noble House* (1845).

Billacois, F., *The Duel: Its Rise and Fall in Early Modern France*, trans. T. Selous (New Haven, 1990).

Bitton, D., *The French Nobility in Crisis, 1560–1640* (Stanford, Calif., 1969).

Brown, K. M., *Bloodfeud in Scotland, 1573–1625: Violence, Justice and Politics in an Early Modern Society* (Edinburgh, 1986).

—— *Kingdom or Province? Scotland and the Regal Unon, 1603–1715* (New York, 1992).

—— *Noble Society in Scotland: Wealth, Family and Culture, from Reformation to Revolution* (Edinburgh, 2000).

Bryson, A., *From Courtesy to Civility: Changing Codes of Conduct in Early Modern England* (Oxford, 1998).

Bush, M. L., *Rich Noble, Poor Noble* (Manchester, 1988).

Caball, M., *Poets and Politics: Continuity and Reaction in Irish Poetry, 1585–1625* (Notre Dame, Ind., 1998).

Carlton, C., *Going to the Wars: The Experience of the British Civil Wars, 1638–1651* (1992).

Childs, J., *Nobles, Gentlemen and the Profession of Arms in Restoration Britain, 1660–1688: A Biographical Dictionary of British Army Officers in Foreign Service* (Soc. for Army Hist. Research, Special Publication 13; 1987).

Clark, Sir G., *War and Society in the Seventeenth Century* (Cambridge, 1958).

Clark, S., *State and Status: The Rise of the State and Aristocratic Power in Western Europe* (Montreal, 1995).

Cockayne, G. E., *The Complete Peerage of England, Scotland and Ireland, Great Britain and the United Kingdom, Extant, Extinct or Dormant*, 13 vols. (rev. edn.; 1910–59; repr. New York, 1984).

Colley, L., *Britons: Forging the Nation, 1707–1837* (New Haven, 1992).

Cooper, J. P., 'Retainers in Tudor England', in G. E. Aylmer and J. S. Morrill (eds.), *Land, Men and Beliefs: Studies in Early Modern History* (1983).

Corvisier, A., *Armies and Societies in Europe, 1494–1789*, trans. A. T. Siddall (Bloomington, Ind., 1979).

Cowan, E. J., *Montrose: For Covenant and King* (1977).

Creveld, Martin van, *Technology and War from 2000 BC to the Present* (New York, 1989).

Dalton, C., *Life and Times of General Sir Edward Cecil, Viscount Wimbledon*, 2 vols. (1885).

—— *The Scots Army, 1661–1688* (1909).

Davies, J. D., *Gentlemen and Tarpaulins: The Officers and Men of the Restoration Navy* (Oxford, 1991).

Dawson, J., 'The Gaidhealtachd and the Emergence of the Scottish Highlands', in Brendan Bradshaw and Peter Roberts (eds.), *British Consciousness and Identity: The Making of Britain, 1537–1707* (Cambridge, 1998).

Dewald, J., *Aristocratic Experience and the Origins of Modern Culture: France, 1590–1715* (Berkeley, Calif., 1993).

*Dictionary of National Biography*, 22 vols. (Oxford, 1990 edn.).

Dodgshon, R. A. ' "Pretense of Blude" and "Place of their Duelling": The Nature of Scottish Clans, 1500–1745', in R. A. Houston and I. D. Whyte (eds.), *Scottish Society, 1500–1800* (Cambridge, 1989).

Donagan, B., 'Halcyon Days and the Literature of War: England's Military Education before 1642'. *P&P* 147 (May 1995).

Dunham, W. H., 'William Camden's Commonplace Book', *Yale University Library Gazette*, 43 (1969).

Elias, N., *The Court Society*, trans. E. Jephcott (paperback edn.; New York, 1983).

Esler, A., *The Aspiring Mind of the Elizabethan Younger Generation* (Durham, NC, 1966).

*European Nobilities in the Seventeenth and Eighteenth Centuries*, ed. H. M. Scott, 2 vols. (1995).

Fedosov, D., *The Caledonian Connection: Scotland–Russia Ties, Middle Ages to Early Twentieth Century* (Aberdeen, 1996).

Ferguson, A. B., *The Indian Summer of English Chivalry: Studies in the Decline and Transformation of Chivalric Idealism* (Durham, NC, 1960).

—— *The Chivalric Tradition in Renaissance England* (Cranbury, NJ, 1986).

Fischer, T. A., *The Scots in Sweden* (Edinburgh, 1907).

Fissel, M. C., *English Warfare, 1511–1642* (2001).

—— (ed.), *War and Government in Britain, 1598–1650* (Manchester, 1991).

Fraser, G. M., *The Steel Bonnets: The Story of The Anglo-Scottish Border Reivers* (1971).

Fraser, J., *Chronicles of the Frasers*, ed. W. Mackay (SHS, 1st ser., 47; Edinburgh, 1905).

Fraser, Sir W., *The Sutherland Book*, 3 vols. (Edinburgh, 1892).

Frevert, U., *Men of Honour: A Social and Cutural History of the Duel*, trans. A. Williams (Cambridge, 1995).

—— 'The Taming of the Noble Ruffian: Male Violence and the Dueling in Early Modern Germany', in Pieter Spierenburg (ed.), *Men and Violence: Gender, Honor, and Rituals in Early Modern Europe and America* (Columbus, Oh., 1998).

Grafton, A., 'Portrait of Justus Lipsius', *American Scholar*, 56 (1986–7).

Grant, J., *The Memoirs and Adventures of Sir John Hepburn* (Edinburgh, 1851).

Graves, T. S., 'Some Pre-Mohock Clansmen', *Studies in Philology*, 20 (1923).

Guy, J. (ed.), *The Reign of Elizabeth I: Court and Culture in the Last Decade* (Cambridge, 1995).

Hale, Sir J. R., 'The Military Education of the Officer Class in Early Modern Europe', in his *Renaissance War Studies* (1983).

—— *War and Society in Renaissance Europe, 1450–1620* (New York, 1985).

Hanlon, G., *The Twilight of a Military Tradition: Italian Aristocrats and European Conflicts, 1560–1800* (New York, 1998).

Hardacre, P. H., 'The Earl Marshal, the Heralds, and the House of Commons, 1604–1641', *International Review of History*, 2 (1957).

Harding, R. R., *Anatomy of a Power Elite: The Provincial Governors of Early Modern France* (New Haven, 1978).

Heal, F., and Holmes, C., *The Gentry in England and Wales, 1500–1700* (Stanford, Calif., 1994).

Heinemann, M., 'Rebel Lords, Popular Playwrights and Political Culture: Notes on the Jacobean Patronage of the Earl of Southampton', *The Yearbook of English Studies: Politics, Patronage and Literature in England: Special Number*, 21 (1991).

Henry, G., *The Irish Military Community in Flanders, 1586–1621* (Dublin, 1992).

Hill, J. M., 'The Distinctiveness of Gaelic Warfare, 1400–1705', *European Studies Review*, 22.3 (1992).

Hill, J. M., *Celtic Warfare, 1595–1763* (Edinburgh, 1986).

Houlding, J. A., *Fit for Service: The Training of the British Army, 1715–1795* (Oxford, 1981).

Hunt, W., 'Civic Chivalry and the English Civil War', in A. Grafton and A. Blair (eds.), *The Transmission of Culture in Early Modern Europe* (Philadelphia, 1990).

James, M. E., *English Politics and the Concept of Honour, 1485–1642* (*P&P* Supplement, 3; Oxford, 1978).

—— *Change and Continuity in the Tudor North: The Rise of Thomas, Lord Wharton* (Borthwick Papers, 27; York, 1965).

Johnson, J. T., *Just War Tradition and the Restraint of War: A Moral and Historical Inquiry* (Princeton, 1981).

Jones, G. H., *Charles Middleton: The Life and Times of a Restoration Politician* (Chicago, 1967).

Keegan, J., *A History of Warfare* (New York, 1993).

Keen, M. H., *The Laws of War in the Late Middle Ages* (1965).

—— *Chivalry* (New Haven, 1984).

Kelly, J., *'That Damn'd Thing Called Honour': Duelling in Ireland, 1570–1860* (Cork, 1995).

Kelso, R., *The Doctrine of the English Gentleman in the Sixteenth Century* (Univ. of Illinois Studies in Language and Literature, 14.1–2; Urbana, Ill., 1929).

Kiernan, V. G., *The Duel in European History: Honour and the Reign of Aristocracy* (Oxford, 1988).

Kipling, G., *The Triumph of Honour: Burgundian Origins of the Elizabethan Renaissance* (The Hague, 1977).

Lenihan, P. (ed.), *Conquest and Resistance: War in Seventeenth-Century Ireland* (Leiden, 2001).

Lewis, M., *England's Sea Officers: The Story of the Naval Profession* (1939).

Lindsay, A., Lord Lindsay, *Lives of the Lindsays*, 3 vols. (1849).

Lynch, K. M., *Roger Boyle, First Earl of Orrery* (Knoxville, Ten., 1965).

Lynn, J. A., *Giant of the* Grand Siècle: *The French Army, 1610–1715* (Cambridge, 1997).

McCoy, R. C., 'A Dangerous Image: The Earl of Essex and Elizabethan Chivalry', *Journal of Medieval and Renaissance Studies*, 13.2 (1983).

—— *The Rites of Knighthood: The Literature and Politics of Elizabethan Chivalry* (Berkeley, Calif., 1989).

—— 'Old English Honour in an Evil Time: Aristocratic Principle in the 1620s', in R. M. Smuts (ed.), *The Stuart Court and Europe: Essays in Politics and Political Culture* (Cambridge, 1996).

MacDongall, N. (ed.), *Scotland and War* (Savage, Md., 1991).

Macinnes, A. I., *Clanship, Commerce and the House of Stuart, 1603–1788* (East Linton, East Lothian, 1996).

—— *Charles I and the Making of the Covenanting Movement, 1625–1641* (Edinburgh, 1991).

—— 'Crown, Clans and Fine: The Civilising of Scottish Gaeldom, 1587–1638', *Northern Scotland*, 13 (1983).

—— 'Gaelic Culture in the Seventeenth Century: Polarization and Assimilation', in S. G. Ellis and S. Barber (eds.), *Conquest and Union: Fashioning a British State, 1485–1725* (1995).

Malcolm, J., *To Keep and Bear Arms: The Origins of an Anglo-American Right* (Cambridge, Mass., 1994).

Manning, R. B., *Village Revolts: Social Protest and Popular Disturbances in England, 1509–1640* (Oxford, 1988).

—— *Hunters and Poachers: A Cultural and Social History of Unlawful Hunting in England, 1485–1640* (Oxford, 1993).

Marshal, A., 'Colonel Thomas Blood and the Restoration Political Scene', *HJ* 32.3 (1989).

—— *Intelligence and Espionage in the Reign of Charles II, 1660–1685* (Cambridge, 1994).

Mayes, C. R., 'The Early Stuarts and the Irish Peerage', *EHR* 73 (1958).

Mettam, R., 'Definitions of Nobility in Seventeenth-Century France', in Penelope J. Corfield (ed.), *Language, History and Class* (Oxford, 1991).

Morah, P., *Prince Rupert of the Rhine* (1976).

Motley, M., *Becoming a French Aristocrat: The Education of the Court Nobility, 1580–1715* (Princeton, 1990).

Murdoch, S., 'The House of Stuart and the Scottish Professional Soldier', in B. Taithe and T. Thornton (eds.), *War: Identities in Conflict, 1300–2000* (Stroud, 1998).

Neuschel, K. B., *Word of Honor: Interpreting Noble Culture in Sixteenth-Century France* (Ithaca, NY, 1989).

Newman, P. R., *The Old Service: The Royalist Regimental Colonels and the Civil Wars, 1642–46* (Manchester, 1993).

Nichols, K., *Gaelic and Gaelicized Ireland in the Middle Ages* (Dublin, 1972).

Oestereich, G., *Neostoicism and the Early Modern State* (Cambridge, 1982).

Ohlmeyer, J. H., ' "Civilizing of those Rude Parts": Colonization within Britain and Ireland, 1580s–1640s', in N. Canny (ed.), *The Origins of Empire: British Overseas Enterprise to the Close of the Seventeenth Century* (Oxford, 1998).

Parker, G., *The Army of Flanders and the Spanish Road, 1567–1659: The Logistics of Spanish Victory and Defeat in the Low Countries War* (Cambridge, 1972).

—— *The Military Revolution: Military Innovation and the Rise of the West, 1500–1800* (2nd edn.; Cambridge, 1996).

Peck, L. L., *Northampton: Patronage and Policy at the Court of James I* (1982).

Peltonen, M., *Classical Humanism and Republicanism in English Political Thought, 1570–1640* (Cambridge, 1995).

—— *The Duel in Early Modern England: Civility, Politeness and Honour* (Cambridge, 2003).

*Political Ideology in Ireland, 1541–1641*, ed. H. Morgan (Dublin, 1999).

Porter, S. (ed.), *London and the Civil War* (1996).

Raa, F. J. S. ten, and Bas, F. de, *Het Staatsche Leger*, 8 vols. (Breda, 1911–80).

Rae, T. I., *The Administration of the Scottish Frontier, 1513–1603* (Edinburgh, 1966).

Redlich, F., *De Praeda Militari: Looting and Booty, 1500–1815* (Vierteljahrschrift für Sozial- und Wirtschaftsgeschichte, 39; Wiesbaden, 1956).

—— *The German Military Enterpriser and his Work Force*, 2 vols. (Vierteljahrschrift für Sozial- und Wirtschaftsgeschichte, 47–8; Wiesbaden, 1964–5).

Rubinstein, H. L., *Captain Luckless: James, First Duke of Hamilton, 1606–1649* (Edinburgh, 1975).

Schalk, E., *From Valour to Pedigree: Ideas of Nobility in France in the Sixteenth and Seventeenth Centuries* (Princeton, 1986).

Schwoerer, L. G., *'No Standing Armies!' The Antiarmy Ideology in Seventeenth-Century England* (Baltimore, 1974).

Scott, H. M. (ed.), *European Nobilities in the Seventeenth and Eighteenth Centuries*, 2 vols. (1995).

Sharpe, K., and Lake, P. (eds.), *Culture and Politics in Early Stuart England* (Stanford, Calif., 1993).

Shaw, W. A., *The Knights of England*, 2 vols. (1906).

Simms, K., 'Warfare in the Medieval Gaelic Lordships'. *IS* 12 (1975–6).

Smith, J. M., *The Culture of Merit: Nobility, Royal Service and the Making of Absolute Monarchy in France, 1600–1789* (Ann Arbor, Mich., 1996).

Smuts, R. M., *Court Culture and the Origins of a Royalist Tradition in Early Stuart England* (Philadelphia, 1987).

—— (ed.), *The Stuart Court and Europe: Essays in Politics and Political Culture* (Cambridge, 1996).

Snow, V. F., *Essex the Rebel: The Life of Robert Devereux, the Third Earl of Essex, 1591–1646* (Lincoln, Neb., 1970).

Squib, G. D., *The High Court of Chivalry* (Oxford, 1959).

Stater, V., *Duke Hamilton is Dead! A Story of Aristocratic Life and Death in Stuart Britain* (New York, 1999).

Stevenson, D. *Alasdair MacColla and the Highland Problem in the Seventeenth Century* (Edinburgh, 1980).

Stone, L., *The Crisis of the Aristocracy, 1558–1641* (Oxford, 1965).

———— and Stone, J. C. F., *An Open Elite? England, 1540–1880* (Oxford, 1984).

Storrs, C., and Scott, H. M., 'The Military Revolution and the European Nobility, *c.*1600–1800', *War in History*, 3 (1996).

Stoye, J. W., *English Travellers Abroad, 1604–1667: Their Influence in English Society and Politics* (1952; repr. 1968).

Tayler, A., and Tayler, H., *The House of Forbes* (Spalding Club, 3rd ser., 8; Aberdeen, 1937).

Teitler, G., *The Genesis of Professional Officer Corps* (Beverley Hills, Calif., 1977).

Tough, D. L. W., *The Last Years of a Frontier: A History of the Borders during the Reign of Elizabeth* (Oxford, 1928).

Treadwell, V., *Buckingham and Ireland, 1616–1628* (Dublin, 1998).

Tucker, T. J., 'Eminence over Efficacy: Social Status and Cavalry Service in Sixteenth-Century France', *Sixteenth Century Journal*, 32.4 (2001).

Vagts, A., *A History of Militarism* (rev. edn.; New York, 1959).

Vale, M., *War and Chivalry: Warfare and Aristocratic Culture in England, France and Burgundy at the End of the Middle Ages* (London and Athens, Ga., 1981).

Verney, F. P., and Verney, M. M., *Memoirs of the Verney Family during the Seventeenth Century*, 2 vols. (1907).

Wagner, A. R., *Heralds and Heraldry in the Middle Ages* (2nd edn.; Oxford, 1956).

Walton, C., *A History of the British Standing Army, 1660–1700* (1894).

Webb, S. S., 'Brave Men and Servants to his Royal Highness: The Household of James Stuart in the Evolution of English Imperialism', *Perspectives in American History*, 8 (1974).

Wernham, R. B., *After the Armada: Elizabethan England and the Struggle for Western Europe, 1588–1595* (Oxford, 1984).

Worden, B., *The Sound of Virtue: Philip Sidney's* Arcadia *and Elizabethan Politics* (New Haven, 1996).

*V. Database (online)*

Murdoch, S., and Grosjean, A., 'Scotland, Scandinavia and Northern Europe, 1580–1707'. (database@www.abdn.ac.uk/history/datasets/ssne).

# Index

Henry, prince of Wales 49, 77, 206–7,
214 n.
Herbert of Cherbury, Edward Herbert,
1st Lord 37, 43–4, 127–8, 200,
235
*hidalgos* 108
hierarchies, social and military 6–7,
23–4, 50, 105
Higford, William 235
highwaymen 157, 163 n., 166
Hoby, Sir Thomas Posthumous 219
Holland, Henry Rich, Lord Kensington
and 1st earl of 38, 50, 126, 137,
239
Holles, family of 211–12
Denzil Holles, 1st Lord 44
Francis 123
Sir George 43, 77–8, 129, 238
Gervase 44–5, 77–8, 123, 213, 234
Thomas 129–30
Hope, Sir William 201
Hume of Eccles, Sir James 23
Hume of Godscroft, David 52–3, 83–4
hunting 40, 77, 112, 122–3, 169–70,
175, 206
Hutcison, Lucy 36, 40

Inchiquin, Murrough O'Brien, 6th
baron and 1st earl of 115
Ireland, lords deputy and lords justices
of 99

Jacobean peace 9–10, 35, 77, 110, 123
Jacobitism 244, 249
James VI and I, king of England, Ireland
and Scotland 24, 26–7, 35, 81–2,
86, 89, 92, 100–1, 107, 142, 144,
161, 166–7, 178, 180, 183, 190–1,
194–5, 201, 206, 216, 221–3
James VII and II, king of England,
Ireland and Scotland, duke of York
41, 63, 72, 132, 134, 167, 227,
229, 243–4, 249
Johnson, Samuel 1
Jonson, Ben 120, 126–7, 153 n.
jousting 7, 205–7, 220
judicial combat 205, 224, 228

Kellie, Sir Thomas 59
Kirke, George 230–1
Königsmarck, family of 163–4
Count Karl-Johann von 163–5
kidnapping 124, 162

Languet, Hubert 55, 66
Lauder, George 30
law cases:
*Claxton v Lilburne* 219
*Lowe and Kyme v Paramour* 219–20
Law of Lauriston, John 232
Lee, Sir Henry 206
Leicester, Robert Dudley, 1st earl of 3,
7, 23, 38–9, 66, 95, 169, 206
Lennard, Samson 76
Leslie, Sir Alexander, 1st earl of Leven
25–6, 156, 185
John, bishop of Ross 175
Lindsay, family of 46
Lindsey, Robert Bertie, 14th Lord
Willoughby and 1st earl of 99, 225
Lipsius, Justus 75, 120–1
Lloyd, Sir Philip 231–2
Locke, John 72, 236
London, City of 48, 147–54, 158,
162–5, 211, 214
apprentices 58, 121–2
gangs 149–52
Honourable Artillery Company 77
Tower of 223
Loque, Bertrand de 222, 233
Lovat, Simon Fraser, 6th Lord 186
Hugh Fraser, 7th Lord 185
Hugh Fraser, 8th Lord 186
master of 185
Thomas, tutor of 185
Lucas, Sir Thomas 193–4
Ludlow, Edmund 132
Lupton, Donald 135–6

Macartney, George 244
MacColla, Alasdair 188
Mackqueen, John 244
Machiavelli, Niccolò 11, 21, 71, 75
Malby, Sir Nicholas 109
Mandeville, Bernard 30, 53
Mantua, Vincentio di Gonzaga, prince
of 212
Markham, Francis 121, 129
Gervase 35, 83, 126
Mary, queen of Scots 144
Maurice of Nassau, prince of Orange 8,
69, 103, 116, 128–9, 208, 211–12,
238
Medina Sidonia, Alonso Pérez de
Guzman, 7th duke of 209
Melville, Andrew 160, 238
memoirs, military 35–7